STRENGTH AND CONDITIONING FOR FOOTBALL

The game of football is one of the most popular in the world and is followed by millions of spectators on all continents. In recent years, football has undergone technical, tactical and physical evolution, whereby players are subjected to ever higher physical stimuli. To be properly prepared, strength and conditioning coaches must use the most advanced scientific evidence to help inform decision-making regarding conditioning their players.

Strength and Conditioning for Football: From Science to Practice summarizes the current scientific evidence in the field for the sport. This evidence serves as a rationale for the decisions practitioners make with their football players to monitor and develop training programs that will help drive improvements in the relevant physical capacities for the game. This new book develops important arguments in football training with chapters examining such questions as (1) game model and training, (2) monitoring and testing, (3) recovery and match preparation and (4) youth and disability in football.

This book offers critical information to readers aiming to succeed as strength and conditioning coaches in football, and it will be required reading for students and practitioners alike in the fields of football, strength and conditioning, coaching, physiotherapy and sport science.

Marco Beato, PhD, is an Associate Professor (MSc, BSc, CPSS, CSCS, SFHEA) and Head of Sport and Exercise Science in the School of Allied Health Sciences, University of Suffolk Ipswich, UK. Marco has published over 160 peer-reviewed journal articles, and he is an Associate Editor for the NSCA's *Journal of Strength and Conditioning Research* (USA) and a fellow and reviewing panel member of the European College of Sport Science (Germany). He is also a scientific and performance consultant of professional football. Marco is qualified as a UEFA coach and professional football fitness coach with the FIGC (Italy).

Chris Bishop, PhD, is an Associate Professor of Strength and Conditioning (MSc, ASCC, SFHEA) at the London Sport Institute, Middlesex University, UK, and is the programme leader for MSc in Strength and Conditioning and the Head of the Department. Chris has published over 250 peer-reviewed journal articles, co-edited two textbooks and serves as a Senior Editor for the NSCA's *Journal of Strength and Conditioning Research* and an Associate Editor for the *Strength and Conditioning Journal*. Chris served on the Board of Directors for the UK Strength and Conditioning Association.

Anthony Turner, PhD, is a Professor of Strength and Conditioning (MSc, ASCC, CSCS*D, SFHEA) and the postgraduate research lead at the London Sport Institute, Middlesex University, UK. Anthony was a sports science consultant and strength and conditioning coach to Olympic and Paralympic athletes and was head of physical preparation for GBR fencing for the Rio Olympic Games. Anthony is a consultant in human performance for the British military and a physical performance coach for Tottenham Hotspur Women's Academy.

STRENGTH AND CONDITIONING FOR FOOTBALL

From Science to Practice

Edited by Marco Beato, Chris Bishop and Anthony Turner

NEW YORK AND LONDON

Designed cover image: Getty images

First published 2026
by Routledge
605 Third Avenue, New York, NY 10158

and by Routledge
4 Park Square, Milton Park, Abingdon, Oxon, OX14 4RN

Routledge is an imprint of the Taylor & Francis Group, an informa business

© 2026 selection and editorial matter, Marco Beato, Chris Bishop and Anthony Turner; individual chapters, the contributors

The right of Marco Beato, Chris Bishop and Anthony Turner to be identified as the authors of the editorial material, and of the authors for their individual chapters, has been asserted in accordance with sections 77 and 78 of the Copyright, Designs and Patents Act 1988.

All rights reserved. No part of this book may be reprinted or reproduced or utilised in any form or by any electronic, mechanical, or other means, now known or hereafter invented, including photocopying and recording, or in any information storage or retrieval system, without permission in writing from the publishers.

Trademark notice: Product or corporate names may be trademarks or registered trademarks, and are used only for identification and explanation without intent to infringe.

ISBN: 978-1-032-46827-3 (hbk)
ISBN: 978-1-032-46826-6 (pbk)
ISBN: 978-1-003-38347-5 (ebk)

DOI: 10.4324/9781003383475

Typeset in Times New Roman
by codeMantra

CONTENTS

List of Figures	*vii*
List of Tables	*xi*
List of Contributors	*xiii*

Introduction   1

1 Physical and Physiological Demands of Football   3
Carlo Castagna, Peter Krustrup, George P. Nassis,
Morten B. Randers, João Brito, and Magni Mohr

2 Analytical and Ecological Approaches to Aerobic
and Anaerobic Conditioning in Football   21
Ryland Morgans, Rafael Oliveira, and Rui Miguel Silva

3 Strength, Power, and Plyometric Training in Football   40
Benjamin Rosenblatt and Martin Evans

4 Speed and Agility Training in Football   53
Filipe Manuel Clemente, Jason Moran,
Rodrigo Ramirez-Campillo, Helmi Chaabene,
and Javier Sanchez-Sanchez

5 Periodization: Planning Fitness Training in Football   74
Magni Mohr, Carlo Castagna, Lars Nybo,
Pawel Chmura, and Peter Krustrup

vi Contents

6 Fitness Testing and Physical Profiling in Football 89
*Nikolaos D. Asimakidis, Chris Bishop, Anthony Turner, and
Marco Beato*

7 Training Load Monitoring in Football 107
*Matthew Weston, Antonio Dello Iacono,
and Shaun J. McLaren*

8 Wellness Monitoring and Readiness in Football 124
Jo Clubb and Amber E. Rowell

9 Match-Day Strategies to Enhance Football Performance:
Warming-Up, Priming, and Extra Time 140
*Samuel P. Hills, Natalie Smith, Liam P. Kilduff,
and Mark Russell*

10 Recovery Strategies after Matches 153
Robin Thorpe and Robert Allan

11 Optimizing Return to Performance Following Injury 181
Luca Maestroni and Paul Read

12 Nutrition and Soccer 202
Andrew T. Hulton and Don P.M. MacLaren

13 Basic Psychology for Coaches in Talent Development and
Elite Football 219
Alexander T. Latinjak and Eduardo Morelló Tomás

14 Considerations for Working with Female Players 238
*Stacey Emmonds, Ric Lovell, Dawn Scott,
Georgie Bruinvels, and Jo Clubb*

15 Strength and Conditioning for Youth Football 252
*Perry Stewart, Thomas John, and
Charlie Norton-Sherwood*

16 Considerations for Disability Football 272
Dave Sims

Postscript 303
Barry Drust

Index *305*

FIGURES

2.1	Categorization of high-intensity interval training types. *SSG: small-sided games	23
2.2	Intensity and duration of work and rest during long intervals (2–5 minutes)	24
2.3	Intensity and duration of work and rest during short intervals (<60 seconds)	25
2.4	Intensity and duration of work and rest during repeated-sprint training (3–10 seconds maximum effort)	25
2.5	Intensity and duration of work and rest during sprint interval training (20–30 seconds all-out)	26
2.6	Running-based HIIT bout using only maximal aerobic speed for different athletes	27
2.7	Running-based HIIT bout using the anaerobic speed reserve (ASR) percentage	28
2.8	Effects of number of players and field size in small-sided games	30
2.9	Impact of encouragement during small-sided games	32
3.1	A biomechanical framework for football	45
3.2	A principle-based approach to train for strength, power and plyometrics within professional football	51
4.1	Weekly football training plan	67
6.1	Key objectives of fitness testing in football	91
6.2	Overview of fitness testing protocols in football	101
6.3	Comprehensive fitness testing framework for football	102
7.1	Nomological network showing the role of monitoring in the training process of football players. Understanding planned training content and anticipated training loads is crucial for a robust interpretation of training monitoring data	108

viii Figures

7.2	Publication timeline for training load studies in football from 2000 to 2022 (PubMed search = [training load] AND [football]) along with landmark studies and events	109
7.3	Variation of daily (matchday, MD) external (HSRD, $\geq$14.4 km·h^{-1}) and internal (session RPE training load, [sRPE-TL]) training load across the training micro-cycle of a professional football team	110
7.4	Matchday training heart rates before and after feedback to coaches on session intensity	113
7.5	Limited variation in match sRPE despite substantial match-to-match variation in high-speed running distance (HSRD, $\geq$19.8 km·h^{-1})	115
7.6	Visualisation of daily (matchday, MD) and microcycle (Cycle) external (relative high-speed running distance [HSRD]) and internal (session RPE training load, [sRPE-TL]) training loads across three one-match micro-cycles for a professional football player	116
7.7	Factors to consider when selecting training load metrics in football. While simple, there are deeper considerations around some areas such as validity (e.g., validity of the construct, validity of the technology)	118
7.8	Speed thresholds for classifying high-speed running (HSR) and sprinting in elite football (open circles = individual studies (see Gualtieri et al., [2023]), orange diamond = zone mean)	119
7.9	The Training Load Tactics Whiteboard. A best-practice approach for the planning, monitoring, and evaluation of training load in football	120
8.1	Example monitoring periodisation in a (A) one-game week and (B) two-game week	135
9.1	A timeline of typical match-day routines for football players, with the addition of suggested strategies for improving football performance	150
10.1	A conceptual model of how recovery choices might influence subsequent performances and training adaptations	157
10.2	Predominant demands and reciprocal stressed physiological systems in football alongside associated typical symptoms and recovery interventions	168
10.3	An example of a decision-making selection process aimed at outlining the most appropriate (adaptation-recovery) modality	169
10.4	An example of the timeline of recovery modality selection and implementation in the hours and days post-match	170

11.1	Return to play progression scheme. Each rehabilitation emphasis is decided according to a targeted test-training integration process. CSA = cross sectional area, ROM = range of motion, RFD = rate of force development, ACC = acceleration, COD = change of direction	182
11.2	Strength, power and reactive strength values and standardized scores for a hypothetical, individual player	194
11.3	Strength, power and reactive strength values and standardized scores for a hypothetical, individual player	194
11.4	Strength, power and reactive strength values and standardized scores for a hypothetical, individual player	195
12.1	(A) Muscle glycogen use throughout a football match (B) Time of five 30 m sprints before the game (●), after the first half (○), and after the game (▲) with Danish fourth-division players (Krustrup et al., 2006)	204
12.2	CHO requirements for varying fuelling requirements and around MD	205
12.3	Glucose profile throughout the postprandial period and a simulated soccer protocol. *significant differences between HGI and LGI (Hulton et al., 2012)	210
12.4	Schematic of the recommendations on MD for a 15:00 kick-off (Hulton et al., 2022)	215
13.1	Sequence 1, from a club's culture and a team's motivational climate to fair play and effort expenditure	221
13.2	Sequence 2, from players' home environment and multidisciplinary coaching to in-game performance	223
13.3	Sequence 3, from psychological loads in training to players' self-regulation within and outside sport	226
13.4	Sequence 4, from coach feedback to in-game performance	228
13.5	Sequence 5, from coaches' half-time talks to players' in-game coping with challenges	230
14.1	Potential physiological mechanisms for the sex difference in muscle fatigability (or time to task failure). The figure shows those potential mechanisms that can contribute to women being more fatigue-resistant than men (Hunter et al., 2014)	240
14.2	Summary of hormonal, morphological, and performance measures change during the adolescent growth spurt for boys and girls (Emmonds and Beech, unpublished)	244
14.3	Considerations required when developing an evidence-based approach to practice in female sport (Emmonds et al., 2019)	247

x Figures

16.1 A 9 panel matrix of a hemiplegic FT2 footballer performing
a goblet, front, and back squat on a flat ground, 15 and 30
wedges. White lines provide a simple kinematic observation of
joint positions at the bottom position of the squat; joint centres
are estimated as the lateral malleolus, lateral epicondyle, great
trochanter, and acromion process 292

16.2 A 9 panel matrix of a diplegic FT1 footballer performing
a goblet, front, and back squat on a flat ground, 15 and 30
wedges. White lines provide a simple kinematic observation of
joint positions at the bottom position of the squat; joint centres
are estimated as the lateral malleolus, lateral epicondyle, great
trochanter, and acromion process 293

16.3 Demonstration of a Romanian Deadlift (RDL) in an FT2 (top
two panels) and an FT1 CP footballer. Note in both the bottom
positions, there is pronounced 'rounding' of the lumber to reach
end range and excessive knee flexion in the FT2 athlete (top
right panel). White lines provide a simple kinematic observation
of joint positions at the bottom position; joint centres are
estimated as the lateral malleolus, lateral epicondyle, great
trochanter, and acromion process 295

16.4 Demonstration of a hamstring rollout in an FT2 (top two panels)
and an FT1 CP footballer. Note in both athletes, there is good
hip extension position at the end range (right panels) which help
target the proximal aspect of the hamstring which may have
a limited range due to spasticity, demonstrated here in the top
right panel for the FT2 athlete who has increased knee flexion.
White lines provide a simple kinematic observation of joint
positions at the bottom position; joint centres are estimated as
the lateral malleolus, lateral epicondyle, great trochanter, and
acromion process 296

TABLES

1.1	Muscle and Blood Metabolites during a Football Match	13
2.1	Physiological Responses of Small-Sided Games	33
3.1	Examples of Football-Specific Tasks and the Associated Force Conditions and Required Co-contractions	47
3.2	Gym-Based Loading Strategies for the Development of Braking Force	48
3.3	Field-Based Loading Strategies for the Development of Braking Force	49
3.4	Considerations and Actions for Manipulating Volume and Intensity	50
5.1	Fitness Training Categories Important for Football	75
5.2	Recovery Times after Various Types of Training in Targeted Body Systems	77
5.3	An Example of a One-Week Training Schedule Three Weeks Prior to the Competitive Season	80
5.4a	An Example of a One-Week Training Schedule during the Season – with One Match per Week	81
5.4b	An Example of a One-Week Training Schedule during the Season – with Two Matches per Week	82
10.1	Current Evidence of the Proposed Mechanisms of Action and Practical Applications of Commonly Used Recovery Modalities	160
11.1	Physical Characteristics Threshold of a Cohort of Professional Soccer Players Returned to Sports Following ACL Reconstruction in Each Tertile	193
12.1	Example from Hulton et al. (2022) Demonstrating a Nutritional Plan to Attain a CHO Intake of 6 g/kg BM for a 75 kg Player on MD-1	208
12.2	Suggestions for Nutritional Support in the Changing Room after a Match and for a Post-match Meal	214

xii Tables

14.1 Suggestions for Closing the Gender Data Gap in Football Physical Preparation across Research and Applied Practice   247
15.1 Speed Development Considerations for Youth Football   257
15.2 Sample Speed Sessions   259
15.3 Agility Development Considerations for Youth Football   261
15.4 Sample Agility Sessions   262
15.5 Suggested Resistance Training Guidance Youth Football Players   265
15.6 Sample Strength and Power Sessions   266
16.1 Para Football Formats, Rules and Key   275
16.2 Global Positioning System Characteristics of Para Football and Able-Bodied Formats Found in the Literature. Key Variables Stated as Mean (SD) or Median [IQR]   282
16.3 GPS Speed Zone Metrics between Manufactures. Zones Given in km/h   286
16.4 Definitions of Speed Zones to Analyse Movement Patterns of Para Football Formats   287
16.5 Physical Performance Variables Found in the Literature within Para Football Players. Variables Stated as Mean (SD) or Median [25th–75th Percentile]   289
16.6 Example Strength Session Plan for an FT3 Para Footballer with the Aim of the Session to Develop Lower Limb Strength   297
16.7 Example Strength Session Plan for an FT1 Para Footballer with the Aim of the Session to Develop Lower Limb Strength   298

CONTRIBUTORS

Robert Allan
School of Health, Social Work and Sport, University of Central Lancashire, Lancashire, UK

Nikolaos D. Asimakidis
Faculty of Science and Technology, London Sport Institute, Middlesex University, London, UK

Marco Beato
School of Allied Health Sciences, University of Suffolk, and Performance Department, Ipswich Town Football Club, Ipswich, UK

Chris Bishop
Faculty of Science and Technology, London Sport Institute, Middlesex University, London, UK

João Brito
Portugal Football School, Portuguese Football Federation, Oeiras, Portugal

Georgie Bruinvels
Orreco Ltd, Business Innovation Unit, NUI Galway, Ireland, and Institute of Sport, Exercise and Health, University College London, London, UK

xiv Contributors

Carlo Castagna
Department of Biomolecular Sciences, School of Exercise and Health Sciences, University of Urbino Carlo Bo, Urbino, Italy, and Fitness Training and Biomechanics Laboratory, Italian Football Federation (FIGC), Technical Department, Coverciano, Italy, and Department of Sports Science and Clinical Biomechanics, Faculty of Health Sciences, SDU Sport and Health Sciences Cluster, University of Southern Denmark, Copenhagen, Denmark

Helmi Chaabene
Division of Training and Movement Sciences, Research Focus Cognition Sciences, University of Potsdam, Potsdam, Germany, and High Institute of Sports and Physical Education of Kef, University of Jendouba, Jendouba, Tunisia

Pawel Chmura
Department of Sports Science and Clinical Biomechanics, Faculty of Health Sciences, SDU Sport and Health Sciences Cluster, University of Southern Denmark, Copenhagen, Denmark

Filipe Manuel Clemente
Escola Superior Desporto e Lazer, Instituto Politécnico de Viana do Castelo, Viana do Castelo, Portugal, and Research Center in Sports Performance, Recreation, Innovation and Technology (SPRINT), Rio Maior, Portugal, and Instituto de Telecomunicações, Delegação da Covilhã, Aveiro, Portugal

Jo Clubb
Sports Science Consultant, Global Performance Insights Ltd, UK

Stacey Emmonds
Carnegie School of Sport, Leeds Beckett University, Leeds, UK

Martin Evans
The Football Association (UK), London, UK

Samuel P. Hills
Faculty of Health and Social Sciences, Bournemouth University, Bournemouth, UK

Andrew T. Hulton
Department of Food, Nutrition and Exercise Sciences, Faculty of Health and Medical Sciences, University of Surrey, Guildford, UK

Antonio Dello Iacono
Institute for Clinical Exercise and Health Science, School of Health and Life Sciences, University of the West of Scotland, Hamilton, UK

Contributors **xv**

Thomas John
Arsenal Performance and Research Team, Arsenal Football Club, London, UK

Liam P. Kilduff
Applied Sports Technology, Exercise Medicine Research Centre (A-STEM), and Welsh Institute of Performance Science, Faculty of Science and Engineering, Swansea University, UK

Peter Krustrup
Department of Sports Science and Clinical Biomechanics, Faculty of Health Sciences, SDU Sport and Health Sciences Cluster, and Danish Institute for Advanced Study (DIAS), University of Southern Denmark, Copenhagen, Denmark, and Sport and Health Sciences, University of Exeter, Exeter, UK

Alexander T. Latinjak
School of Allied Health Sciences, University of Suffolk, Ipswich, UK

Ric Lovell
Faculty of Science, Medicine and Health, University of Wollongong, Wollongong, Australia, and School of Health Sciences, Western Sydney University, Sydney, Australia

Don P.M. MacLaren
Research Institute for Sport and Exercise Sciences, Liverpool John Moores University, Liverpool, UK

Luca Maestroni
London Sport Institute, School of Science and Technology, Middlesex University, and Institute of Sport, Exercise and Health, London, UK

Shaun J. McLaren
Newcastle Falcons Rugby Club, Newcastle upon Tyne, UK, and Institute of Sport, Metropolitan University, London, UK

Magni Mohr
Department of Sports Science and Clinical Biomechanics, Faculty of Health Sciences, SDU Sport and Health Sciences Cluster, University of Southern Denmark, Copenhagen, Denmark, and Centre of Health Science, Faculty of Health, University of the Faroe Islands, Tórshavn, Faroe Islands

Jason Moran
School of Sport, Rehabilitation and Exercise Sciences, University of Essex, Essex, UK

xvi Contributors

Eduardo Morelló Tomás
Athletic Club Bilbao, Department of Sport Science, Bilbao, Spain

Ryland Morgans
School of Sport and Health Sciences, Cardiff Metropolitan University, Cardiff, UK

George P. Nassis
Department of Physical Education, College of Education, Kalba, Sharjah, United Arab Emirates

Charlie Norton-Sherwood
Arsenal Performance and Research Team, Arsenal Football Club, London, UK

Lars Nybo
Department of Nutrition, Exercise and Sports, University of Copenhagen, Copenhagen, Denmark

Rafael Oliveira
Sports Science School of Rio Maior, Polytechnic Institute of Santarém, Santarém, Portugal, and Research Centre in Sports Sciences, Health Sciences and Human Development, Vila Real, Portugal

Rodrigo Ramirez-Campillo
Exercise and Rehabilitation Sciences Institute, School of Physical Therapy, Faculty of Rehabilitation Sciences, Universidad Andres Bello, Santiago, Chile

Morten B. Randers
Department of Sports Science and Clinical Biomechanics, Faculty of Health Sciences, SDU Sport and Health Sciences Cluster, University of Southern Denmark, Copenhagen, Denmark

Paul Read
Institute of Sport, Exercise and Health, London, UK, and School of Sport and Exercise, University of Gloucestershire, Cheltenham, UK, and Division of Surgery and Interventional Science, University College London, London, UK, and Faculty of Sport, Allied Health and Performance Science, St. Mary's University, Twickenham, UK

Benjamin Rosenblatt
292 Performance Ltd, London, UK

Amber E. Rowell
Sports Science Lead, Adelaide Football Club, West Lakes, Australia

Contributors **xvii**

Mark Russell
Department of Sport and Wellbeing, Leeds Trinity University, Leeds, UK

Javier Sanchez-Sanchez
Research Group Planning and Assessment of Training and Athletic Performance, Faculty of Education, Universidad Pontificia de Salamanca, Salamanca, Spain

Dawn Scott
School of Health Sciences, Western Sydney University, Sydney, Australia

Rui Miguel Silva
Escola Superior Desporto e Lazer, Instituto Politécnico de Viana do Castelo, Viana do Castelo, Portugal, and Innovation and Technology (SPRINT), Rio Maior, Portugal

Dave Sims
The Para Football Research Centre, The FA Group, Wembley, UK

Natalie Smith
Department of Sport and Wellbeing, Leeds Trinity University, Leeds, UK

Perry Stewart
Arsenal Performance and Research Team, Arsenal Football Club, London, UK

Robin Thorpe
Research Institute for Sport and Exercise Sciences, School of Sport and Exercise Sciences, Liverpool John Moores University, Liverpool, UK, and College of Health Solutions, Arizona State University, Tempe, Arizona, USA, and Red Bull Athlete Performance Center, Santa Monica, California, USA

Anthony Turner
London Sport Institute, Middlesex University, London, UK

Matthew Weston
Institute for Sport, Physical Education and Health Science, Moray House School of Education and Sport, University of Edinburgh, Edinburgh, UK

INTRODUCTION

In the realm of competitive football, the quest for peak performance is a journey that never ceases. This book *Strength and Conditioning for Football: From Science to Practice* emerges as a beacon of knowledge, meticulously bridging the gap between scientific theory and the gritty reality of the pitch. Under the editorial guidance of *Marco Beato, Chris Bishop*, and *Anthony Turner*, this book is poised to become an indispensable asset for all coaches, support staff practitioners, and researchers, who are all united by a common goal – to develop football players of unparalleled prowess.

Spanning 16 comprehensive chapters, the book is a deep dive into the multifaceted world of all things physical and athletic performance for football. It commences with an exploration of the game model and the physical demands of football in Chapter 1, laying down the strategic framework that underpins all subsequent conditioning efforts. This foundational knowledge is crucial, as it sets the tone for a nuanced understanding of the sport's requirements. Chapter 2 delves into the heart of football conditioning. Here, the reader is introduced to both aerobic and anaerobic training methodologies, including innovative ball-based drills that marry technical skill with physical conditioning. The chapter serves as a testament to the evolving nature of football training, where the integration of skill work and fitness is paramount. The narrative then progresses to the raw power behind the sport in Chapter 3, which focuses on strength, power, and plyometrics. This section is a treasure trove of information on how to cultivate the explosive strength that is so vital on the football field. Speed and agility, the cornerstones of a footballer's arsenal, are dissected in Chapter 4. The training techniques discussed here are designed to sharpen the athlete's reflexes and enhance their ability to navigate the chaos of the game with grace and precision. Periodization, the art and science of training planning, is the subject of Chapter 5. It is here that the book delves into

DOI: 10.4324/9781003383475-1

2 Strength and Conditioning for Football

the meticulous orchestration of training cycles, ensuring that athletes reach their pick. Chapters 6 and 7 are dedicated to the critical aspects of fitness testing and training load monitoring. These chapters underscore the importance of data-driven approaches to training, where every sprint, every jump, and every stride is quantified and analyzed for the betterment of the athlete. Wellness monitoring and readiness take center stage in Chapter 8, emphasizing the need for a holistic approach to athlete management. This chapter highlights the importance of mental and physical health, alongside physical readiness, as key indicators of an athlete's capacity to perform. The prelude to performance – warming up, priming, and considerations for extra time – is the focus of Chapter 9. This chapter provides insights into the preparatory rituals that can make the difference between a good start and a great one. Post-match recovery strategies are explored in Chapter 10, offering guidance on how to effectively replenish and rejuvenate the athlete's body after the rigors of the game. This chapter is a crucial read for those looking to minimize downtime and maximize the quality of training sessions. Returning to play after an injury is a delicate process, and Chapter 11 addresses this with the care it deserves. Rehabilitation protocols and return-to-play criteria are discussed, providing a roadmap for injured athletes to make their comeback safely and effectively. Nutrition is the subject of Chapter 12. This chapter goes beyond the basics of sports nutrition, delving into the specific dietary needs of football players to ensure optimal performance and recovery. The psychological landscape of football is vast and complex, and Chapter 13 navigates this terrain with expertise. Mental toughness, resilience, and the psychological strategies that can give players the edge are examined in detail. Chapters 14 and 15 are devoted to the unique considerations for female and youth players. These sections acknowledge the diversity of the sport and provide specialized advice that respects the distinct physiological and developmental needs of these groups. Finally, Chapter 16 rounds out the book with a discussion on disability football. This chapter is a celebration of inclusivity, offering insights into how the beautiful game adapts to embrace athletes of all abilities.

Strength and Conditioning for Football: From Science to Practice is more than a collection of chapters; it is a manifesto for the modern football coach and player. It is a call to action to embrace the science of training, to apply it with wisdom, and to elevate the game to unprecedented heights. As readers embark on this journey, they will find themselves equipped with the knowledge to transform potential into excellence on the football field. This extended introduction aims to provide a thorough overview of the book's content, emphasizing the depth and breadth of topics covered, and setting the stage for the detailed exploration of each subject in the subsequent chapters. It is designed to be engaging and informative, reflecting the book's blend of scientific rigor and practical application.

Marco Beato, Chris Bishop, and Antony Turner

1

PHYSICAL AND PHYSIOLOGICAL DEMANDS OF FOOTBALL

Carlo Castagna, Peter Krustrup, George P. Nassis, Morten B. Randers, João Brito, and Magni Mohr

Introduction

Football stands as the world's most widely played and beloved team sport (Milanovic et al., 2015; Nassis et al., 2020; Stølen et al., 2005). Success in this sport hinges on a multitude of factors spanning technical, tactical, physical, physiological, and psychological domains. The intricate makeup of football performance poses several training challenges, which can be effectively addressed through a thorough understanding of the game's demands. However, despite the growing body of research within the scientific community, a definitive consensus on the most optimal approach for achieving success in competitive football continues to remain elusive.

Football spans across multiple levels of competition, including professional, amateur, and recreational settings, and encompasses championships and tournaments for both men and women. Despite the gender-distinctive participation, the same rules apply for men's and women's matches giving rise to concern about competitive scaling (Pedersen et al., 2019). Competitive football is proposed as a scaled version at youth level, with modified pitch dimensions and playing time duration aiming to account for biological growth. As a result, providing a "one size fit all" model to identify the physical and physiological demands of football can likely be considered misleading and reductive, at best. However, profiling the demands of elite football may be useful for strength and conditioning coaches and sports scientists. The knowledge of the physiological demands of the game enables the fitness and technical coaches to understand the physical abilities to prioritize during training, both at the group and individual levels. Match time-motion analysis data, coupled with sound physiological variables, collected in selected parts of the game, are crucial to develop training interventions (Bangsbo and

DOI: 10.4324/9781003383475-2

4 Strength and Conditioning for Football

Andersen, 2013). The detection of the most intense periods of the match and the keen analysis of physical and physiological demands involved in the game constitute a useful approach to guide on-pitch training in the form of different format ball drills (Fereday et al., 2020; Novak et al., 2021; Rico-González et al., 2022). The preparation for the match aims to develop players who are fit for their specific roles in the team (i.e., field players or goalkeepers), taking into account their individual physical and physiological characteristics (Stølen et al., 2005). Match participation may be characterized by the activity produced by players (e.g., distances covered at various speeds and accelerations) to gain competitive success, and the physiological adaptations required to sustain those activities for the duration of a match (and season). Using the current training methodology terminology, game demands may be defined as describing the internal load sustained by players to produce actual match-play considered as the external load (Jeffries et al., 2020).

Over the past few years, there has been a notable transformation in men's and women's football, resulting in heightened requirements in terms of technique, strategy, and physical prowess within the sport (Mohr et al., 2022; Nassis et al., 2020, 2022). These alterations in match-play tactics and the introduction of new initiatives by FIFA and UEFA, such as the substantial rise in match frequency due to greater participation and the rate of recurrence of European club and national team tournaments, are anticipated to significantly impact the physiological and psychological demands placed on modern men's and women's football players (Nassis et al., 2020). Consequently, the escalated demands of the game may have implications not only for physical performance levels but also for injury rates (Datson et al., 2014; Nassis et al., 2020, 2022). Therefore, the remaining content of this chapter will provide an outline of the demands imposed by football on players during competitive matches (acute load), and in the hours following competition (residual load), leading to the subsequent training sessions or games. The contextual representation of match demands and effects will serve as a reference for elite football.

Match External Load

Football represents an intermittent high-intensity activity, with a typical duration of around 90–100 minutes, which can extend to over 120 minutes in the case of matches that include extra time (Mohr et al., 2023). This intermittent nature of football is characterized by fluctuations in match activities, with reported values ranging from 1,000 to 1,650 activity changes, depending on factors like competitive level and sex (Andersson et al., 2007, 2010; Mohr et al., 2008; Stølen et al., 2005). These fluctuations lead to a change in match activity every 3–5 seconds, involving a mix of orthodox and unorthodox running (e.g., laterally and backwards), as well as directional changes in conjunction with various technical actions such as tackling, dribbling, kicking, and heading, each performed at different intensities (Reilly and Bowen, 1984; Schimpchen et al., 2021; Stølen et al., 2005).

To gain a broad overview of the external load experienced during a match, we often look at the total distance covered by players. In a standard 90-minute match, this distance typically falls within the range of 10–12 km, regardless of a player's role or gender (Andrzejewski et al., 2012; Datson et al., 2014; Mohr et al., 2003, 2008; Panduro et al., 2022; Stølen et al., 2005). For a more comprehensive assessment of match day total distance covered, it is of interest to account for various factors such as allowance for time lost (i.e., extended time), match extra-time, distance accumulated performing pre-match warm-up, and post-match cool-down routines. Match activities are typically measured by calculating the distance covered or time spent at various intensities, which are categorized using arbitrary speed thresholds. Regrettably, there is no consensus on the specific speed thresholds that should be used to define match performance (Gualtieri et al., 2023). This lack of agreement has led to challenges when comparing studies, as there are discrepancies in the speed thresholds employed to describe match intensity (Bradley and Vescovi, 2015; Carling et al., 2012).

High-intensity activities, such as sprints and intense running, are key components of the external load profile in football matches. However, obtaining consistent data on high-intensity activities in matches can be challenging due to varying speed thresholds used in different studies. Research indicates that these high-intensity activities typically constitute 10%–20% of the total distance covered by players during a match (Carling et al., 2012; Gualtieri et al., 2023; Mohr et al., 2023; Panduro et al., 2022; Paul et al., 2015; Riboli and Castagna, 2023; Stølen et al., 2005). Notably, when comparing studies using identical speed thresholds to define match external load, significant gender differences emerge (Bradley and Vescovi, 2015; Krustrup et al., 2005). For instance, female players at the same competitive level accumulate only two-thirds of the high-intensity workload compared to their male counterparts (Krustrup et al., 2005; Panduro et al., 2022).

Competitive level and players' roles in the team affect match high-intensity activities (Paul et al., 2015). In a study examining players from an Italian Serie A team, players were found to cover more high-intensity running with the ball compared to lower-ranked players reporting greater overall coverage (Rampinini et al., 2009). When comparing players at different competitive levels, contrasting results have been reported (Bradley et al., 2013; Mohr et al., 2003). In a study comparing players of different competitive levels and national leagues, it becomes evident that higher-level players cover significantly greater distances at high-intensity activities (2,430 m) and sprinting (650 m) compared to lower-level players (1.90 km and 410 m, respectively) (Mohr et al., 2003), representing a substantial difference of 28% and 58%, respectively (Mohr et al., 2003). However, Bradley and colleagues reported an inverse association between competitive level and match intensity across the professional English football leagues (Bradley et al., 2013). English professional football data contrasts with most of the studies that examined match activities in Scandinavian players of different competitive levels and genders (Andersson et al., 2010; Bangsbo, 1994; Bangsbo et al., 1991; Bradley

6 Strength and Conditioning for Football

et al., 2013; Mohr et al., 2008; Stølen et al., 2005). Differences in research designs (i.e., across country comparisons versus same country leagues comparisons), player professional status, and style of play have been proposed as possible reasons for the reported differences (Bradley et al., 2013). Interestingly, the counter-intuitive difference reported in English professional leagues was not reflective of football-specific fitness levels suggesting a diverse team approach to the game (Bradley et al., 2013; Rampinini et al., 2009). Midfielders have been reported to cover more distance at high intensity compared to attackers and central defenders (Krustrup et al., 2005; Mohr et al., 2008; Panduro et al., 2022). Attackers complete the greatest amount of sprinting during the matches, followed by midfielders and defenders (Mohr et al., 2008). However, a large amount of intra and inter-player variability in the high-intensity domain should be expected suggesting individual performance profiling when dealing with professional footballers (Fransson et al., 2017; Paul et al., 2015). The above considerations also apply to women's football, suggesting a relative construct of similarities when considering football itself (Andersson et al., 2007; Mohr et al., 2008).

The current use of arbitrary speed thresholds underestimates the real temporal and spatial length of sprint bouts, as it does not allow for the detection of the accelerations leading up to when players are sprinting at or near maximal velocity (Gualtieri et al., 2023). Furthermore, accelerations and decelerations are notably costly from a physiological standpoint, when performed during running, even if at low intensity (Sonderegger et al., 2016). With this in mind, the information coming from external load variables may be misleading if not coupled with objective physiological measurements.

Individual speed thresholds have been proposed to account for between-player differences in physical and physiological performance, and the use of mathematical algorithms to convert biomechanical loads into metabolic (i.e., metabolic power) values has been proposed (Abt and Lovell, 2009; Castagna, Varley, et al., 2017; Rago et al., 2020). Interestingly, commonly used procedures using arbitrary speed thresholds and metabolic power variables to characterize match high-intensity resulted in an almost perfect association ($r = 0.93$), suggesting procedures may be able to be used interchangeably (Castagna, Varley, et al., 2017). Currently, no consensus has been gained regarding the optimal procedure to be considered to perform an objective evaluation of match external load despite efforts made to provide principle-derived speed thresholds proposing criteria underpinning physiological constructs (Bradley and Vescovi, 2015; Gualtieri et al., 2023).

Match running intensity fluctuations have been reported to indicate temporary and cumulative performance decrement in elite football (Fransson, Vigh-Larsen, et al., 2018; Mohr et al., 2023). However, variations in match performance can be the result of physical and cognitive fatigue as well as technical–tactical fluctuations (Paul et al., 2015). Profiling the activity performed at high intensity as discrete match micro-periods (e.g., 1–5 minutes) revealed a significant decrement of distance covered in the periods immediately following the most intense moments

Physical and Physiological Demands of Football **7**

of the match (Fransson et al., 2017; Mohr et al., 2003). Provided that consistent metrics and a valid tracking system are considered, the discrete analysis of match high-intensity phases may result in a viable strategy to profile players' physiological resilience across the match (Jones, 2023).

Temporary and Cumulative Fatigue

The ability to repeat sprints across the match with limited performance decrements (i.e., repeated sprint ability) is also considered a key fitness component relevant to match success in football (Impellizzeri et al., 2008; Rampinini et al., 2007). Interestingly, repeated sprint performance (i.e., 30-m sprints with ~30 s of active recovery) has been shown to track temporary and cumulative fatigue during the match and residual fatigue in the hours following the competition (Castagna, Francini, Krustrup, et al., 2017; Krustrup et al., 2006, 2022; Mohr et al., 2015). Furthermore, repeated sprint ability has also been shown to be strongly correlated with match high intensity ($r = -0.60$) and sprint distance ($r = -0.65$) in male professional football (Rampinini et al., 2007). Despite the reported recurrence of high-intensity bouts across the match, the actual sequence of sprint bouts seems to only partially mimic the paradigms used to test the ability to repeatedly sprint in football players (Carling et al., 2012; Schimpchen et al., 2016). Nevertheless, studies have once more highlighted differences in sprint recovery times among players based on their team roles, with midfielders experiencing 20% of match sprint bouts with less than 30 s of recovery (Schimpchen et al., 2021). Again, caution must be applied when considering match sprint bouts as they may result in underestimations in duration and distance, and only rarely will players reach their maximum velocity (Schimpchen et al., 2016). Sprint performance and distances covered at high-intensity were reported to discriminate between competitive levels in professional male and female football players (Krustrup et al., 2005; Mohr et al., 2003, 2008). Interestingly, sprint activities may decrease in the latter stages of the match, reflecting the expected match-related fatigue (Krustrup et al., 2006, 2022). This reduction in sprinting could be indicative of the physiological strain experienced by players as the game progresses.

Muscle fiber composition, particularly the ratio of MHCII to MCHI, has been linked to sprint performance in matches (Mohr et al., 2016). This association applies both to the total number of sprints accumulated during the match and to the sprints performed during the most intensive peak 1-minute period. A substantial decrement (35%–45%) of high-intensity activities during the final part (5–15 min) of the match was reported (Fransson et al., 2017; Mohr et al., 2003). Motor and cognitive fatigue, have been reported to be the cause of activity decrement during the match (Behrens et al., 2023; Krustrup et al., 2006; Mohr et al., 2022, 2023). The occurrence of high-intensity phases during a football match can happen at various moments due to the unpredictable nature of the sport (Novak et al., 2021; Varley et al., 2012). The intensity of these moments is closely tied to the timeframe

8 Strength and Conditioning for Football

granularity considered for analyses, cautioning against an over-reliance on time-motion analysis for training prescription (Connor et al., 2022). Moreover, the sporadic and variable nature of peak match demands challenges the use of benchmark moments for specific training drill implementation (Novak et al., 2021). In light of such findings, the use of match data to build training drills to replicate what a player may face during the games cannot be performed without consideration for the physiological demands imposed during its application (Novak et al., 2021). Match activity during the peak 5-minute period of a match has been reported to be simulated during 4 vs 4 small-sided games (Dalen et al., 2021). However, the utilization of this information for functional training might be questionable if not contextualized within the match and coupled with internal load measurements. Studies have shown that the use of small-sided games can be effective when conducted at selected intensities, underscoring the significance of physiologically principled training in football (Hill-Haas et al., 2011; Impellizzeri et al., 2006). This highlights the priority of internal load monitoring when aiming to improve players' ability to cope with demands and fluctuating match tempos.

Comparing match external load with training paradigms, used by technical coaches to prepare players for match demands, showed an under-representation of drills promoting demands similar to or higher than the competitive scenario (Riboli and Castagna, 2023). This meaningful information, collected in highly competitive teams across the season, highlights the importance of an accurate check and regulation of training activities to warrant training specificity. In this regard, external load metrics should be accurately chosen according to the aim of the training session. Specifically, high-intensity actions, sprints, accelerations, and decelerations should be used to analyze sessions aiming to develop football-specific drills. Variables referring to high-intensity speed should be considered when specific drills are used to improve players' aerobic fitness.

Match Internal Load

The physiological demands on players during matches are assessed primarily through exercise heart rate and blood lactate levels, due to the limited invasiveness of these measures (Stølen et al., 2005). Reports of elite football matches have shown the attainment of average heart rates of 85%–90% of individual maximums, whilst achieving maximal or near maximal values in crucial parts of the game (Panduro et al., 2022; Stølen et al., 2005). While it is suggested that the assessment of maximal heart rate takes a multicomponent approach, casting doubt on the assumption that the reported heart rate ranges represent true maximal values, these ranges bear witness to a significant engagement of the cardiovascular system during competitive matches (Póvoas et al., 2019).

Interestingly, the average heart rate was similar to that found in amateur, recreational, and youth football matches, suggesting the existence of similar relative cardiovascular match demands in football (Milanovic et al., 2015). Despite the

Physical and Physiological Demands of Football **9**

similarities of the reported average match heart rate with the anaerobic threshold construct, the stochastic nature of competitive football warns against this reductionist approach (Stølen et al., 2005). However, training studies have reported moderate to large effects on match activities, mainly considered as distances covered at various speeds, by improvement in players' aerobic fitness variables (Helgerud et al., 2001; Impellizzeri et al., 2006). The aerobic contribution to global match metabolism has been estimated to be >90% of the total required match energy (Bangsbo, 1994; Stølen et al., 2005). Descriptive studies carried out with elite women's football players showed that match external load was very largely associated (r = 0.76–0.83) with the aerobic fitness variables such as VO_{2max}, speed at selected blood lactate concentrations (i.e., 2 mM), and aerobic performance tests (i.e., Yo-Yo intermittent recovery test level 1) (Krustrup et al., 2005).

Although the overall energy contribution from anaerobic metabolism during a match is relatively minor, its impact on performance is substantial, especially since key activities leading to goal opportunities are predominantly anaerobic in nature (Faude et al., 2012; Schulze et al., 2022; Stølen et al., 2005). Determining the anaerobic involvement in a match requires the sampling of blood and, occasionally, muscle specimens during the competition. Despite the minimal association between blood and muscle lactate during matches, reporting blood lactate concentration remains a viable strategy for estimating match anaerobic metabolism (Krustrup et al., 2006). Given the discreet nature of match lactate concentration assessment, the magnitude of reported values is a consequence of the activity performed before sampling (Bangsbo et al., 1991). Competitive matches have occasionally reported peak blood-lactate concentrations in the range of 10–15 mM, albeit average values are around 5 mM, suggesting the relevance that anaerobic capacity may have in competitive football (Castagna, Francini, Povoas, et al., 2017; Castagna et al., 2019; Stølen et al., 2005).

Fatigue assumed as variations in match repeated sprint ability variables have been shown to be largely associated with muscle glycogen concentration depletion in male (r = −0.56) and female players (r = 0.60) (Krustrup et al., 2022; Mohr et al., 2023). Muscle lactate concentration has also been shown to be associated with sprint performance, but only in women's football (Krustrup et al., 2022). This lending credit to the effect of high-intensity and sprint activities on metabolic perturbations (mainly glycolytic dependent) in women's football. Repeated-sprint paradigms have been employed to characterize match fatigue, serving as a physiological descriptor of the demands faced by outfield players during competition (Krustrup et al., 2006, 2021). Specifically, decrements in repeated sprint ability after high-intensity phases in the first half of the match are considered signs of temporary fatigue (i.e., adenosine-tri-phosphate [ATP]- creatine phosphate (CP) pathway), with cumulative fatigue emerging in the latter stages of matches, due to documented glycogen depletion in type II fibers (Krustrup et al., 2006, 2022). Understanding fluctuations in match high-intensity activity may provide useful insights into critical match scenarios, facilitating considerations for enhancing

10 Strength and Conditioning for Football

players' physical and physiological abilities (Castagna, Francini, Povoas, et al., 2017; Castagna et al., 2019; Fransson et al., 2017; Fransson, Nielsen, et al., 2018). The sequential analysis of discrete 1- to 5-minute match segments, considering high-intensity activity as the dependent variable and comparing them with match average values to identify match fatigue, has been suggested as a viable strategy (Bradley et al., 2010; Mohr et al., 2003; Varley et al., 2012).

Match blood glucose concentration has been reported to remain elevated during men's and women's football (Krustrup et al., 2006, 2022). Interestingly, free fatty acid concentrations have also been reported to increase during the second half in both men's and women's football matches (Krustrup et al., 2006, 2022). This suggests a shift to lipid metabolism as a result of the ongoing muscle glycogen depletion as matches progress. Muscle creatine phosphate fluctuation during a match is a natural consequence of the intense and intermittent nature of the game. During men's and women's football matches, creatine phosphate concentration has been reported to decrease across the match and particularly, during the second half, in accordance with the high-intensity bouts of activity (Krustrup et al., 2006, 2022). Muscle inosine monophosphate has also been shown to increase during matches but may be considerably lower than those observed during exhaustive exercise (Krustrup et al., 2006). Adenosine-tri-phosphate (ATP) turnover rarely shows a large drop in muscle concentration after high-intensity phases of the second half in women's football (Krustrup et al., 2022). In men's football, muscle ATP concentrations are typically more stable (Krustrup et al., 2006). However, despite similar muscle and blood metabolite variability across matches, the magnitude of the reported ATP concentration was lower in women's compared to men's football (Krustrup et al., 2022). Considering match relative effort, using sex-related maximal values may prove useful in better understanding some of the key differences in physiological demands, in both men's and women's football (Castagna, Francini, Povoas, et al., 2017).

Residual Fatigue

While acute match fatigue can inform appropriate training strategies, such as examining the most intense periods during matches, post-match fatigue becomes valuable in structuring training interventions throughout the subsequent weekly micro-cycle. This involves accounting for the recovery profile of players based on the unique demands of the game (Fransson, Vigh-Larsen, et al., 2018). Studies have documented the lingering impact of match demands on players' physiology, extending several hours/days post-match (Silva et al., 2017). This leads to a subsequent decrease in physical performance and variations in muscle physiology functions during the hour following the match, termed residual fatigue (Silva et al., 2017).

Residual match fatigue has been monitored in the hours following competitive matches, employing physical performance paradigms that are indicative of football physiological performance (Mohr et al., 2015; Silva et al., 2017). These paradigms include repeated sprinting, maximal voluntary force, explosive strength, flexibility, and intermittent high-intensity endurance (Fransson, Vigh-Larsen, et al., 2018; Silva et al., 2017). Notably, residual match fatigue demonstrates a progressive dissipation within at least 72 hours post-competition, with a full homeostatic recovery requiring 96 hours (Silva et al., 2017). These findings underscore the importance of players' physical and psychological resilience, especially during congested match schedules (Nassis et al., 2020). Further to this, in modern football (irrespective of sex), fixture schedules often require players to compete again less than 96 hours after the previous match, inducing incomplete recovery in players on a continual basis throughout the season.

Physiological resilience has been reported as a dimension of endurance performance (Jones, 2023). Considering football as an unpredictable, high-intensity, intermittent endurance exercise, physiological resilience should be considered when preparing elite competitive players. This prepares players to cope with the repeated demands imposed on them throughout the congested match season and helps limit performance decrements during competition. This is of specific urgency in modern football as frequent competition with less than four days of break has been reported to increase injury risk (Bengtsson et al., 2013, 2018). This may mean that young players should be trained and/or selected to improve their aerobic fitness as this has been reported to foster enhanced resilience between matches (i.e., greater immune system response) and to enhance their ability to store muscle glycogen (Areta and Hopkins, 2018; Malm et al., 2004).

The documented decrease in physical performance and physiological functions reported as a sign of post-match residual fatigue is said to be partly the result of the remarkable muscle glycogen depletion caused by match activities (Mohr et al., 2015, 2022, 2023). After an experimental men's football match, a 43% decrement in muscle glycogen was reported, resulting in 47% of the vastus lateralis muscle fibers being almost depleted (Krustrup et al., 2006). Similar post-match glycogen decrements (42%) have been reported in women's football with 80% of type I fibers and 70% of type II fibers being almost empty or completely empty after the match (Krustrup et al., 2022). These findings add to the seminal biopsy studies conducted with professional players in the early 1970s and 1980s, confirming the importance of players having fully replenished muscle glycogen stores before competitive fixtures (Jacobs et al., 1982; Saltin, 1973; Stølen et al., 2005). Post-match muscle glycogen concentration, tissue inflammation, oxidative stress and muscle damage may be some of the variables that should be considered in the pursuit of building competitive resilience in modern football. The type of training intervention during the weekly macrocycle following the match may potentially affect the restoration of muscle glycogen concentration (Areta and Hopkins, 2018; Fransson, Nielsen, et al., 2018; Impey et al., 2020). The role of muscle glycogen concentration on match physical performance (i.e., external load, sprint performance) and post-match residual fatigue has been shown to be exacerbated when extra time is

12 Strength and Conditioning for Football

played (Mohr et al., 2023). There is consensus in promoting proper pre-match and post-match nutritional strategies to ensure optimal glycogen repletion (Abreu et al., 2021; Collins et al., 2020; Mohr et al., 2022). Glycogen resynthesis is delayed after competitive match-play with a total of three days required for full supercompensation (Table 1.1), and even four days after extraordinarily intense matches, probably due to micro muscle damage related to specific intense activities such as decelerations and changes of direction occurring during match-play (Mohr et al., 2022, 2023).

Practical Applications

Over the past few decades, elite football has evolved into a notably more intense sport compared to the past, featuring increased instances of sprinting, high-speed running, and a greater prevalence of high-impact actions throughout the entire match (Nassis et al., 2020, 2022). Moreover, there is a rise in the intensity of peak periods, marked by more extended durations of "serial high-intensity action," often induced by strategies such as high pressing, repressing, and counterattacks.

Elite football match demands and the related performance decrements may be profiled accounting for three main fatigue paradigms namely:

- Temporary fatigue;
- Cumulative fatigue.
- Residual fatigue

Temporary fatigue performance decrements, characterized by a decline in sprint abilities, are reported to occur after peak intensity periods, with a distinct manifestation during the initial 5–10 min of the second half (Mohr et al., 2005). This decline is attributed to the reduction in leg muscle and core temperature during the halftime period suggesting re-warm up during the interval (Mohr et al., 2004). Notably, temporary fatigue can undergo partial recovery during the first phase of the match (i.e., the first half), particularly when it is primarily related to the ATP-PC pathway, and a re-warm-up is conducted during the match interval (Krustrup et al., 2006, 2022; Mohr et al., 2004). Cumulative fatigue refers to the performance decrements that manifests during the last 15–20 min of the match caused by a selective muscle fiber depletion in glycogen. Elite football match-play results in a substantial depletion of glycogen in a significant portion of both slow-twitch and fast-twitch fibers in the thigh muscles. By the end of match-play, approximately 70%–80% of individual fibers are either empty or nearly depleted of glycogen (Mohr et al., 2022). Inter-player variability in the magnitude of muscle glycogen depletion is reduced when considering selective fiber-type glycogen uptake. Indeed, high-intensity and sprint bouts, occurring occasionally and persistently during a match, are reported to affect players' type II fibers, impairing sprint performance, particularly in the second half of the match (Krustrup et al., 2006). The pattern of glycogen depletion

Physical and Physiological Demands of Football **13**

TABLE 1.1 Muscle and Blood Metabolites during a Football Match

						Changes (%)			
Variable	Sex	Baseline	After	First	Second	After	First	Second	Extended
ATP Muscle [mM kg^{-1}dw]	Male	26.4	23.0	25.6	22.6	13	3	14	
IMP Muscle [mM kg^{-1}dw]	Male	0	0.3	0.2	0.6	300	200	600	
CP [mM kg^{-1}dw]	Male	88	79	76	67	10	14	24	
	Female	79	80	67	70				
Lactate Muscle [mM kg^{-1}dw]	Male	4.2	13.0	15.9	16.9	210	279	302	300
	Female	6.4	12.9	14.3	9.8				
H$^+$ Muscle [µM kg^{-1}dw]	Male	57	69	111	86	21	95	51	
Muscle pH [-logH$^+$]	Male	7.24	7.17	6.96	7.07	1	4	2	
	Female	7.25	7.17	7.20	7.21				
Muscle Glycogen [mM kg^{-1}dw]	Male	449	255	296	241	43	34	46	−50
	Female	409	236	318	248	42	22	39	
Lactate Blood [mM]	Male	1.3	3.9	6.0	5.0	−200	−362	−285	500
	Female	1.3	8.4			−546			
Glucose Blood [mM]	Male	4.5	4.9	6.1	5.3	−9	−36	−18	−13
	Female	4.7	7.9			−68			
Plasma FFA [µM]	Male	390	1365	555	740	−250	−42	−90	
	Female	509	521			−2			
Plasma Glycerol [µM]	Male	81		185	234		−128	−189	137
	Female	63.1	146.2						
Plasma NH$_3$ [µM]	Male	59	199	203	217	−237	−244	−268	191
	Female	62.3	115.3						
Plasma K$^+$ [mM]	Male	3.9	4.3	4.9	4.8	−10	−26	−23	
	Female	3.9	4.6						
Plasma Insulin [µM]	Male	15.2		7.4	6		51	61	

% = percentage of baseline or pre-match values; after = after the first end of the match; half first = after high-intensity phases during the first half; second = after high-intensity phases during the second half; extended = extended match time. Male = (Krustrup et al., 2006); Female = (Krustrup et al., 2022).

14 Strength and Conditioning for Football

undergoes notable shifts during football match-play, with a considerably higher rate of utilization observed in the initial 15 minutes compared to the rest of the game. This aligns with the peak intensity exercise periods for over three-quarters of the players. The observed increase in plasma-free fatty acid accumulation in the second half suggests that elite football players may employ pacing strategies to sustain optimal performance throughout the entire match duration (Krustrup et al., 2006, 2022). The etiology of temporary fatigue is intricate and not fully elucidated, but it may, in part, be associated with intramuscular ionic perturbations. These perturbations can impact excitation-contraction coupling, muscle metabolite alterations, and a decrease in enzyme function induced by acidity. Elite football match-play relies on a combination of aerobic and anaerobic energy sources. Notably, there is a predominant average aerobic energy turnover at both whole-body and leg muscle levels, supplemented by periodic spikes in anaerobic energy turnover. These spikes involve the utilization of energy-rich phosphates and glycolysis, with lactate as the end product. While the anaerobic energy turnover rates are moderate compared to other high-intensity sports, the cumulative values are substantial, leading to significant glycogen depletion. The elevated aerobic component is achieved during exercise conditions that heavily engage both slow-twitch and fast-twitch fibers in the leg muscles. This places substantial demands on the aerobic power and capacity of the fast-twitch fibers in the thigh and calf muscles. Consequently, muscle force, and rapid muscle force, may not be fully recovered after competitive match-play until three days after the match (72 hours) (Silva et al., 2017). This suggests caution when the implementation of strength training sessions is planned in the first days of the training micro-cycle following the match (Fransson, Vigh-Larsen, et al., 2018; Lovell et al., 2018). Fluid loss during elite football match-play is large, but controllable, under normal environmental conditions, but it can result in performance deterioration and potentially heat shock in hot and humid environment (Mohr et al., 2010; Racinais et al., 2012).

Recovery following football training is contingent on the nature of the activity. Generally, full recovery occurs in less than a day after aerobic low- and medium-intensity exercise drills, within one day after aerobic high-intensity low-impact drills, within two days after high-intensity medium-impact aerobic exercise drills and anaerobic sprint endurance maintenance training, and within three days after anaerobic sprint endurance production training. For speed training, recovery is less than a day for short sprints (>2 s) and up to two days for longer sprints (4–5 s). This practical evidence should be considered when dealing with match residual fatigue to organize the post-match training micro-cycle. The time interval between matches should inform decisions on training load, encompassing goals, intensity, and volume, to ensure optimal match performance and player well-being. Individualized training and recovery procedures should be considered according to the reported effect of match-play and structured according to player's sex, physiology, and training status.

References

Abreu, R., Figueiredo, P., Becker, P., Marques, J. P., Amorim, S., Caetano, C., . . . Brito, J. (2021). Portuguese Football Federation consensus statement 2020: nutrition and performance in football. *BMJ Open Sport Exercise Medicine, 7*(3), e001082. https://doi.org/10.1136/bmjsem-2021-001082

Abt, G., and Lovell, R. (2009). The use of individualized speed and intensity thresholds for determining the distance run at high-intensity in professional soccer. *Journal of Sports Sciences, 27*(9), 893–898. https://www.ncbi.nlm.nih.gov/entrez/query.fcgi?cmd=Retrieve&db=PubMed&dopt=Citation&list_uids=19629838

Andersson, H., Krustrup, P., and Mohr, M. (2007). Differences in movement pattern, heart rate and fatigue development in international versus national league matches of Swedish and Danish elite female soccer players. *Journal of Sports Science and Medicine, 6*(Suppl. 10), 109.

Andersson, H. A., Randers, M. B., Heiner-Moller, A., Krustrup, P., and Mohr, M. (2010). Elite female soccer players perform more high-intensity running when playing in international games compared with domestic league games [Comparative Study Research Support, Non -U.S. Gov't]. *Journal of Strength and Conditioning Research, 24*(4), 912–919. https://doi.org/10.1519/JSC.0b013e3181d09f21

Andrzejewski, M., Chmura, J., Pluta, B., and Kasprzak, A. (2012). Analysis of motor activities of professional soccer players. *Journal of Strength and Conditioning Research, 26*(6), 1481–1488. https://doi.org/10.1519/JSC.0b013e318231ab4c

Areta, J. L., and Hopkins, W. G. (2018). Skeletal muscle glycogen content at rest and during endurance exercise in humans: a meta-analysis. *Sports Medicine, 48*(9), 2091–2102. https://doi.org/10.1007/s40279-018-0941-1

Bangsbo, J. (1994). The physiology of soccer--with special reference to intense intermittent exercise. *Acta Physiologica Scandinavica Supplementum, 619*, 1–155. https://www.ncbi.nlm.nih.gov/pubmed/8059610

Bangsbo, J., and Andersen, J. L. (2013). *Power Training in Football: A Scientific and Practical Approach.* Espergærde: Bangsbosport.

Bangsbo, J., Norregaard, L., and Thorso, F. (1991). Activity profile of competition soccer. *Canadian Journal of Sports Sciences, 16*(2), 110–116. https://www.ncbi.nlm.nih.gov/pubmed/1647856

Behrens, M., Gube, M., Chaabene, H., Prieske, O., Zenon, A., Broscheid, K. C., . . . Weippert, M. (2023). Fatigue and human performance: an updated framework. *Sports Medicine, 53*(1), 7–31. https://doi.org/10.1007/s40279-022-01748-2

Bengtsson, H., Ekstrand, J., and Hagglund, M. (2013). Muscle injury rates in professional football increase with fixture congestion: an 11-year follow-up of the UEFA Champions League injury study. *British Journal of Sports Medicine, 47*(12), 743–747. https://doi.org/10.1136/bjsports-2013-092383

Bengtsson, H., Ekstrand, J., Walden, M., and Hagglund, M. (2018). Muscle injury rate in professional football is higher in matches played within 5 days since the previous match: a 14-year prospective study with more than 130 000 match observations. *British Journal of Sports Medicine, 52*(17), 1116–1122. https://doi.org/10.1136/bjsports-2016-097399

Bradley, P. S., Carling, C., Gomez Diaz, A., Hood, P., Barnes, C., Ade, J., . . . Mohr, M. (2013). Match performance and physical capacity of players in the top three competitive standards of English professional soccer. *Human Movement Science, 32*(4), 808–821. https://doi.org/10.1016/j.humov.2013.06.002

16 Strength and Conditioning for Football

Bradley, P. S., Di Mascio, M., Peart, D., Olsen, P., and Sheldon, B. (2010). High-intensity activity profiles of elite soccer players at different performance levels. *Journal of Strength and Conditioning Research*, *24*(9), 2343–2351. https://doi.org/10.1519/JSC.0b013e3181aeb1b3

Bradley, P. S., and Vescovi, J. D. (2015). Velocity thresholds for women's soccer matches: sex specificity dictates high-speed running and sprinting thresholds - Female Athletes in Motion (FAiM). *International Journal of Sports Physiology and Performance*, *10*(1), 112–116. https://doi.org/10.1123/ijspp.2014-0212

Carling, C., Le Gall, F., and Dupont, G. (2012). Analysis of repeated high-intensity running performance in professional soccer. *Journal of Sports Sciences*, *30*(4), 325–336.

Castagna, C., Francini, L., Krustrup, P., Fenarnandes-da-Silva, J., Povoas, S. C. A., Bernardini, A., and D'Ottavio, S. (2017). Reliability characteristics and applicability of a repeated sprint ability test in male young soccer players. *Journal of Strength and Conditioning Research*, *32*(6), 1538–1544. https://doi.org/10.1519/JSC.0000000000002031

Castagna, C., Francini, L., Povoas, S. C., and D'Ottavio, S. (2017). Long sprint abilities in soccer: ball vs running drills. *International Journal of Sports Physiology and Performance*, *12*(9), 1–22. https://doi.org/10.1123/ijspp.2016-0565

Castagna, C., Stefano, D. O., Stefano, C., and Cristina, A. P. S. (2019). The effects of long sprint ability-oriented small-sided games using different ratios of players to pitch area on internal and external load in soccer players. *International Journal of Sports Physiology and Performance*, *14*, 1265–1272. https://doi.org/10.1123/ijspp.2018-0645

Castagna, C., Varley, M., Povoas, S. C. A., and D'Ottavio, S. (2017). Evaluation of the match external load in soccer: methods comparison. *International Journal of Sports Physiology and Performance*, *12*(4), 490–495. https://doi.org/10.1123/ijspp.2016-0160

Collins, J., Maughan, R. J., Gleeson, M., Bilsborough, J., Jeukendrup, A., Morton, J. P., . . . McCall, A. (2020). UEFA expert group statement on nutrition in elite football. Current evidence to inform practical recommendations and guide future research. *British Journal of Sports Medicine*, *55*(8). https://doi.org/10.1136/bjsports-2019-101961

Connor, M., Mernagh, D., and Beato, M. (2022). Quantifying and modelling the game speed outputs of English Championship soccer players. *Research in Sports Medicine*, *30*(2), 169–181. https://doi.org/10.1080/15438627.2021.1888108

Dalen, T., Sandmæl, S., Stevens, T. G. A., Hjelde, G. H., Kjøsnes, T. N., and Wisløff, U. (2021). Differences in acceleration and high-intensity activities between small-sided games and peak periods of official matches in elite soccer players. *Journal of Strength and Conditioning Research*, *35*(7), 2018–2024. https://doi.org/10.1519/jsc.0000000000003081

Datson, N., Hulton, A., Andersson, H., Lewis, T., Weston, M., Drust, B., and Gregson, W. (2014). Applied physiology of female soccer: an update. *Sports Medicine*, *44*(9), 1225–1240. https://doi.org/10.1007/s40279-014-0199-1

Faude, O., Koch, T., and Meyer, T. (2012). Straight sprinting is the most frequent action in goal situations in professional football. *Journal of Sports Science*, *30*(7), 625–631. https://doi.org/10.1080/02640414.2012.665940

Fereday, K., Hills, S. P., Russell, M., Smith, J., Cunningham, D. J., Shearer, D., . . . Kilduff, L. P. (2020). A comparison of rolling averages versus discrete time epochs for assessing the worst-case scenario locomotor demands of professional soccer match-play. *Journal of Science and Medicine in Sport*, *23*(8), 764–769. https://doi.org/10.1016/j.jsams.2020.01.002

Fransson, D., Krustrup, P., and Mohr, M. (2017). Running intensity fluctuations indicate temporary performance decrement in top-class football. *Science and Medicine in Football*, *1*(1), 10–17. https://doi.org/10.1080/02640414.2016.1254808

Fransson, D., Nielsen, T. S., Olsson, K., Christensson, T., Bradley, P. S., Fatouros, I. G., . . . Mohr, M. (2018). Skeletal muscle and performance adaptations to high-intensity training in elite male soccer players: speed endurance runs versus small-sided game training. *European Journal of Applied Physiology*, *118*(1), 111–121. https://doi.org/10.1007/s00421-017-3751-5

Fransson, D., Vigh-Larsen, J. F., Fatouros, I. G., Krustrup, P., and Mohr, M. (2018). Fatigue responses in various muscle groups in well-trained competitive male players after a simulated soccer game. *Journal of Human Kinetics*, *61*, 85–97.

Gualtieri, A., Rampinini, E., Dello Iacono, A., and Beato, M. (2023). High-speed running and sprinting in professional adult soccer: current thresholds definition, match demands and training strategies. A systematic review. *Frontiers in Sports and Active Living*, *5*, 1116293. https://doi.org/10.3389/fspor.2023.1116293

Helgerud, J., Engen, L. C., Wisloff, U., and Hoff, J. (2001). Aerobic endurance training improves soccer performance. *Medicine and Science in Sports and Exercise*, *33*(11), 1925–1931. https://www.ncbi.nlm.nih.gov/pubmed/11689745

Hill-Haas, S. V., Dawson, B., Impellizzeri, F. M., and Coutts, A. J. (2011). Physiology of small-sided games training in football: a systematic review. *Sports Medicine*, *41*(3), 199–220. https://doi.org/10.2165/11539740-000000000-00000

Impellizzeri, F. M., Marcora, S. M., Castagna, C., Reilly, T., Sassi, A., Iaia, F. M., and Rampinini, E. (2006). Physiological and performance effects of generic versus specific aerobic training in soccer players. *International Journal of Sports Medicine*, *27*(6), 483–492. https://doi.org/10.1055/s-2005-865839

Impellizzeri, F. M., Rampinini, E., Castagna, C., Bishop, D., Ferrari Bravo, D., Tibaudi, A., and Wisloff, U. (2008). Validity of a repeated-sprint test for football. *International Journal of Sports Medicine*, *29*(11), 899–905. https://doi.org/10.1055/s-2008-1038491

Impey, S. G., Jevons, E., Mees, G., Cocks, M., Strauss, J., Chester, N., . . . Morton, J. P. (2020). Glycogen utilization during running: intensity, sex, and muscle-specific responses. *Medicine and Science in Sports and Exercise*, *52*(9), 1966–1975. https://doi.org/10.1249/mss.0000000000002332

Jacobs, I., Westlin, N., Karlsson, J., Rasmusson, M., and Houghton, B. (1982). Muscle glycogen and diet in elite soccer players. *European Journal of Applied Physiology and Occupational Physiology*, *48*(3), 297–302. https://doi.org/10.1007/BF00430219

Jeffries AC, Marcora SM, Coutts AJ, Wallace L, McCall A, Impellizzeri FM. Development of a Revised Conceptual Framework of Physical Training for Use in Research and Practice. Sports Med. 2022 Apr;52(4):709–724. doi: 10.1007/s40279-021-01551-5. Epub 2021 Sep 14. PMID: 34519982.

Jones, A. M. (2023). The fourth dimension: physiological resilience as an independent determinant of endurance exercise performance. *Journal of Physiology*, *602*(17), 4113–4128. https://doi.org/10.1113/JP284205

Krustrup, P., Mohr, M., Ellingsgaard, H., and Bangsbo, J. (2005). Physical demands during an elite female soccer game: importance of training status. *Medicine and Science in Sports and Exercise*, *37*(7), 1242–1248.

Krustrup, P., Mohr, M., Nybo, L., Draganidis, D., Randers, M. B., Ermidis, G., . . . Fatouros, I. G. (2022). Muscle metabolism and impaired sprint performance in an elite women's football game. *Scandinavian Journal of Medicine and Science in Sports*, *32*(Suppl 1), 27–38. https://doi.org/10.1111/sms.13970

Krustrup, P., Mohr, M., Steensberg, A., Bencke, J., Kjaer, M., and Bangsbo, J. (2006). Muscle and blood metabolites during a soccer game: implications for sprint performance. *Medicine and Science in Sports and Exercise*, *38*(6), 1165–1174.

18 Strength and Conditioning for Football

Lovell, R., Whalan, M., Marshall, P. W. M., Sampson, J. A., Siegler, J. C., and Buchheit, M. (2018). Scheduling of eccentric lower limb injury prevention exercises during the soccer micro-cycle: Which day of the week? *Scandinavian Journal of Medicine and Science in Sports*, *28*(10), 2216–2225. https://doi.org/10.1111/sms.13226

Malm, C., Ekblom, O., and Ekblom, B. (2004). Immune system alteration in response to increased physical training during a five day soccer training camp. *International Journal of Sports Medicine*, *25*(6), 471–476. https://doi.org/10.1055/s-2004-821119

Milanovic, Z., Pantelic, S., Covic, N., Sporis, G., and Krustrup, P. (2015). Is recreational soccer effective for improving VO_{2max}? A systematic review and meta-analysis. *Sports Medicine*, *45*(9), 1339–1353. https://doi.org/10.1007/s40279-015-0361-4

Mohr, M., Draganidis, D., Chatzinikolaou, A., Barbero-Alvarez, J. C., Castagna, C., Douroudos, I., . . . Fatouros, I. G. (2015). Muscle damage, inflammatory, immune and performance responses to three football games in 1 week in competitive male players. *European Journal of Applied Physiology*, *116*, 179–193. https://doi.org/10.1007/s00421-015-3245-2

Mohr, M., Ermidis, G., Jamurtas, A. Z., Vigh-Larsen, J. F., Poulios, A., Draganidis, D., . . . Fatouros, I. G. (2023). Extended match time exacerbates fatigue and impacts physiological responses in male soccer players. *Medicine and Science in Sports and Exercise*, *55*(1), 80–92. https://doi.org/10.1249/MSS.0000000000003021

Mohr, M., Krustrup, P., Andersson, H., Kirkendal, D., and Bangsbo, J. (2008). Match activities of elite women soccer players at different performance levels. *Journal of Strength and Conditioning Research*, *22*(2), 341–349. https://doi.org/10.1519/JSC.0b013e318165fef6

Mohr, M., Krustrup, P., and Bangsbo, J. (2003). Match performance of high-standard soccer players with special reference to development of fatigue. *Journal of Sports Sciences*, *21*, 519–528.

Mohr, M., Krustrup, P., and Bangsbo, J. (2005). Fatigue in soccer: a brief review. *Journal of Sports Sciences*, *23*(6), 593–599.

Mohr, M., Krustrup, P., Nybo, L., Nielsen, J., and Bangsbo, J. (2004). Muscle temperature and sprint performance during soccer matches – beneficial effect of re-warm-up at half-time. *Scandinavian Journal of Medicine and Science in Sports*, *14*, 156–162.

Mohr, M., Mujika, I., Santisteban, J., Randers, M. B., Bischoff, R., Solano, R., . . . Krustrup, P. (2010). Examination of fatigue development in elite soccer in a hot environment: a multi-experimental approach. *Scandinavian Journal of Medicine and Science in Sports*, *20*(Suppl 3), 125–132. https://doi.org/10.1111/j.1600-0838.2010.01217.x

Mohr, M., Thomassen, M., Girard, O., Racinais, S., and Nybo, L. (2016). Muscle variables of importance for physiological performance in competitive football. *European Journal of Applied Physiology*, *116*(2), 251–262. https://doi.org/10.1007/s00421-015-3274-x

Mohr, M., Vigh-Larsen, J. F., and Krustrup, P. (2022). Muscle glycogen in elite soccer - a perspective on the implication for performance, fatigue, and recovery. *Frontiers in Sports and Active Living*, *4*, 876534. https://doi.org/10.3389/fspor.2022.876534

Nassis, G. P., Brito, J., Tomas, R., Heiner-Moller, K., Harder, P., Kryger, K. O., and Krustrup, P. (2022). Elite women's football: evolution and challenges for the years ahead. *Scandinavian Journal of Medicine and Science in Sports*, *32*(Suppl. 1), 7–11. https://doi.org/10.1111/sms.14094

Nassis, G. P., Massey, A., Jacobsen, P., Brito, J., Randers, M. B., Castagna, C., . . . Krustrup, P. (2020). Elite football of 2030 will not be the same as that of 2020: preparing players, coaches, and support staff for the evolution. *Scandinavian Journal of Medicine and Science in Sports, 30*(6), 962–964. https://doi.org/10.1111/sms.13681

Novak, A. R., Impellizzeri, F. M., Trivedi, A., Coutts, A. J., and McCall, A. (2021). Analysis of the worst-case scenarios in an elite football team: towards a better understanding and application. *Journal of Sports Sciences, 39*(16), 1850–1859. https://doi.org/10.1080/026 40414.2021.1902138

Panduro, J., Ermidis, G., Røddik, L., Vigh-Larsen, J. F., Madsen, E. E., Larsen, M. N., . . . Randers, M. B. (2022). Physical performance and loading for six playing positions in elite female football: full-game, end-game, and peak periods. *Scandinavian Journal of Medicine and Science in Sports, 32*(Suppl 1), 115–126. https://doi.org/10.1111/ sms.13877

Paul, D. J., Bradley, P. S., and Nassis, G. P. (2015). Factors affecting match running performance of elite soccer players: shedding some light on the complexity. *International Journal of Sports Physiology and Performance, 10*(4), 516–519. https://doi.org/10.1123/ IJSPP.2015-0029

Pedersen, A. V., Aksdal, I. M., and Stalsberg, R. (2019). Scaling demands of soccer according to anthropometric and physiological sex differences: a fairer comparison of men's and women's soccer. *Frontiers in Psychology, 10*, 762. https://doi.org/10.3389/ fpsyg.2019.00762

Póvoas, S. C., Krustrup, P., Pereira, R., Vieira, S., Carneiro, I., Magalhaes, J., and Castagna, C. (2019). Maximal heart rate assessment in recreational football players: a study involving a multiple testing approach. *Scandinavian Journal of Medicine and Science in Sports, 29*(10), 1537–1545. https://doi.org/10.1111/sms.13472

Racinais, S., Mohr, M., Buchheit, M., Voss, S. C., Gaoua, N., Grantham, J., and Nybo, L. (2012). Individual responses to short-term heat acclimatisation as predictors of football performance in a hot, dry environment. *British Journal of Sports Medicine, 46*(11), 810–815. https://doi.org/10.1136/bjsports-2012-091227

Rago, V., Brito, J., Figueiredo, P., Krustrup, P., and Rebelo, A. (2020). Application of individualized speed zones to quantify external training load in professional soccer. *Journal of Human Kinetics, 72*, 279–289.

Rampinini, E., Bishop, D., Marcora, S. M., Ferrari Bravo, D., Sassi, R., and Impellizzeri, F. M. (2007). Validity of simple field tests as indicators of match-related physical performance in top-level professional soccer players. *International Journal of Sports Medicine, 28*(3), 228–235.

Rampinini, E., Impellizzeri, F. M., Castagna, C., Coutts, A. J., and Wisløff, U. (2009). Technical performance during soccer matches of the Italian Serie A league: effect of fatigue and competitive level. *Journal of Science and Medicine in Sport, 12*(1), 227–233. https:// doi.org/10.1016/j.jsams.2007.10.002

Reilly, T., and Bowen, T. (1984). Exertional cost of changes in directional modes of running. *Perceptual and Motor Skills, 58*, 49–50.

Riboli, A., and Castagna, C. (2023). Soccer-drill specificity in top-class male players with reference to peak match locomotor demands. *Journal of Sports Sciences, 41*(6), 1–11. https://doi.org/10.1080/02640414.2023.2228131

Rico-González, M., Oliveira, R., Palucci Vieira, L. H., Pino-Ortega, J., and Clemente, F. M. (2022). Players' performance during worst-case scenarios in professional soccer matches: a systematic review. *Biology of Sport, 39*(3), 695–713. https://doi.org/10.5114/ biolsport.2022.107022

Saltin, B. (1973). Metabolic fundamentals in exercise. *Medicine and Science in Sports*, *5*(3), 137–146. https://www.ncbi.nlm.nih.gov/pubmed/4270581

Schimpchen, J., Gopaladesikan, S., and Meyer, T. (2021). The intermittent nature of player physical output in professional football matches: an analysis of sequences of peak intensity and associated fatigue responses. *European Journal of Sport Science*, *21*(6), 793–802.

Schimpchen, J., Skorski, S., Nopp, S., and Meyer, T. (2016). Are "classical" tests of repeated-sprint ability in football externally valid? A new approach to determine in-game sprinting behaviour in elite football players. *Journal of Sports Sciences*, *34*(6), 519–526. https://doi.org/10.1080/02640414.2015.1112023

Schulze, E., Julian, R., and Meyer, T. (2022). Exploring factors related to goal scoring opportunities in professional football. *Science and Medicine in Football*, *6*(2), 181–188. https://doi.org/10.1080/24733938.2021.1931421

Silva, J. R., Rumpf, M. C., Hertzog, M., Castagna, C., Farooq, A., Girard, O., and Hader, K. (2017). Acute and residual soccer match-related fatigue: a systematic review and meta-analysis. *Sports Medicine*, *48*, 539–583. https://doi.org/10.1007/s40279-017-0798-8

Sonderegger, K., Tschopp, M., and Taube, W. (2016). The challenge of evaluating the intensity of short actions in soccer: a new methodological approach using percentage acceleration. *PLoS One*, *11*(11), e0166534. https://doi.org/10.1371/journal.pone.0166534

Stølen, T., Chamari, K., Castagna, C., and Wisløff, U. (2005). Physiology of soccer: an update. *Sports Medicine*, *35*(6), 501–536.

Varley, M. C., Elias, G. P., and Aughey, R. J. (2012). Current match-analysis techniques' underestimation of intense periods of high-velocity running. *International Journal of Sports Physiology and Performance*, *7*(2), 183–185. https://doi.org/10.1123/ijspp.7.2.183

2

ANALYTICAL AND ECOLOGICAL APPROACHES TO AEROBIC AND ANAEROBIC CONDITIONING IN FOOTBALL

Ryland Morgans, Rafael Oliveira, and Rui Miguel Silva

Introduction

Research in professional football has shown that the physical demands of competitive match-play have substantially increased over the last few decades (Carling et al., 2016; Morgans et al., 2024) as well as training demands (Oliveira et al., 2022). As such, the role of support staff has developed to provide theoretical, scientific, and practical support to the manager in a variety of areas. These include performance analysis, strength and conditioning, and the integration of technical and tactical elements. The role of fitness and conditioning staff is to have knowledge of scientific literature and analyze performance data to condition and recover players appropriately to deal with the ever-evolving demands of elite football competition.

Various football actions stress the different physiological energy systems (Malone et al., 2015). Football is characterized by intermittent bouts of low- and high-intensity activities (Drust et al., 2007) in which aerobic metabolism is predominant from 80% to 90% of a full match (Stolen et al., 2005), while high-intensity anaerobic activity accounts for the remaining 10–20% (Rienzi et al., 2000). Professional players cover approximately 10–13 km during a football match (Di Salvo et al., 2007; Morgans et al., 2022), in which central midfielders typically cover the most and central defenders the least (Bradley et al., 2009; Di Salvo et al., 2007). Therefore, the need to perform intense, repeated actions requires enhanced physical capabilities (e.g., speed, muscle strength, anaerobic power, agility, and maximal aerobic power) (Clemente et al., 2014a; Rampinini et al., 2009).

Regarding the analytical and ecological high-intensity interval training (HIIT) approaches to aerobic and anaerobic conditioning, arguably both traditional HIIT, small-sided games (SSG), and circuit-type drills produce comparable effects on enhancing endurance performance and maximal oxygen uptake in soccer players

DOI: 10.4324/9781003383475-3

22 Strength and Conditioning for Football

(Clemente et al., 2023). Thus, this chapter highlights relevant insights on both analytical and ecological approaches to HIIT programming, for aerobic and anaerobic conditioning in football.

Aerobic and Anaerobic Contributions to Football

Football has specific characteristics related to both anaerobic and aerobic profiles, as it is played at a minimum of 75% of maximum heart rate (HR). Moreover, it encompasses extended durations of aerobic activities interspersed with brief high-intensity actions, necessitating elevated levels of both aerobic and anaerobic fitness. Additionally, neuromuscular-oriented activities such as changes of direction, high-speed running, and sprints are pivotal factors that must be considered when programming aerobic/anaerobic conditioning (Buchheit and Laursen, 2013a).

To repeat high-intensity actions, drills should feature explosive, short-duration work bouts followed by short recovery periods. This type of action has been referred to as "repeated sprint ability" (RSA) (Clemente, Ramirez-Campillo, Afonso, Sarmento, Rosemann, and Knechtle, 2021). To develop this ability, it is relevant to know which aerobic or anaerobic determinants are related to performance, and to what extent. Some research showed negative associations between relative maximal oxygen uptake (VO_{2max}) and RSA mean and total [$r = -0.591$ to -0.655, $p < 0.001$] (Jones et al., 2013). For instance, a higher VO_{2max} may contribute to a better RSA by allowing the replenishment of phosphocreatine stores during recovery between sprints, and consequently helping to maintain higher performance through several high-intensity actions (Bogdanis et al., 1996). However, in another study, VO_{2max} appears to be moderately related to RSA (in terms of total work [kJ]; $r = 0.79$, $p < 0.05$) (Bishop et al., 2003). This suggests that factors other than VO_{2max} contribute to RSA performance, including anaerobic fitness.

High-Intensity Interval Training Methods for Aerobic and Anaerobic Conditioning

HIIT comprises six types, each meticulously crafted to elicit diverse demands on the aerobic, anaerobic, or neuromuscular systems. The existing body of literature categorizes these six HIIT variants, as depicted in Figure 2.1. This classification serves as a valuable tool for coaches and athletes, offering a spectrum of options to cater to specific training needs and goals when utilizing HIIT interventions (Buchheit and Laursen, 2013a).

As depicted in Figure 2.1, HIIT type 1 is characterized by aerobic metabolic processes that heavily rely on oxygen transport and utilization mechanisms, notably involving the cardiopulmonary system and oxidative muscle fibers. HIIT type 2, shares the metabolic characteristics with type 1 but exhibits a heightened level of neuromuscular strain. HIIT type 3, displays metabolic traits akin to type 1 but with a substantial contribution from anaerobic glycolysis and limited neuromuscular

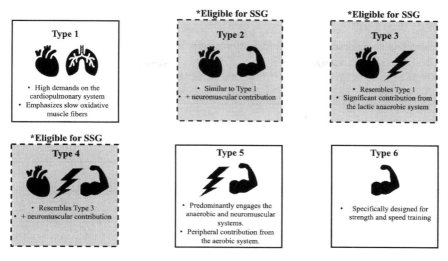

FIGURE 2.1 Categorization of high-intensity interval training types. *SSG: small-sided games.

strain. HIIT type 4, mirrors the metabolic profile of type 3 but features elevated neuromuscular strain. HIIT type 5 is characterized by limited aerobic response yet significant anaerobic glycolytic energy contribution and neuromuscular strain. Finally, HIIT type 6, distinct from traditional HIIT, involves exclusively high neuromuscular strain, typically associated with speed and strength training. The selection of HIIT types to elicit specific HIIT-targeted responses encompasses short intervals, long intervals, repeated sprint training, sprint interval training (SIT), and game-based HIIT sessions (Laursen and Buchheit, 2019).

Furthermore, it is important to note that four primary HIIT formats can be employed to correspond with each of the six principal HIIT types. These formats are defined as short intervals (lasting less than 60 seconds), long intervals (above 60 seconds), SIT, and repeated-sprint training (Buchheit and Laursen, 2013a). It is noteworthy that short intervals can be effectively applied to accommodate the requirements of the first to the fourth HIIT types, whereas long intervals are best suited for the third and fourth types. Repeated-sprint training is particularly well-suited to match the fourth and fifth types, while SIT primarily aligns with the sixth type (Buchheit and Laursen, 2013a).

Long and Short Intervals

Distinguishing between short intervals and long intervals of HIIT highlights the disparate physiological effects during exercise. In the case of long intervals, exercising continuously at intensities surpassing the lactate threshold results in incremental disturbances to homeostasis, leading to a gradual onset of muscular fatigue and diminishing the body's capacity for effective muscular contraction (Poole et al., 2021). However, short intervals include briefer but more frequent recovery intervals, allowing for rapid restoration of homeostasis during these breaks (Gunnarsson et al., 2013).

The differential impact stems from the role of myoglobin within muscle cells. In short intervals, myoglobin functions as an oxygen reservoir, accumulating oxygen at the commencement of each brief exercise interval (Atakan et al., 2021). These recovery periods then facilitate the reloading of myoglobin with oxygen, minimizing the build-up of anaerobic by-products, such as lactate, during subsequent exercise intervals. This pattern in short intervals enables improved oxygen utilization, extraction, and swift re-establishment of homeostasis, resulting in a heightened average oxygen uptake and power output (Laursen and Jenkins, 2002). This contrasts with long intervals, where the progressive disturbance of homeostasis leads to a prolonged and gradual onset of fatigue (Buchheit and Laursen, 2013a).

The long intervals represent protracted work segments focusing on a more extended phase of the intensity-time spectrum, typically within the range of 95–105% of the individual maximal aerobic speed (MAS) or 80–90% of the final velocity reached during the 30-15 intermittent fitness test (30-15 IFT), known as V_{IFT} (Buchheit, 2010). To effectively execute long intervals of >2 minutes at 80–85% of V_{IFT}, brief recovery intervals of 1–2 minutes of passive rest should be interspersed or more extended periods of active recovery reaching up to 45% of V_{IFT} from 2 to 4 minutes (Figure 2.2).

While short intervals encompass set periods of less than 60 seconds, recurring within a comparably brief time span. To ensure short intervals achieve objectives, they should be executed repeatedly at intensities ranging between 90% and 105% of V_{IFT}, lasting 10–60 seconds and interspersed with less than 1 minute of recovery which may be passive or active up to 45% of V_{IFT} (Figure 2.3).

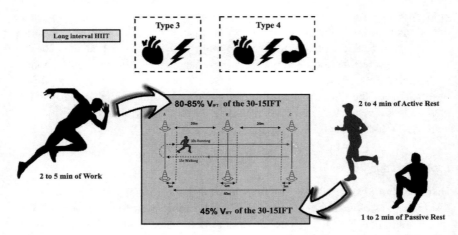

FIGURE 2.2 Intensity and duration of work and rest during long intervals (2–5 minutes).

Repeated-sprint training is characterized by the repetition of more than two brief (≤10 seconds) maximum-effort sprints, interspersed with a brief recovery interval lasting less than 1 minute (Buchheit and Laursen, 2013a) (Figure 2.4). The high-intensity nature of the repeated-sprint training naturally triggers substantial stress on the acute neuromuscular response, allowing for the pursuit of HIIT types 4 and 5 objectives. In repeated-sprint training, the decline in running speed demonstrates an escalating overall stress on the locomotor system, evidenced by diminished force production, altered stride patterns, decreased musculoskeletal stiffness, and a combination of neuromuscular adjustments and metabolic disruptions at the muscular level (Haugen et al., 2014).

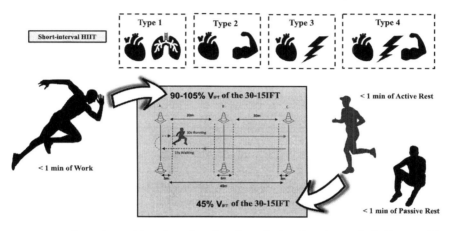

FIGURE 2.3 Intensity and duration of work and rest during short intervals (<60 seconds).

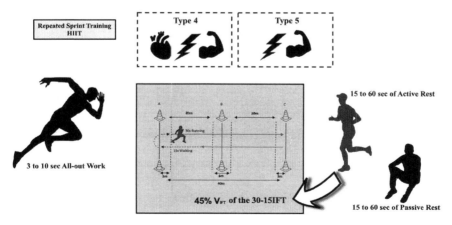

FIGURE 2.4 Intensity and duration of work and rest during repeated-sprint training (3–10 seconds maximum effort).

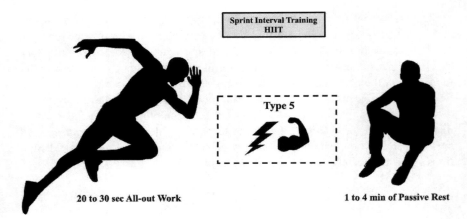

FIGURE 2.5 Intensity and duration of work and rest during sprint interval training (20–30 seconds all-out).

Sprint interval training involves maximal effort sprints, but the duration is extended, typically ranging from 20 to 45 seconds. These efforts are highly demanding, and the recovery period is passive and prolonged, usually spanning between 1 and 4 minutes (Figure 2.5). The SIT method is another variant of HIIT that involves more extended efforts and recovery periods, for instance, repeated 30-second sprints with 2 to 4 minutes of passive recovery. Sprint interval training demands a maximum performance, allowing it to be prescribed without individual pre-testing (i.e., MAS is not specifically required to determine the intensity). Therefore, SIT targets specific acute responses, particularly in type 5 responses, requiring primarily anaerobic glycolytic and neuromuscular reactions (Hoffmann et al., 2014).

The Maximal Aerobic Speed and Anaerobic Speed Reserve for HIIT Programming

Given the profoundly aerobic nature of various field sports, necessitating athletes to sustain high-intensity performance levels throughout the game's duration, the significance of elevated aerobic power in overall performance becomes apparent. For this reason, MAS is commonly utilized for running-based HIIT prescription (Bok et al., 2023). However, using only MAS for running-based HIIT prescription raises an important issue, as it does not consider the athletes' individual maximal sprinting speed (Sandford et al., 2021). Specifically, MAS can be considered as the "lowest" speed when reaching VO_{2max} (Bentley et al., 2002; Rampinini et al., 2009). However, during a VO_{2max} assessment, it is still possible to increase speed without increasing oxygen consumption. The difference between the lowest and the maximum speed when reaching VO_{2max} is known as anaerobic speed reserve

(ASR). Thus, other speeds of ASR can also be used for training prescriptions as a better tool to estimate the time required for exhaustion (Buchheit, 2010). Even so, there is scarce research employing this approach (Julio et al., 2019) while most studies use MAS (Kavanagh et al., 2023; Mallol et al., 2015; Munoz et al., 2015; Paquette et al., 2017; Silva et al., 2011).

An example of how HIIT prescription based on MAS can be particularly misleading is illustrated in Figure 2.6. Two different athletes (athletes A and B), both of whom have exactly the same MAS (16 km/h), but different maximal sprinting speed (athlete A = 28 km/h; Athlete B = 35 km/h). Considering that ASR is calculated as the difference between MAS and maximal sprinting speed, athlete A has an ASR of 12 km/h, while athlete B has an ASR of 19 km/h.

Consequently, if a coach prescribes the same HIIT exercise (e.g., 10-second run at 120% of MAS, representing a running speed of 19.2 km/h) for both athletes A and B, athlete A will be running closer to his maximal sprinting speed (28 km/h), athlete B will be running further from his maximal sprinting speed (35 km/h). In this scenario, athlete A may be exerting a lot of effort, while athlete B may be 'cruising'.

However, it is possible to individualize the HIIT bout by using percentages of each athlete's ASR. The potential lies in modifying interval prescription based on a proportion of the ASR as opposed to solely depending on MAS percentages. For instance, rather than executing a 10-second run at 120% MAS, the sane run could be performed at 20% of the ASR. An athlete with a greater reserve is likely to engage in a more strenuous run at a higher speed compared to another athlete possessing an equivalent MAS but with a lower ASR (Sandford et al., 2021). As depicted in Figure 2.7, by considering the ASR percentage HIIT prescription method, athlete A avoids excessive strain during his conditioning session.

Focusing on ASR is crucial for HIIT programming to optimize athletes' preparedness, for instance, a previous study investigated the factors that influence the

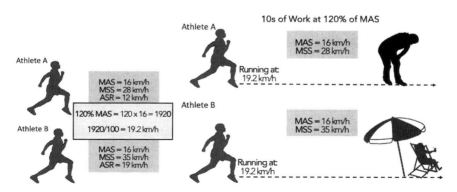

FIGURE 2.6 Running-based HIIT bout using only maximal aerobic speed for different athletes.

28 Strength and Conditioning for Football

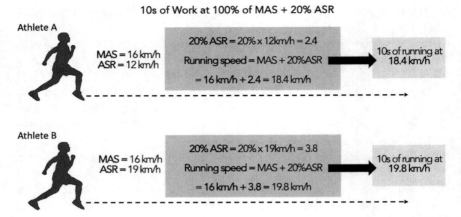

FIGURE 2.7 Running-based HIIT bout using the anaerobic speed reserve (ASR) percentage.

time an athlete can continue running at high intensities, specifically in the range of 90–140% of MAS (Blondel et al., 2001). The authors found that the athlete's ASR was a better predictor of endurance at these high intensities compared to MAS alone. Put simply, if an athlete was running at, 120% of MAS, what determined how long they could keep going at that intensity was not just the percentage above MAS, but also how effectively ASR was utilized at that level of effort. A significant portion of the variation in the time an athlete could sustain exercise at 120% and 140% of MAS could be explained by how much of the ASR was utilized (Blondel et al., 2001). This, in turn, suggests that ASR becomes particularly important when exercising at very high intensities, even more so than MAS.

SSG-Based HIIT Types

It is noteworthy that SSG is primarily associated with types 2, 3, and 4 of HIIT. Consequently, coaches may opt to design SSG with the intention of promoting cardiorespiratory adaptations, with variable emphasis on the neuromuscular system. The convergence of HIIT types 2, 3, and 4 with SSG highlights the complexity of targeting distinct physical attributes in isolation within the context of SSG (Clemente, 2020). SSG can be strategically designed to highlight the emphasis on HIIT types 2, 3, or 4, according to the coaches' aims. However, it is of paramount importance to consider the influencing factors that affect the imposed intensity during SSGs (Clemente, 2020).

SSG consist of a reduction in the dynamic structure of the conventional football game. Consequently, these games may assume a more tactical and/or physical character, depending on the type of modifications and constraints of the task implemented by the coach (Clemente, 2016; Davids et al., 2013). SSG have increased theoretical and operational popularity in football, as perception and learning of players regarding important technical-tactical determinants is achieved, as well as allowing a relevant variation of physiological stimuli (Clemente et al., 2014a, 2021).

Moreover, SSG have the advantage of producing greater motivation, motor efficiency, tactical concentration, and technical ability of football players (Arslan et al., 2020; Sarmento et al., 2018). However, it is also necessary to highlight the greater variability that SSG presents in terms of exercise intensity when compared to traditional methods such as non-football-specific running. Thus, despite the SSG demonstrating significant value, the coach must supplement these games with some tasks of an analytical nature, as these present greater control regarding the intensity of the exercise (Clemente, Afonso, and Sarmento, 2021).

Generally, SSG present differentiated forms of HIIT (Buchheit and Laursen, 2013a, 2013b). In turn, these produce biological adaptations, also differentiated, in the medium to long term (Moran et al., 2019). The format of SSG is related to different types of task constraints (Clemente, 2016; Davids et al., 2013) which include (Morgans et al., 2014; Sarmento et al., 2018):

- Changes in the number of players involved;
- Field configuration (individual area per player, width/length ratio, and field size);
- Presence or not of scoring a goal (goal scoring in mini goals or conventional goals);
- The presence or not of goalkeepers;
- Type of actions allowed (limitation of touches on the ball or movements);
- Number of sets, repetitions, effort/recovery ratio.

All these types of constraints promote different physiological adaptations, especially in the cardiorespiratory system (internal load responses) (Gonçalves et al., 2017; Hammami et al., 2018). However, there are other factors that can affect adaptations at the cardiorespiratory level, such as age, competitive level, sex, physical fitness level, and/or psychological/mental aspects (Clemente, Ramirez-Campillo, Afonso, Sarmento, Rosemann, and Knechtle 2021; Kunrath et al., 2020). In the next subchapters, different conditioning/constraints that the coach can implement in SSG will be presented, as well as the physiological impact on the players, especially at the cardiorespiratory level.

Number of Players and Pitch Size

The general finding in the literature is that as player numbers increase, exercise intensity decreases (Morgans et al., 2014; Dello Iacono et al., 2023). This relationship is, however, partly dependent on whether the pitch size also increases. Nevertheless, it is important to consider that the relationship between HR and blood lactate (La-) presents notable inter-individual variability. Generally, the lactate threshold is approximately 50–60% of HRmax in untrained individuals and 80% of HRmax in trained individuals (Janssen, 2001). The anaerobic threshold occurs on average with an La- of approximately 4 mmol/L, although it may be higher than this value. In this way, when the coach's objective is to develop an SSG with greater aerobic emphasis, it is important to consider the pitch size, number of players, sets and repetitions (Morgans et al., 2014) to avoid higher HRmax and La- values, also reducing a level of exacerbated fatigue, which will not meet the training objectives of the coach (Clemente et al., 2014b).

However, previous studies have not clearly shown the same RPE response during exercise (e.g., 2 vs 2 = 7.6 arbitrary units [AU], while 4 vs 4 = 7.9 AU) (Aroso et al., 2004; Dellal et al., 2012; Hill-Haas et al., 2009; Köklü, 2012; Rampinini et al., 2007; Randes et al., 2012). However, this variable cannot be considered in isolation, as the size of the field may also influence the intended stimulus. In this sense, it is noteworthy that games reduced to 4 vs 4 seem to be more adjusted to a high-intensity level, probably to work the glycolytic system (Clemente, 2016).

Some studies show that the larger the field, the greater the physiological stimulus, regardless of the number of players, showing that this variable can be decisive in the type of training and stimulus that is intended to be imposed. Likewise, the larger field size allows for exploring longitudinal and lateral areas, which allows the development of important technical-tactical issues (Aroso et al., 2004; Casamichana and Castellano, 2010; Kelly and Drust, 2009; Owen et al., 2011; Rampinini et al., 2007). Figure 2.8 presents an example of SSG acute responses in terms of HR and La- concentrations for different SSG formats.

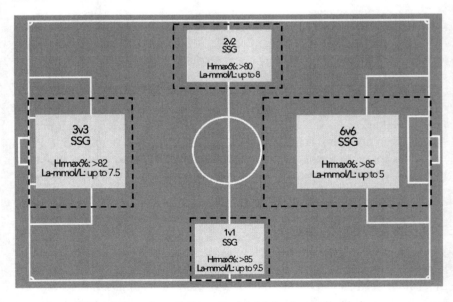

FIGURE 2.8 Effects of number of players and field size in small-sided games.

Task Constraints of SSG

As mentioned previously, there are other types of constraints such as rules related to ball possession, whether or not to score a goal, whether or not to use goalkeepers, whether or not to use additional players, often referred to as neutral players or floaters that play for the team in possession, who play with the team in possession of the ball), goal size, number of goals, restrictions on the number of touches on the ball, goal line, or even the use or not of coach's encouragement. The literature suggests that the use of small goals and different types of scoring (goal scoring, use of goalkeepers, ball possession, goal size, etc.) can significantly increase the physiological impact when compared to traditional goal formats or the use of goalkeepers. However, there are few studies that have compared these issues (Casamichana et al., 2013; Clemente et al., 2014a, 2014b; Halouani et al., 2014; Mallo and Navarro, 2008). As for the existence or absence of goals during SSG, the physiological stimulus increases in the absence of goals (for example, in an SSG where the objective will be to maintain ball possession). Regarding the number of touches on the ball, the more limited the number of touches, the greater the physiological stimulus. This specific rule modification was tested with data suggesting that limiting the number of consecutive touches compared to free play significantly enhances acute physiological responses, by increasing HR, La- and RPE values blood lactate concentrations, and subjective perceived exertion (Casamichana et al., 2014; Dellal et al., 2011). Please see Figure 2.2 and Table 2.1 (Casamichana et al., 2014; Dellal et al., 2011).

The type of marking (i.e., man-to-man, double marking, zonal) has also an influence on physiological responses. In a study carried out with amateur players in the 3 vs 3, 6 vs 6, and 9 vs 9 formats, the mean (HRmean) and HRmax increased in the 3 vs 3 when the marking was made man-to-man from 163 to 169 (HRmean) and 180 to 183 (HRmax) (Casamichana et al., 2015). Also in young players, comparisons between free marking and man-to-man marking or even 2 vs 1 marking revealed a greater HR effort (167 vs 178 vs 185 bpm), RPE (2.0 vs 4.3 vs 7.2 arbitrary units) and distances covered (e.g., total distance, 1,612 vs 1,751 vs 1,783 m and distance >18 km/h, 48 vs 74 vs 125 m) (Cihan, 2015). Therefore, man-to-man marking seems to promote a greater physiological stimulus. While, not using goalkeepers, the use of mini-goals, and limiting the number of touches and man-to-man marking increase the intensity of the reduced game. However, the use of goalkeepers, conventional goals, unlimited touches on the ball, and zone marking, decreases the intensity (Cihan, 2015).

Another variable to consider is the verbal encouragement given by coaches, which also has a physiological impact on reduced games. Higher values of HR, La- and RPE (Figure 2.9), were found in SSG with verbal coach encouragement when compared to games without encouragement (Rampinini et al., 2007; Sampaio et al., 2007). To summarize the contents related to the topic of this subsection, Figure 2.9 illustrates the athletes' internal responses to the presence or absence of verbal encouragement by the coach.

32 Strength and Conditioning for Football

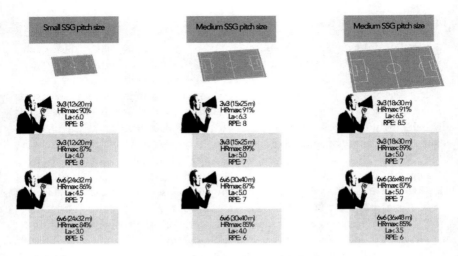

FIGURE 2.9 Impact of encouragement during small-sided games.

Active or passive rest also influences the physiological impact produced by SSG. The results of another study (Arslan et al., 2017) demonstrated an increasing physiological response with passive rest when compared to active rest in terms of RPE and La-. Furthermore, 2 vs 2 with passive rest induced significantly lower %HRmax and total distance covered than with active recovery. Additionally, the distance covered at high intensity was significantly greater in the 4 vs 4 active recovery games than in the 4 vs 4 passive recovery games (Arslan et al., 2017).

The use of neutral players or "jokers" is related to the support that is intended to be given to offensive or defensive positions, causing a numerical superiority. Normally, the neutral player only participates in offensive or defensive moments with the attacking or defensive team, respectively. In this situation, there are few studies available (Bekris et al., 2012a, 2012b). Therefore, a clear trend of the physiological impact is not available. For example, in 1 vs 1 and 4 vs 4 games, the highest HR values were observed without a neutral player. In the 3 vs 3 games, the highest HR values were achieved with a defensive neutral, and in the 2 vs 2 games, the highest HR was observed with an offensive neutral player (Bekris et al., 2012a, 2012b). Thus, more research is needed on this topic to expand the previous findings. Table 2.1 summarizes the main physiological stimuli depending on the type of SSG.

Practical Applications

The knowledge derived from the preceding sections offers valuable insights for practitioners in designing and implementing training and conditioning sessions in

Analytical and Ecological Approaches **33**

TABLE 2.1 Physiological Responses of Small-Sided Games

Condition Type	Higher ↑ / Lower ↓ Using ✓ / Not Using X	Physiological Stimuli
Number of players	↑	↓
4 vs 4 or ↓ number	↑ anaerobic	↑
5 vs 5 or ↑ number	↑ aerobic	↓
Field size	↑	↑
Goal scoring	X	↑
Number of ball touches	↓	↑
Marking type	man-to-man	↑
Marking type	free	↓
Goalkeeper utilization	Not clear	Not clear
Neutral player utilization	Not clear	not clear
Coach encouragement	✓	↑
Active recovery		↑ (HR%)
Passive recovery		↓ (RPE and La-)

football, catering to both aerobic and anaerobic fitness. The following practical applications provide tangible guidance for enhancing athletes' performance:

- **Analytical HIIT programming:** Coaches should employ HIIT methods that meet individual athlete profiles. To ensure effective HIIT programming, consider utilizing the ASR as a crucial parameter, concurrent with the use of MAS values. Individualize HIIT bouts by adjusting the percentage of the ASR, focusing on specific endurance, strength, or anaerobic power objectives.
- **Long and short intervals:** Distinguish between long and short intervals for HIIT programming. Long intervals are ideal for prolonged, high-intensity exercise phases and should be interspersed with short recovery periods. Short intervals with shorter but more frequent recovery intervals, help maintain oxygen utilization and improve power output. Coaches should select the interval type according to training objectives and individual athlete capabilities.
- **Understanding SSG-based HIIT:** SSG serve as an excellent method for implementing HIIT of various types. Coaches should strategically design SSG to align with specific physiological and technical/tactical goals, from HIIT types 2 to 4.
- **SSG task constraints:** Manipulate rules and task constraints in SSG to elicit desired physiological responses. The number of players, pitch and goal size, scoring rules, working and rest periods, and ball touches can impact SSG intensity. Understanding how each constraint influences physiological stimuli

34 Strength and Conditioning for Football

is crucial for crafting tailored training sessions. Hence, customization of SSG attributes is pivotal to achieving targeted training outcomes.

- **Verbal encouragement:** Coaches can employ verbal encouragement to elevate the physiological response during SSG-based HIIT. Providing feedback, motivation, and instructions during training can increase HR, La-, and RPE. Utilizing encouragement carefully aligns with specific training objectives.
- **Rest types:** Active and passive rest intervals have differing effects on exercise intensity during both analytical and ecological HIIT approaches. The choice between active and passive rest depends on the desired physiological response. Passive rest can lead to higher HR and La- levels, while active rest may be more suitable for moderate-intensity training. Coaches should select the appropriate rest type according to the training objectives.

References

Aroso, J., Rebelo, A. N., and Gomes-Pereira, J. (2004). Physiological impact of selected game-related exercises. *Journal of Sports Sciences*, *22*, 522.

Arslan, E., Alemdaroglu, U., Koklu, Y., Hazir, T., Muniroglu, S., and Karakoc, B. (2017). Effects of passive and active rest on physiological responses and time motion characteristics in different small sided soccer games. *Journal of Human Kinetics*, *60*(1), 123–132. https://doi.org/10.1515/hukin-2017-0095

Arslan, E., Orer, G. E., and Clemente, F. M. (2020). Running-based high-intensity interval training vs. small-sided game training programs: Effects on the physical performance, psychophysiological responses and technical skills in young soccer players. *Biology of Sport*, *37*(2), 165–173. https://doi.org/10.5114/BIOLSPORT.2020.94237

Atakan, M. M., Li, Y., Koşar, Ş. N., Turnagöl, H. H., and Yan, X. (2021). Evidence-based effects of high-intensity interval training on exercise capacity and health: A review with historical perspective. *International Journal of Environmental Research and Public Health*, *18*(13), 7201. https://doi.org/10.3390/ijerph18137201

Bekris, E., Eleftherios, M., Aris, S., Ioannis, G., Konstantinos, A., and Natalia, K. (2012b). Supernumerary in small sided games 3Vs3 and 4Vs4. *Journal of Physical Education and Sport*, *12*(3), 398–406. https://doi.org10.7752/jpes.2012.03059

Bekris, E., Gissis, I., Sambanis, M., Milonys, E., Sarakinos, A., and Anagnostakos, K. (2012a). The physiological and technical-tactical effects of an additional soccer player's participation in small sided games training. *Physical Training*, *11*(1–3), 1–14.

Bentley, D. J., Newell, J., and Bishop, D. (2002). Methods to determine aerobic endurance. *Sports Medicine*, *32*(11), 675–700.

Bishop, D., Lawrence, S., and Spencer, M. (2003). Predictors of repeated-sprint ability in elite female hockey players. *Journal of Science and Medicine in Sport*, *6*(2), 199–209. https://doi.org/10.1016/S1440-2440(03)80255-4

Blondel, N., Berthoin, S., Billat, V., and Lensel, G. (2001). Relationship between run times to exhaustion at 90, 100, 120, and 140% of $v\dot{V}O_{2max}$ and velocity expressed relatively to critical velocity and maximal velocity. *International Journal of Sports Medicine*, *22*(1), 27–33. https://doi.org/10.1055/s-2001-11357

Bogdanis, G. C., Nevill, M. E., Boobis, L. H., and Lakomy, H. K. A. (1996). Contribution of phosphocreatine and aerobic metabolism to energy supply during repeated sprint exercise. *Journal of Applied Physiology*, *80*(3), 876–884. https://doi.org/10.1152/jappl.1996.80.3.876

Bok, D., Gulin, J., Škegro, D., Šalaj, S., and Foster, C. (2023). Comparison of anaerobic speed reserve and maximal aerobic speed methods to prescribe short format high-intensity interval training. *Scandinavian Journal of Medicine and Science in Sports*, *33*(9), 1638–1647. https://doi.org/10.1111/sms.14411

Bradley, P. S., Sheldon, W., Wooster, B., Olsen, P., Boanas, P., and Krustrup, P. (2009). High-intensity running in English FA Premier League soccer matches. *Journal of Sports Sciences*, *27*, 159–168.

Buchheit, M. (2010). The 30-15 Intermittent Fitness Test: 10 year review. *1*, 1–9.

Buchheit, M., and Laursen, P. B. (2013a). High-intensity interval training, solutions to the programming puzzle: Part I: Cardiopulmonary emphasis. *Sports Medicine*, *43*(5), 313–338. https://doi.org/10.1007/s40279-013-0029-x

Buchheit, M., and Laursen, P. B. (2013b). High-intensity interval training, solutions to the programming puzzle: Part II: Anaerobic energy, neuromuscular load and practical applications. *Sports Medicine*, *43*(10), 927–954. https://doi.org/10.1007/s40279-013-0066-5

Carling, C., Bradley, P., and McCall, A. D. G. (2016). Match-to-match variability in high-speed running activity in a professional soccer team. *Journal of Sports Sciences*, *34*(24), 2215–2223. https://doi.org/10.1080/02640414.2016.1176228

Casamichana, D., and Castellano, J. (2010). Time-motion, heart rate, perceptual and motor behaviour demands in small-sides soccer games: Effects of pitch size. *Journal of Sports Sciences*, *28*(14), 1615–1623. https://doi.org/10.1080/02640414.2010.521168

Casamichana, D., Castellano, J., and Dellal, A. (2013). Influence of different training regimes on physical and physiological demands during small-sided soccer games: Continuous vs. intermittent format. *Journal of Strength and Conditioning Research*, *27*(3), 690–697. https://doi.org/10.1519/JSC.0b013e31825d99dc

Casamichana, D., Román-Quintana, J. S., Castellano, J., and Calleja-González, J. (2015). Influence of the type of marking and the number of players on physiological and physical demands during sided games in soccer. *Journal of Human Kinetics*, *47*(1), 259–268. https://doi.org/10.1515/hukin-2015-0081

Casamichana, D., Suarez-Arrones, L., Castellano, J., and Román-Quintana, J. S. (2014). Effect of number of touches and exercise duration on the kinematic profile and heart rate response during small-sided games in soccer. *Journal of Human Kinetics*, *41*(1), 113–123. https://doi.org/10.2478/hukin-2014-0039

Cihan, H. (2015). The effect of defensive strategies on the physiological responses and time-motion characteristics in small-sided games. *Kinesiology*, *47*(2), 179–187.

Clemente, F. M. (2016). Small-sided and conditioned games: An integrative training approach. In *Small-Sided and Conditioned Games in Soccer Training* (SpringerBriefs in Applied Sciences and Technology). Singapore: Springer, pp. 1–13. https://doi.org/10.1007/978-981-10-0880-1_1

Clemente, F. M. (2020). The threats of small-sided soccer games: A discussion about their differences with the match external load demands and their variability levels. *Strength and Conditioning Journal*, *42*(3), 100–105. https://doi.org/10.1519/SSC.0000000000000526

Clemente, F. M., Afonso, J., and Sarmento, H. (2021). Small-sided games: An umbrella review of systematic reviews and meta-analyses. *PLoS ONE*, *16*(2), e0247067. https://doi.org/10.1371/journal.pone.0247067

Clemente, F. M., Lourenço Martins, F. M., and Mendes, R. S. (2014a). Developing aerobic and anaerobic fitness using small-sided soccer games: Methodological

36 Strength and Conditioning for Football

proposals. *Strength and Conditioning Journal*, *36*(3), 76–87. https://doi.org/10.1519/SSC.0000000000000063

Clemente, F. M., Lourenço Martins, F. M., and Mendes, R. S. (2014b). Periodization based on small-sided soccer games. *Strength and Conditioning Journal*, *36*(5), 34–43.

Clemente, F. M., Moran, J., Ramirez-Campillo, R., Beato, M., and Afonso, J. (2023). Endurance performance adaptations between SSG and HIIT in soccer players: A meta-analysis. *International Journal of Sports Medicine*, *45*(3), 183–210. https://doi.org/10.1055/a-2171-3255

Clemente, F. M., Ramirez-Campillo, R., Afonso, J., and Sarmento, H. (2021). Effects of small-sided games vs. running-based high-intensity interval training on physical performance in soccer players: A meta-analytical comparison. *Frontiers in Physiology*, *12*(February). https://doi.org/10.3389/fphys.2021.642703

Clemente, F. M., Ramirez-Campillo, R., Afonso, J., Sarmento, H., Rosemann, T., and Knechtle, B. (2021). A meta-analytical comparison of the effects of small-sided games vs. running-based high-intensity interval training on soccer players' repeated-sprint ability. *International Journal of Environmental Research and Public Health*, *18*(5), 2781. https://doi.org/10.3390/ijerph18052781

Davids, K., Araújo, D., Correia, V., and Vilar, L. (2013). How small-sided and conditioned games enhance acquisition of movement and decision-making skills. *Exercise and Sport Sciences Reviews*, *41*(3), 154–161. https://doi.org/10.1097/JES.0b013e318292f3ec

Dellal, A., Chamari, K., Lee Owen, A., Wong, D. P., Lago-Penas, C., and Hill-Haas, S. (2011). Influence of technical instructions on the physiological and physical demands of small-sided soccer games. *European Journal of Sport Science*, *11*(5), 341–346. https://doi.org/10.1080/17461391.2010.521584

Dellal, A., Hill-Haas, S. V., Lago-penas, C., and Chamari, K. (2012). Small-sided games in soccer: Amateur vs. professional players' physiological responses, physical and technical analysis. *Journal of Strength and Conditioning Research*, *25*(9), 2371–2381.

Dello Iacono, A., McLaren, S. J., Macpherson, T. W., Beato, M., Weston, M., Unnithan, V. B., and Shushan, T. (2023). Quantifying exposure and intra-individual reliability of high-speed and sprint running during sided-games training in soccer players: A systematic review and meta-analysis. *Sports Medicine*, *53*(2). https://doi.org/10.1007/s40279-022-01773-1

Di Salvo, V., Baron, R., Tschan, H., Calderon Montero, F. J., Bachl, N., and Pigozzi, F. (2007). Performance characteristics according to playing position in elite soccer. *International Journal of Sports Medicine*, *28*(3), 222–227. https://doi.org/10.1055/s-2006-924294

Drust, B., Atkinson, G., and Reilly, T. (2007). Future perspectives in the evaluation of the physiological demands of soccer. *Sports Medicine*, *37*(9), 783–805. https://doi.org/10.2165/00007256-200737090-00003

Gonçalves, B., Esteves, P., Folgado, H., Ric, A., Torrents, C., and Sampaio, J. (2017). Effects of pitch area-restrictions on tactical behavior, physical, and physiological performances in soccer large-sided games. *Journal of Strength and Conditioning Research*, *31*(9), 2398–2408. https://doi.org/10.1519/JSC.0000000000001700

Gunnarsson, T. P., Christensen, P. M., Thomassen, M., Nielsen, L. R., and Bangsbo, J. (2013). Effect of intensified training on muscle ion kinetics, fatigue development, and repeated short-term performance in endurance-trained cyclists. *American Journal of Physiology - Regulatory Integrative and Comparative Physiology*, *305*(7), 811–821. https://doi.org/10.1152/ajpregu.00467.2012

Halouani, J., Chtourou, H., Dellal, A., Chaouachi, A., and Chamari, K. (2014). Physiological responses according to rules changes during 3 vs. 3 small-sided games in youth soccer players: Stop-ball vs. small-goals rules. *Journal of Sports Sciences*, *32*(15), 1485–1490. https://doi.org/10.1080/02640414.2014.899707

Hammami, A., Gabbett, T. J., Slimani, M., and Bouhlel, E. (2018). Does small-sided games training improve physical fitness and team-sport-specific skills? A systematic review and meta-analysis. *Journal of Sports Medicine and Physical Fitness*, *58*(10), 1446–1455. https://doi.org/10.23736/S0022-4707.17.07420-5

Haugen, T. A., Tønnessen, E., Hisdal, J., and Seiler, S. (2014). The role and development of sprinting speed in soccer. *International Journal of Sports Physiology and Performance*, *9*(3), 432–441. https://doi.org/10.1123/IJSPP.2013-0121

Hill-Haas, S. V., Coutts, A. J., Rowsell, G. J., and Dawson, B. T. (2009). Generic versus small-sided game training in soccer. *International Journal of Sports Medicine*, *30*(9), 636–642. https://doi.org/10.1055/s-0029-1220730

Hoffmann, J. J., Reed, J. P., Leiting, K., Chiang, C. Y., and Stone, M. H. (2014). Repeated sprints, high-intensity interval training, small-sided games: Theory and application to field sports. *International Journal of Sports Physiology and Performance*, *9*(2), 352–357. https://doi.org/10.1123/IJSPP.2013-0189

Janssen, P. (2001). *Lactate Threshold Training*. I. H. K. Champaign.

Jones, R. M., Cook, C. C., Kilduff, L. P., Milanović, Z., James, N., Sporiš, G., Fiorentini, B., Fiorentini, F., Turner, A., and Vučković, G. (2013). Relationship between repeated sprint ability and aerobic capacity in professional soccer players. *The Scientific World Journal*, *2013*(1), 952350. https://doi.org/10.1155/2013/952350

Julio, U. F., Panissa, V. L. G., Paludo, A. C., Alves, E. D., Campos, F. A. D., and Franchini, E. (2019). Use of the anaerobic speed reserve to normalize the prescription of high-intensity interval exercise intensity. *European Journal of Sport Science*, *20*(2), 166–173. https://doi.org/10.1080/17461391.2019.1624833

Kavanagh, R., McDaid, K., Rhodes, D., McDonnell, J., Oliveira, R., and Morgans, R. (2023). An analysis of positional generic and individualized speed thresholds within the most demanding phases of match play in the English Premier League. *International Journal of Sports Physiology and Performance*, *19*(2), 116–126. https://doi.org/10.1123/ijspp.2023-0063

Kelly, D. M., and Drust, B. (2009). The effect of pitch dimensions on heart rate responses and technical demands of small-sided soccer games in elite players. *Journal of Science and Medicine in Sport*, *12*(4), 475–479. https://doi.org/10.1016/j.jsams.2008.01.010

Köklü, Y. (2012). A comparison of physiological responses to various intermittent and continuous small-sided games in young soccer players. *Journal of Human Kinetics*, *31*(1), 89–96.

Kunrath, C. A., Nakamura, F. Y., Roca, A., Tessitore, A., and Teoldo Da Costa, I. (2020). How does mental fatigue affect soccer performance during small-sided games? A cognitive, tactical and physical approach. *Journal of Sports Sciences*, *38*(15), 1818–1828. https://doi.org/10.1080/02640414.2020.1756681

Laursen, P., and Buchheit, M. (2019). *Science and Application of High-Intensity Interval Training* (1st ed.). Champaign: Human Kinetics.

Laursen, P. B., and Jenkins, D. G. (2002). The scientific basis for high-intensity interval training: Optimising training programmes and maximising performance in highly trained endurance athletes. *Sports Medicine*, *32*(1), 53–73. https://doi.org/10.2165/00007256-200232010-00003

Mallo, J., and Navarro, E. (2008). Physical load imposed on soccer players during small-sided training games. *The Journal of Sports Medicine and Physical Fitness*, *42*, 166–171.

38 Strength and Conditioning for Football

Mallol, M., Bentley, J. D., Lynda, N., Kevin, N., Mejuto, G., and Yanci, J. (2015). Comparison of reduced volume-high intensity interval training compared to high volume training on endurance performance in triathletes. *International Journal of Sports Physiology and Performance, 14*(2), 239–245.

Malone, J. J., Di Michele, R., Morgans, R., Burgess, D., Morton, J. P., and Drust, B. (2015). Seasonal training-load quantification in elite English Premier League soccer players. *International Journal of Sports Physiology and Performance, 10*(4), 489–497. https://doi.org/10.1123/ijspp.2014-0352

Moran, J., Blagrove, R. C., Drury, B., Fernandes, J. F. T., Paxton, K., Chaabene, H., and Ramirez-Campillo, R. (2019). Effects of small-sided games vs. conventional endurance training on endurance performance in male youth soccer players: A meta-analytical comparison. *Sports Medicine, 49,* 731–742. https://doi.org/10.1007/s40279-019-01086-w

Morgans, R., Bezuglov, E., Orme, P., Burns, K., Rhodes, D., Babraj, J., Di Michele, R., and Oliveira, R. F. S. (2022). The physical demands of match-play in academy and senior soccer players from the Scottish premiership. *Sports, 10,* 150. https://doi.org/10.3390/sports10100150

Morgans, R., Orme, P., Anderson, L., and Drust, B. (2014). Principles and practices of training for soccer. *Journal of Sport and Health Sciences, 13,* 1–7. https://doi.org/10.1016/j.jshs.2014.07.002

Morgans, R., Radnor, J., Fonseca, J., Haslam, C., King, M., Rhodes, D., Zmijewski, P., and Oliveira, R. (2024). Match running performance is influenced by possession and team formation in an English Premier League team. *Biology of Sport, 41*(3), 275–286.

Munoz, I., Seiler, S., Alcocer, A., Carr, N., and Esteve-Lanao, J. (2015). Specific intensity for peaking: Is race pace the best option? *Asian Journal of Sports Medicine, 6*(3). https://doi.org/10.5812/asjsm.24900

Oliveira, R., Martins, A., Moreno-Villanueva, A., Brito, J. P., Nalha, M., Rico-González, M., and Clemente, F. M. (2022). Reference values for external and internal training intensity monitoring in professional male soccer players: A systematic review. *International Journal of Sports Science and Coaching, 17*(6), 1506–1530. https://doi.org/10.1177/17479541211072966

Owen, A. L., Wong, D. P., Mckenna, M., and Dellal, A. (2011). Heart rate responses and technical comparison between small-vs. large-sided games in elite professional soccer. *Journal of Strength and Conditioning Research, 25*(8), 2104–2110. https://doi.org/10.1519/JSC.0b013e3181f0a8a3

Paquette, M., Le Blanc, O., Lucas, S. J. E., Thibault, G., Bailey, D. M., and Brassard, P. (2017). Effects of submaximal and supramaximal interval training on determinants of endurance performance in endurance athletes. *Scandinavian Journal of Medicine and Science in Sports, 27*(3), 318–326. https://doi.org/10.1111/sms.12660

Poole, D. C., Rossiter, H. B., Brooks, G. A., and Gladden, L. B. (2021). The anaerobic threshold: 50+ years of controversy. *Journal of Physiology, 599*(3), 737–767. https://doi.org/10.1113/JP279963

Rampinini, E., Impellizzeri, F. M., Castagna, C., Abt, G., Chamari, K., Sassi, A., and Marcora, S. M. (2007). Factors influencing physiological responses to small-sided soccer games. *Journal of Sports Sciences, 25*(6), 659–666.

Rampinini, E., Impellizzeri, F. M., Castagna, C., Coutts, A. J., and Wisløff, U. (2009). Technical performance during soccer matches of the Italian Serie A league: Effect of fatigue and competitive level. *Journal of Science and Medicine in Sport, 12*(1), 227–233. https://doi.org/10.1016/j.jsams.2007.10.002

Randes, M., Heitmann, A., and Muller, L. (2012). Physical responses of different small-sided game formats in elite youth soccer players. *Journal of Strength and Conditioning Research, 26*(5), 1353–1360.

Rienzi, E., Drust, B., Reilly, T., Carter, J. E., and Martin, A. (2000). Investigation of anthropometric and work-rate profiles of elite South American international soccer players. *Journal of Sports Medicine and Physical Fitness, 40*(2), 162–169.

Sampaio, J., Garcia, G., Maças, V., Ibanez, J., Abrantes, C., and Caixinha, P. (2007). Heart rate and perceptual responses to 2 × 2 and 3 × 3 small-sided youth soccer games. *Journal of Sports Sciences and Medicine, 6*(10), 121–122.

Sandford, G. N., Laursen, P. B., and Buchheit, M. (2021). Anaerobic speed/power reserve and sport performance: Scientific basis, current applications and future directions. *Sports Medicine, 51*(10), 2017–2028. https://doi.org/10.1007/s40279-021-01523-9

Sarmento, H., Clemente, F. M., Harper, L. D., da Costa, I. T., Owen, A., and Figueiredo, A. J. (2018). Small sided games in soccer–A systematic review. *International Journal of Performance Analysis in Sport, 18*(5), 693–749. https://doi.org/10.1080/24748668.2018.1517288

Silva, P., Lott, R., Wickrama, K. a S., Mota, J., and Welk, G. (2011). VO$_2$ at maximal and supramaximal intensities: Lessons to high interval training in swimming. *International Journal of Sport Nutrition and Exercise Metabolism, 32*, 1–44.

Stolen, T., Chamari, K., and Castagna, C. (2005). Physiology of soccer: An update. *Sports Medicine, 35*, 501–536.

Williams, K., and Owen, A. (2007). The impact of player numbers on the physiological responses to small sided games. *Journal of Sports Science and Medicine, 10*, 99–102.

3

STRENGTH, POWER, AND PLYOMETRIC TRAINING IN FOOTBALL

Benjamin Rosenblatt and Martin Evans

Introduction

The purpose of any physical training programme in sport is to improve an athlete's capability of excelling within the technical and tactical constraints of their sport. This involves improving the effectiveness of critical actions and also reducing the biomechanical and physiological cost of these actions to reduce fatigue and mitigate injury risk. The most unique feature of elite football is not only the physical attributes that are required to dominate 1v1 scenarios and critical actions within the game all over the pitch, but also the requirement to repeat this across a high volume of training sessions and a densely congested fixture schedule. This context has led to debates about the most appropriate methods of developing strength and power abilities for football players. With this in mind, the purpose of this chapter is to identify the key actions which take place within football, the biomechanical framework and neuromuscular demand which underpins their effectiveness, and then to align the different training strategies available (i.e., strength, power, and plyometrics) within the conceptual framework to the principles of training. Put simply, our aim is to provide strength and conditioning (S and C) coaches with a decision-making framework and a way of thinking which allows them to improve the effectiveness of their exercise selection and the associated periodization strategies.

Demands of the Game

It is common when looking at the match demands of football to quantify the total distance covered alongside distances covered at high intensities (Bradley and Ade, 2018). Whilst this approach can yield some insight that may be helpful in designing

DOI: 10.4324/9781003383475-4

a physical preparation plan, it does not fully capture the match demands; therefore, limiting the physical preparation plan design process. For example, in the 2022 FIFA World Cup in Qatar, the average team distance covered was 108.1 km with 9,001 m covered at >20 km/h and 2,345 m at >25 km/h, respectively. These data represent large variations in distance covered at differing intensities, highlighting the importance of contextualizing this type of information alongside the tactical aspects of the game. To further elaborate, teams that tend to sit in low or mid-blocks typically cover less total distance, whilst teams that tend to transition frequently will cover greater distances. Another consideration is that there is large match-to-match variation in each team's output which indicates that the opposition has a strong influence on a team's output as well – likely because of a modified gameplan. This highlights that these outputs are not necessarily a reflection of what players are capable of, but are more reflective of what players have been asked to do. Ultimately, a team's success is based on the organization of the team to optimize individuals' physical and technical capabilities (Bradley and Noakes, 2013).

Within a team, there are several specialized roles or positions and each of these positions tends to have its own unique output. Match analysis reveals that central midfielders tend to cover the most distance with centre-backs covering the least (Beato et al., 2024). This makes sense when you consider their roles within the game where the centre-backs are primarily involved during out of possession phases, whereas central midfielders tend to be active both in and out of possession. Further to this, players in wide positions tend to cover greater distance at higher speeds than central players, which highlights the opportunities that they are afforded to accelerate into space and reach higher peak speeds than players in central positions where space is more limited. In terms of preparing players to perform, this illustrates the predominant types of work they need to be prepared for. However, as with team outputs, there is considerable variation between players within the same position, which again, comes back to what are players being asked to do tactically. Trends tend to point that the high-intensity work is increasing for all positions in recent years, which has implications for the physical development of players now and in the future if this trend is to continue increasing.

An additional method sometimes used to quantify the work done by football players is video capture techniques. However, a major limitation of this type of analysis is the inability to quantify acceleration and deceleration metrics which are a large component of the demand placed on players. Interest in acceleration for football performance has become more frequent in recent years (Akenhead and Nassis, 2016; Morin, 2021). This is completely understandable given that acceleration ability may be one of the most important capabilities for match-defining moments such as winning the race to a ball, moving into open space to create an opportunity to shoot, or being able to aggressively press an opponent to win the ball back (Faude et al., 2012). From a physical preparation perspective, it is essential that players are prepared for the mechanical and metabolic demands of acceleration which are over and above what is typically observed in constant speed running

42 Strength and Conditioning for Football

(di Prampero et al., 2023). Similarly, the impact of deceleration activities is poorly understood with recent research illustrating the unique biomechanical demands of these actions (e.g. very large braking forces applied in very small periods of time) (Harper et al., 2022). Consequently, players are often underprepared to cope with these actions at high magnitudes and high frequencies.

Beyond these volume-based metrics, which typically underestimate the locomotive demands (Bradley et al., 2013), research has started to investigate the physical outputs in different time epochs (Ju et al., 2022). This type of analysis looks at the physical trends in the most demanding (peak) periods of match-play (e.g., 1-min, 3-min, 5-min), and can help practitioners design drills that reflect the most demanding passages of play (Connor et al., 2022). As with volume-based metrics, this type of analysis can be performed for the different positions to provide information to design optimal physical preparation programmes for players. This is an essential step for practitioners looking to optimally prepare players for football performance as it is determined by the interaction of technical, tactical, physical, and psychological components (Stølen et al., 2005).

From a tactical perspective, an individual within a team is either manipulating their own body or an opponent's in order to create or deny space. To achieve this, a player has a variety of different movement solutions available to them which will depend on the context in which they sit. Typically, actions that involve creating space require an athlete to deceive an opponent and perform a sprint (Bloomfield et al., 2007). Conversely, actions that are intended to deny space typically involve hard accelerations and attempting to couple themselves with an opponent. Additionally, each individual within a team will have a unique injury history, in addition to tactical strengths and weaknesses which require bespoke training to improve. By using a biomechanical framework, it becomes possible for a player or coach to identify an area of the game that the team or specific players within the team need to improve or cope with, and then provide a conditioning stimulus which drives the necessary adaptation – which is the primary aim of this chapter.

A Biomechanical Framework for Football

Sprinting to Generate Space

When generating space, a player has to bring the ball or their body rapidly away from an opponent. This can be done immediately after changing direction or from a variety of initial conditions. Fundamentally, it requires a player to generate the distance they require as fast as possible in order to be in the position they require. The fundamental biomechanical demand of sprinting requires an athlete to increase their system stiffness in order to reduce their ground contact, reduce the vertical displacement of the centre of mass, and project it horizontally, by applying a large propulsive impulse with each step (Weyand et al., 2000). This occurs through the neuromuscular system producing large co-contractions around the hip extensors generating a large propulsive impulse, with the knee extensors maintaining vertical centre of mass displacement, and the ankle joint producing a large plantar-flexion moment to minimize ground contact time. The unique feature of these co-contractions is the requirement to maintain postural control and to produce these contractions in a proximal to distal sequence. These actions require the ankle and knee joints, and lumbar-pelvic region to act like stiff springs by producing large amounts of force isometrically, whilst also resisting length change. Whilst this is happening, the hip extensors also need to generate large amounts of power to propel the athlete forward. The unique feature of sprinting within football is that players may be required to do this when their centre of mass is outside of their base of support in a variety of directions and also whilst dribbling the ball.

Braking to Deny Space

In order to effectively reduce their velocity rapidly to either change direction or apply direct pressure to an opponent, a player must have the capability to brake effectively. From a biomechanical perspective, this requires the compression of the spring mass system by generating a large braking impulse in the steps prior to stopping (Harper et al., 2022). This is typically achieved by reducing the height of the centre of mass whilst trying to align it in the frontal plane towards the new direction of travel, prior to a directional change (Harper et al., 2022). Effective strategies to achieve this include: rapid flexion of the knee and hip with vertical trunk alignment during ground contact. Conversely to sprinting, these contractions occur in a distal to proximal sequence (Harper et al., 2022). This places high magnitudes of force through the ankle plantar flexors, knee and hip extensors, whilst requiring high force generation of the hip and pelvis rotators and lateral flexors, in order to maintain centre of mass alignment for the following action.

Action Coupling and Decoupling

Research from 1v1 situations across a variety of sports has shown that successful defence requires the defender to couple the lateral and anterior motion of their centre of mass with that of the attacker. This scenario can also be applied to the goalkeeper who is attempting to win a 1v1 situation or match the trajectory of the ball with the trajectory of their centre of mass (Fujii et al., 2014). When defenders are successful in coupling their centre of mass with an attacker's (which often results in them winning a duel), they have to generate rapid braking co-contractions in response to the attacker's movement whilst maintaining postural control to retain their gaze. As these movements are often unanticipated, the time available to produce these co-contractions is limited which increases the braking impulse required to maintain coupling (Spiteri et al., 2015). From a neuromuscular perspective, this increases the demand on the tissues to resist length change and can increase the potential for tissue damage (Harper et al., 2022). This capacity for greater strain

44 Strength and Conditioning for Football

resistance (commonly known as braking strength) is critical for defensive actions (Harper et al., 2022). Conversely, the role of the attacker is to try and decouple the action of their centre of mass from the defender to try and generate space. This is achieved through effective postural control and unexpected changes in rhythm and motion, and requires deliberate action to notice when they have generated space for them to move into. Once the space is available to the attacker, their capacity to generate system stiffness through rapid proximal to distal contractions, whilst their centre of mass may not be orientated towards their direction of travel, will be critical to success (Fujii et al., 2014). In both attacking and defending scenarios, there is a much greater demand for lateral and rotational movement which requires force closure around the pelvis in order to keep control of the centre of mass. This requires the hip ab/adductors and lateral trunk muscular structure to work in synergy and tolerate high quasi-isometric forces (Jeong et al., 2021).

Manipulating an Opponent's Body

In many attacking and defending scenarios, there is a need for a player to manipulate their opponent to try to win or protect the ball. During these actions, the players must identify when their opponent's centre of mass is outside of their base of support and aim to destabilize this (within the rules of the game)! This requires the ability to rapidly generate force through the kinetic chain to the point of contact with the opponent. Conversely, when a player's body position is being manipulated, they must produce even greater levels of force throughout the kinetic chain to overcome the momentum of their opponent, whilst their centre of mass is outside of their base of support. Both of these types of actions require forceful contractions to retain postural control to both absorb and generate force through the transverse and frontal planes.

Ball Striking

Kicking a football is clearly the most unique feature of the game. The control a player has over the direction of the ball will be dependent on how long they can keep their foot in contact with the ball when striking, and their potential to increase ball striking velocity will be dependent on the foot velocity at impact (Janani et al., 2023). The ball-kicking sequence is a proximal to distal action of the lower limb kinetic chain which often occurs when the centre of mass is not over the base of support. In order to be effective at this, the standing leg must produce a large co-contraction around the lateral hip and pelvis whilst the trunk flexors resist length change and allow the adductor and hip flexors to generate high power.

Consequently, by presenting a biomechanical conceptual framework (Figure 3.1) for the critical actions within the game, it's possible to identify the necessary sites of adaptation for strength, power, and plyometric training. With this in mind, S and C coaches can work with technical coaches to increase their understanding of the game model and the needs of each individual within, and then use the

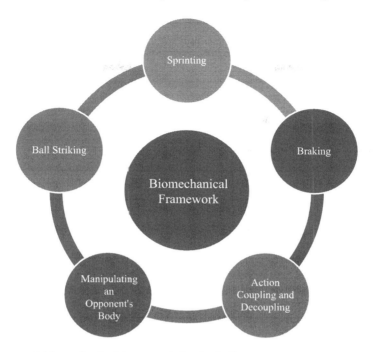

FIGURE 3.1 A biomechanical framework for football.

biomechanical framework to identify appropriate training activities. However, in order to design a training programme which is unique for each individual, physical profiling can help S and C coaches gain an insight into the physical capability of an individual might enable or limit an athlete's performance in these actions.

Physical Profiling

Physical profiling is the process of understanding the athlete's capability to cope with and thrive within the demands of the game. The tests selected by the S and C coach should represent the biomechanical and metabolic demand of the critical tasks within the game and the neuromuscular system's capability of performing them effectively. Ultimately, this should help the S and C coach select appropriate exercises and write an effective training programme for the player. When profiling a footballer, it's useful to set clear thresholds prior to the test and have a decision-making framework in place to improve the reliability and efficiency of training prescription.

Once a practitioner has identified what the important physical characteristics of the team are then an appropriate testing battery can be compiled. It is important to ensure that the pros and cons of each test are clearly understood. From a practical perspective, it is important to consider the feasibility of repeating these tests throughout a season. Football typically has a busy calendar that makes it

46 Strength and Conditioning for Football

challenging to run maximal testing routinely, which can then limit the practitioners, understanding of what the players' response to a training intervention is. In the authors' experience, creating situations where *training = testing* is the most easily incorporated. This might mean a trade-off from a 'gold standard' approach, but if this is acknowledged and the bandwidths and reliability of the testing protocol are identified, then this can form an invaluable set of information from which programming can be monitored and adjusted accordingly.

Once the testing battery is compiled, practitioners should seek to understand the 'noise' in the test so that meaningful change can be detected. It is all too common for practitioners to celebrate or commiserate a small magnitude of change that is within the inherent error of the test. Once a baseline for an individual is established (which will help to identify their strengths and weaknesses across the important characteristics), a training programme can be developed and then routinely monitored to assess changes in response to training and other factors that may influence some physical characteristics (e.g., the influence of fatigue). Tests can be organized into flows that allow practitioners to understand the underpinning characteristics of the action. For example, if acceleration is the action of interest, there could be a test of acceleration that looks at the player's time to cover 10 m. The next layer could then look to examine some of the key aspects as to how they performed that acceleration (e.g., looking into the ability of the individual to project their CoM forward, their ability to react off the floor, and their capacity to switch their limbs). The next layer can then look at isolated physical tests that underpin these strategies.

Using the aforementioned biomechanical framework, tests and appropriate benchmarks can be established using practitioner experience and peer-reviewed research to identify how an athlete's physical capability might limit their capability to perform a skill. This process of identifying limiting and enabling factors within performance is the most critical aspect of identifying which activities to prioritize for strength, power, and plyometric training.

Principles of Training

Specificity and Exercise Selection

Specificity is a key principle to the success of an intervention aiming to change a player's physical qualities. Therefore, understanding the demands of the game and the framework of critical game actions is a vitally important step to be able to identify both the physical profiling tests and variables to be monitored, and the subsequent intervention that follows. This understanding will allow practitioners to identify the appropriate strength qualities.

Strength is defined as the ability to create force under specific conditions (Zatsiorsky, 2008). Therefore, defining the conditions in which force must be produced is crucial to developing a programme for players to be able to cope with and excel in the demands placed on them. Consideration must be given to the amount of

Strength, Power, and Plyometric Training in Football **47**

force, the timing of the force application, the type of muscular action, and the sequencing of the contractions (Table 3.1).

The use of an appropriately developed physical profiling battery that is aligned to the biomechanical framework can be used to understand how players display the relevant strength qualities. This can then be utilized to develop an appropriate intervention to maximize a player's strength and minimize their weaknesses or those factors that limit the performance of critical game actions. If the limiting factor is the local tissue's capacity to produce and resist high forces at high rates, then utilizing strength and power training modalities will overload the specific tissue characteristics. Conversely, if the limiting factor comes from the capacity to coordinate contractions and retain postural control in a task-specific manner, then plyometric training might be a preferable option.

Once the S and C coach has identified the limiting factors of performance for the individual and their relevant tasks, the next stage is to select exercises which are aligned with the capability of the athlete and the need for the tasks they need to perform. Below is an example series of diagrams and tables to help coaches select loading methods and exercises based on the tasks they are trying to improve and the force conditions they are trying to change. These examples are taken from work undertaken by the authors in collaboration with Damian Harper (The FA Training Solutions Manual), with a focus on braking strength specifically. The subsequent tables (Tables 3.2 and 3.3) then provide an overview of what loading methods and exercises could be used to develop braking force specifically. This same approach can be used to create similar models for other critical game actions (e.g., acceleration or sprinting).

TABLE 3.1 Examples of Football-Specific Tasks and the Associated Force Conditions and Required Co-contractions

Task	Force Conditions	Co-Contraction Region
Shielding the ball from an opponent	A task which challenges the tissue or joint system to generate high forces.	Co-contraction of hip and trunk muscles
Minimizing GCT during acceleration	A task which challenges the tissue or joint system to generate force within a constrained period of time.	Co-contraction around the ankle joint
Decrease the CoM during penultimate step when pressing	A task where force is produced to resist length change.	Co-contraction around the hip and knee joint
Lower the CoM height when evading an opponent	A task where force is produced to rapidly resist length change within a constrained time period.	Co-contraction around the knee joint

GCT = ground contact time; CoM = centre of mass.

48 Strength and Conditioning for Football

TABLE 3.2 Gym-Based Loading Strategies for the Development of Braking Force

Gym-Based Loading Strategies for the Development of Braking Force			
Training Strategies	*Equipment Required*	*Example Exercises*	*Coaching and Loading Comments*
Targeted Eccentrics (TAR-EOC)	N/A	Reverse Nordic	Coaching: • Resist the fall • Slow and steady in descent Loading: • Band assisted or resisted • Eccentric only • Assisted concentric
	TMR Belt	Squat and Hip Extension	
	Leg Extension Machine	Leg Extension	
	TMR Belt	Good Morning	
	Hip Extension machine	Hip Extension	
	Calf raise machine	Calf Raise	
Slow Accentuated Eccentric Loaning (S-AEL)	Weight Releasers or Smith Machine	Reverse Nordic	Coaching: • Resist movement • Slow and steady in descent Loading: • Different squat variation • Delayed eccentric action • Impulse overload • Assisted concentric • 2/1 technique • Increase inertia
	Flywheel	Squat and Hip Extension	
	Flywheel	Leg Extension	
	Flywheel	Good Morning	
	Flywheel	Hip Extension	
	Flywheel	Calf Raise	
SA-EL (2/1 Technique)	Free weight	Skater Squat	Coaching: • Push up fast • Get out of hole quick Loading: • Combine with an ISO pause to create ECC-ISO
	Free weight	SL dead stop squat	
	Free weight	Kickstand squat	
	Free weight	Single leg RDL	
	Free weight	Split Stance RDL	
	Free weight	Lunges	
	Free weight	Back/Front Squat	
	Free weight	Kickstand deadlift	
Yielding-Isometrics (Y-ISO)	Low pulley	Ankle ISO yield	Coaching: • Maintain posture • Loading: • Horizontal band resistance • Combine with AEL • Progress duration to intensity • Change joint angle
	Leg press or smith machine	Ankle ISO yield Straight leg calf raise	
	Leg Extension Machine	Knee ISO-yield Leg extension	
	Leg press, smith machine, free weight	Knee ISO-yield SL squat	
	Free weight	Knee ISO-yield RFESS	
	Free weight	Hip ISO-yield (split stance deadlift, good morning)	

Strength, Power, and Plyometric Training in Football **49**

TABLE 3.3 Field-Based Loading Strategies for the Development of Braking Force

Field-Based Loading Strategies for the Development of Braking Force			
Training Strategies	*Equipment Required*	*Example Exercises*	*Coaching and Loading Comments*
Assisted braking	Cable pulley, resistance bands, 1,080 sprint, Vertimax Raptor	Horizontal braking steps	Coaching: • Feel each braking step • Foot rocker – heel or flat foot • Push hard no ground contact
	Cable pulley, resistance bands, 1,080 sprint, Vertimax Raptor	Horizontal hops and jumps	Loading: • Progressive increase in amount of assistance • Increased number of braking steps in sequence • Perform in complex with planned decelerations
Planed decelerations	Cones, poles	Linear decelerations	Coaching: • Brake quick • Feel each braking step Loading:
	Cones, poles	Decelerations into change of directions ($>60°$)	• Different linear deceleration distances

Intensity, Volume, and Overload

Manipulating training volume and intensity are fundamental components of periodizing a training programme over time to elicit a chronic adaptive response, whilst mitigating acute fatigue when a player is preparing for a match. There are several macro- and micro-periodization strategies that are available to an S and C coach when trying to help a player improve their performance. Fundamentally, the volume and intensity should be progressive over time to ensure that the stimulus is initially tolerable and then remains above the athlete's habitual level and respites in the training cycle exist, to enable the super compensation effect and mitigate fatigue to prepare for the upcoming fixture. During periods of fixture congestion, it might be prudent to take a micro-dosing approach to training (Cuthbert et al., 2024). This requires the athlete to retain the intensity of exercises but split the total volume up over multiple sessions. This approach decreases the acute session fatigue, whilst maintaining the total cycle training volume which is required to retain the training adaptations developed during the previous cycle.

A fundamental concept in exercise selection is matching the intensity of the exercise to the athlete's physical capability. Fundamentally, intensity only needs to be above a certain threshold in order to trigger an adaptive response. Therefore, the exercise (and how it is executed) must stimulate the neuromuscular system above its habitual level, but this doesn't need to be in excess of its maximal tolerable level. This has important implications not only for the amount of load an

50 Strength and Conditioning for Football

TABLE 3.4 Considerations and Actions for Manipulating Volume and Intensity

Considerations	Low	High
Athlete Training Tolerance	Undulating, but linear increase in training volume on a weekly basis over the training cycle may be required for progressive overload	Higher volumes of work may be required over a training cycle may be required compared to athletes with lower training history
Exercise Intensity	Higher volumes can be tolerated over the cycle	Lower volumes are required for desired training response
Fixture Congestion	Opportunity to increase volume of higher intensity exercises	Very low volume of high intensity exercises. Retain volume of lower intensity exercises
Football Training Demand	Opportunity for higher S and C volume	Reduce S and C volume

athlete should lift but also which exercise you should select to help them develop their task-specific physical capability. For example, the Nordic Hamstring Curl is a very common exercise used to prevent hamstring injuries by increasing the amount of strain the hamstrings can tolerate. However, compliance is often limited due to DOMS associated with the novelty of the intensity of the exercise. For athletes that have low training histories and levels of eccentric hamstring strength, the exercise can be modified by using a band or an alternative exercise such as a slider can be used, to overload the hamstrings without resulting in a response which has an acute negative effect on training capability and football performance. Some key considerations for manipulating volume and intensity are provided in Table 3.4.

Practical Applications

We recognize that football is a complex sport with a high volume of multiple types of actions taking place at different intensities, over the course of multiple matches and training sessions throughout the season. We also recognize that each head coach will have a unique vision of how to approach the physical preparation of their team. Therefore, the purpose of this chapter was to provide coaches with a framework to select exercises and prescribe strength, power, and plyometric training in order to improve athlete's performance within the unique context of professional football. This process will be unique for each coach, but should always be dependent on the biomechanical demands of the game, the needs of the player, the competition schedule, and ultimately, the adaptations which the coach believes are required for improved football performance. Taking a principle-based approach, using physical

Strength, Power, and Plyometric Training in Football

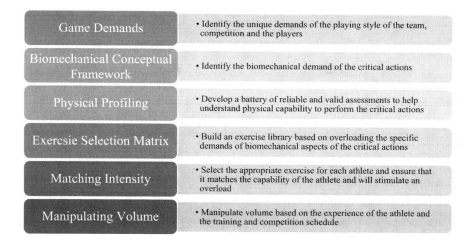

FIGURE 3.2 A principle-based approach to train for strength, power and plyometrics within professional football.

profiling to objectively identify performance gaps and having exercise selection frameworks will help coaches improve the effectiveness, efficiency, and reliability of their training programmes. The process that coaches can deploy to build their own physical performance framework is outlined in Figure 3.2.

References

Akenhead, R., and Nassis, G. P. (2016). Training load and player monitoring in high-level football: Current practice and perceptions. *International Journal of Sports Physiology and Performance*, 11, 587–593.

Beato, M., Youngs, A., and Costin, A. J. (2024). The analysis of physical performance during official competitions in professional English Football: Do positions, game locations, and results influence players' Game Demands? *Journal of Strength and Conditioning Research*, 38(5), e226–e234.

Bloomfield, J., Polman, R., and O'Donoghue, P. (2007). Physical demands of different positions in FA Premier League Soccer. *Journal of Sports Science and Medicine*, 6(1), 63–70.

Bradley, P., Carling, C., Gómez-Díaz, A., et al. (2013). Match performance and physical capacity of players in the top three competitive standards of English professional soccer. *Human Movement Science*, 32(4), 808–821.

Bradley, P. S., and Ade, J. D. (2018). Are current physical match performance metrics in elite soccer fit for purpose or is the adoption of an integrated approach needed? *International Journal of Sports Physiology and Performance*, 13, 656–664.

Bradley, P. S., and Noakes, T. D. (2013). Match running performance fluctuations in elite soccer: Indicative of fatigue, pacing or situational influences? *Journal of Sports Sciences*, 31, 1627–1638.

Connor, M., Mernagh, D., and Beato, M. (2022). Quantifying and modelling the game speed outputs of English Championship soccer players. *Research in Sports Medicine*, 30(2), 169–181.

52 Strength and Conditioning for Football

Cuthbert, M., Haff, G., McMahon, J., Evans, M., and Comfort, P. (2024). Microdosing: A conceptual framework for use as programming strategy for resistance training in team sports. *Strength and Conditioning Journal*, 46(2), 180–201,

di Prampero, P., Osgnach, P., Morin, J. B., Zamparo, P., and Pavei, G. (2023). Mechanical and metabolic power in accelerated running–PART I: The 100-m dash. *European Journal of Applied Physiology*, 123(11), 1–9.

Faude, O., Koch, T., and Meyer, T. (2012). Straight sprinting is the most frequent action in goal situations in professional football. *Journal of Sports Science*, 30, 625–631.

Fujii, K., Yamashita, D., Yoshioka, S., Isaka, T., and Kouzaki, M. (2014). Strategies for defending a dribbler: Categorisation of three defensive patterns in 1-on-1 basketball. *Sports Biomechanics*, 13, 1–11.

Harper, D. J., McBurnie, A. J., Santos, T. D., et al. (2022). Biomechanical and neuromuscular performance requirements of horizontal deceleration: A review with implications for random intermittent multi-directional sports. *Sports Medicine*, 52, 2321–2354.

Janani, G., Vigneshmoorthy, K., Nimishaanth, S. S., Vikram, R., Thiagarajan, A., and Arumugam, S. (2023). Biomechanical factors influencing post-strike ball velocity in football players: A cross-sectional Study. *Journal of Clinical and Diagnostic Research*, 17(11), 10–14.

Jeong, J., Choi, D. H., and Shin, C. S. (2021). Core strength training can alter neuromuscular and biomechanical risk factors for anterior cruciate ligament injury. *American Journal of Sports Medicine*, 49(1), 183–192.

Ju, W., Doran, D., Hawkins, R., et al. (2022). Contextualised peak periods of play in English Premier League matches. *Biology of Sport*, 39(4), 973–983.

Morin, J. B., Le Mat, Y., Osgnach, C., Barnabò, A., Pilati, A., Samozino, P., and di Prampero, P. (2021). Individual acceleration-speed profile in-situ: A proof of concept in professional football players, *Journal of Biomechanics*, 123, 110524.

Spiteri, T., Newton, R., Hart, N., Binetti, M., Sheppard, J., and Nimphius, S. (2015). Mechanical determinants of faster change of direction and agility performance in female basketball athletes. *The Journal of Strength and Conditioning Research*, 29, 2205–2214.

Stølen, T., Chamari, K., Castagna, C., and Wisløff, U. (2005). Physiology of soccer. *Sports Medicine*, 35, 501–536.

Weyand, P., Sternlight, D., Bellizzi, M., and Wright, S. (2000). Faster top running speeds are achieved with greater ground forces not more rapid leg movements. *Journal of Applied Physiolofy (1985)*, 89(5), 1991–1999.

Zatsiorsky, V. (2008). Biomechanics of strength and strength training. In Paavo V. Komi (ed), *Stregnth and Power in Sport*, 2nd Edition. Wiley-Blackwell. https://doi.org/10.1002/9780470757215.ch23

4

SPEED AND AGILITY TRAINING IN FOOTBALL

Filipe Manuel Clemente, Jason Moran,
Rodrigo Ramirez-Campillo, Helmi Chaabene,
and Javier Sanchez-Sanchez

Introduction

Sprint running and change of direction (COD) ability are critical components of football players' repertoire of motor skills [1]. The performance of these skills is typically associated with key moments during a match when a player must overcome the physical challenge of an opponent or create a goal-scoring chance from a counter-attack [2]. For example, linear sprinting is the most frequent action that is performed prior to an open-play goal-scoring opportunity and is also common when assisting a player during such a scenario [3]. In addition to linear sprinting, it is essential to highlight the importance of curvilinear sprint trajectories which are typically performed to evade, track, or draw an opponent during open play [4]. Interestingly, curvilinear sprint trajectories may represent 85% of the total number of actions undertaken at a maximum speed [4] while most sprints are performed at an angle of between $3.7°$ and $6.2°$ [5].

Considering the multidirectional nature of movement in football, changing direction is also a very common action during play. Football players perform an average of about 100 turns between $90°$ and $180°$ per game [3] and of those, around 8.5% occur while sprinting. Accordingly, players must demonstrate proficient COD ability so they can effectively perform fast and sudden directional changes [6] and "cut" at acute angles during play [7].

Determinants of Sprint Performance

Sprint performance depends on players' ability to accelerate, express maximal speed, and sustain high speed against the emergence of fatigue [8]. Performance in the different sprint phases is governed by stride length (i.e., distance travelled

DOI: 10.4324/9781003383475-5

54 Strength and Conditioning for Football

by each stride) and stride rate (i.e., number of strides executed per second) [8,9]. Generally, stride length and rate are mediated by neural (e.g., motor unit recruitment and rate coding), morphological (e.g., muscle fiber types, muscle cross-sectional area), metabolic (e.g., decreased ATP and CP), anthropometric (e.g., body fat, extremities' length), and technical (e.g., direction of force application during ground contact) factors [8]. Regarding the latter point, there exists substantial evidence supporting the notion that the capacity to generate a substantial magnitude of ground reaction force in the horizontal plane plays a pivotal role in achieving optimal acceleration and overall superior sprint performance [10].

However, it is worth noting that stride length is primarily influenced by the amount of force generated during the contact phase of the gait cycle [11]. It is during this phase that the muscles push against the ground to propel the body forward and generate the necessary force to produce a longer stride. Consequently, training efforts should prioritize the attainment of an optimal stride length, as opposed to excessively lengthening an athlete's stride, as this may lead to the foot being positioned too far ahead of the body's center of mass. Such a scenario can compromise an athlete's power generation capabilities and ultimately result in a reduction of running speed. Stride rate, on the other hand, is influenced by both ground contact times and flight times, although research suggests that the greatest variation in stride rate is mainly attributed to differences in ground contact rather than flight time [12]. In this sense, there is evidence suggesting that a faster stride rate is associated with shorter ground contact times which can be attributed to the ability to produce force rapidly through high rates of neural activation during the gait cycle [11].

Determinants of Change of Direction and Agility Performance

COD performance is determined by multiple factors as displayed in the model previously proposed by Sheppard and Young [13]. These factors pertain to movement technique (e.g., forward lean during acceleration and low center of gravity and shorter stride length during deceleration), the magnitude of straight sprinting speed and leg muscle qualities (i.e., left-right asymmetries, concentric strength and power, and reactive strength) [13]. Of note, these factors are sensitive to changes due to training, which can improve COD speed performance. On the contrary, anthropometric characteristics (e.g., body height, body fat, body segments' length, and height of the athlete's center of gravity), constitute other determining factors that are largely not changeable through training [13]. Furthermore, an additional crucial factor in determining COD speed is eccentric strength [14], which enables an athlete to quickly decelerate their body during high-speed movement, facilitating early reacceleration in a different direction; thus, contributing to better overall COD performance [14].

Agility has two distinct major components. The first is the physical component, related to COD speed capabilities, and the aforementioned moderating factors. The second is the perceptual and decision-making process components [13]. The latter factor is deemed to be more determinant of good agility performance than the physical component. This cognitive component involves factors such as anticipation, visual scanning, pattern recognition, and knowledge of a given situation [13]. Also, there is evidence that COD and agility are independent skills [15]. This would mean that COD training does not necessarily enhance agility performance so coaches must adopt distinct training strategies to focus on each component. This seems to be mainly due to the cognitive element of agility which is largely absent in COD tasks [13,15].

Assessment of Sprint Performance

Instruments for Measuring Sprint Running

Sprint running can be tested by using different instruments and technologies. Among the potential tools coaches can use are: (i) fully automatic timing systems; (ii) manual timing (e.g., stopwatch); (iii) photocell timing; (iv) floor pods; (v) audio and visual start sensors; (vi) video timing; (vii) laser and radar devices; and (viii) global positioning systems (GPS) [16].

Fully automatic timing systems are considered the most accurate and precise systems [17] consisting of a silent gun, photo-finish camera, and pressure-sensitive start blocks for detecting false starts. Despite being considered the gold standard in terms of testing, these systems are expensive and potentially not appropriate for use in a football setting due to their lack of specificity in terms of the starting point and their high cost. Accordingly, in football practice, coaches typically use photocell timing, video timing, laser and radar devices, or GPS.

Concerns in the Setup of Sprint Running Tests

Testing sprint performance requires attention to the configuration of the adopted data collection processes. Here, some critical issues that may minimize error during assessments, are highlighted.

Photocells' height can affect sprint time: a study [18] comparing two different photocell heights (60 and 80 cm) in 10 m and 20 m linear sprint tests showed significant differences in the sprint time (~0.7 seconds) observed by the instruments over these distances. Specifically, faster sprint times were consistently recorded when the photocell was positioned at hip height, as opposed to shoulder height, owing to the action of the legs interrupting the timing beam as they extend in front of the upper body during running [18]. Accordingly, it is recommended that coaches be consistent in the way the photocells are mounted each time they are used. In addition, the positioning of a photocell at hip height can minimize the chances of triggering the beam with an outstretched limb.

Start positions may affect the ultimate sprint performance: a study [19] comparing parallel stance, false-step stance, staggered stance, and staggered false-step

56 Strength and Conditioning for Football

stance revealed that starting with a staggered stance (whether employing a false-step or not) resulted in the fastest forward sprints over an initial 15 m sprint distance. It is also important that when taking repeated measures, players always start in the same position to maximize consistency and reliability in the collected data.

Surface conditions: in the case of repeated measures (e.g., pre-season vs mid-season), it is to be expected that different environmental conditions will be experienced and that this can affect the surface that is utilized during testing (e.g., weather, environmental factors). It is suggested that where possible, coaches avoid comparing and measuring linear sprints executed under disparate environmental conditions, particularly those affected by rain, high humidity, or wind as such conditions may play a significant role in floor traction and the ultimate running performance.

Linear Sprint Tests

To measure peak sprinting speed in football, coaches should utilize linear sprint tests between 10 m and 40 m [20]. In a study comparing peak velocities attained in a linear 40-m sprint test to those attained in competitive matches and large, medium, and small-sided games, it was observed that greater speeds were achieved in the linear 40 m sprint test [20]. However, contradictory findings have also been shown in separate research [21] which showed that the peak speed attained in matches was faster than in a 40 m linear sprint test. Despite this, the use of the 40-m linear sprint test, exhibits lower heterogeneity and variability than that which is observed in a match scenario.

Independent of the distance selected, it is worth mentioning that linear sprints performed without any other task in combination are highly reliable tests. This finding is supported by a comprehensive systematic review dedicated to this specific topic [22]. An intraclass correlation test demonstrated values exceeding 0.75, indicating a high level of agreement between repeated measurements [22]. Furthermore, the coefficient of variation remained below 3.0%, indicating minimal variability and enhancing the overall reliability of the measurements [22]. However, the integration of linear sprint tests into complex tests or match-simulations may reduce this reliability.

Linear sprint tests can be conducted in two different ways in terms of how movement is initiated: (i) static-start tests, which are more useful for assessing an athlete's ability to accelerate and, over longer distances, their ability to achieve maximum speed; (ii) flying-start tests, which enable the athlete to "pre-accelerate" in a designated zone prior to initiation of the test and focus only on the measurement of a player's maximum speed. It has been hypothesized that very fast players, while possessing greater acceleration capacity, can reach peak speeds relatively faster, and for that reason, a 20- to 30-m flying start test can be effective for estimating this capability [23]. Despite this, a static-start 40-m linear sprint test is also appropriate to measure a players accelerative and maximal sprinting qualities. Coaches can also use timing gates placed at various intervals along the 40-m course to measure split times (e.g., 5, 10, 20, and 30 m points), which can be useful in further breaking down the acceleration and maximal speed phases for analysis. In the case of flying starts, if coaches do not possess the necessary equipment to do this, video-based analysis with markers placed at the appropriate points on the course can be used to serve the purpose of deriving split times. Flying starts can be particularly advantageous for achieving maximal speed earlier in a sprint. With a flying start, athletes can reach their maximum speed over a shorter distance compared to a static start which requires a longer distance to attain the same speed.

Curvilinear Sprint Test

Considering that most sprints are performed in curvilinear trajectories [5], a curvilinear sprint test was previously designed for football players [24]. This test utilizes the arc of the penalty area on a regulation football field as the trajectory for sprint performance, covering a distance of 17 m [24]. The original study [24] positioned photocells at the start, mid (8.5 m), and at the end of the 17 m course. The front foot was placed one meter behind the first timing gate providing the athlete with a clear starting point for the test. The reliability of this curvilinear sprint test was confirmed with an intra-class correlation coefficient of between 0.75 and 0.96 while the coefficient of variation ranged from 0.5% to 1.97% [24]. The relationships between the curvilinear sprint test and the linear sprint test of 17 m were limited with the coefficient of determination being between 0.34 and 0.37 [24]. These findings suggest that curvilinear and straight-line sprinting abilities demonstrate a certain level of independence from each other. Accordingly, this validates the inclusion of both linear and curvilinear sprints in football players' training programs. It is also worth noting the implications for kinematic analysis in the context of curve sprinting actions. Evidence suggests that there is a longer foot contact time observed in the inside leg compared to the outside leg during such movements (4). Additionally, electromyographic activity analysis has revealed significant differences between the outside and inside legs during curve sprinting. Specifically, the outside leg exhibits higher activity in the biceps femoris and gluteus medius muscles, while the inside leg demonstrates increased activity in the semitendinosus and adductor muscles (4). These findings shed light on the distinct muscle activation patterns and asymmetries that arise during curve sprinting; thus, highlighting the importance of considering these factors in kinematic analyses.

Assessment of Change-of-Direction and Agility Performance

As previously mentioned, the concept of agility is more complex and multi-dimensional than that of COD ability. COD speed represents the speed at which a player can execute pre-planned movements that require little cognitive input. Agility places demands on the perceptual and decision-making ability of the player and challenges their propensity to anticipate specific on-field events while using COD

58 Strength and Conditioning for Football

ability to underpin the execution of a subsequent action. These factors should be considered when choosing an appropriate test.

For example, the traditional 5-0-5 or the 5-10-5 (also known as "pro-agility test") tests are examples of COD tests that do not assess agility capability because they do not challenge the perceptual or cognitive component of the athlete's movement. Conversely, the original reactive agility test combines COD ability with a given response to a stimulus that is provided by a video, person, arrow, or light [25]. In a reactive test condition, a departure from the conventional pre-determined movement patterns often seen in agility tests is implemented. Instead, participants are instructed to respond to passes generated by a player on a video display [25]. This dynamic and interactive configuration aims to simulate real-time decision-making and reactive agility, providing a more ecologically valid assessment of an individual's agility performance [25]. This testing approach has previously demonstrated favorable test-retest reliability, as indicated by a strong intra-class correlation coefficient ($r = 0.83$) [25]. However, it is important for coaches to consider the time and effort required to administer such a test when deciding whether or not to implement it in their training program.

The coach should consider what each test is designed to assess and the measures that fit into their perspective for such assessments. Moreover, other requirements and criteria should be considered for choosing the appropriate test, specifically if that test focuses on a player's abilities to maintain speed and tolerate highly demanding braking while performing COD at different angles. Similarly, if coaches want to isolate COD ability, this should be considered in the selection of the appropriate test.

Finally, and importantly, although most tests quantitatively evaluate a player's COD or agility ability, it is worth employing qualitative observation of movement to enhance the translation of testing performance to playing performance. Such assessment may involve observation of trunk control and position, the orientation of the hips relative to the intended direction of travel, rear or front foot strike during the stance phase, or flexion of the knees [26]. Dos Santos et al. [27, 28] introduced the Cutting Movement Assessment Score (CMAS) Qualitative Screening Tool as a recently validated field-based instrument for qualitative analysis. The tool aims to identify athletes exhibiting high-risk postures associated with an increased risk of non-contact anterior cruciate ligament injuries during side-step cutting. The CMAS comprises nine items that qualitatively evaluate hip, knee, foot, and trunk postures during side-step cutting, focusing on the technical factors influencing peak knee abduction moments [27].

The CMAS test is designed based on several components, including the penultimate foot contact braking strategy, as well as trunk, hip, knee, and foot postures and motions during the final "plant" step [28]. Seven of the CMAS criteria employ a dichotomous scale (yes or no), while lateral leg plant distance and frontal/transverse plane trunk positioning involve a descriptive classification with three and four possible descriptors, respectively [28]. Athletes are assigned a score when they demonstrate any of the CMAS criteria with higher scores indicating suboptimal technique and greater peak knee abduction moments. It is important to note that the CMAS is specifically applicable to side-step cuts within the range of 30° to 90° [28].

To ensure ecological validity, CMAS screening should be conducted on the same surface on which athletes perform their sport, such as a synthetic field-turf, or grass, under similar weather conditions [28]. Additionally, it is recommended that athletes wear sport-specific footwear during the screening process. As a minimum recommendation, practitioners are encouraged to utilize two high-speed cameras for qualitative screening, positioned on tripods approximately three meters apart in the frontal plane and five meters away, in the sagittal plane, from the cutting zone [28]. This type of analysis is best conducted retrospectively as it requires observational data and very thorough analysis. Implementing such an analysis in real time would be challenging due to the need for careful observation and detailed data collection.

Change-of-Direction Tests: Examining Principal Parameters

Straight COD tests are commonly utilized in football with the 5-0-5 test being one of the most common choices. This test offers valuable insights to coaches, specifically in assessing an individual's isolated COD ability and analyzing the COD deficit as the primary outcome. The traditional 5-0-5 consists of a 10 m untimed acceleration phase, followed by a timed 10-m sprint with a 180° COD. Typically, the main outcome variables associated with this test are velocity and time. Time is commonly measured using photocells to accurately gauge the duration of an athlete's movement from its initiation to reaching a specific point. Measuring instantaneous velocity during the test can be more challenging as it requires advanced equipment. However, average velocity can be obtained by analyzing the distance covered over a specified timeframe.

The 5-0-5 test presents good levels of reliability [29]. However, the construct validity may be compromised. Although the 5-0-5 test time provides information about COD ability, the result may depend on maximum linear speed [30]. This suggests that COD time during the test is biased by linear sprint performance and may therefore not be a completely independent component of COD performance [30]. However, the COD deficit [31] introduces a novel perspective to address the collinearity challenge which arises from the high correlation observed between linear speed and COD time [31]. This measure consists of the 10 m linear sprint time being subtracted from the 10 m COD time (in the 5-0-5 test as an example):

COD deficit = mean time 505 time − mean 10 m time

A recent addition to the repertoire of measures is the deceleration deficit [32], which offers valuable insights into an athlete's deceleration capabilities. The

60 Strength and Conditioning for Football

deceleration deficit is calculated as the difference between a 15-m linear sprint and 15-m deceleration times (+50% ground contact time) [32,33]. Notably, a large correlation was observed between the deceleration deficit and the COD deficit (Dominant: $r = 0.59$; $p < 0.01$; Non-dominant: $r = 0.62$; $p < 0.01$) [32]. However, 78% of the subjects exhibited discrepancies between these deficit measures that exceeded the threshold for moderate worthwhile changes [32]. The deceleration deficit holds promise as a more distinct construct when compared to the COD deficit, as it specifically focuses on an athlete's deceleration capabilities, whereas COD deficit time is inclusive of both deceleration and re-acceleration ability.

Coaches can employ an asymmetry index in addition to the COD parameters. This may facilitate an understanding of functional imbalances occurring while braking [34]. A simple way to measure the asymmetry index is by using the formula:

$$AI = \frac{D \text{ time (s)} - ND \text{ time (s)}}{D \text{ time (s)}} \times 100$$

where "D" represents the dominant leg, and "ND" represents the non-dominant leg. For some researchers, the dominant leg is the plant foot with the fastest completion time [34]. Along with this example, coaches may replace the measured "time" with the COD deficit or deceleration deficit as an example. There are other alternatives to calculate the asymmetry index, which can be found in research by Bishop et al. [35].

Agility Tests

A reactive agility test has previously been proposed for the sport of netball [25]. This test uses a pre-recorded video of various sport-specific movements. After the player crosses a timing gate, they must move either left or right in response to a video-communicated stimulus triggered by the timing gate being broken [13]. Accordingly, this test aims to combine the element of perceptual-cognitive speed with one's ability to change direction. Although some researchers believe that this test can be critical to evaluate the difference between physical and perceptual abilities [36], others have questioned whether using a light or a video cue can be a valid or ecological approach to evaluate agility performance in sports given that neither occurs during competitive play [13]. Accordingly, some alternative approaches [37] have employed human movement (e.g., a sidestep to the side in which the player must decide to move) to make the test organic to the scenarios encountered in a true sporting situation.

Training Methods for Enhancing Sprinting Performance

There seems to be agreement amongst football strength and conditioning coaches that sprint development exercises are a key element of preparation for competition.

Indeed, sprint performance is among the most assessed physical fitness qualities by coaches in the sport. The methods that a coach can utilize to enhance sprint speed should be specifically reflective of the demands of the game. Field sports such as football, are characterized by sprints of different distances with highly specific demands placed on the player. Sprint movements in football may involve running short distances to dispossess opponents or to track players down to defend against their attacks. In the case of longer-distance sprints, there is a greater dependence on short ground contact times and the use of the stretch-shortening cycle. Conversely, short-distance activity is more specifically characterized by longer ground contact times and concentric force production. Accordingly, when coaches target these activities through training, they must choose appropriate methods that exhibit these same characteristics, particularly the magnitude and orientation of forces [38,39].

Different categorizations have previously been put forth for sprint training [39–41] which are broadly classified as: (i) specific [40], including free sprinting, resisted sprinting, and assisted sprinting, (ii) non-specific, including plyometric training, strength training, and power training, and (iii) combined [41] (i.e., a combination of two or more of the six previously mentioned training methods).

Specific Training Methods

The term "specific training methods" refers to those methods which directly incorporate the movement patterns utilized in the sport. For example, short sprints are commonly executed by professional players undertaking an average of approximately 11 per game. Of these, 90% are shorter than 5 seconds in duration [42]. In addition to professional players, sprint training is highly effective in youth playing populations. A meta-analysis that included 14 studies (11 from football) showed that sprint training was moderately effective at improving sprint times in youths (effect size = 1.01), particularly amongst more physically mature participants. The authors recommended twice-weekly training sessions with up to 16 sprints of around 20 m and a work-to-rest ratio of 1:25 (or greater than 90 seconds) over a program duration of eight weeks [43].

From a practical standpoint, so-called free sprinting can be an effective training method, however, manipulations of the dynamics of sprinting with the utilization of resistive loads and assistive equipment can also be very beneficial to the football player.

Free-unresisted Sprinting Methods

In team sports such as football, accelerative sprinting speed over very short distances (i.e., <10 m) is important because during competitive play, many movements are executed in brief bouts of rapid activity. Accordingly, free-unresisted sprinting activities over the distances that are most often covered by football players (21 ± 3 m) must be performed in training to ensure sufficient physical preparation

62 Strength and Conditioning for Football

for competition. Nevertheless, football players are still required to sprint at full speed in matches and so coaches must program exercises that concentrate on free-unresisted sprinting over both short and long distances, as reflected during play. Beato et al. [44] report that even though distances of less than 30 m can be used to enhance acceleration ability, they are not suitable to prepare football players for maximum speed demands. This seems to be particularly important in the prevention of injury with a lack of exposure to sprints over longer distances serving as a potential marker for soft tissue (e.g., hamstrings) injuries risk [44].

Resisted and Assisted Sprinting Methods

Resisted sled training seems to be effective for sprint performance improvement. However, this is not the only method that can be utilized for this type of training as previous work has shown that training with a weighted vest, equivalent to approximately 18.9% of a player's body mass, resulted in similar increases in 10 m and 30 m speed, as did sprinting with no additional load [45]. Previous work also showed that the use of alternative tools to sleds, such as parachutes, can present players with a highly specific speed training stimulus as only small changes to biomechanical movement have been reported, despite training overload being induced by decreased stride length and running speed [46].

There is conflicting evidence on the benefits of using resistance elastic bands to enhance sprint speed in football players. A previous systematic review reported that the use of resistance bands did not result in any improvement in sprint speed when compared to regular sprint training [47]. Another study in well-trained female players found that resistance bands had little to no significant impact on tests including the 20 m acceleration (ES = −0.2), 20 m maximum sprinting speed (ES = 0.0), and 40 m sprint (ES = 0.1) [48]. On the contrary, a more recent investigation [49] in young football players supported the inclusion of elastic resistance in sprint training, with the results suggesting significant improvements in sprint time, maximal speed, and maximal power output related to enhanced anterior-posterior force production during the final phase of acceleration. Elastic bands may enhance the stretch-shortening cycle capability which is reinforced by increasing the ability of soft tissue structures to store and utilize elastic energy. Recent systematic reviews with meta-analyses that included studies of football codes (~72%–79%) reported favorable effects on 0–5–10–20–30 m and up to 50 m sprint performance following both assisted (and resisted) training [38,39].

Non-specific Training Methods

Compared to specific sprint training methods, non-specific methods have had considerable scientific support [40]. Non-specific training methods involve non-sprint training exercises such as plyometrics and resistance training. Such methods can elicit a combination of biological changes which can result in transference to a players' sprint performance.

Plyometric Jump Training

Though plyometric jump training can be considered a non-specific method of training [41], plyometric muscle actions usually involve a rapid stretch-shortening cycle of the lower-limb muscles, common during sprinting and jumping actions. Such specificity of plyometric jumps in relation to sprinting may explain the high transference of plyometric jump-induced adaptations to sprint performance improvement. Indeed, plyometric jump training has been classified as a safe, ecologically sound, and effective method for increasing sprint speed in players of different ages, sex, and playing standards [50,51]. To maximize the transfer of adaptations, it is important that the programmed jumps share common characteristics with the action of sprinting, such as stretch-shortening cycle duration (e.g., ground contact times) and the direction of force application. By matching the biomechanical pattern of a particular jump to that which is exhibited during a particular phase of sprinting (e.g., maximal speed), the coach can fine-tune the specificity of the training stimulus to the characteristics of the athletic task in question. For example, if a player needs to improve sprint acceleration, a greater training emphasis may be considered for jumps involving relatively "slower" stretch-shortening cycle muscle actions (e.g., longer foot ground contact times). Among biomechanical variables, the measurement of ground contact time is usually logistically feasible and affordable in lower-resource environments. Indeed, ground contact time can be calculated for individual players using contact mats, portable force plates, or a smart phone application within any practical setting. In support of the use of plyometric jump training to enhance sprint speed, recent systematic reviews and meta-analyses noted a favorable effect on the time to complete sprints distances of up to 5 m (ES = 0.66), 10 m (ES = 0.65), 20 m (ES = 0.46), 30 m (ES = 0.47), >30 m (ES = 0.49), and maximal velocity (ES = 0.32) [38,39].

Strength Training

Strength training for the enhancement of sprint speed typically includes exercises focused on the lower body such as squat variations (back squat, front, squat, split squat), deadlift variations (conventional, trap bar, Romanian, Sumo style), and lunges. Exercises such as these can enhance the force-producing capability of the muscles that are predominantly used during sprinting (i.e., quadriceps, hamstrings, and gluteal muscles). Accordingly, this assists a player in propelling their body forward during movement, thus enhancing sprint speed. Despite its effects, strength training for speed development is still considered to be a non-specific training method due to several key limitations of its use. For example, although meta-analyses reported favorable effects on sprint performance after strength training [38,39], their effects on female football players' sprint speed were not supported in similar research [50]. The expression of speed during movement represents a complex motor skill that involves more than just one's ability to exert force maximally. The short ground contact times that are exhibited during full-speed sprinting

64 Strength and Conditioning for Football

allow just a very short timeframe for force to be applied to the ground by the player. Similarly, specific elements of sprinting such as technique, coordination, and neuromuscular efficiency also play a crucial part in performance. A player could exhibit excellent muscular strength and power in comparison to their rivals, however, if their sprint mechanics and coordination are not of the required level, they may be unable to translate that strength into "usable" sprint speed. Accordingly, while strength training can be a highly effective tool for increasing sprint speed in football, it should be programmed alongside methods that target other factors that contribute to optimal performance. This may include sprinting technique refinement, plyometric jump training, and football-specific agility exercises. However, it is worth mentioning that strength forms the foundation that gradually enables players to effectively perform specific drills.

Power Training

Strength training that is programmed such that the emphasis is on the rate of force development, as opposed to slow, sustained force production, is a vital component of football players' training regimen. Increases in muscle power can have a transfer effect on sprinting and other dynamic movements, such as jumping, on the field of play. For example, Olympic weightlifting exercises, such as the snatch and clean and jerk, are very effective for the development of muscular power which transfers to dynamic performance. These exercises require a player to move a barbell from the ground to an overhead position in a highly dynamic manner that places a coordinative demand on multiple muscle groups in a complex synergistic fashion. Furthermore, movements such as jump squats (barbell and trap bar) are somewhat easier for a player to execute but also serve as a highly effective exercise for the development of lower body power. The jump squat exercise requires the player to execute a squat movement (to varying degrees of knee flexion as determined by the coach or self-selected by the player) before jumping as high as possible, using the legs to generate maximal power in an explosive manner. Corroborating the potential benefits of power training exercises, previous systematic reviews with meta-analyses reported a favorable effect (up to large [i.e., >0.8]) on short, medium, and long sprint distances after power training [38,39].

Combined Training Methods

Combined training methods enable the player to work on several methods (e.g., strength, power, plyometrics), all within the same training session. This time-efficient approach may be relatively more practically-relevant as the competition demands placed on the player increase. For example, in the professional setting, potentially congested competition schedules can limit the training time that could be devoted to the execution of separate individual preparation methods, thus a combined approach may be warranted.

Speed and Agility Training in Football **65**

Among combined training methods, complex training has received considerable attention within the research sphere in recent years. Regular football training programs may be supplemented with complex training to enhance sprint performance in players of various ages and playing levels. Furthermore, neuromuscular training includes a combination of strength training, plyometrics, proprioception, core, sprinting, and COD movements which replicate the demands of football and physically develop the player accordingly.

In addition to specific, non-specific, and combined sprint training methods, general training principles should be considered in a player's training program and these include progressive overload, specificity of the training stimulus, variation and periodization, individualization, tapering and the prevention of injuries and recovery from training/injury.

Training Methods for Enhancing Change-of-Direction and Agility Performance

The ability to change direction can be differentiated from that to be agile, in that the latter entails swift whole-body movements combined with changes in velocity or direction in response to an extraneous stimulus [52]. Agility encompasses perceptual and decision-making abilities, as well as COD speed which means that performers can be classified into four distinct profiles: (i) fast movers, fast thinkers; (ii) slow movers, fast thinkers; (iii) fast movers, slow thinkers; and (iv) slow movers, slow thinkers. Consequently, the training priorities that are required for each of these individuals vary depending on player type. Developing training drills for agility poses a challenge for coaches and therefore requires careful contextual consideration. Three primary categories can be identified [53]: (i) pre-planned COD movements, (ii) agility activities with a general stimulus, and (iii) agility training with a specific stimulus.

Planned Change-of-Direction Movements

Effective COD training should incorporate stages comprising both static positions and dynamic linear running followed by a COD. In the static position phase, players can be exposed to various starting techniques such as plyo steps, crossover steps, or drop steps. When considering dynamic linear running actions, players can engage in cutting or crossover drills. When it comes to dynamic linear running, the movement direction holds paramount significance. In recognition of the vital role played by shorter contact times, the incorporation of a rapid stretch-shortening cycle assumes considerable importance. Consequently, unilateral multi-planar exercises are recommended for the training of the qualities inherent to these types of movements. In the 45°–60° range, ground contact times increase alongside lower velocity of movement. Here, players may benefit from both fast and slow ground contact time plyometric drills, while the development of eccentric strength

66 Strength and Conditioning for Football

to assist with braking requirements is also highly beneficial. Finally, within the 60°–180° range of COD movement, substantial braking occurs, resulting in longer ground contact times and emphasizing the eccentric strength component and necessitating power-based plyometric jump training drills with longer ground contact times, such as the counter movement jump. Consequently, COD training necessitates breaking down the training process based on the specific phases that the coach wishes to target. In addition to this, players need to enhance their visual scanning abilities, deceleration skills during directional changes, braking capabilities (emphasizing eccentric strength), and the ability to re-accelerate (highlighting concentric strength and explosiveness).

When coaches emphasize training for smaller COD angles (0°–45°), reactive strength training should be prioritized. Conversely, when addressing greater COD angles (180°), training emphasis should shift towards eccentric training (to sustain braking ability) and concentric training to enhance the ability to re-accelerate following the slowing of movement.

To support the programming of COD ability, coaches can incorporate specific training drills involving different COD patterns, supplementing them with relevant strength training exercises. Technique considerations are also crucial when training for COD speed. For instance, during deceleration, athletes should gradually lower their center of mass while tilting their trunk backward. During braking or directional changes, the body's weight should be focused on the inside foot, thus aligning the body appropriately for the intended destination. Upon exiting the braking phase, the emphasis should shift to rapid trunk rotation in conjunction with sound acceleration mechanics.

Agility Activities with a Generic Stimulus

Stimuli such as lights, physical gestures, or sounds can serve as generic stimuli to incorporate a reactive component into agility drills. While not necessarily "sport-specific" in nature, these stimuli can be integrated into regular COD drills, introducing a stimulus that occurs at the initiation of, or during, an agility drill. Players can react to simple indications such as a physical gesture or a light signal, or they can respond to the specific body movement of an opponent.

In more complex scenarios, coaches may find it beneficial to utilize chasing drills in a 1v1 setting, whereby players can pursue their opponent while running, before deciding their direction of movement based on that of said opponent. Although the specificity to match-based scenarios may be limited in some cases, integrating the ability to COD with a stimulus can enhance the task complexity for the player.

Agility Training with a Specific Stimulus

Agility training with a specific stimulus can be effectively implemented through the utilization of small-sided games. These games can facilitate a high frequency of directional changes, accelerations, decelerations, and re-accelerations which can adequately replicate the demands of a match. While the degree of stimulus provided to each player may vary in these games, the smaller format and confined space naturally create numerous opportunities for players to engage in frequent dynamic movements that can enhance agility in scenarios that are reminiscent of match situations.

It is important to note that the frequency and intensity of specific actions cannot necessarily be precisely controlled in small-sided games. However, such games serve as a valuable component within the continuum of agility training, ranging from isolated and decontextualized drills to specific and non-controlled training scenarios. Research [54] has indicated that small-sided games can contribute to improvements in agility performance, not solely by enhancing the ability to physically change direction, but also by enhancing the decision-making speed of the player.

Practical Case

Considering a standard weekly microcycle, from Sunday to Sunday (Figure 4.1), a proposal for sprint and agility training could follow the following recommendations:

The player should have 48 hours of recovery following a competitive match (i.e., day off and match day plus 2 [MD+2]). Accordingly, sprint and agility training are not usually scheduled to occur on these days. However, some training, such as neuromuscular training, may be programed for players who accumulated fewer than 60 minutes of play on the day of the match. Such stimuli may involve repeated sprints and small-sided games using pitch size parameters of <75 m^2 per player in 3 vs 3 to 5 vs 5 formats, focusing on accelerative actions.

MD-4 should include the methods described for improving sprint and agility in this chapter. These exercises are usually programmed after warm-up and activation, the main exception being strength and power training (e.g., gym-based training) which is usually executed prior to on-field training activity. Some examples of training drills that can be applied at MD-4

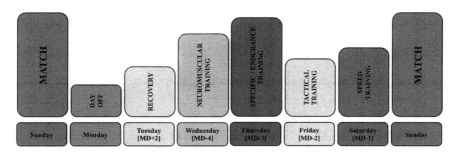

FIGURE 4.1 Weekly football training plan.

68 Strength and Conditioning for Football

Linear or COD sprinting: 5, 15, and 25 m linear sprints, involving 6–10, 4–8, and 2–6 repetitions, respectively, with inter-sprint recovery of 30, 45, and 60 s, respectively, and 4 minutes of full recovery between sets. Also, multi-planar drills can be programmed including frontal, lateral, and backwards movement executed at different angles (e.g., 45° and 90°) of turning and trajectories (i.e., linear and curvilinear). The previous training method examples can also be performed using resistive loads, usually in the form of weighted sleds, parachutes, or elastic bands, followed by a sprint (without any additional resistance). It is recommended to use distances of <10 m incorporating varying trajectories and technical actions or, as an alternative, participation in game situations of short duration and with few players (e.g., 1 vs 1 with finishing on goal).

Technical actions such as passing, dribbling, ball reception, and shooting can be executed for a more football-specific training stimulus. In such drills, it is also recommended that actions with the ball in possession be carried out at maximum speed and that the recovery between these efforts be sufficient to avoid excessive fatigue that could impair the execution of subsequent actions. To include technical-tactical stimuli it is recommended to program game drills on a field with relatively large dimensions (i.e., >150 m² per player). To this end, game formats of 5 vs 5 up to 10 vs 10 are also recommended with work:rest ratios of 1:2 or 1:3. Formats with fewer players and lower work-rest ratios of 1:1 to 1:0.5 may be used to stimulate glycolytic pathways (e.g., muscular- local-endurance training). For a COD stimulus, relatively smaller field sizes (i.e., <100 m² per player) with game formats up to 4 vs 4 may be adequate as this may increase ball contact time, contact with opponents, and number of accelerations and decelerations. In this case, the total volume of work may be less than that used in training for high speed but the recovery time between repetitions must remain relatively high to ensure the development of maximum intensity in each game sequence.

Plyometric training and strength training: plyometric drills can be performed in isolation, or within game scenarios with controlled opposition to improve individual and collective execution of powerful movements in pressurized situations. Vertical and horizontal jumps can be included, together with accelerations and decelerations, CODs, sprints, passing, dribbling, and shooting actions. To maintain high intensity, it is recommended that each sequence is programmed for 10 s or less. Recovery times between non-repeated jumps may be 15 s or less and if jumps are combined with other specific football drills, recovery can be 90 s or less with around 5 minutes or less between sets. Strength and power can be developed using loads between 30% and 80% of one repetition maximum (depending on the exercise, speed-strength 30%–60%, for strength speed 70%–80%) performing the repetitions at maximum speed. In addition, flywheel devices can induce an eccentric stimulus that can generate positive neuromuscular adaptations [55]. Coaches can plan some multi-joint strength training exercises such as back squats, core exercises, dowel hinge exercises and split squats, which can have direct application to the mechanics of acceleration and deceleration.

During MD-3 and MD-2 sessions, coaches frequently incorporate 11 vs 11 matches (using the squad players), which can promote high-speed actions and provide neuromuscular stimuli. Finally, MD-1 can include a low dose of sprint and COD training integrated into game-based scenarios, which replicates what players need to do on MD. The density (work:recovery ratio) of this training should also be low, with at least a 1:3 work:rest ratio used so as to avoid metabolic and neuromuscular fatigue.

Practical Applications

Sprinting and agility are integral physical components in soccer players. Coaches should prioritize the implementation of specifically-oriented sprint and agility training drills within the weekly schedule. It is crucial to recognize that both components require not only specific drills but also complementary training interventions that primarily target the development of strength and power.

In sprint training, emphasis should be placed on distinctly-identified phases such as those of acceleration and maximal speed, and consequently, it is important to differentiate training interventions for these elements of performance. Acceleration training necessitates a higher focus on concentric-based power exercises, maximal strength development, and specific exercises such as resisted sprints. Also, maximal speed can be increased through the execution of power and reactive strength exercises, as well as specific exercises like assisted sprints.

Regarding agility training, coaches must establish a continuum of training that progresses from controlled drills with a primary focus on COD ability and associated technique. As training progresses, the inclusion of specific stimuli should gradually increase, aligning with a strategy that aims to closely replicate the physiological demands of soccer. By integrating these targeted training approaches, coaches can optimize the development of sprinting and agility capabilities in soccer players, ultimately enhancing their on-field performance.

References

1. Haugen TA, Breitschädel F, Seiler S. Sprint mechanical properties in soccer players according to playing standard, position, age and sex. *J Sports Sci* [Internet]. 2020;38(9):1070–1076. Available from: https://www.tandfonline.com/doi/full/10.1080/02640414.2020.1741955
2. Oliva-Lozano JM, Martínez-Puertas H, Fortes V, López- Del Campo R, Resta R, Muyor JM. Is there any relationship between match running, technical-tactical performance, and team success in professional soccer? A longitudinal study in the first and second divisions of LaLiga. *Biol Sport* [Internet]. 2023;40(2):587–594. Available from: https://www.termedia.pl/doi/10.5114/biolsport.2023.118021
3. Faude O, Koch T, Meyer T. Straight sprinting is the most frequent action in goal situations in professional football. *J Sports Sci.* 2012;30(7):625–631.
4. Filter A, Olivares-Jabalera J, Santalla A, Morente-Sánchez J, Robles-Rodríguez J, Requena B, et al. Curve sprinting in soccer: Kinematic and neuromuscular analysis. *Int*

J Sports Med [Internet]. 2020;41(11):744–750. Available from: https://www.thieme-connect.de/DOI/DOI?10.1055/a-1144-3175

5. Fitzpatrick JF, Linsley A, Musham C. Running the curve: A preliminary investigation into curved sprinting during football match-play. *Sport Perform Sci Rep.* 2019;55, v1.

6. Chaouachi A, Manzi V, Chaalali A, Wong DP, Chamari K, Castagna C. Determinants analysis of change-of-direction ability in elite soccer players. *J Strength Cond Res* [Internet]. 2012;26(10):2667–2676. Available from: https://journals.lww.com/00124278-201210000-00008

7. Dos'Santos T, Thomas C, Comfort P, Jones PA. The effect of angle and velocity on change of direction biomechanics: An angle-velocity trade-off. *Sports Med* [Internet]. 2018;48(10):2235–2253. Available from: https://link.springer.com/10.1007/s40279-018-0968-3

8. Ross A, Leveritt M, Riek S. Neural influences on sprint running. *Sports Med.* 2001;31(6):409–425.

9. Mero A, Komi PV, Gregor RJ. Biomechanics of sprint running. *Sports Med.* 1992;13(6):376–392.

10. Morin JB, Bourdin M, Edouard P, Peyrot N, Samozino P, Lacour JR. Mechanical determinants of 100-m sprint running performance. *Eur J Appl Physiol* [Internet]. 2012;112(11):3921–3930. Available from: https://link.springer.com/10.1007/s00421-012-2379-8

11. Salo AIT, Bezodis IN, Batterham AM, Kerwin DG. Elite sprinting: Are athletes individually step-frequency or step-length reliant? *Med Sci Sports Exerc.* 2011;43(6):1055–1062.

12. Weyand PG, Sternlight DB, Bellizzi MJ, Wright S. Faster top running speeds are achieved with greater ground forces not more rapid leg movements. *J Appl Physiol.* 2000;89(5):1991–1999.

13. Sheppard JM, Young WB. Agility literature review: Classifications, training and testing. *J Sports Sci* [Internet]. 2006;24(9):919–932. Available from: https://www.tandfonline.com/doi/abs/10.1080/02640410500457109

14. Chaabene H, Prieske O, Negra Y, Granacher U. Change of direction speed: Toward a strength training approach with accentuated eccentric muscle actions. *Sports Med.* 2018;48(8):1773–1779.

15. Young WBWB, Dawson B, Henry GJGJ. Agility and change-of-direction speed are independent skills: Implications for training for agility in invasion sports. *Int J Sports Sci Coach.* 2015;10(1):159–169.

16. Haugen T, Buchheit M. Sprint running performance monitoring: Methodological and practical considerations. *Sports Med* [Internet]. 2016;46(5):641–656. Available from: https://link.springer.com/10.1007/s40279-015-0446-0

17. Haugen TA, Tønnessen E, Seiler SK. The difference is in the start: Impact of timing and start procedure on sprint running performance. *J Strength Cond Res* [Internet]. 2012;26(2):473–479. Available from: https://journals.lww.com/00124278-201202000-00021

18. Cronin JB, Templeton RL. Timing light height affects sprint times. *J Strength Cond Res* [Internet]. 2008;22(1):318–320. Available from: https://journals.lww.com/00124278-200801000-00046

19. Johnson TM, Brown LE, Coburn JW, Judelson DA, Khamoui A V, Tran TT, et al. Effect of four different starting stances on sprint time in collegiate volleyball players. *J Strength Cond Res* [Internet]. 2010;24(10):2641–2646. Available from: https://journals.lww.com/00124278-201010000-00009

20. Kyprianou E, di Salvo V, Lolli L, al Haddad H, Villanueva AM, Gregson W, et al. To measure peak velocity in soccer, let the players sprint. *J Strength Cond Res* [Internet]. 2019;36(1):273–276. Available from: https://journals.lww.com/10.1519/JSC.0000000000003406

21. Massard T, Eggers T, Lovell R. Peak speed determination in football: Is sprint testing necessary? *Sci Med Footb* [Internet]. 2018;2(2):123–126. Available from: https://www.tandfonline.com/doi/full/10.1080/24733938.2017.1398409

22. Altmann S, Ringhof S, Neumann R, Woll A, Rumpf MC. Validity and reliability of speed tests used in soccer: A systematic review. *PLoS One* [Internet]. 2019;14(8):e0220982. Available from: https://dx.plos.org/10.1371/journal.pone.0220982

23. Buchheit M, Simpson BM, Hader K, Lacome M. Occurrences of near-to-maximal speed-running bouts in elite soccer: Insights for training prescription and injury mitigation. *Sci Med Footb* [Internet]. 2021;5(2):105–110. Available from: https://www.tandfonline.com/doi/full/10.1080/24733938.2020.1802058

24. Fílter A, Olivares J, Santalla A, Nakamura FY, Loturco I, Requena B. New curve sprint test for soccer players: Reliability and relationship with linear sprint. *J Sports Sci* [Internet]. 2020;38(11–12):1320–1325. Available from: https://www.tandfonline.com/doi/full/10.1080/02640414.2019.1677391

25. Farrow D, Young W, Bruce L. The development of a test of reactive agility for netball: A new methodology. *J Sci Med Sport* [Internet]. 2005;8(1):52–60. Available from: https://linkinghub.elsevier.com/retrieve/pii/S1440244005800246

26. Nimphius S, Callaghan SJ, Bezodis NE, Lockie RG. Change of direction and agility tests. *Strength Cond J* [Internet]. 2018;40(1):26–38. Available from: https://journals.lww.com/00126548-201802000-00004

27. Dos'Santos T, McBurnie A, Donelon T, Thomas C, Comfort P, Jones PA. A qualitative screening tool to identify athletes with 'high-risk' movement mechanics during cutting: The cutting movement assessment score (CMAS). *Physical Therapy in Sport*. 2019;38:152–161.

28. Dos'Santos T, Thomas C, McBurnie A, Donelon T, Herrington L, Jones PA. The Cutting Movement Assessment Score (CMAS) qualitative screening tool: Application to mitigate anterior cruciate ligament injury risk during cutting. *Biomechanics*. 2021;1(1):83–101.

29. Stewart PF, Turner AN, Miller SC. Reliability, factorial validity, and interrelationships of five commonly used change of direction speed tests. *Scand J Med Sci Sports* [Internet]. 2014;24(3):500–506. Available from: https://onlinelibrary.wiley.com/doi/10.1111/sms.12019

30. Ryan C, Uthoff A, McKenzie C, Cronin J. Traditional and modified 5-0-5 change of direction test: Normative and reliability analysis. *Strength Cond J* [Internet]. 2022;44(4):22–37. Available from: https://journals.lww.com/10.1519/SSC.0000000000000691

31. Nimphius S, Callaghan SJ, Spiteri T, Lockie RG. Change of direction deficit: A more isolated measure of change of direction performance than total 505 time. *J Strength Cond Res*. 2016;30(11):3024–3032.

32. Clarke R, Read PJ, De Ste Croix MBA, Hughes JD. The deceleration deficit: A novel field-based method to quantify deceleration during change of direction performance. *J Strength Cond Res*. 2022;36(9):2434–2439.

33. Bishop C, Clarke R, Freitas TT, Arruda AFS, Guerriero A, Ramos MS, et al. Change-of-direction deficit vs. deceleration deficit: A comparison of limb dominance and inter-limb asymmetry between forwards and backs in elite male rugby union players. *J Sports Sci*. 2021;39(10):1088–1095.

34. Dos'Santos T, Thomas C, Jones PA, Comfort P. Assessing asymmetries in change of direction speed performance: Application of change of direction deficit. *J Strength Cond Res* [Internet]. 2019;33(11):2953–2961. Available from: https://journals.lww.com/10.1519/JSC.0000000000002438

35. Bishop C, Read P, Chavda S, Turner A. Asymmetries of the lower limb: The calculation conundrum in strength training and conditioning. *Strength Cond J* [Internet]. 2016;38(6):27–32. Available from: https://journals.lww.com/00126548-201612000-00003

36. Gabbett T, Benton D. Reactive agility of rugby league players. *J Sci Med Sport* [Internet]. 2009;12(1):212–214. Available from: https://linkinghub.elsevier.com/retrieve/pii/S1440244007001971

37. Sheppard JM, Young WB, Doyle TLA, Sheppard TA, Newton RU. An evaluation of a new test of reactive agility and its relationship to sprint speed and change of direction speed. *J Sci Med Sport* [Internet]. 2006;9(4):342–349. Available from: https://linkinghub.elsevier.com/retrieve/pii/S1440244006001198

38. Nicholson B, Dinsdale A, Jones B, Till K. The training of medium- to long-distance sprint performance in football code athletes: A systematic review and meta-analysis. *Sports Med.* 2022;52(2):257–286.

39. Nicholson B, Dinsdale A, Jones B, Till K. The training of short distance sprint performance in football code athletes: A systematic review and meta-analysis. *Sports Med.* 2021;51(6):1179–1207.

40. Haugen T, Seiler S, Sandbakk Ø, Tønnessen E. The training and development of elite sprint performance: An integration of scientific and best practice literature. *Sports Med Open.* 2019;5(1):44.

41. Rumpf MC, Lockie RG, Cronin JB, Jalilvand F. Effect of different sprint training methods on sprint performance over various distances. *J Strength Cond Res.* 2016;30(6):1767–1785.

42. Andrzejewski M, Chmura J, Pluta B, Strzelczyk R, Kasprzak A. Analysis of sprinting activities of professional soccer players. *J Strength Cond Res* [Internet]. 2013;27(8):2134–2140. Available from: https://journals.lww.com/00124278-201308000-00012

43. Moran J, Sandercock G, Rumpf M, Parry D. Variation in responses to sprint training in male youth athletes: A meta-analysis. *Int J Sports Med.* 2016;38(1):1–11.

44. Beato M, Drust B, Iacono AD. Implementing high-speed running and sprinting training in professional soccer. *Int J Sports Med* [Internet]. 2020;42(4):295–299. Available from: https://www.thieme-connect.de/DOI/DOI?10.1055/a-1302-7968

45. Rey E, Padrón-Cabo A, Fernández-Penedo D. Effects of sprint training with and without weighted vest on speed and repeated sprint ability in male soccer players. *J Strength Cond Res.* 2017;31(10):2659–2666.

46. Alcaraz PE, Palao JM, Elvira JLL, Linthorne NP. Effects of three types of resisted sprint training devices on the kinematics of sprinting at maximum velocity. *J Strength Cond Res.* 2008;22(3):890–897.

47. Hrysomallis C. The effectiveness of resisted movement training on sprinting and jumping performance. *J Strength Cond Res.* 2012;26(1):299–306.

48. Shalfawi SAI, Haugen T, Jakobsen TA, Enoksen E, Tønnessen E. The effect of combined resisted agility and repeated sprint training vs. strength training on female elite soccer players. *J Strength Cond Res.* 2013;27(11):2966–2972.

49. Le Scouarnec J, Samozino P, Andrieu B, Thubin T, Morin JB, Favier FB. Effects of repeated sprint training with progressive elastic resistance on sprint performance and

anterior-posterior force production in elite young soccer players. *J Strength Cond Res.* 2022;36(6):1675–1681.

50. Pardos-Mainer E, Lozano D, Torrontegui-Duarte M, Cartón-Llorente A, Roso-Moliner A. Effects of strength vs. plyometric training programs on vertical jumping, linear sprint and change of direction speed performance in female soccer players: A systematic review and meta-analysis. *Int J Environ Res Public Health.* 2021;18(2):401.

51. Ramirez-Campillo R, Gentil P, Negra Y, Grgic J, Girard O. Effects of plyometric jump training on repeated sprint ability in athletes: A systematic review and meta-analysis. *Sports Med.* 2021;51(10):2165–2179.

52. Young WB, Farrow D. A review of agility: Practical applications for strength and conditioning. *Strength Cond J.* 2006;28(5):24–29.

53. Mota T, Afonso J, Sá M, Clemente FM. An agility training continuum for team sports. *Strength Cond J* [Internet]. 2021;44(1):46–56. Available from: https://journals.lww.com/10.1519/SSC.0000000000000653

54. Young W, Rogers N. Effects of small-sided game and change-of-direction training on reactive agility and change-of-direction speed. *J Sports Sci* [Internet]. 2014;32(4):307–314. Available from: https://www.tandfonline.com/doi/abs/10.1080/02640414.2013.823230

55. Allen WJC, De Keijzer KL, Raya-González J, Castillo D, Coratella G, Beato M. Chronic effects of flywheel training on physical capacities in soccer players: A systematic review. *Res Sport Med.* 2023;31(3):228–248.

5

PERIODIZATION

Planning Fitness Training in Football

Magni Mohr, Carlo Castagna, Lars Nybo, Pawel Chmura, and Peter Krustrup

Introduction

Elite football has undergone a significant evolution in recent decades, marked by a substantial increase in the number of matches played, as well as increased training duration and intensity, indicative of the ongoing development which is likely to continue in the future (Nassis et al., 2020, 2022). This surge in physical demands and exposure to training and match environments has correspondingly heightened the risk of injuries, as evidenced by epidemiological studies initiated by UEFA (Ekstrand et al., 2020, 2022). This evolution has been accompanied by an ever-increasing use of technology and sports science. Currently, the number of support staff in top national teams and clubs often surpasses the number of players, with coaches, assistants, goalkeeper coaches, sports scientists, fitness coaches, medical personnel, psychologists, match analysts, and dieticians all working to try and optimize health and performance. Consequently, the process of planning training sessions in elite football today differs markedly from that of a decade ago.

Designing fitness training regimens for football and team sports presents distinct challenges compared to individual sports like athletics, swimming, or cycling, where performance is primarily linked to specific physical domains such as endurance or power. In football, performance is shaped by a complex interplay of physical, technical, tactical, cognitive, and psychological factors (Rico-González et al., 2022). Furthermore, football can be classified as a hybrid sport, where performance depends on the entire spectrum of physical capabilities. This renders the prioritization of various training modalities a highly intricate task. Moreover, significant individual variability exists in the demands placed on players during matches, influenced by tactical roles, physical capacities, playing styles, and contextual factors. This often presents a dilemma, as football necessitates both team-oriented

DOI: 10.4324/9781003383475-6

tactical training and individual-focused physiological training, which may not always align perfectly. Thus, the planning of fitness training in hybrid sports like football is inherently complex.

Therefore, this chapter aims to offer insights into the planning of fitness training in elite football, employing an exercise and training physiological perspective while also providing practically applied examples. There are different approaches from one country/culture to another, and the use of new technology has provided possibilities to base a substantial part of the training evaluation on tracking data. This variability in the definition of fitness training and data-driven approaches is important; however, it is essential to include advanced exercise and training physiology as a key pillar in planning and periodization in elite football, regardless of the country or culture in question. The chapter also covers general training guidelines in the preseason and in-season periods, as well as principles in planning a session and weekly microcycles for regular players and substitutes are included, also extending to match-play scenarios beyond 90 minutes.

Categorization of Fitness Training in Football

In this chapter, we categorize fitness training according to Bangsbo and Mohr (2014), with associated categories shown in Table 5.1. Aerobic training covering endurance or durability training is divided into three categories based on exercise intensity: low-, moderate-, and high-intensity training, which are determined by classical heart rate zones (see Bangsbo and Mohr, 2014). Anaerobic training covering high-intensity intermittent training is divided into speed training and speed endurance training, which is further divided into speed endurance production (aiming to develop anaerobic power) and speed endurance maintenance training, which also has been deemed training of anaerobic capacity or tolerance. Strength/power training is classified as per Bangsbo and Andersen (2015). Strength training is performed in the gym using external resistance (e.g., weights), while power training is performed at a greater speed using low external resistance or natural

TABLE 5.1 Fitness Training Categories Important for Football

Training Type
Aerobic training (moderate intensity, 75%–85% HRmax)
Aerobic training (high-intensity, >90% HRmax)
Anaerobic speed endurance maintenance training (work-rest ratio, 1:1)
Anaerobic speed endurance production training (work-rest ratio, 1:3/4)
Speed training (short sprints; <4 seconds in duration)
Speed training (long sprints; >4 seconds in duration)
Strength training (2–3 sets, 3–8 reps, 1–2 days per week)
Football-specific strength/power training (sprints, change of direction, accelerations/ decelerations, etc.)

76 Strength and Conditioning for Football

body mass exercises (following the principle of the force-velocity curve). Finally, football-specific strength/power training is performed on the pitch focusing on specific game events demanding a high rate of force development (sprints, change of direction, accelerations/decelerations, shots, jumps, etc.). Prevention training and rehabilitation training will also be covered briefly in this chapter.

It is critical to consider the recovery time from different training types, which will help form the basis of the number of weekly sessions for each component of fitness. A few studies have tested the recovery kinetics from different training categories in an isolated manner. For example, it has been demonstrated that speed endurance production training induces short-term neuromuscular fatigue but causes a prolonged deterioration of jump ability (24 hours), strength (48 hours), and speed (72 hours) (Tzatzakis et al., 2020). Moreover, speed endurance production training is associated with a prolonged (72 hours) and elevated delayed onset of muscle soreness (DOMS) (Tzatzakis et al., 2020; Papanikolaou et al., 2021). The recovery time is also affected by the types of intervals performed. For instance, a reduction in recovery time has been shown when longer work-to-rest ratios are applied. Finally, the same study also indicated that fitness status may affect the recovery kinetics from a speed endurance production session in trained male players (Tzatzakis et al., 2020). In support of these findings, it has been shown by Wiig et al. (2019) that of all the conventionally applied external load markers, the volume of high-speed running is the best predictor of prolonged post-game recovery in football. Thus, high-intensity training and high running speeds are likely to prolong the recovery time. Also, small-sided games (SSGs) are related to a prolonged rise of exercise-induced muscle damage (EIMD), provoke short-term neuromuscular fatigue, and slow recovery kinetics of strength, jump, and sprinting performance. Moreover, the type of SSG plays a role, with not surprisingly, the time for complete recovery being longer for SSGs of lower density (i.e., using greater pitch sizes) (Papanikolaou et al., 2021).

It is important to include speed and strength/power training using maximal or near maximal intensity, low volume (few bouts/repetitions), and long resting periods to prioritize intensity and reduce the acute fatigue and the subsequent recovery time associated with these training components (see Bangsbo and Mohr, 2014; Bangsbo and Andersen, 2015). Based on estimations from these types of studies and the scientific literature on post-exercise recovery kinetics, Table 5.2 shows a schematic overview of recovery times from different training categories.

Planning the Week and Individual Sessions

Balancing training stimulus and recovery is crucial in sessions and weekly microcycle planning, especially during the competitive season, while during the preseason there is more flexibility in relation to physiological overload. Recovery from a football game can take up to 4 days (Mohr et al., 2005, 2016; Silva et al., 2018) due to factors like slow muscle glycogen resynthesis (Krustrup et al., 2011; Mohr et al.,

Periodization: Planning Fitness Training in Football **77**

TABLE 5.2 Recovery Times after Various Types of Training in Targeted Body Systems

Recovery Times after Various Types of Training	Recovery Time
Aerobic moderate intensity training:	Heart 3 hours (1–12 h)
	Legs 1 day (3 h–2 days)
Aerobic high-intensity training:	Heart 1 day (12 h–1 day)
	Legs 2 days (1–2 days)
Anaerobic speed endurance maintenance training	Heart 1 day (12 h–1 day)
	Legs 1–2 days (1–3 days)
Anaerobic speed endurance production training	Legs 2 days (2–4 days)[a]
Speed training, short sprints, <4 seconds	Legs 1 day (12 h–2 days)
Speed training, long sprints, >4 seconds	Legs 2 days (2–3 days)
Leg strength training, plyometrics	Legs 2 days (1–3 days)*
Core/upper body strength training	Core/upper body, 2 days (1–3 days)

[a] It should be emphasized that some training types are not to be introduced during the competitive season due to extended recovery periods (3–4 days), such as certain types of speed endurance production training and plyometric strength training.

2022), muscle damage, oxidative stress, and elevated inflammation (Mohr et al., 2016; Wiig et al., 2022). Also, previous research has shown that while some parameters are fully recovered (e.g. hormonal and technical), a period of 72 hours after a game is not long enough to completely restore homeostatic balance (e.g. muscle damage, physical and well-being status) (Silva et al., 2018). Thus, players who play a full game should be managed carefully, especially in the following 48 hours. The game serves as a significant session of aerobic high-intensity training, speed training, and speed endurance training. For example, on MD +1, players who played 90 minutes may perform a brief power training session (approx. 30 minutes), aiming to maintain power and potentially aid recovery through increased growth hormone and testosterone (Vingren et al., 2010; Bangsbo and Andersen, 2015). On MD +2, they can rest or have a short aerobic high-intensity training session (e.g., 5 × 2 minutes at ~90% HRmax with 1 minute recovery, performed as SSGs). Substitute players should perform additional high-intensity runs (speed endurance production) immediately after the game and a 30–45 minutes basic power training session on MD +1, along with a full aerobic high-intensity training session.

By MD +3, all players should be nearly fully recovered and can train together, performing aerobic high-intensity training (e.g., 6 × 3 minutes at ~90% HRmax with 1 minute recovery) and speed endurance production training (e.g., 7 × 20-s at 90% of maximal intensity with 2 minutes recovery), plus a 20–30 minutes game on a large pitch. Thirty minutes of power (gym or on the pitch) training session can also be included. On MD-3, players should have a shorter session with aerobic high-intensity training on a small pitch or a speed endurance maintenance training

78 Strength and Conditioning for Football

session. It has been demonstrated that the games on large pitch sizes (i.e., 11 vs 11 format) induce greater magnitudes of perceptual DOMS and muscle damage (Silva et al., 2018). Moreover, high-intensity running, which is increased with large pitch sizes is the best external load predictor of a delayed post-training/game recovery (Wiig et al., 2019). Finally, MD-2 should focus on team tactics with speed training or football-specific power training (e.g., accelerations, sprints) included, while MD-1 should be a brief session with agility and short sprints.

In order to avoid the potential negative impact of concurrent training on strength and power parameters (Bangsbo and Andersen, 2015), it is recommended to avoid performing power training prior to football training, which has a marked aerobic component. If for example a gym-based power training session is executed in the morning, it is recommended to have 4–6 hours of rest or recovery before a football field session is initiated.

Planning the Preseason

The preseason spans from the last game of one season to the first competitive game of the next. Its length varies by league, but this chapter uses a ten-week model. The first four weeks are the individual period (usually defined as the off-season), where players train independently to maintain physical capacity predominately focusing on preserving endurance and power. During this period, players are advised to engage in aerobic moderate-intensity and aerobic high-intensity training to preserve aerobic capacity components like maximum oxygen uptake, blood volume, haemoglobin mass, oxygen uptake kinetics, muscle capillarization, and mitochondrial oxidative capacity (Joyner and Coyle, 2008). A study by Thomassen et al. (2010) with Danish football players showed that those who detrained for two weeks after the season experienced a ~25% decline in Yo-Yo Intermittent Recovery level 2 (Yo-Yo IR2) test performance, as well as impairment in repeated sprint ability. Conversely, those who reduced training volume, but increased intensity maintained their Yo-Yo IR2 performance but increased repeated sprint ability by ~2%. This underscores the importance of maintaining training intensity during the individual period. Thus, having three weekly sessions (approx. 30 minutes) of aerobic moderate-intensity training in the first week and progressively changing towards aerobic high-intensity training (one session in week 2, two sessions in week 3, and then three sessions in week 4) in the individual period, is deemed important to hit the ground running when the team reconvenes. Players should also engage in strength/power (gym-based) training two to three times per week during this period to maintain muscle mass and neural drive (Andersen et al., 2005; Bangsbo and Andersen, 2015). The strength/power training should primarily focus on the lower body, but some upper body and core strength exercises should also be included. Specific needs, such as rehabilitation, muscular asymmetries, or specialized fitness areas, should be addressed with tailored programs from fully qualified professionals in their respective disciplines.

The subsequent rebuilding period lasts six weeks (after the end of the off-season), during which the team trains together. Having maintained aerobic, strength, and power capacities in the individual period (off-season), players can now intensify their training with a focus on aerobic high-intensity training, speed training, and speed endurance training to rebuild and enhance fitness levels (Silva, 2022; Bangsbo and Mohr, 2014; Bangsbo et al., 2006; Hostrup and Bangsbo, 2023). Recommended frequencies are typically three times weekly for aerobic high-intensity training, three times for speed training, and two to three times for speed endurance training. Intensified training (i.e., >90% HRmax aerobic high-intensity training) can induce beneficial adaptations in aerobic power and capacity and it has shown to be highly efficient for football players (see Hostrup and Bangsbo, 2023). A study by Fransson et al. (2017), with Swedish players, compared groups performing speed endurance production training executed as runs with the ball and aerobic moderate-intensity training executed as SSG during the rebuilding period of the preseason. Results showed that speed endurance production training resulted in ~40% greater improvements in Yo-Yo IR2 performance as well as a greater upregulation in muscle oxidative capacity compared to the aerobic moderate intensity training group. Hence, anaerobic speed endurance maintenance and production training (see Table 5.1), should be prioritized in the rebuilding period for elite football populations. Strength and power training should also be emphasized, with gym-based power sessions gradually reduced from three to one to two per week (e.g., using a total body approach when only one session a week is possible), while sport-specific power exercises and football-specific (e.g., on pitch accelerations, decelerations, sprint exercises) sessions are introduced and step by step replacing some of the gym-based power sessions (in this period there will be a shift from general training to sport-specific training). Table 5.3 illustrates a training week, three weeks before the season starts for an elite football team.

Planning the Season

Season planning varies by league; therefore, this section provides general guidelines for fitness training throughout the season, considering both one and two-game weekly scenarios for regular players and substitutes. This section discusses the priority of some training methods over others during the course of the season, such as aerobic training (low, moderate, and high-intensity), anaerobic training (e.g., speed, speed endurance production, and speed endurance maintenance) and strength/power training (e.g., hypertrophy, gym-based, and pitch-based power exercises).

A high priority should be given to aerobic high-intensity training, speed training, and speed endurance training throughout the entire season, with up to three sessions weekly (in particular for players who did not play the previous match) to maintain preseason fitness levels or to even further develop this general physical capacity. A full game can count as one session of aerobic high-intensity, speed,

80 Strength and Conditioning for Football

TABLE 5.3 An Example of a One-Week Training Schedule Three Weeks Prior to the Competitive Season

	Morning	*Afternoon/Evening*
Sunday	Free	Free
Monday	WU/TT (40 minutes)	WU/TT 15 minutes
	AHI 12 × 1 minutes 30 seconds recovery (20 minutes)	Set pieces (30 minutes)
	SEP 5 × 30 s, 3 minutes recovery (20 minutes)	FP (4 × 5 max effort) (15 minutes)
Tuesday	Free	WU/TT 45 min
		AHI 12 × 1 minutes 30 seconds recovery (20 minutes)
		FP (4 × 5 max effort) (15 minutes)
Wednesday	Free	Free
Thursday	WU/TT (30 minutes)	WU/AMI (20 minutes)
	SP 10 × 2–3 s, 45 seconds recovery (10 minutes)	ST (2 ×6 × 8RM)
	Play 11v11 (30 minutes)	PT 2 × 10 max effort (40 minutes)
	SEM 2 × 10 reps, 15–15 seconds runs (15 minutes)	
Friday	WU/TT (45 minutes)	WU (15 minutes)
	AHI 8 × 2 minutes, 1 minute recovery (25 minutes)	Upper body strength and core (30 minutes)
Saturday	WU/TT (30 minutes)	Free
	SP (15 minutes)	
	Play (30 minutes)	
Sunday	Free	Training game
		Top-up runs for players playing less than 45 minutes

Training categories: WU (warm-up), TT (technical/tactical training), AHI (aerobic high-intensity), AMI (aerobic moderate intensity), SEP (speed endurance production), SEM (speed endurance maintenance), SP (speed), FP (football power), ST (strength training), PT on the pitch (power training).

Note: The table shows the distribution of different fitness training sessions in three week prior to the start of the season. A "day-off" means that the players do not meet at the club, while "free" means that the players meet at the club for meetings, treatment, mental training, etc.

and speed endurance training. Although that, it is well known that it is difficult to maintain a stable fitness level throughout a season. For example, Mohr and Krustrup (2014) found significant variability in training loads across a competitive season, which affects performance markedly. This variability in physical performance was team-specific and also linked to playing position, seasonal period, and even physical capacity during the start of the preseason (Mohr and Krustrup, 2014). Moreover, a case study by Rago et al. (2020) demonstrated that a team in the Spanish LaLiga increased training volume and intensity in the last three months of a season. Results showed marked performance improvements defined as a significant

Periodization: Planning Fitness Training in Football **81**

reduction in heart rate loading during a submaximal Yo-Yo IR1 test. In addition, increased prioritization of fitness training post-season (in preparation for national team competitions) showed a similar significant improvement in Yo-Yo IR1 or IE2 submaximal performance. This highlights the importance of sustaining high training loads (especially intensity) throughout the season. Table 5.4 exemplifies weekly schedules for one (a) and two-game (b) weeks for one elite football team.

Table 5.4a shows that the team in the model above prioritizes recovery after a game in the one-game-per-week scenario. Thus, after the game on Sunday afternoon, the regular players have free time from training the entire Monday and Tuesday morning, taking into consideration the aforementioned slow post-game recovery parameters (e.g., strength, speed, and jump). Then there is time to prioritize fitness training during the week with some power sessions, aerobic moderate intensity, aerobic high-intensity, speed endurance, and speed training. In contrast, with two weekly games and only 72 hours between games one and two, and 96 hours between games two and three, there is limited room for fitness training for the starting 11 (Table 5.4b). Therefore, a short gym-based power session is included as part of the recovery on MD+1. Moreover, a relatively short session with aerobic high-intensity

TABLE 5.4a An Example of a One-Week Training Schedule during the Season – with One Match per Week

	Morning	*Afternoon/Evening*
Sunday	Free	Match
Monday	Free	Free
Tuesday	Free	WU/TT 20 minutes
		PT (2×10 max effort) (15 minutes)
		SE (SEP or SEM; 20 minutes)
Wednesday	WU/TT (45 minutes)	ST ($6 \times 6 \times 6$RM) (60 minutes)
	AHI 12×1 minutes,	
	30 seconds recovery	
	(20 minutes)	
Thursday	Free	WU/AMI (20 minutes)
		FP (4×5 max effort) (15 minutes)
		Play 11v11 (30 minutes)
Friday	WU/TT (45 minutes)	WU (15 minutes)
	AHI 8×2 minutes, 1 minute recovery (25 minutes)	Free
Saturday	WU/TT (30 minutes)	Free
	SP (15 minutes)	
	TT/play (45 minutes)	Free
Sunday	Free	Match

Training categories: WU (warm-up), TT (technical/tactical training), AHI (aerobic high intensity), AMI (aerobic moderate intensity), SE (speed endurance) SEP (speed endurance production), SEM (speed endurance maintenance), SP (speed), FP (football power), ST (strength training), PT on the pitch (power training).

82 Strength and Conditioning for Football

TABLE 5.4b An Example of a One-Week Training Schedule during the Season – with Two Matches per Week

	Morning	Afternoon/Evening
Sunday	Free	Match
Monday	Free	WU/AMI (30 minutes)
		ST (2 × 6 × 8 RM) (30 min)
Tuesday	WU/TT 30 minutes	Free
	SP (15 minutes)	
	AHI 4 × 2 minutes, 1 minute recovery (11 minutes)	
Wednesday	Free	Match
Thursday	Free	WU/AMI (30 minutes)
		ST (2 × 6 × 8 RM) (30 minutes)
Friday	WU/TT (20 minutes)	Free
	FP (4 × 5 max effort) (15 minutes)	
	AHI 6 × 2 minutes, 1 minute recovery (20 minutes)	
Saturday	WU (15 minutes)	Free
	TT/play (30 minutes)	
Sunday	Free	Match

Training categories: WU (warm-up), TT (technical/tactical training), AHI (aerobic high intensity), AMI (aerobic moderate intensity), SE (speed endurance) SEP (speed endurance production), SEM (speed endurance maintenance), SP (speed), FP (football power), ST (strength training), PT on the pitch (power training).

training is included together with speed training and football-specific pitch-based training with the aim of developing power abilities (accelerations, decelerations, and sprints). Finally, speed endurance training is avoided for regular players in this week, since the Sunday-Wednesday-Sunday games are expected to provide a sufficient anaerobic stimulus, and due to the load and high muscle glycogen degradation in this type of training (Mohr et al., 2007).

Planning for Peak Performance – International Tournaments and Cup Games

Extended match-play or 120 minute games is an increasing and underestimated component in modern football (Krustrup, 2017; Field et al., 2020). For example, in the knockout stages of the 2018 Men's World Cup in Russia, Croatia reached the final having played three consecutive matches with extra time. Also, in the last World Cup for men, five knockout games went into overtime. Moreover, since 1992, in all EURO and World Cup tournaments, 85% of the semi-finalists have participated in 120 minute games. In line with these trends, in the Champions League tournament 2023, 8 out of 15 knockout games ended as 120 min. Thus, when planning for international tournaments, it is highly relevant to consider preparation strategies that go beyond 90 minutes.

Periodization: Planning Fitness Training in Football **83**

It was recently shown for the first time that the fatigue response and the performance impairment from a 120 minute game is highly exacerbated compared to 90 minute games (Mohr et al., 2022). Indeed, both sprint and jump performance are further compromised (2 vs 7% and 19 vs 27%, respectively) as a result of the extra 30 minutes, and muscle glycogen falls to 150-200 mmol·kg^{-1} (Mohr et al., 2022) and is not recovered after 3 days (Ermidis et al., 2024). We know from previous studies that repeated 90 minute games result in profound fatigue, muscle soreness, inflammation, and performance deterioration (Mohr et al., 2016). There is limited available information about recovery in response to possible consecutive 120 minute games. Therefore, we recently studied the impact of consecutive game scenarios with a 72 hour recovery interval between games, showing an elevated systemic muscle damage marker response, inflammation, and rise in oxidative stress, as well as augmented fatigue (Ermidis et al., 2024). Thus, planning of training needs to account for the unpredictable appearance of 120 minute games during domestic and international cup scenarios. It is recommended that the training load is adjusted during the MD-2 and MD-1 training sessions leading up to a potential 120 minute game to reduce the amount of high-speed running, which as aforementioned is associated with prolonged recovery (Wiig et al., 2019), and the acceleration and deceleration loads, as well as other vigorous eccentric movements, to lower pre-game EIMD.

A central part of counteracting the exacerbated fatigue response and prolonged recovery after 120 minute games is proper planning of substitutions. This is especially important because FIFA introduced a modification of the regulations in 2020, which increased the number of substitutions from 3 to 5, which was finally officially approved in 2022 (to protect the recovery and health of the players). More than 20 years ago, it was shown that players substituted during the second half performed markedly more high-intensity running during the last 15 minutes of a normal game in comparison to players playing a full 90 minute game (Mohr et al., 2005). Several other studies have investigated the role of substitutes in modern football. For example, running performance has been shown to increase due to the use of five substitutes instead of three in the Japanese top league (Ayabe et al., 2022), as well as high-speed running in the Spanish LaLiga (López-Valenciano et al., 2023). Also, the use of substitutions for certain player types is a major area of focus among coaching staff in modern football (Wittkugel et al., 2022). Thus, player-specific fatigue patterns and detailed analysis of the high-intensity phases of a game (Leifsson et al., 2024) using tracking data should be used to plan substitutions in games that may go into extra time.

Planning of Injury Prevention

As previously highlighted, the risk of injury in elite football has increased during the last two decades; thus, football staff have an emphasis on injury prevention strategies to mitigate the risk of injuries as best as they can. This training aims to increase the strength of the muscles around the major joints, correct an imbalance

84 Strength and Conditioning for Football

in strength between muscles and limbs, and develop some specific neuromuscular adaptations which lead to having players ready for the sport-specific demands of the game, with the overall final aim to reduce the likelihood of injuries. Prevention training can be split into at least three categories: (1) pre-activation exercises incorporating balance, agility, and strength-based exercises, such as what is suggested in the FIFA 11+ protocol, (2) concentric and eccentric strength training, including the Nordic hamstring, Copenhagen adductor exercises or flywheel resistance training, and (3) 80%–90% of individual maximal speed sprints.

Prevention training should be performed one to two times a week with two to three sets of four to ten repetitions per exercise, and apart from the initial familiarization one to two weeks in pre-season, the loading does not have to be progressively increased like in strength or power training. However, some specific exercises may require following the general principle of progressive overload and reversibility (or progress will be lost when an athlete stops training) to keep being effective during the season. In contrast, when players are already experiencing some muscular or tendinous issues (which is very common during the season) but are still taking part in training, the practitioners should put in place the best training programme possible, working around player 'niggles' so that they can return to training and compete in the absence of pain or limitations. As a case example, a player with pain in the patella tendon (jumper's knee) may implement some specific gym-based training with the aim of strengthening the muscle groups and reducing the inflammation around the knee. An option to be implemented may consist of 4 sets of 12 repetitions of an eccentric quadriceps exercise at a moderate load (around 15 RM) in the first week. Following this, the number of repetitions may be progressively reduced while the load is increased every week, culminating in six sets of six repetitions, after six to eight weeks. Since the strength and conditioning coach is a member of the multidisciplinary team, other practitioners will also play a part in the training of the players. For instance, performing some conservative therapies to reduce excessive inflammation and sensations of pain. Regarding return-to-play strategies and rehab, further information can be found in Chapter 11.

Practical Applications

The present chapter provides a perspective on the planning of fitness training in football that is exercise and training physiologically based. The chapter advocates the use of well-defined training categories that are originally derived from basic exercise physiology but have been tested and adopted to football training models. A major component to take into account when planning training microcycles is the recovery time of muscle function, performance and key physiological systems from match-play, but also in relation to the different training modalities and types of training load. The preseason should be separated into an early individual period aiming to maintain aerobic capacity or fatigue resilience, as well as power that precedes the rebuilding period, when the squad trains together. In the rebuilding periods, the main focus is on rebuilding the physiological systems that determine exercise durability (i.e. cardiac function, blood volume, capillarization, mitochondrial function), high-intensity exercise performance (i.e. muscle ion transporters, glycolytic enzymes) and performance during ballistic/explosive movements (i.e. neural drive, muscle hypertrophy). During the season different models can be applied in relation to game fixtures, where the training volume is varied. However, it is highly essential to maintain the high-intensity in the training with major emphasis on aerobic high-intensity training, speed endurance training, speed/agility, and power training. During periods when a team may face 120 minute games, which are becoming more frequent in modern football, the training volume and type of training need to be adjusted to respect the great fatigue responses and prolonged recovery from these games. The planning of substitutions to counteract end-game and post-game fatigue and recovery kinetics is important in normal games but becomes central in 120 minute games.

References

Andersen LL, Andersen JL, Magnusson SP, Suetta C, Madsen JL, Christensen LR, Aagaard P. Changes in the human muscle force-velocity relationship in response to resistance training and subsequent detraining. *J Appl Physiol (1985)*. 2005;99(1):87–94.

Ayabe M, Sunami S, Kumahara H, Ishizaki S. Effects of substitute allowance on match activity characteristics in Japanese professional football across 2019, 2020, and 2021 seasons. *J Sports Sci*. 2022;40(23):2654–2660. https://doi.org/10.1080/02640414.2023.2182878.

Bangsbo, J., & Andersen, J. L. (2013). *Power Training in Football: A Scientific and Practical Approach*. Bangsbosport. Fitness Training in Soccer Vol. 3

Bangsbo, J., & Mohr, M. (2014). *Individual Training in Football*. Bangsbosport.

Bangsbo J, Mohr M, Poulsen A, Perez-Gomez J, Krustrup P. Training and testing the elite athlete. *J Exerc Sci Fit*. 2006;4(1):1–14.

Bradley PS, Bendiksen M, Dellal A, Mohr M, Wilkie A, Datson N, Orntoft C, Zebis M, Gomez-Diaz A, Bangsbo J, Krustrup P. The application of the Yo-Yo intermittent endurance level 2 test to elite female soccer populations. *Scand J Med Sci Sports*. 2014;24(1):43–54.

Bradley PS, Mascio MD, Mohr M, Fransson D, Wells C, Moreira A, Castellano J, Gomez A, Ade JA. Can modern football match demands be translated into novel training and testing modes. link: https://journal.aspetar.com/en/archive/volume-7-targeted-topic-football-revolution/can-modern-football-match-demands-be-translated-into-novel-training-and-testing-modes *Aspetar Sport Med J*. 2018. Volume 7, Topic 16, 2018.

Bradley PS, Mohr M, Bendiksen M, Randers MB, Flindt M, Barnes C, Hood P, Gomez A, Andersen JL, Di Mascio M, Bangsbo J, Krustrup P. Sub-maximal and maximal Yo-Yo intermittent endurance test level 2: Heart rate response, reproducibility and application to elite soccer. *Eur J Appl Physiol*. 2011;111(6):969–978.

Ekstrand J, Bengtsson H, Waldén M, Davison M, Khan KM, Hägglund M. Hamstring injury rates have increased during recent seasons and now constitute 24% of all injuries in men's professional football: The UEFA Elite Club Injury Study from 2001/02 to 2021/22. *Br J Sports Med*. 2022;57(5):292–298.

86 Strength and Conditioning for Football

Ekstrand J, Krutsch W, Spreco A, van Zoest W, Roberts C, Meyer T, Bengtsson H. Time before return to play for the most common injuries in professional football: A 16-year follow-up of the UEFA Elite Club Injury Study. *Br J Sports Med*. 2020;54(7):421–426.

Ermidis G, Mohr M, Jamurtas AZ, Draganidis D, Poulios A, Papanikolaou K, Vigh-Larsen JF, Loules G, Sovatzidis A, Nakopoulou T, Tsimeas P, Douroudos II, Papadopoulos C, Papadimas G, Rosvoglou A, Liakou C, Deli CK, Georgakouli K, Chatzinikolaou A, Krustrup P, Fatouros IG. Recovery during successive 120-min football games: Results from the 120-min placebo/carbohydrate randomized controlled trial. *Med Sci Sports Exerc*. 2024;56(6):1094–1107.

Field A, Corr LD, Haines M, Lui S, Naughton R, Michael R, Harper LD. Biomechanical and physiological responses to 120 min. of football-specific exercise. *Res Q Exerc Sport*. 2020;91(4):692–704.

Fransson D, Krustrup P, Mohr M. Running intensity fluctuations indicate temporary performance decrement in top-class football. *Sci Med Footb*. 2017;1:10–17.

Hostrup M, Bangsbo J. Performance adaptations to intensified training in top-level football. *Sports Med*. 2023;53(3):577–594.

Joyner MJ, Coyle EF. Endurance exercise performance: The physiology of champions. *J Physiol*. 2008;586(1):35–44.

Krustrup P. The physical, tactical and mental challenge of 120-minute matches in elite football—historical development, coaches' perception and up-to-date match analyses. *UEFA Pro-Licence assignment Danish FA*. 2017;1–86.

Krustrup P, Bradley PS, Christensen JF, Castagna C, Jackman S, Connolly L, Randers MB, Mohr M, Bangsbo J. The Yo-Yo IE2 test: physiological response for untrained men versus trained soccer players. Med Sci Sports Exerc. 2015 Jan;47(1):100-8. doi: 10.1249/MSS.0000000000000377. PMID: 24824774.

Krustrup P, Mohr M, Ellingsgaard H, Bangsbo J. Physical demands during an elite female soccer game: Importance of training status. *Med Sci Sports Exerc*. 2005;37(7):1242–1248.

Krustrup P, Mohr M, Nybo L, Jensen JM, Nielsen JJ, Bangsbo J. The Yo-Yo IR2 test: Physiological response, reliability, and application to elite soccer. *Med Sci Sports Exerc*. 2006;38(9):1666–1673.

Krustrup P, Ortenblad N, Nielsen J, Nybo L, Gunnarsson TP, Iaia FM, Madsen K, Stephens F, Greenhaff P, Bangsbo J. Maximal voluntary contraction force, SR function and glycogen resynthesis during the first 72 h after a high-level competitive soccer game. *Eur J Appl Physiol*. 2011;111(12):2987–2995.

Leifsson EN, Krustrup P, Mohr M, Randers MB. Effect of peak intensity periods on temporary fatigue and recovery kinetics in professional male football. J Sports Sci. 2024 May;42(9):769-775. doi: 10.1080/02640414.2024.2364135. Epub 2024 Jun 12. PMID: 38864394.

López-Valenciano A, Moreno-Perez V, Campo RL, Resta R, Coso JD. The five-substitution option enhances teams' running performance at high speed in football. *Int J Sports Med*. 2023;44(5):344–351.

Mohr M, Draganidis D, Chatzinikolaou A, Barbero-Álvarez JC, Castagna C, Douroudos I, Avloniti A, Margeli A, Papassotiriou I, Flouris AD, Jamurtas AZ, Krustrup P, Fatouros IG. Muscle damage, inflammatory, immune and performance responses to three football games in 1 week in competitive male players. *Eur J Appl Physiol*. 2016;116(1):179–193. https://doi.org/10.1007/s00421-015-3245-2.

Mohr M, Krustrup P. Yo-Yo intermittent recovery test performances within an entire football league during a full season. *J Sports Sci*. 2014;32(4):315–327.

Mohr M, Krustrup P, Bangsbo J. Fatigue in soccer: A brief review. *J Sports Sci.* 2005;23(6):593–599.

Mohr M, Krustrup P, Nielsen JJ, Nybo L, Rasmussen MK, Juel C, Bangsbo J. Effect of two different intense training regimens on skeletal muscle ion transport proteins and fatigue development. *Am J Physiol Regul Integr Comp Physiol.* 2007 Apr;292(4):R1594–602.

Mohr M, Vigh-Larsen JF, Krustrup P. Muscle glycogen in elite soccer – A perspective on the implication for performance, fatigue, and recovery. *Front Sports Act Living.* 2022;4:876534. https://doi.org/10.3389/fspor.2022.876534.

Nassis GP, Brito J, Tomás R, Heiner-Møller K, Harder P, Kryger KO, Krustrup P. Elite women's football: Evolution and challenges for the years ahead. *Scand J Med Sci Sports.* 2022;32(Suppl 1):7–11. https://doi.org/10.1111/sms.14094.

Nassis GP, Massey A, Jacobsen P, Brito J, Randers MB, Castagna C, Mohr M, Krustrup P. Elite football of 2030 will not be the same as that of 2020: Preparing players, coaches, and support staff for the evolution. *Scand J Med Sci Sports.* 2020;30(6):962–964. https://doi.org/10.1111/sms.13681.

Papanikolaou K, Tsimeas P, Anagnostou A, Varypatis A, Mourikis C, Tzatzakis T, Draganidis D, Batsilas D, Mersinias T, Loules G, Poulios A, Deli CK, Batrakoulis A, Chatzinikolaou A, Mohr M, Jamurtas AZ, Fatouros IG. Recovery kinetics following small-sided games in competitive soccer players: Does player density size matter? *Int J Sports Physiol Perform.* 2021;16(9):1270–1280. https://doi.org/10.1123/ijspp.2020-0380.

Rago V, Krustrup P, Martín-Acero R, Rebelo A, Mohr M. Training load and submaximal heart rate testing throughout a competitive period in a top-level male football team. *J Sports Sci.* 2020;38(11–12):1408–1415. https://doi.org/10.1080/02640414.2019.1618534.

Rico-González M, Pino-Ortega J, Praça GM, Clemente FM. Practical applications for designing soccer' training tasks from multivariate data analysis: A systematic review emphasizing tactical training. *Percept Mot Ski.* 2022;129(3):892–931.

Silva JR. The soccer season: Performance variations and evolutionary trends. *PeerJ.* 2022;10:e14082. https://doi.org/10.7717/peerj.14082.

Silva JR, Rumpf MC, Hertzog M, Castagna C, Farooq A, Girard O, Hader K. Acute and residual soccer match-related fatigue: A systematic review and meta-analysis. *Sports Med.* 2018;48(3):539–583. https://doi.org/10.1007/s40279-017-0798-8.

Thomassen M, Christensen PM, Gunnarsson TP, Nybo L, Bangsbo J. Effect of 2-wk intensified training and inactivity on muscle Na+-K+ pump expression, phospholemmal (FXYD1) phosphorylation, and performance in soccer players. *J Appl Physiol (1985).* 2010;108(4):898–905. https://doi.org/10.1152/japplphysiol.01015.2009.

Tzatzakis T, Papanikolaou K, Draganidis D, Tsimeas P, Kritikos S, Poulios A, Laschou VC, Deli CK, Chatzinikolaou A, Batrakoulis A, Basdekis G, Mohr M, Krustrup P, Jamurtas AZ, Fatouros IG. Recovery kinetics after speed-endurance training in male soccer players. *Int J Sports Physiol Perform.* 2020;15(3):395–408. https://doi.org/10.1123/ijspp.2018-0984.

Vingren JL, Kraemer WJ, Ratamess NA, Anderson JM, Volek JS, Maresh CM. Testosterone physiology in resistance exercise and training: The up-stream regulatory elements. *Sports Med.* 2010;40(12):1037–1053. https://doi.org/10.2165/11536910-000000000-00000.

Wiig H, Cumming KT, Handegaard V, Stabell J, Spencer M, Raastad T. Muscular heat shock protein response and muscle damage after semi-professional football match. *Scand J Med Sci Sports.* 2022;32(6):984–996. https://doi.org/10.1111/sms.14148.

Wiig H, Raastad T, Luteberget LS, Ims I, Spencer M. External load variables affect recovery markers up to 72 h after semiprofessional football matches. *Front Physiol*. 2019;10:689. https://doi.org/10.3389/fphys.2019.00689.

Wittkugel J, Memmert D, Wunderlich F. Substitutions in football – what coaches think and what coaches do. *J Sports Sci*. 2022;40(15):1668–1677. https://doi.org/10.1080/02640414.2022.2099177.

6

FITNESS TESTING AND PHYSICAL PROFILING IN FOOTBALL

Nikolaos D. Asimakidis, Chris Bishop, Anthony Turner, and Marco Beato

Introduction

Football is a game that requires players to have a combination of technical, tactical, physical, and psychological factors to compete at a high standard. When focused on the physical aspect of the sport, a thorough understanding of the demands imposed on players is paramount to designing training programs that prepare the players to meet the specific physical requirements of the game. This in-depth analysis highlights potential areas of focus and prioritization, enabling practitioners to adopt an evidence-based and systematic approach in the physical preparation process. In addition, the identification of the biomechanical and physiological demands of the sport assists in the determination of the most relevant physical attributes, which in turn, form the basis for the development of a physical test battery. Therefore, this chapter aims, firstly, to briefly summarize the physical demands of football match-play, and secondly, to suggest the most relevant tests that practitioners can use to evaluate their players.

Physical Demands

The intermittent nature of football requires players to intersperse explosive bursts (i.e., rapid accelerations to chase the ball, change direction to evade opponents, jumps for a header, shots and tackles) with lower intensity activities (i.e., walking and jogging) (Dolci et al., 2020). Although these high-intensity activities constitute a small fraction of the total game duration, their role is crucial as they precede some of the most decisive moments of the game. An analysis of the goals scored in the English Premier League revealed that 83% of player's sequence of movements before scoring a goal included at least one explosive action, such as linear sprints, decelerations, turns, and jumps (Martínez-Hernández, Quinn and Jones, 2023).

DOI: 10.4324/9781003383475-7

Moreover, players need to frequently execute these power-related actions consistently throughout a 90-minute match, with brief recovery periods during the most demanding passages of play (Vigne et al., 2010). A decline in physical performance has been shown to occur in the second half (Vigne et al., 2010; Bradley, 2024). For instance, data has shown that at the 2022 FIFA World Cup in Qatar, there was a 7.4% reduction in total distance covered per minute (109.8 vs 101.7 m/min) and a 10.2% reduction in distance at speeds exceeding 20 km/h (9.2 vs 8.2 m/min) in the second half (Bradley, 2024). Thus, high levels of aerobic and anaerobic capacity are crucial to counteract fatigue during the last stages of the game, especially in environments where extremely high ambient temperatures are present.

In terms of the specific physical demands of an elite football match, individuals have been reported to cover total distances between 10 and 13 km, and for some players up to 14 km (Dolci et al., 2020), with approximately 900 m at speeds higher than 19.8 km/h, and 200–300 m at speeds higher than 25.2 km/h (Allen et al., 2023). The physical demands in the top European leagues have substantially increased over time, especially in terms of running at higher speeds (Allen et al., 2023), with further increases being anticipated over this decade. These increases may be attributable to tactical changes in the game, such as the high-intensity pressing and the increased number of offensive transitions, which typically increase the demands of high-intensity (i.e., >19.8 km/h) running.

Elite football players have been shown to sprint (>25.2 km/h) around 80 times per match, with the vast majority of sprints lasting less than 5 seconds (Vigne et al., 2010). On top of that, numerous accelerations, decelerations, and turns are performed during the game. Bloomfield, Polman and O'Donoghue (2007) found that over 700 directional changes are made during a game, with the majority of them being less than 90°. In terms of higher intensity accelerations and decelerations, the systematic review of Harper, Carling and Kiely (2019) found that elite football players exhibit a greater number of high (>2.5 m/s^2) and very high (>3.5 m/s^2) decelerations in comparison to accelerations, illustrating the high mechanical demands of elite football.

Tactical factors such as different playing positions result in different physical outputs. Players positioned in the centre of the pitch (i.e., defensive and centre midfielders) generally perform a greater amount of total running. In contrast, those playing in wider and forward positions (i.e., full backs, wide midfielders, and centre forwards) cover greater distances at higher intensities (Allen et al., 2023; Bradley, 2024). A recent analysis of the 2022 FIFA World Cup revealed that wide midfielders and wide forwards covered 16–92% and 36–138% greater distances compared to central defenders, defensive and central midfielders, at speeds above 20 km/h and 25 km/h, respectively (Bradley, 2024). Moreover, players of the same playing position have been found to display different outputs across different playing formations (Arjol-Serrano et al., 2021). Therefore, it seems logical to suggest that practitioners may wish to consider a more bespoke level of positional analysis when it comes to evaluating the physical demands of the sport.

Fitness Testing and Physical Profiling in Football 91

Why Do We Test?

Being physically robust can facilitate coping with the ever-increasing physical demands and number of matches per season, reduce post-match fatigue and increase training load capacity, and support the successful completion of the required technical and tactical actions. Fitness testing is integral to the physical development process to obtain a comprehensive understanding of a player's physical profile and longitudinal progress (Figure 6.1).

Fitness testing allows the benchmarking of an athlete with normative data, the identification of strengths and areas in need of improvement, and the determination of the effectiveness of a training intervention. Furthermore, fitness testing can support the talent identification and player recruitment process by highlighting players with specific physical attributes that fit the club's overall game model. For example, a playing style that relies heavily on the successful execution of attacking transitions may require the selection of forward players characterized by high levels of speed and power, as opposed to physically strong target men with exceptional aerial and ball-holding ability. Moreover, fitness testing can be a valuable tool to

FIGURE 6.1 Key objectives of fitness testing in football.

92 Strength and Conditioning for Football

increase the motivation and overall buy-in of an individual into the training process, fostering a culture of improvement and competitiveness.

The role of fitness testing is multifactorial, and not limited to the performance domain. Certain deficits and imbalances can render a player more prone to certain injuries, and fitness testing can play a pivotal role in the identification of modifiable risk factors for common football-related injuries (Timmins et al., 2016; Ribeiro-Alvares et al., 2020). In this sense, the recent work of Maestroni et al. (Maestroni et al., 2023) highlights the importance of establishing baseline pre-injury values for a successful return-to-play process in professional football players. Besides informing the return-to-play process, baseline fitness testing values can be used for neuromuscular fatigue monitoring purposes and determination of readiness to train (Bishop et al., 2023), facilitating the appropriate management of the training load placed.

Several factors can influence testing selection, including equipment availability, number of athletes, age and training status of the athlete, time constraints, simplicity, practicality, timing, and whether the test is fatiguing or not. It is crucial for practitioners to select the most relevant tests for assessing the fitness level of their athletes and avoid conducting testing just for the sake of testing. The following sections discuss the different types of tests that can be used to assess fitness parameters in football.

Aerobic Tests

The large amount of total distance that players need to cover during the game, combined with the need to quickly recover from high-intensity actions (Dolci et al., 2020), highlights the necessity for high aerobic capacity levels. A higher aerobic capacity can have a protective effect against lower-limb injuries, as players with enhanced aerobic capacity levels can better tolerate greater high-speed running volumes (Malone et al., 2018). A higher aerobic capacity allows players to sustain their technical performance, enabling consistent execution of high-quality technical actions throughout the game.

$\dot{V}O2max$ measurement during incremental treadmill exercise represents the gold-standard assessment of aerobic capacity (Bok and Foster, 2021), which takes place in a laboratory setting. Although there is not a clear minimum $\dot{V}O_{2max}$ value to have to play football at an elite level, professional football players typically have $\dot{V}O_{2max}$ values around 55–60 mL/kg/min. During an incremental treadmill test, is also possible to determine the maximum heart rate and the maximal aerobic speed (MAS) (km/h), which is the lowest running speed at which $\dot{V}O_{2max}$ occurs. Nevertheless, aerobic assessments in a laboratory setting are time-consuming and associated with an increased cost and limited accessibility. With this in mind, on-field tests and time trials for certain distances (e.g., 1,500 m) have been developed as potential alternatives. However, the main limitation of time-trial tests is that they

Fitness Testing and Physical Profiling in Football **93**

are not sport-specific because they do not replicate the specific intermittent pattern of football (Bok and Foster, 2021).

In the last 20 years, some intermittent field tests have been proposed. The Yo-Yo intermittent recovery tests, consisting of level 1 (YYIR1) and level 2 (YYIR2), and 30-15 Intermittent Fitness Test (30-15 IFT) are intermittent shuttle-based tests that may better resemble the activity profile of football. The Yo-Yo intermittent tests follow a standardized protocol with repeated 2 × 20-m shuttle runs at increasing speeds, dictated by audio signals, with the total distance covered during the test being the primary outcome variable that is recorded. Both the YYIR1 and YYIR2 are designed to provoke a maximal stimulation of the aerobic system, yet their main differences lie in their underlying mechanisms stemming from the different starting speeds. More specifically, YYIR2 starts at a higher speed, resulting in a lower exhaustion time and a higher contribution from the anaerobic system (Bangsbo, Iaia and Krustrup, 2008).

Another valid option to assess intermittent running is the 30-15 IFT, which has garnered increased attention in the field of elite football during the last seven years (Malone et al., 2018; Asimakidis et al., 2024), possibly attributed to its high sensitivity to assess fitness changes (Bok and Foster, 2021). The 30-15 IFT consists of 30-s shuttle runs, interspersed with 15-s passive recovery periods, and an increase in velocity by 0.5 km/h at the end of each 45-s stage. The final velocity achieved during the test can be used to prescribe high-intensity interval training.

The demanding training schedules and the fixture congestion encountered during the in-season phase in elite football environments pose significant challenges in the administration of fitness testing. As such, submaximal fitness tests have emerged as practical solutions, possibly owing to their short duration, nondisruptive and non-fatiguing nature. Their potential for a seamless integration into the warm-up process can enable a more frequent assessment (e.g., weekly) of athletes' physiological state. Common submaximal protocols in elite football players include a submaximal version of YYIR1, which consists of running for 6 minutes at a velocity of 14.5 km/h, and a total distance of 720 m, as well as a submaximal 4-minute warm-up test at a speed of 12 km/h. HR during exercise (HRex) and HR recovery represent the main outcome variables derived from these tests (Shushan et al., 2022).

Overall, special importance should be placed on the ability of a test to guide training prescription. While laboratory tests provide a detailed assessment of aerobic capacity under controlled conditions, field tests are often preferred due to their practical relevance. In this sense, shuttle-based intermittent field tests, such as the YYIR1 and the 30-15 IFT, may better replicate the football-specific demands, yet the value of more straightforward field tests, such as certain time trials (e.g., 1,000–1,500 m), should not be underestimated in practical settings. Finally, the administration of submaximal fitness testing can facilitate ongoing monitoring, especially during congested fixture periods.

Strength and Power Tests

Strength is a fundamental capacity in football, since it has been shown to represent an underlying factor for the successful completion of many in-game high-intensity actions, such as sprinting, jumping, and changing direction, whereas power is the product of strength and speed. Training interventions consisting of strength and power exercises have been shown to be a highly effective way of improving the performance of a range of football-related physical qualities such as acceleration, top speed, jumping, and change of direction (COD) ability (Otero-Esquina et al., 2017).

Strength Testing

Practitioners have a variety of options to evaluate muscular strength, including isokinetic (i.e., quadriceps and hamstring), isometric (i.e., isometric mid-thigh pull [IMTP], isometric squat, adductor squeeze), eccentric (i.e., Nordic hamstring and flywheel hamstring), and dynamic (e.g., back squat) strength testing. Isokinetic dynamometry, Nordic hamstring strength, and adductor squeeze represent popular testing options that are highly effective tools in determining the strength of isolated muscle groups, such as hamstring, quadriceps, and adductor muscles, which represent some of the most injury-prone areas in football (Bahr, Clarsen and Ekstrand, 2018; Ekstrand et al., 2020). Due to their pivotal role in the injury screening process, these tests are discussed in detail in the "Injury screening assessments" section. Therefore, this section will focus on strength assessments that provide a more global insight into a player's maximal force production capability.

Repetition maximum (RM) testing, which determines the maximum load that can be lifted for a given number of repetitions (typically 1–5) in exercises such as the back squat, represents a widely recognized method of identifying an athlete's dynamic strength ability, particularly in the absence of any specialized equipment. Furthermore, dynamic strength testing can be useful in training prescription, since the implementation of loads expressed as percentages of the RM allows for individualized strength programming. Although 1RM testing is often considered the gold standard and the most accurate method of dynamic strength testing, a high level of resistance training experience and familiarity with the overall process is required. As a consequence, elite football practitioners seem to favour the use of multiple repetitions maximum testing, such as the 3RM squat (Asimakidis et al., 2024), to eliminate any potential safety concerns associated with 1RM squat testing. Subsequently, a 1RM value can be predicted with various estimation equations. Nevertheless, RM testing is time-consuming, especially when it comes to large groups of athletes, which is often the case in football teams. The rise of measuring devices that can track barbell velocity, such as motion capture systems, linear position transducers, accelerometers, and smartphone apps, has enabled the estimation of 1RM based on the velocity achieved at submaximal loads (Balsalobre-Fernández

Fitness Testing and Physical Profiling in Football **95**

and Torres-Ronda, 2021). Consequently, strength assessment can be seamlessly integrated during the training session without the need to conduct maximal testing. Moreover, the development of time-efficient load-velocity profiling methods such as the two-point system, where a lighter (40–60% 1RM) and heavier load (80–90% 1RM) are applied, has made lower-body load-velocity profiling more time-efficient, without compromising reliability (intraclass correlation coefficient [ICC]: 0.82–0.99, coefficient of variation [CV]: 4.42–4.50%) and validity ($R^2 = 0.70$) (Çetin et al., 2022).

Isometric strength tests, such as the IMTP and the isometric squat, can serve as quicker and less fatiguing alternatives to dynamic strength testing. During isometric strength testing (performed on a force plate), multiple variables such as peak force, force at specific time points, rate of force development (RFD), and impulse can be recorded within a single trial, providing a nuanced insight into an individual's force generation capacity. The IMTP test, which replicates the position of the second pull in weightlifting, is a highly reliable isometric strength assessment, especially in terms of peak force (ICC: 0.98, CV: 4.3%, SEM: 89 N) (Brady et al., 2018), that has been shown to correlate with 1RM squat performance ($r = 0.86$, $p < 0.05$) (Wang et al., 2016). In addition, the IMTP has been found to be the most frequently used strength test by elite football practitioners (Asimakidis et al., 2024), which may be indicative of the increased availability and affordability of force plates, as well as the popularity of isometric testing in the applied environment. In the same vein, the isometric squat at knee angles of 90° and 120° could represent an additional reliable isometric strength testing alternative. In particular, the isometric squat removes the involvement of the upper body, having the potential to provide a true reflection of lower body strength. Nevertheless, caution is warranted for an increased risk of lower back injury through increased axial loading. Ultimately, careful use of time-dependent metrics such as RFD and impulse during isometric strength testing is recommended, as they have been found to be less reliable than non-time-dependent metrics such as peak force (Brady et al., 2018).

Power Testing

Power, defined as the ability to generate force quickly, is an important physical attribute for soccer players. Given its multifaceted nature, which involves a complex interplay of biomechanical, physiological, and neuromuscular factors, a single test is unlikely to provide a comprehensive assessment of power ability. Jump tests, such as the countermovement jump (CMJ), squat jump (SJ), single-leg CMJ (SLCMJ), drop jump (DJ), standing broad jump (SBJ) and single-leg repeated hops, represent the common methods used in the field to provide an estimation of a player's lower-limb muscular capacity. Jump height is typically the primary variable of interest, with take-off velocity and flight-time methods constituting the two primary methods to calculate jump height (Xu et al., 2023).

The CMJ is an easy-to-administer and time-efficient test, requiring minimal familiarization, that provides an insight into neuromuscular function and slow stretch-shortening cycle (SSC) performance. In particular, the CMJ has been shown to exhibit high within- (i.e., ICC: 0.94–0.97, CV: 2.7–3.1%, SEM: 1.4 cm) (Maestroni et al., 2023) and between-day (i.e., ICC: 0.83, CV: 4.3%, SEM: 1.7 cm) reliability (Enright et al., 2018) in elite football players. In contrast, the SJ theoretically evaluates an athlete's jumping ability without the use of SSC, as no countermovement is allowed, providing different insights compared to the CMJ. Compliance with the SJ protocol (i.e., the isometric hold of 2–3 seconds prior to the jump) is necessary, since a small amplitude counter-movement (SACM) has been shown to affect the jump height achieved (Sheppard and Doyle, 2008). More importantly, Sheppard and Doyle (2008) found that 55% of the SJ trials in their study consisted of a SACM when a gross observation was used. Nevertheless, the percentage of the SJ trials consisting of a SACM was considerably higher when additional analyses were performed with force plates (89%) and linear position transducers (99%). This can have significant implications in practical settings, where access to specialized equipment and resources to analyse each jump are limited. In light of these considerations, practitioners should critically evaluate the value of the information provided by the SJ. In addition, the DJ can be employed to assess an athlete's reactive strength, which is defined as the ability to change quickly from an eccentric to a concentric contraction, providing insight into an athlete's fast SSC capability. In particular, reactive strength index (RSI) – the ratio of jump height to ground contact time in a DJ – has been shown to correlate with key football movements, such as sprinting and COD (Jarvis et al., 2022), making it a useful complement to the CMJ for a comprehensive power assessment. Further to this, the SLCMJ allows for the assessment of unilateral jump performance, which can be of particular value considering a number of movement patterns in football require some degree of unilateral movement competency. Notably, valuable insights into potential inter-limb asymmetries can also be obtained. Ultimately, combining information from the SLCMJ with the CMJ has been suggested to provide a broader picture of an athlete's neuromuscular performance, thereby guiding more effectively the return-to-play process (Maestroni et al., 2023).

While vertical jumping is a valuable tool for assessing SSC characteristics, horizontal jump assessments can provide unique information that is not obtainable through vertical jumping. Among the various horizontal jump assessments, the SBJ test is the most commonly used. The SBJ can be an appealing choice to assess power ability in a large group of athletes in the field in the absence of any specialized equipment, as only a measurement tape is required. Additionally, the triple hop test provides insights into horizontal reactive strength ability and can play a significant role in the return-to-play process (Kotsifaki et al., 2022).

Force plates are considered gold-standard equipment to assess jumping ability (Xu et al., 2023), providing force-time data that enable a more detailed evaluation of jump strategy. In fact, there has been a growing emphasis recently on exploring

Fitness Testing and Physical Profiling in Football **97**

metrics beyond jump height, such as peak power, peak force, impulse, and duration prior to take-off, to allow for individualized training prescription. Careful consideration is required when selecting some of these variables though, due to their higher degree of variability compared to jump height (Bishop et al., 2023). Nevertheless, force plates may not always be accessible in the field due to increased cost. As such, jump mats, optoelectronic devices, and smartphone apps represent reliable and valid alternatives to estimate jump height from flight time (Rago et al., 2018). In addition, the latest version of a smartphone app (i.e., My Jump Lab) has been shown to be valid and reliable for assessing jump strategy metrics, such as the time to take-off and the RSI modified, with the use of a correction equation (Bishop, Jarvis, et al., 2022). Finally, it is crucial to adhere to a standardized procedure using the same equipment to enable informative longitudinal comparisons within and between athletes.

Linear Speed, Multidirectional Speed, and Repeated Sprint Ability Tests

Linear Speed Testing

Within the context of a football match, straight-line sprinting has been found to be the most frequent action preceding goal scoring (Martínez-Hernández, Quinn and Jones, 2023). Linear speed consists of the acceleration and the maximum speed phases, with the two being separate physical qualities with distinct kinetic and kinematic characteristics. Therefore, it is crucial to investigate each of those two components.

The assessment of linear speed in football involves the use of different distances (0–40 m) with split times to facilitate the concurrent assessment of acceleration and maximum speed. Various equipment methods can be employed for linear speed assessment, such as hand-held timing devices, radar gun and laser devices, global positioning systems (GPS) photocell systems (i.e., timing gates), and fully automated camera systems, with the latter representing the gold-standard equipment method (Haugen and Buchheit, 2016). Nevertheless, it is costly and impractical for use in the applied setting due to its time-consuming process, and as such, timing gates are typically used. Although timing gates allow for the reliable assessment of certain split times and average speed (ICC: 0.91–0.98, CV: 0.65–2.26%) (Krespi, Sporiš and Trajković, 2020), they cannot provide an indication of peak velocity achieved. GPS enables the valid and reliable (ICC: 0.99, CV: 1.8–2.3%) assessment of peak velocity (Beato et al., 2018), and its seamless assessment at the end of the warm-up and during speed sessions, which is of particular value considering the challenges existing in fitness testing in elite football.

Regardless of the methods used, it is important for practitioners to administer sprint testing under standardized conditions, including running surfaces, starting methods and distances behind the starting line, measuring equipment and equipment calibration (e.g., height of timing gates) (Haugen and Buchheit, 2016).

98 Strength and Conditioning for Football

Changes of Direction Tests

Football requires the ability to turn effectively with both limbs at different angles across various defensive and offensive situations (Bloomfield, Polman and O'Donoghue, 2007). COD ability has been defined as "the ability to decelerate, reverse or change movement direction and accelerate again", providing the physical and mechanical basis of multidirectional speed. COD tests have been previously categorized into two types: (1) "COD speed" tests, which involve a "cutting" movement, such as 505 COD tests, and (2) "manoeuvrability" tests, referring to those without a clear "plant" step and/or involving a change in the mode of travel to and from transitional movements (i.e., side shuffle or backpedalling), such as Illinois agility test and Zig-Zag test (Nimphius et al., 2018). Additionally, the agility T-test can be considered a "hybrid" test, as it contains features of both the COD speed and manoeuvrability tests.

Overall, COD ability is reported to be angle dependent and influenced by the entry velocity. In particular, different COD angles present distinct kinetic and kinematic characteristics, with sharper COD angles ($\geq 90°$) being associated with longer braking distances and ground contact times, as well as an increased trunk lean and pelvic rotation during the plant step. Furthermore, the 180° turn performed during the 505 COD test can serve as a proxy of an athlete's deceleration capacity, since the high-velocity braking ability is significantly challenged (Nimphius et al., 2018). This could be of particular importance for practitioners given the frequency of high-intensity deceleration in football (Harper, Carling and Kiely, 2019).

Completion time is typically used as the main outcome variable of interest in COD testing. However, relying solely on completion time may not fully capture the whole picture of an athlete's COD proficiency, as it does not provide insights into the key technical performance indicators of the turning action. In addition, most of the COD tests are reported to include a significant proportion of linear sprinting, thus influencing the final outcome by compensating for a poor turning ability. Consequently, the use of change of direction deficit (CODD) (i.e., the difference of COD completion time and linear sprint time over an identical distance) has been proposed to remove the influence of linear speed and provide an isolated measure of COD ability (Nimphius et al., 2018). However, the low to moderate reliability levels of CODD reported in young football players (ICC: 0.19–0.79, CV: 7.1–12%, MDC [95% CI]: 17.7–33.3%) suggests some caution should be applied in using it (Taylor et al., 2019).

Technological advancements like 3D motion analysis, force platforms, high-speed cameras, and mobile applications, such as CODTimer app, can provide a more detailed analysis of an athlete's turning ability. More specifically, kinetic (e.g., joint angles, centre of mass velocity, contact time during the plant step) and kinematic aspects (e.g., ground reaction forces) insights of the COD task of interest can be obtained, which can be used to inform individualized training programming. However, the extensive use of resources (i.e., financial and time) associated

Fitness Testing and Physical Profiling in Football **99**

with the implementation of those methods, may impede the assessment of multiple athletes, and as such, it may need to be employed only in specific scenarios where an in-depth analysis of turning mechanics is required (e.g., return to play process).

A single test that can assess all the COD requirements of football does not exist. Hence, practitioners need to consider several factors, such as test duration, whether a clear plant step exists, the complexity of the task (e.g., number of directional changes), and the assessment of the underlying physical quality.

Repeated Sprint Ability Testing

Repeated sprint ability (RSA) refers to the ability to perform multiple short sprints with a limited decline in performance. No gold-standard testing protocol seems to exist, as RSA is generally assessed with various directions (linear vs multidirectional), sprint distances (20–40 m), sprint repetitions (3–15), recovery durations (10–60 seconds), and recovery type (active vs passive) (Kyles et al., 2023). Nevertheless, the 6 × 40 m (20 + 20 m, 180° COD) shuttle sprints with 20 s passive recovery, the 6 × 20 m sprint with 25 s active recovery, and 7 × 30 m sprint with 25 s active recovery are commonly employed RSA protocols used in elite football players. Percentage of performance decrement (i.e., the ratio of mean sprint time [RSAmean] to best sprint time [RSAbest]), total sprint time (RSAtotal), RSAbest, and RSAmean are the main outcome variables used to quantify RSA performance (Altmann et al., 2019; Kyles et al., 2023). Caution should be practiced with the use of a percentage of performance decrement as a fatigue indicator, as it has been shown to have low reliability levels (ICC: 0.11–0.49, CV: 16.8–51.0%) (Altmann et al., 2019), which is likely due to the inherent variability of ratio measures. Ultimately, practitioners need to be aware that the various sprint distances, repetitions, the inclusion of CODs, their angle and number, and the type of recovery impose a distinct neuromuscular and physiological load on the athletes.

Injury Screening Assessments

The presence of injuries in professional football carries significant implications, resulting in increased financial burdens for clubs and organizations. Conversely, lower injury rates are associated with better team performance, leading to greater overall club success and higher league rankings (Hägglund et al., 2013). The overarching aim of injury screening is to identify individuals predisposed to injuries by investigating the intrinsic modifiable injury risk factors, such as neuromuscular control, range of motion, and muscle strength (Timmins et al., 2016; Ribeiro-Alvares et al., 2020). As such, baseline measurements and objective markers can be established, enabling the implementation of targeted injury minimization programs.

In order to determine the screening battery, a thorough examination of the most common injuries is required. Epidemiological studies in professional football players have identified hamstring (17.4% of total injuries) and groin muscle groups

100 Strength and Conditioning for Football

(11.2% of total injuries) as the two most commonly injured muscle areas (Ekstrand et al., 2020). In addition, although low in terms of frequency, anterior cruciate ligament (ACL) injury presents the highest injury severity (Bahr, Clarsen and Ekstrand, 2018), resulting in long periods of absence (around 200 days). Last but not least, the ankle has been shown to represent another injury-prone region in football players (Bahr, Clarsen and Ekstrand, 2018), with ankle lateral ligaments representing 6.3% of total injuries in professional football players (Ekstrand et al., 2020).

Although movement screening has been reported to have a limited ability as an injury prediction tool (Moran et al., 2017), certain areas predisposing an individual to a greater injury risk can be identified. Given the time constraints associated with the movement screening process, the overhead squat test represents a time-efficient test providing insights into overall movement quality, by challenging the mobility and the stability of the entire kinetic chain. In addition, the Y-Balance test is an easy-to-administer assessment of dynamic balance, proprioception and neuromuscular control, which has been proven to be a valuable tool in identifying athletes at a higher risk for lower-limb injury (Manoel et al., 2020).

Assessment of the strength of the relevant muscle groups is crucial for the establishment of an injury risk profile (Timmins et al., 2016). Isokinetic dynamometry testing of knee extensors and flexors provides valuable insights into the force-generation capacity of these muscles at different angular velocities (i.e., 30°, 60°, 180°, 240°, 300°/s) and contraction types (concentric vs eccentric). As such, side-to-side strength differences and muscle strength imbalances around the knee joint can be identified, which have been shown to associate with an increased hamstring strain injury (HSI) risk in elite football players (Ribeiro-Alvares et al., 2020). Nevertheless, isokinetic dynamometers are costly, lack portability, and demand a significant amount of time to complete their various testing protocols. Consequently, clubs with limited resources may not have access to this equipment.

Nordic hamstring testing enables the functional assessment of eccentric hamstring strength (Timmins et al., 2016) – a critical factor given the high prevalence of hamstring injuries in football as well as the constantly increased demands of the modern game in the amount of high-speed running performed. The increased familiarity with the Nordic hamstring exercise as part of an injury prevention program, the growing availability of Nordic measurement devices in elite football environments (e.g., Nordbord), and the ability to reliably (ICC: 0.54–0.73, CV: 7.2–10.06%) assess large groups of athletes in a time-efficient manner are significant advantages that can facilitate its use in practice (Bishop, Manuel, et al., 2022).

Higher levels of isometric adductor strength can assist in reducing groin injury risk in elite football players (Light and Thorborg, 2016). The adductor squeeze test is a widely used test to assess the isometric strength of adductor muscles in football players (Asimakidis et al., 2024), which can discriminate between players with and without groin pain (Mosler et al., 2015). It can be reliably performed using a sphygmomanometer cuff and a portable hand-held dynamometer (HHD). Nevertheless, the growing accessibility specialized equipment in the field, such as the ForceFrame

FITNESS TESTING FOR FOOTBALL

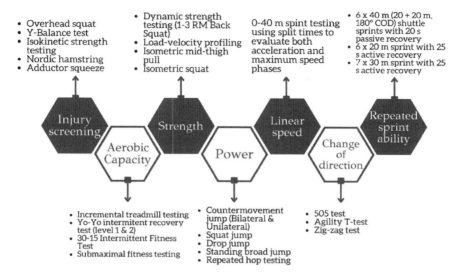

FIGURE 6.2   Overview of fitness testing protocols in football.

Strength Testing System and the Kangatech KT360 may facilitate an easier evaluation of the adductor strength. These tools can help in overcoming some of the limitations of the sphygmomanometer (i.e., ceiling effect in stronger individuals) and the HHD (i.e., subject to tester's strength biases when not externally fixated). Different hip angles have been used across the literature in adductor squeeze testing in elite football players, including 0° (i.e., extended legs), 45°, and 60°. Yet, the different hip angles result in different reliability and output levels (Delahunt et al., 2011), and as such comparisons between different positions should be avoided.

Injury screening is a dynamic and ever-evolving process, as individual's risk factors may change over time. Hence, screening should be performed at regular intervals during the season, and training interventions should be adapted accordingly, where possible. In addition, if time permits, additional screening based on individual's intrinsic risk factors (i.e., previous injuries, age, gender, race) can offer valuable complementary insights to practitioners. Figure 6.2 provides a visual summary of the available testing options for football practitioners.

Practical Considerations in the Delivery of Fitness Testing Protocols

Core principles such as validity (i.e., the degree to which a test measures what it is intended to measure), reliability (i.e., the repeatability of a test), and sensitivity (i.e., the ability of a test to detect changes greater than the measurement error) are essential for the use of a fitness test in the practice. The administration of fitness testing under standardized conditions will ensure that reliable data across multiple testing sections is obtained, enabling decisions to be made on the basis of accurate information. It is recommended that practitioners who are less familiar with these testing pillars take the time to develop a deeper understanding of these concepts and start establishing their own reliability measures within their specific settings.

The hectic schedule and the time constraints of the applied environments necessitate the implementation of time-efficient and informative testing batteries. In this sense, a "flexible" testing approach, where fitness testing is embedded within the training sessions using a multiday microdosing approach during the microcycle, could be also implemented to minimize any disruption in the training schedule, whilst allowing on-going data collection. In addition, practitioners must be equipped with robust data analysis – both at the individual and team level – and data visualization skills to ensure that testing results are not only accurately analysed, but also effectively communicated to the key stakeholders (i.e., coaches, players). Ultimately, it should be acknowledged that physical development and fitness testing are the key aspects of competitive success, but they are not the only determinants, therefore, data and decisions should be interpreted within the technical, tactical, and psychological context (Figure 6.3).

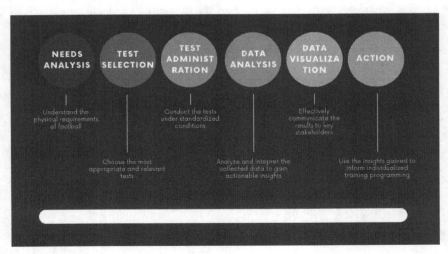

FIGURE 6.3 Comprehensive fitness testing framework for football.

References

Allen, T. *et al.* (2023) 'Running More than Before? The Evolution of Running Load Demands in the English Premier League', *International Journal of Sports Science and Coaching*, 19(2), p. 174795412311645. Available at: https://doi.org/10.1177/17479541231164507.

Altmann, S. *et al.* (2019) 'Validity and Reliability of Speed Tests Used in Soccer: A Systematic Review', *PLOS ONE*, 14(8), p. e0220982. Available at: https://doi.org/10.1371/journal.pone.0220982.

Arjol-Serrano, J.L. *et al.* (2021) 'The Influence of Playing Formation on Physical Demands and Technical-Tactical Actions According to Playing Positions in an Elite Soccer Team', *International Journal of Environmental Research and Public Health*, 18(8), p. 4148. Available at: https://doi.org/10.3390/ijerph18084148.

Asimakidis, N.D. *et al.* (2024) 'A Survey into the Current Fitness Testing Practices of Elite Male Soccer Practitioners: From Assessment to Communicating Results', *Frontiers in Physiology*, 15, p. 1376047. Available at: https://doi.org/10.3389/fphys.2024.1376047.

Bahr, R., Clarsen, B. and Ekstrand, J. (2018) 'Why We Should Focus on the Burden of Injuries and Illnesses, Not Just their Incidence', *British Journal of Sports Medicine*, 52(16), pp. 1018–1021. Available at: https://doi.org/10.1136/bjsports-2017-098160.

Balsalobre-Fernández, C. and Torres-Ronda, L. (2021) 'The Implementation of Velocity-Based Training Paradigm for Team Sports: Framework, Technologies, Practical Recommendations and Challenges', *Sports*, 9(4), p. 47. Available at: https://doi.org/10.3390/sports9040047.

Bangsbo, J., Iaia, F.M. and Krustrup, P. (2008) 'The Yo-Yo Intermittent Recovery Test: A Useful Tool for Evaluation of Physical Performance in Intermittent Sports', *Sports Medicine*, 38(1), pp. 37–51. Available at: https://doi.org/10.2165/00007256-200838010-00004.

Beato, M. et al. (2018) 'The Validity and Between-Unit Variability of GNSS Units (STATSports Apex 10 and 18 Hz) for Measuring Distance and Peak Speed in Team Sports', *Frontiers in Physiology*, 9, p. 1288. Available at: https://doi.org/10.3389/fphys.2018.01288.

Bishop, C. et al. (2023) 'Selecting Metrics That Matter: Comparing the Use of the Countermovement Jump for Performance Profiling, Neuromuscular Fatigue Monitoring, and Injury Rehabilitation Testing', *Strength and Conditioning Journal*, 45(5), 545–553.

Bishop, C., Jarvis, P., *et al.* (2022) 'Validity and Reliability of Strategy Metrics to Assess Countermovement Jump Performance Using the Newly Developed My Jump Lab Smartphone Application', *Journal of Human Kinetics*, 83, pp. 185–195. Available at: https://doi.org/10.2478/hukin-2022-0098.

Bishop, C., Manuel, J., *et al.* (2022) 'Assessing Eccentric Hamstring Strength Using the NordBord: Between-Session Reliability and Interlimb Asymmetries in Professional Soccer Players', *Journal of Strength and Conditioning Research*, 36(9), pp. 2552–2557. Available at: https://doi.org/10.1519/JSC.0000000000004303.

Bloomfield, J., Polman, R. and O'Donoghue, P. (2007) 'Physical Demands of Different Positions in FA Premier League Soccer', *Journal of Sports Science and Medicine*, 6(1), pp. 63–70.

Bok, D. and Foster, C. (2021) 'Applicability of Field Aerobic Fitness Tests in Soccer: Which One to Choose?', *Journal of Functional Morphology and Kinesiology*, 6(3), p. 69. Available at: https://doi.org/10.3390/jfmk6030069.

Bradley, P.S. (2024) '"Setting the Benchmark" Part 1: The Contextualised Physical Demands of Positional Roles in the FIFA World Cup Qatar 2022', *Biology of Sport*, 41(1), pp. 261–270. Available at: https://doi.org/10.5114/biolsport.2024.131090.

104 Strength and Conditioning for Football

Brady, C.J. *et al.* (2018) 'A Comparison of the Isometric Midthigh Pull and Isometric Squat: Intraday Reliability, Usefulness, and the Magnitude of Difference Between Tests', *International Journal of Sports Physiology and Performance*, 13(7), pp. 844–852. Available at: https://doi.org/10.1123/ijspp.2017-0480.

Çetin, O. *et al.* (2022) 'Reliability and Validity of the Multi-point Method and the 2-point Method's Variations of Estimating the One-Repetition Maximum for Deadlift and Back Squat Exercises', *PeerJ*, 10, p. e13013. Available at: https://doi.org/10.7717/peerj.13013.

Delahunt, E. *et al.* (2011) 'Intrarater Reliability of the Adductor Squeeze Test in Gaelic Games Athletes', *Journal of Athletic Training*, 46(3), pp. 241–245. Available at: https://doi.org/10.4085/1062-6050-46.3.241.

Dolci, F. et al. (2020) 'Physical and Energetic Demand of Soccer: A Brief Review', *Strength and Conditioning Journal*, 42(3), pp. 70–77. Available at: https://doi.org/10.1519/SSC.0000000000000533.

Ekstrand, J. *et al.* (2020) 'Time before Return to Play for the Most Common Injuries in Professional Football: A 16-year Follow-up of the UEFA Elite Club Injury Study', *British Journal of Sports Medicine*, 54(7), pp. 421–426. Available at: https://doi.org/10.1136/bjsports-2019-100666.

Enright, K. *et al.* (2018) 'Reliability of "in-season" Fitness Assessments in Youth Elite Soccer Players: A Working Model for Practitioners and Coaches', *Science and Medicine in Football*, 2(3), pp. 177–183. Available at: https://doi.org/10.1080/24733938.2017.1411603.

Hägglund, M. et al. (2013) 'Injuries Affect Team Performance Negatively in Professional Football: an 11-year Follow-up of the UEFA Champions League Injury Study', *British Journal of Sports Medicine*, 47(12), pp. 738–742. Available at: https://doi.org/10.1136/bjsports-2013-092215.

Harper, D.J., Carling, C. and Kiely, J. (2019) 'High-Intensity Acceleration and Deceleration Demands in Elite Team Sports Competitive Match Play: A Systematic Review and Meta-Analysis of Observational Studies', *Sports Medicine*, 49(12), pp. 1923–1947. Available at: https://doi.org/10.1007/s40279-019-01170-1.

Haugen, T. and Buchheit, M. (2016) 'Sprint Running Performance Monitoring: Methodological and Practical Considerations', *Sports Medicine*, 46(5), pp. 641–656. Available at: https://doi.org/10.1007/s40279-015-0446-0.

Jarvis, P. *et al.* (2022) 'Reactive Strength Index and Its Associations with Measures of Physical and Sports Performance: A Systematic Review with Meta-Analysis', *Sports Medicine*, 52(2), pp. 301–330. Available at: https://doi.org/10.1007/s40279-021-01566-y.

Kotsifaki, A. *et al.* (2022) 'Symmetry in Triple Hop Distance Hides Asymmetries in Knee Function After ACL Reconstruction in Athletes at Return to Sports', *The American Journal of Sports Medicine*, 50(2), pp. 441–450. Available at: https://doi.org/10.1177/03635465211063192.

Krespi, M., Sporiš, G. and Trajković, N. (2020) 'Effects of Two Different Tapering Protocols on Fitness and Physical Match Performance in Elite Junior Soccer Players', *Journal of Strength and Conditioning Research*, 34(6), pp. 1731–1740. Available at: https://doi.org/10.1519/JSC.0000000000002861.

Kyles, A. *et al.* (2023) 'Linear and Change of Direction Repeated Sprint Ability Tests: A Systematic Review', *Journal of Strength and Conditioning Research*, 37(8), pp. 1703–1717. Available at: https://doi.org/10.1519/JSC.0000000000004447.

Light, N. and Thorborg, K. (2016) 'The Precision and Torque Production of Common Hip Adductor Squeeze Tests Used in Elite Football', *Journal of Science and Medicine in Sport*, 19(11), pp. 888–892. Available at: https://doi.org/10.1016/j.jsams.2015.12.009.

Maestroni, L. *et al.* (2023) 'Comparison of Strength and Power Characteristics Before ACL Rupture and at the End of Rehabilitation before Return to Sport in Professional Soccer Players', *Sports Health: A Multidisciplinary Approach*, 15(6), p. 194173812311715. Available at: https://doi.org/10.1177/19417381231171566.

Malone, S. *et al.* (2018) 'High-speed Running and Sprinting as an Injury Risk Factor in Soccer: Can Well-developed Physical Qualities Reduce the Risk?', *Journal of Science and Medicine in Sport*, 21(3), pp. 257–262. Available at: https://doi.org/10.1016/j.jsams.2017.05.016.

Manoel, L.S. *et al.* (2020) 'Identification of Ankle Injury Risk Factors in Professional Soccer Players Through a Preseason Functional Assessment', *Orthopaedic Journal of Sports Medicine*, 8(6), p. 232596712092843. Available at: https://doi.org/10.1177/2325967120928434.

Martínez-Hernández, D., Quinn, M. and Jones, P. (2023) 'Linear Advancing Actions Followed by Deceleration and Turn Are the Most Common Movements Preceding Goals in Male Professional Soccer', *Science and Medicine in Football*, 7(1), pp. 25–33. Available at: https://doi.org/10.1080/24733938.2022.2030064.

Moran, R.W. *et al.* (2017) 'Do Functional Movement Screen (FMS) Composite Scores Predict Subsequent Injury? A Systematic Review with Meta-analysis', *British Journal of Sports Medicine*, 51(23), pp. 1661–1669. Available at: https://doi.org/10.1136/bjsports-2016-096938.

Mosler, A.B. *et al.* (2015) 'Which Factors Differentiate Athletes with Hip/Groin Pain from Those Without? A Systematic Review with Meta-Analysis', *British Journal of Sports Medicine*, 49(12), pp. 810–810. Available at: https://doi.org/10.1136/bjsports-2015-094602.

Nimphius, S. *et al.* (2018) 'Change of Direction and Agility Tests: Challenging Our Current Measures of Performance', *Strength and Conditioning Journal*, 40(1), pp. 26–38. Available at: https://doi.org/10.1519/SSC.0000000000000309.

Otero-Esquina, C. et al. (2017) 'Is Strength-training Frequency a Key Factor to Develop Performance Adaptations in Young Elite Soccer Players?', *European Journal of Sport Science*, 17(10), pp. 1241–1251. Available at: https://doi.org/10.1080/17461391.2017.1378372.

Rago, V. *et al.* (2018) 'Countermovement Jump Analysis Using Different Portable Devices: Implications for Field Testing', *Sports*, 6(3), p. 91. Available at: https://doi.org/10.3390/sports6030091.

Ribeiro-Alvares, J.B. *et al.* (2020) 'Prevalence of Hamstring Strain Injury Risk Factors in Professional and Under-20 Male Football (Soccer) Players', *Journal of Sport Rehabilitation*, 29(3), pp. 339–345. Available at: https://doi.org/10.1123/jsr.2018-0084.

Sheppard, J.M. and Doyle, T.L.A. (2008) 'Increasing Compliance to Instructions in the Squat Jump', *Journal of Strength and Conditioning Research*, 22(2), pp. 648–651. Available at: https://doi.org/10.1519/JSC.0b013e31816602d4.

Shushan, T. *et al.* (2022) 'Submaximal Fitness Tests in Team Sports: A Theoretical Framework for Evaluating Physiological State', *Sports Medicine*, 52(11), pp. 2605–2626. Available at: https://doi.org/10.1007/s40279-022-01712-0.

Taylor, J.M. *et al.* (2019) 'The Reliability of a Modified 505 Test and Change-of-Direction Deficit Time in Elite Youth Football Players', *Science and Medicine in Football*, 3(2), pp. 157–162. Available at: https://doi.org/10.1080/24733938.2018.1526402.

Timmins, R.G. *et al.* (2016) 'Short Biceps Femoris Fascicles and Eccentric Knee Flexor Weakness Increase the Risk of Hamstring Injury in Elite Football (Soccer): A Prospective Cohort Study', *British Journal of Sports Medicine*, 50(24), pp. 1524–1535. Available at: https://doi.org/10.1136/bjsports-2015-095362.

Vigne, G. *et al.* (2010) 'Activity Profile in Elite Italian Soccer Team', *International Journal of Sports Medicine*, 31(5), pp. 304–310. Available at: https://doi.org/10.1055/s-0030-1248320.

Wang, R. *et al.* (2016) 'Isometric Mid-Thigh Pull Correlates with Strength, Sprint, and Agility Performance in Collegiate Rugby Union Players', *Journal of Strength and Conditioning Research*, 30(11), pp. 3051–3056. Available at: https://doi.org/10.1519/JSC.0000000000001416.

Xu, J. *et al.* (2023) 'A Systematic Review of the Different Calculation Methods for Measuring Jump Height during the Countermovement and Drop Jump Tests', *Sports Medicine*, 53(5), pp. 1055–1072. Available at: https://doi.org/10.1007/s40279-023-01828-x.

7

TRAINING LOAD MONITORING IN FOOTBALL

Matthew Weston, Antonio Dello Iacono, and Shaun J. McLaren

Introduction

Be it matches or training, the physical demands of football are complex, requiring frequent changes in the type, speed, intensity, and direction of movement, thus resulting in an intermittent activity profile that requires contributions from aerobic and anaerobic energy systems (Morgans et al., 2014). This suggests the development of well-rounded physical capacities (i.e., speed, agility, strength, and endurance) is a priority for the strength and conditioning coach (Taylor et al., 2022). The completion of a large number of fitness-based training sessions is difficult in football though, given the skill nature of the sport technical and technical sessions take priority over all other training activities (Morgans et al., 2014). As such, daily training sessions often encompass different activities, all of which will likely have distinct physical objectives and profiles. In the interest of time efficiency, training drills that involve a combination of physical and technical/tactical training activities dominate the football training environment. Players' training responses (i.e., training effects) are often, therefore, a consequence of coach-planned training (Weston, 2018) which can a cause disparity between the prescribed (i.e., anticipated) dose and the actual (i.e., monitored) response.

Training load is often associated with the concept of monitoring, but for best practice, it should be both planned and monitored to allow for an optimal review and evaluation as part of best practice (Figure 7.1). At an organisational level, the primary goal of training monitoring should be to assist and inform the coach/ manager of decision-making on player availability for training (Bourdon et al., 2017). At the individual level, the quantification of training is of critical importance for football practitioners aiming to optimise the training process (Martin et al., 2022). The practice of training monitoring and its value for informing

DOI: 10.4324/9781003383475-8

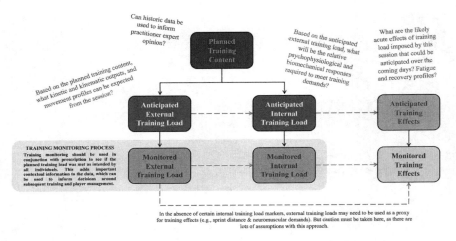

FIGURE 7.1 Nomological network showing the role of monitoring in the training process of football players. Understanding planned training content and anticipated training loads is crucial for a robust interpretation of training monitoring data.

the training process is not new, however. Despite the sport originally relying on fitness tests for training monitoring, Impellizzeri and colleagues long since recognised that further improvements in the physical fitness of football players are achievable by monitoring the training process rather than just the outcome (Impellizzeri et al., 2005). From the early 2000s, the monitoring of players' heart rates during small-sided games showed an intensity (~90% maximal heart rate [HR_{max}]) equivalent to that attained during high-intensity interval running, but a lower intensity (~72%HR_{max}) for technical/tactical drills (Sassi et al., 2004). These data suggested that small-group work with the ball presents a high-intensity training stimulus, whereas technical/tactical training presents only a moderate challenge to the circulatory system.

The number of football training monitoring scientific studies has grown exponentially over the past 20 years (Figure 7.2). This is largely a consequence of technological advancements in activity measurement devices that provide staff with detailed information on the outcomes of the training as a whole and its component parts (e.g., drills) as well as on the players' response to training. The extent of this growth is evidenced by training monitoring now being a daily practice in football clubs, with performance staff responsible for collecting and interpreting large volumes of training data and providing daily feedback to coaches (Akenhead and Nassis, 2016). To perhaps justify the extra time and resources spent on training monitoring, the worth of this practice has been examined beyond the quantification of how players respond to prescribed training. Here, studies have focused on the utility of training monitoring for evidencing and explaining injury risk, dose-response, and readiness to play. Despite some practitioners and coaches

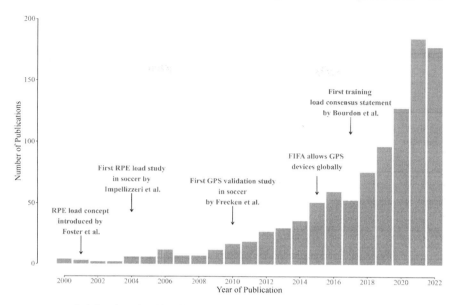

FIGURE 7.2 Publication timeline for training load studies in football from 2000 to 2022 (PubMed search = [training load] AND [football]) along with landmark studies and events.

perceiving the primary purpose of training monitoring to reduce injury (Weston, 2018), training data provide an unreliable assessment of injury risk (Kalkhoven et al., 2020). For example, Lolli et al. (2020) found limited evidence for the role of perceived exertion and training session duration as etiological factors of hamstring injury in professional football. Dose-response investigations provide useful insights into the association between training and fitness changes, with positive relationships reported (Martin et al., 2022; Jaspers et al., 2016). The strength of the relationship between dose and response varies by training mode and metric, however (McLaren et al., 2018), and therefore a direct link between dose and response should not be assumed (Impellizzeri et al., 2019). Numerous observational studies (for a review see Silva et al., 2023) have evidenced player 'readiness to play' via the tapering of training across the shortest planning cycle in football (i.e., tactical periodisation). Irrespective of the monitoring variable, variation across the week is largely consistent with that originally presented by Impellizzeri and colleagues in 2004, whereby training response varied across the week and was lowest for the training session in closest proximity to the match (i.e., matchday-1) (Figure 7.3).

Nonetheless, training monitoring should primarily focus on whether a player is undertaking the prescribed training, along with contributing to the assessment of how they cope with prescribed loads (Kalkhoven et al., 2020). That is, training sessions are monitored to ascertain if session objectives have been met (Weston,

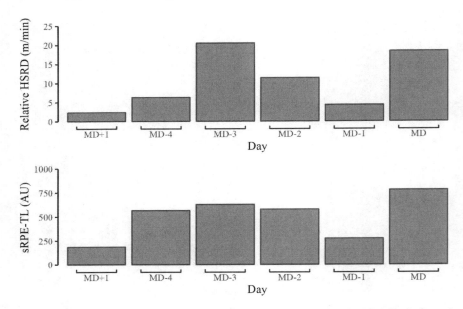

FIGURE 7.3 Variation of daily (matchday, MD) external (HSRD, ≥ 14.4 km·h^{-1}) and internal (session RPE training load, [sRPE-TL]) training load across the training micro-cycle of a professional football team.

2013). The aim of this chapter is therefore to explore some of the most pertinent scientific considerations during the training monitoring process, with a specific focus on enhancing the practice of training load monitoring during pitch-based training sessions in football.

Training Load Monitoring

The training prescribed and performed by players is often categorised as external training load or internal training load. External training load represents the physical outputs performed by the players and, through the use of Global Positioning Systems (GPS), accelerometers, and gyroscopes, (i.e., distance, speed, accelerations, and decelerations) is now relatively straight forward to measure (Impellizzeri et al., 2019). Internal training load represents the response to an external training load and should be an indicator used to prescribe exercise intensity (Impellizzeri et al., 2019); this can be objective, via heart rates and blood lactates, or subjective, via Ratings of Perceived Exertion (RPE). Of these measures, recent surveys in elite professional football reported GPS, heart rates, and RPE as the most frequent methods for training monitoring in elite male and female football (Akenhead and Nassis, 2016; Weston, 2018; Luteberget et al., 2021) and to ensure an equal balance between player perception and quantifiable practice a combination of objective and subjective tools is recommended (Bourdon et al., 2017).

Internal Training Load Monitoring

The importance of training monitoring via measures of internal training load is emphasised by the stimulus for exercise-induced adaptations being the relative stress imposed on players (Impellizzeri et al., 2004). Here, we focus on issues impacting the collection and interpretation of training heart rates and RPE.

Heart Rates

The historical development of heart rate monitoring in football is comprehensively detailed elsewhere (e.g., Dellal et al., 2012). Briefly, however, the rationale for measuring heart rate during exercise is that the measurement provides an indicator of cardiopulmonary stress and given the close relationship with oxygen uptake, heart rate during training provides a good marker of exercise intensity (Buchheit, 2014). In an overview of common training monitoring methods, heart rate monitoring was reported to have a low-to-medium cost, medium-to-high ease of use, reliability, and validity, and can be used to prescribe and interpret training (Bourdon et al., 2017). While heart rate monitoring during training was traditionally associated with endurance sports, the practice lends itself well to the football training environment as the devices used to measure heart rate are non-invasive and can be applied routinely and simultaneously across a large number of athletes (Buchheit, 2014). For example, 40 of 41 worldwide clubs surveyed collected heart rates on all players during every pitch-based training session (Akenhead and Nassis, 2016). Popularity was less within English football ($\sim$15%), a consequence of these practitioners and coaches working with younger players and at clubs with fewer resources for training monitoring (Weston, 2018).

In the context of training prescription, the physical demand of football necessitates high-speed running and sprinting; therefore, the combination of game-based running exercises and football circuit-based drills is advised (Gualtieri et al., 2023). However, alongside factors that impact exercise heart rates (e.g., hydration status, time of day, day-to-day variation, training status, and emotional state), practitioners should be cognisant that during intense intermittent exercise heart rate can respond slowly to rapid changes in intense activity (Impellizzeri et al., 2019). Consequently, heart rate is a less valid indicator of internal training load in the short duration, intermittent high-intensity efforts that constitute many pitch-based football training activities (Dellal et al., 2012; Impellizzeri et al., 2019). Nonetheless, it is still possible for elevated heart rates ($\sim$90%HR_{max}) to be attained during repeated short intervals (i.e., 15 seconds) (Dellal et al., 2012) which makes heart rate monitoring a useful tool for the strength and conditioning coach. The benefits of using heart rates to prescribe training intensity are long established as demonstrated by the early studies on the interpretation of small-sided game intensity (e.g., Sassi et al., 2004) and the prescription of high-intensity interval running for improving fitness and match running performance (e.g., Helgerud et al., 2001).

112 Strength and Conditioning for Football

In the context of training monitoring, the attention of coaches has shifted to examining external loads (Akenhead and Nassis, 2016; Impellizzeri et al., 2019), leading to one practitioner stating that "heart rate monitoring had become forgotten" (Austin, 2018). A possible explanation here is that when using heart rates to prescribe training intensity a visual display (e.g., wrist monitor) is required for players to calibrate running speed to the desired training heart rate. Nowadays, however, it is common for heart rate data to be collected on the same device used to collect GPS data with wrist monitors less likely to be worn during training sessions. In the absence of real-time feedback, either via a wrist monitor or dashboard-driven practitioner feedback, the value of heart rate monitoring during football training may therefore lie in the interpretation of training intensity.

When using heart rates to interpret training, values should ideally be expressed relative to a player's maximal heart rate ($\%HR_{max}$) with maximal being defined as the highest plausible value obtained during matches, training, or fitness tests (Weston et al., 2004). This will facilitate an accurate within-player intensity analysis. Useful metrics for the monitoring of training via heart rates are session peak, session average, or time spent in different zones, either arbitrary (e.g., $<60\%HR_{max}$, 60–75%, 76–85%, 86–93%, >93%) or zones anchored to the individual response obtained from a laboratory, or ideally a field-based fitness assessment.

Given aforementioned challenges of using heart rate monitoring during football training activities, it is recommended that the interpretation of training heart rates is combined with additional measures (Dellal et al., 2012). Valuable information can still be gleaned from the interpretation of heart rates alone, however. For example, Figure 7.4 shows the heart rate response from a wide defender during two training sessions. The session in the lower panel, when first viewed looks like an impressively intensive training session with substantial time spent training between 90% and $100\%HR_{max}$ (red zone). On discussion with the coaches however, the session was actually technical/tactical training performed on the morning of an evening match and the coaches were unaware of the intensity imposed on the player. Following feedback on the intensive nature of the training session, the coaches then subsequently reduced the intensity of these sessions to a level more appropriate for the morning of an evening match. These positive changes in training practice were achieved with heart rate being the club's sole method of training monitoring.

While heart rate provides a measure of exercise intensity, training sessions are the product of intensity and duration. In an attempt to combine these variables into a single metric, a training impulse score (TRIMP) can be derived. For more details on this approach, readers are directed to McLaren et al. (2022b). A pragmatic approach here is the accumulated duration in each of five different heart rate zones multiplied by a weighted score for each zone (i.e., $<60\%HR_{max} = 1$; 60–75% = 2; 76–85% = 3; 86–93% = 4; >93% = 5). The summation of the five scores represents an objective measure of internal training load (i.e., HR load).

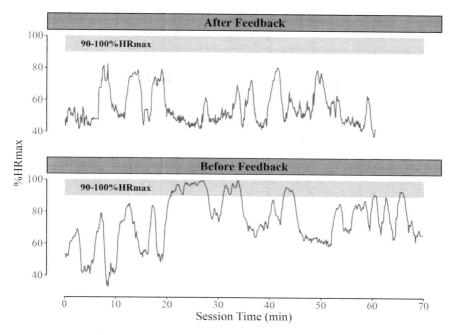

FIGURE 7.4 Matchday training heart rates before and after feedback to coaches on session intensity.

Ratings of Perceived Exertion

RPE represent a low-cost, highly usable measure that possesses moderate-to-high reliability and validity and can be used to prescribe and interpret training intensity (Bourdon et al., 2017). The prescription and interpretation of RPE are invariably linked given that the pre-determined RPE used for regulating exercise intensity are anchored to an intensity determined from the interpretation of previous sessions (Groslambert and Mahon, 2006). RPE are a prominent method for training monitoring in elite male and female football (Akenhead and Nassis, 2016; Weston, 2018; Luteberget et al., 2021). Irrespective of usage (i.e., prescription or interpretation), ratings can be assigned to segments of a training session, or, more commonly, used as a gestalt (referred to as the session RPE [sRPE]), that represents either an approximated average of the entire training session or a summation of session component parts (Foster et al., 2001). While the scientific literature is by no means an accurate representation of club training monitoring practices, research using RPE is predominantly for interpreting training intensity rather than prescription. This may in part be due to football training sessions often being the composite of discrete training activities that likely have different intensity requirements. Other explanations could be the difficulty of precisely estimating an individual's internal training load prior to exercise (Impellizzeri et al., 2019), studies showing

114 Strength and Conditioning for Football

incongruence between sRPE values prescribed with the sRPE reported by players, the practical utility of using sRPE in an attempt to understand dose-response, and the shift toward external training load dominance of training prescription (i.e., running speeds). Irrespective of its designated use, it is important practitioners follow good scientific practices that promote the collection of robust sRPE.

When RPE is collected, the importance of using a validated scale cannot be understated. Non-validated scales, such as those with additional features like colour, facial expressions (e.g., emojis), or images, introduce response bias whereby response is influenced by the perception of a scale feature instead of the perception of exertion (McLaren et al., 2022a). Practitioners are therefore recommended to use the CR10 or CR100 scales (Borg and Kaijser, 2006) and these scales can be used interchangeably (Fanchini et al., 2016). Beyond scale selection, other important issues to consider when collecting sRPE to monitor training are player instructions and the timing of data collection. To focus players' attention on providing an accurate estimation of their training session exertion, it is recommended that players assign their rating according to the verbal anchors (e.g., easy, hard, etc.) and not rely on the numbers associated with each exertion category. This way, integer bias can be avoided. Furthermore, players should be consistently reminded to rate their perceived exertion and not any other exercise-related sensation (i.e., fatigue). While it was initially recommended that sRPE were collected from the players after a period that permitted reflection on the entire session (~30 minutes), this practice is not always possible. A reflection period is not necessarily required however, given that studies have consistently shown the temporal robustness of sRPE (i.e., reliable over time). It is also recommended that data are collected by approaching players in isolation as sRPE is more likely rated higher when collected in a group setting (Minett et al., 2022). For further details on recommendations for collecting sRPE, readers are referred to McLaren and colleagues (2022a).

A limitation of sRPE in football is that when used as a single score it may lack sensitivity to capture the stochastic demands of football training or matches. For example, despite substantial match-to-match variation in an individual's high-speed running distance (HSRD), match sRPE was either 6.0, 6.5, or 7.0 AU (~hard) (Figure 7.5). Although increased sensitivity may be offered using the CR100 instead of the CR10, as evidenced by less verbal anchor clustering (Fanchini et al., 2016; Lovell et al., 2020), from a practical perspective, asking players to provide differentiated RPE (dRPE) (i.e., separate ratings for the perceived central or respiratory exertion (e.g., breathlessness) and peripheral or local exertion (e.g., leg muscle) (McLaren et al., 2022a)) can provide a more detailed interpretation of training intensity. Differential RPE represent distinct psychophysiological exertional constructs in team sports and have demonstrated face, content, and construct validity (McLaren et al., 2022a). Here, the same advice provided for the collection of reliable and valid sRPE is recommended when collecting dRPE.

Similar to heart rate, a TRIMP can be generated when sRPE is multiplied by session duration with the resultant number representing the subjective internal training

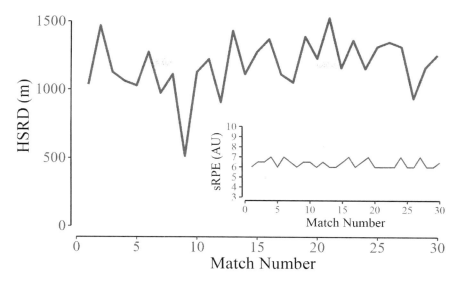

FIGURE 7.5 Limited variation in match sRPE despite substantial match-to-match variation in high-speed running distance (HSRD, ≥ 19.8 km·h^{-1}).

load (sRPE-TL). Despite obvious practical appeal (e.g., dashboard analysis), the integration of training data into one summary score is not without limitation though as this practice may come at the cost of losing relevant information and TRIMP scores may not differentiate between training session types (van der Zwaard et al., 2023). Furthermore, the calculation of dRPE load is not recommended (i.e., sRPE-L × duration), as session duration is constant, so any differences in dRPE load merely represent differences in exercise intensity. The practical utility of sRPE-TL is evident via a visual examination of a player's session-to-session and cycle-to-cycle subjective internal training loads. When interpreted alongside heart rate load, the relationship between the two variables can provide insight into how players are adapting to their training programme. For example, similar heart rate loads from a standardised training session when accompanied with lower sRPE may indicate a positive training adaptation. A similar process of uncoupling between internal and external training loads can provide further insights into how players cope with their training (Impellizzeri et al., 2019). This approach to training monitoring facilitates an easy visual examination of a player's session-to-session and cycle-to-cycle training loads (Figure 7.6), which in turn provides an informed standpoint for the programming of future training sessions and cycles.

External Training Load Monitoring

As the relationship between external and internal training load varies by training type (McLaren et al., 2018), an understanding of the work performed by players

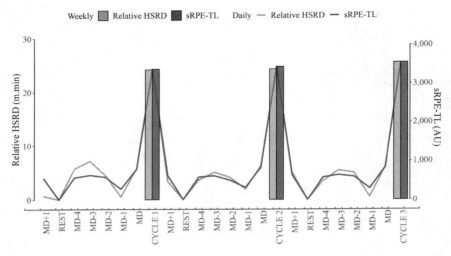

FIGURE 7.6 Visualisation of daily (matchday, MD) and microcycle (Cycle) external (relative high-speed running distance [HSRD]) and internal (session RPE training load, [sRPE-TL]) training loads across three one-match micro-cycles for a professional football player.

is an integral part of the training monitoring process (Impellizzeri et al., 2019). To understand a player's external training load, many measures can be used, ranging from low-cost, high-ease-of-use measures (e.g., time, session frequency) to high cost, low-ease-of-use measures (e.g., automated time-motion video analysis (Bourdon et al., 2017). The non-invasive nature of GPS devices (worn in a custom-made vest located between the scapula) facilitates the routine collection of external load data on football players during training and matches. Therefore, although use is moderated by club resources (Weston, 2018), time motion analysis via GPS technologies, is the most used external training load procedure in football training (Akenhead and Nassis, 2016; Weston, 2018; Luteberget et al., 2021) with focus on the variables of velocity, distance, acceleration, and time in zones (Bourdon et al., 2017).

While GPS-derived measures of external training load can be used to prescribe and interpret training, the science of external training load monitoring in football is weighted more towards training interpretation. For example, a recent retrospective evaluation of training session HSRDs, collected via portable micro-technologies, facilitated the quantification of elite football in-season periodisation strategies (Kelly et al., 2020). While useful, such data provide only an evaluation of practice, which is interesting but nothing more than confirmatory for practitioners in football. Irrespective of whether GPS-derived measures of external training load are used to prescribe or interpret training, it is important that practitioners bridge the gap between science and practice to maximise the quality of their data. For the remainder of this section, we therefore focus on two instances where recent scientific thought may positively influence external training load monitoring procedures in the football training environment; reliability and speed zone calculation.

Reliability

A key consideration with any measurement device is reliability, which can be defined as the consistency of a measure. This issue has dominated the scientific literature and is re-examined with each and every iteration of software and hardware. A certain degree of measurement error will always be present in any measurement device and practitioners need to decide on what represents an acceptable amount of error when making their decisions on external training load monitoring methods. The perception of what constitutes an acceptable amount of measurement error varies substantially between individuals given that 49 expert football practitioners felt the acceptable amount of measurement error when assessing maximal sprinting speed ranged from 0.0 to 0.5 $m \cdot s^{-1}$, with a median value of 0.2 $m \cdot s^{-1}$ (Kyprianou et al., 2019).

The standard error of measurement, expressed in raw units or as a % (i.e., the coefficient of variation [CV]) is often cited as a statistical measure of reliability, with lower values suggestive of greater reliability. Too frequently, however, reliability benchmarks have been used to guide interpretation, with device reliability assumed with a CV < 5%. This does not represent good practice as small, meaningful changes (i.e., the signal) may not be distinguishable from measurement error (i.e., the noise). Therefore, devices used for external training load monitoring should possess sufficient sensitivity to distinguish signal from noise which will facilitate the correct interpretation of meaningful between-training session changes at the individual level. However, another worrying practice here is that measurement sensitivity is often calculated and interpreted via standardisation, whereby CV magnitude is interpreted against the 'smallest worthwhile change' which is frequently calculated by 0.2 × between-player standard deviations. Despite its widespread popularity, practitioners are discouraged from this approach as standardisation can produce unrealistic values within a homogenous, elite squad. For example, only 15/49 of the experts surveyed reported an acceptable amount of measurement error as low as a standardised value (Kyprianou et al., 2019). So, in the context of measurement sensitivity practitioners are encouraged to interpret reliability against meaningful change values derived from personal experience and evidence-based knowledge and not against absolute or standardised thresholds (Ferguson et al., 2023).

Reliability is one of three key measurement properties that any useful training load matrix should possess. Alongside validity and sensitivity, measures of training load should be feasible within the context of implementation, including cost, time efficiency, the requirement of additional resources or skills, and the ability to scale to large playing squads (Figure 7.7).

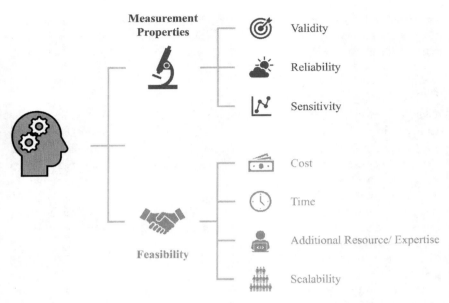

FIGURE 7.7 Factors to consider when selecting training load metrics in football. While simple, there are deeper considerations around some areas such as validity (e.g., validity of the construct, validity of the technology).

Speed Zone Calculation

External training loads are very often expressed in terms of the distances covered in selected speed zones (e.g., high-intensity running [19.8 km·h^{-1}] and sprinting [25.2 km·h^{-1}]) with these speed zones originally delineated by absolute, and often arbitrary speed thresholds (Gualtieri et al., 2023). Unfortunately, the origin of these zones is unclear, most likely a product of commercial companies specialising in tracking data for player monitoring rather than any scientifically agreed criteria (Drust, 2018). Furthermore, there is no consensus in the football scientific literature about standard thresholds defining zones of running intensities (Figure 7.8). Arbitrary speed thresholds fail to individualise external training loads relative to a player's specific movement speeds or physiological capacity (Weston, 2013), potentially underestimating the amount of high-speed running and sprinting performed by less fit, slower players and overestimating in fitter, faster players. This can lead to an incorrect interpretation of player external training loads (Gualtieri et al., 2023).

Such limitations necessitated the investigation of individualised speed zones whereby zones are expressed relative to physical capacities and most GPS software now afford the customisability of speed zones (Malone et al., 2017). Individualised GPS-derived external training loads have been anchored to fitness test performance, with maximal aerobic speed and maximal sprint speed

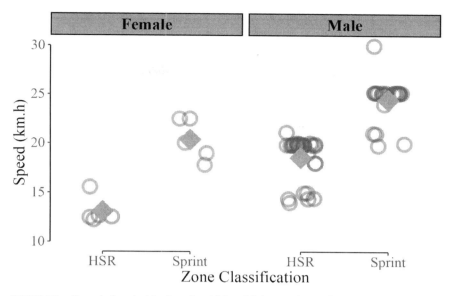

FIGURE 7.8 Speed thresholds for classifying high-speed running (HSR) and sprinting in elite football (open circles = individual studies (see Gualtieri et al., [2023]), orange diamond = zone mean).

as the common metrics (Iacono et al., 2023). The theory here is that external training loads expressed relative to a players' fitness characteristics will better explain the relationship between physical performance and response, i.e., the external-internal training load relationship. While this practice has obvious theoretical merit, its practical value has been questioned. For example, individualised speed thresholds failed to enhance the external-internal training load relationship in elite female football players when compared to the use of arbitrary speed zones (Scott and Lovell, 2018). Current evidence is therefore equivocal on the merit of individualised speed zones, which may explain why football practitioners use predominantly absolute speeds or absolute speeds combined with individualised speeds for determining high-speed running and sprinting thresholds. A final consideration here is that commonly used absolute (e.g., 19.8, 25.2 km·h^{-1}) and individualised (~50%, ~70% of maximal sprinting speed) high-speed running and sprinting speeds may correspond with jogging and striding, thereby underestimating true demands and in turn potentially underpreparing players for matches (Freeman et al., 2023).

Overall, it is recommended that to best monitor a football players' training load, objective and subjective training loads are collected and interpreted in the context of external training loads. Alongside these scientific measures, the value of coach perception of training monitoring should not be underestimated, and fortunately, this method is prevalent in football (Weston, 2018).

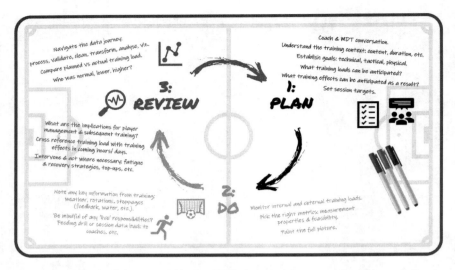

FIGURE 7.9 The Training Load Tactics Whiteboard. A best-practice approach for the planning, monitoring, and evaluation of training load in football.

Practical Applications

Training load monitoring is fundamental to understand the relationships and causal effects of training processes on surrogate measures of football performance or health-related outcomes. Upon adopting reliable technological tools, procedures and measures to monitor training load, the first step is to define the purpose(s) of monitoring strategies for a correct interpretation of the collected outputs. Then, to assess whether players perform, respond, and adapt to training as planned, football practitioners should consider a combination of internal and external training load measures, explore their relationships in the context of training as well as investigate the causal mechanisms linked to the outcome(s) of interest (Figure 7.9). When comprehensive training load monitoring strategies are unavailable, with barriers stemming from the lack of financial resources, designated professional personnel, and the skills required to leverage and analyse sensor-level data, the value of coaches' perception of training monitoring should not be underestimated. However, the accuracy and sensitivity of this practice should be empirically corroborated further as the lack of agreement between the coach-perceived and athlete-perceived (i.e., internal) or actual (i.e., external) training loads may place athletes at a greater risk of maladaptive practices resulting in a deterioration of performance or injury and illness.

References

Akenhead, R., and Nassis, G. P. (2016). Training Load and Player Monitoring in High-Level Football: Current Practice and Perceptions. *International Journal of Sports Physiology and Performance*, *11*(5), 587–593. https://doi.org/10.1123/ijspp.2015-0331

Austin, S. (2018, December 21). How Arsenal Use Heart Rate Monitoring. https://trainingground.guru/articles/how-arsenal-use-heart-rate-monitoring

Borg, E., and Kaijser, L. (2006). A Comparison between Three Rating Scales for Perceived Exertion and Two Different Work Tests. *Scandinavian Journal of Medicine and Science in Sports*, *16*(1), 57–69. https://doi.org/10.1111/j.1600-0838.2005.00448.x

Bourdon, P. C., Cardinale, M., Murray, A., Gastin, P., Kellmann, M., Varley, M. C., Gabbett, T. J., Coutts, A. J., Burgess, D. J., Gregson, W., and Cable, N. T. (2017). Monitoring Athlete Training Loads: Consensus Statement. *International Journal of Sports Physiology and Performance*, *12*(Suppl 2), S2-161–S2-170. https://doi.org/10.1123/ijspp.2017-0208

Buchheit, M. (2014). Monitoring Training Status with HR Measures: Do All Roads Lead to Rome? *Frontiers in Physiology*, *5*, 73. https://doi.org/10.3389/fphys.2014.00073

Dellal, A., da Silva, C. D., Hill-Haas, S., Wong, D. P., Natali, A. J., Lima, J. R. P. D., Filho, M. G. B. B., Marins, J. J. C. B., Garcia, E. S., and Karim, C. (2012). Heart Rate Monitoring in Football. *Journal of Strength and Conditioning Research*, *26*(10), 2890–2906. https://doi.org/10.1519/jsc.0b013e3182429ac7

Drust, B. (2018). An Individual Approach to Monitoring Locomotive Training Load in English Premier League Academy Football Players. *International Journal of Sports Science and Coaching*, *13*(3), 429–430. https://doi.org/10.1177/1747954118771182

Fanchini, M., Ferraresi, I., Modena, R., Schena, F., Coutts, A. J., and Impellizzeri, F. M. (2016). Use of the CR100 Scale for Session Rating of Perceived Exertion in Football and Its Interchangeability with the CR10. *International Journal of Sports Physiology and Performance*, *11*(3), 388–392. https://doi.org/10.1123/ijspp.2015-0273

Ferguson, J., Gibson, N. V., Weston, M., and McCunn, B. (2023). Reliability of Measures of Lower Body Strength and Speed in Academy Male Adolescent Football Players. *Journal of Strength and Conditioning Research*, 2024 Mar 1;*38*(3), e96–103.

Foster, C., Florhaug, J. A., Franklin, J., Gottschall, L., Hrovatin, L. A., Parker, S., Doleshal, P., and Dodge, C. (2001). A New Approach to Monitoring Exercise Training. *Journal of Strength and Conditioning Research*, *15*(1), 109–115.

Freeman, B. W., Talpey, S. W., James, L. P., Opar, D. A., and Young, W. B. (2023). Common High-Speed Running Thresholds Likely Do Not Correspond to High-Speed Running in Field Sports. *Journal of Strength and Conditioning Research*, *37*(7), 1411–1418. https://doi.org/10.1519/jsc.0000000000004421

Groslambert, A., and Mahon, A. D. (2006). Perceived Exertion. *Sports Medicine*, *36*(11), 911–928. https://doi.org/10.2165/00007256-200636110-00001

Gualtieri, A., Rampinini, E., Iacono, A. D., and Beato, M. (2023). High-Speed Running and Sprinting in Professional Adult Football: Current Thresholds Definition, Match Demands and Training Strategies. A Systematic Review. *Frontiers in Sports and Active Living*, *5*, 1116293. https://doi.org/10.3389/fspor.2023.1116293

Helgerud, J., Engen, L. C., Wisloff, U., and Hoff, J. (2001). Aerobic Endurance Training Improves Football Performance. *Medicine and Science in Sports and Exercise*, *33*(11), 1925–1931. https://doi.org/10.1097/00005768-200111000-00019

Iacono, A. D., Beato, M., Unnithan, V. B., and Shushan, T. (2023). Programming High-Speed and Sprint Running Exposure in Football: Beliefs and Practices of More Than 100 Practitioners Worldwide. *International Journal of Sports Physiology and Performance*, *18*(7), 1–16. https://doi.org/10.1123/ijspp.2023-0013

Impellizzeri, F. M., Marcora, S. M., and Coutts, A. J. (2019). Internal and External Training Load: 15 Years On. *International Journal of Sports Physiology and Performance*, *14*(2), 270–273. https://doi.org/10.1123/ijspp.2018-0935

Impellizzeri, F. M., Rampinini, E., Coutts, A. J., Sassi, A., and Marcora, S. M. (2004). Use of RPE-Based Training Load in Football. *Medicine and Science in Sports and Exercise*, *36*(6), 1042–1047. https://doi.org/10.1249/01.mss.0000128199.23901.2f

Impellizzeri, F. M., Rampinini, E., and Marcora, S. M. (2005). Physiological Assessment of Aerobic Training in Football. *Journal of Sports Sciences*, *23*(6), 583–592. https://doi.org/10.1080/02640410400021278

Jaspers, A., Brink, M. S., Probst, S. G. M., Frencken, W. G. P., and Helsen, W. F. (2016). Relationships between Training Load Indicators and Training Outcomes in Professional Football. *Sports Medicine*, *47*(3), 533–544. https://doi.org/10.1007/s40279-016-0591-0

Kalkhoven, J. T., Watsford, M. L., Coutts, A. J., Edwards, W. B., and Impellizzeri, F. M. (2020). Training Load and Injury: Causal Pathways and Future Directions. *Sports Medicine*, *51*, 1–14. https://doi.org/10.1007/s40279-020-01413-6

Kelly, D. M., Strudwick, A. J., Atkinson, G., Drust, B., and Gregson, W. (2020). Quantification of Training and Match-Load Distribution across a Season in Elite English Premier League Football Players. *Science and Medicine in Football*, *4*(1), 59–67. https://doi.org/10.1080/24733938.2019.1651934

Kyprianou, E., Lolli, L., Haddad, H. A., Salvo, V. D., Varley, M. C., Villanueva, A. M., Gregson, W., and Weston, M. (2019). A Novel Approach to Assessing Validity in Sports Performance Research: Integrating Expert Practitioner Opinion into the Statistical Analysis. *Science and Medicine in Football*, *3*(4), 1–6. https://doi.org/10.1080/24733938.2019.1617433

Lolli, L., Bahr, R., Weston, M., Whiteley, R., Tabben, M., Bonanno, D., Gregson, W., Chamari, K., Salvo, V. D., and van Dyk, N. (2020). No Association between Perceived Exertion and Session Duration with Hamstring Injury Occurrence in Professional Football. *Scandinavian Journal of Medicine and Science in Sports*, *30*(3), 523–530. https://doi.org/10.1111/sms.13591

Lovell, R., Halley, S., Siegler, J., Wignell, T., Coutts, A. J., and Massard, T. (2020). Use of Numerically Blinded Ratings of Perceived Exertion in Football: Assessing Concurrent and Construct Validity. *International Journal of Sports Physiology and Performance*, *15*(10), 1430–1436. https://doi.org/10.1123/ijspp.2019-0740

Luteberget, L. S., Houtmeyers, K. C., Vanrenterghem, J., Jaspers, A., Brink, M. S., and Helsen, W. F. (2021). Load Monitoring Practice in Elite Women Association Football. *Frontiers in Sports and Active Living*, *3*, 715122. https://doi.org/10.3389/fspor.2021.715122

Malone, J. J., Lovell, R., Varley, M. C., and Coutts, A. J. (2017). Unpacking the Black Box: Applications and Considerations for Using GPS Devices in Sport. *International Journal of Sports Physiology and Performance*, *12*(Suppl 2), S2-18–S2-26. https://doi.org/10.1123/ijspp.2016-0236

Martin, M., Rampinini, E., Bosio, A., Azzalin, A., McCall, A., and Ward, P. (2022). Relationships Between Internal and External Load Measures and Fitness Level Changes in Professional Football Players. *Research Quarterly for Exercise and Sport*, *94*(3), 1–13. https://doi.org/10.1080/02701367.2022.2053646

McLaren, S. J., Coutts, A. J., and Impellizzeri, F. M. (2022a). Perception of Effort and Subjective Monitoring. In D. French and L. Torres Ronda (Eds.), *NSCA's Essentials of Sports Science* (1st ed., pp. 231–254). Human Kinetics.

McLaren, S. J., Impellizzeri, F. M., Coutts, A. J., and Weston, M. (2022b). *Sport and Exercise Physiology Testing Guidelines: Volume I – Sport Testing*, pp. 405–412. Routledge. https://doi.org/10.4324/9781003045281-74

McLaren, S. J., Macpherson, T. W., Coutts, A. J., Hurst, C., Spears, I. R., and Weston, M. (2018). The Relationships between Internal and External Measures of Training Load and

Intensity in Team Sports: A Meta-Analysis. *Sports Medicine*, *48*(3), 641–658. https://doi.org/10.1007/s40279-017-0830-z

Minett, G. M., Fels-Camilleri, V., Bon, J. J., Impellizzeri, F. M., and Borg, D. N. (2022). Peer Presence Increases Session Ratings of Perceived Exertion. *International Journal of Sports Physiology and Performance*, *17*(1), 106–110. https://doi.org/10.1123/ijspp.2021-0080

Morgans, R., Orme, P., Anderson, L., and Drust, B. (2014). Principles and Practices of Training for Football. *Journal of Sport and Health Science*, *3*(4), 251–257. https://doi.org/10.1016/j.jshs.2014.07.002

Sassi, R., Reilly, T., and Impellizzeri, F. M. (2004). A Comparison of Small-Sided Games and Interval Training in Elite Professional Football Players. *Journal of Sports Sciences*, *22*(6), 521–566. https://doi.org/10.1080/02640410410001675432

Scott, D., and Lovell, R. (2018). Individualisation of Speed Thresholds Does Not Enhance the Dose-Response Determination in Football Training. *Journal of Sports Sciences*, *36*(13), 1523–1532. https://doi.org/10.1080/02640414.2017.1398894

Silva, H., Nakamura, F. Y., Castellano, J., and Marcelino, R. (2023). Training Load Within a Football Microcycle Week—A Systematic Review. *Strength* and *Conditioning Journal*, *45*(5), 568–577. https://doi.org/10.1519/ssc.0000000000000765

Taylor, J. M., Madden, J. L., Cunningham, L. P., and Wright, M. (2022). Fitness Testing in Football Revisited: Developing a Contemporary Testing Battery. *Strength and Conditioning Journal*, *44*(5), 10–21. https://doi.org/10.1519/ssc.0000000000000702

van der Zwaard, S., Otter, R. T. A., Kempe, M., Knobbe, A., and Stoter, I. K. (2023). Capturing the Complex Relationship between Internal and External Training Load: A Data-Driven Approach. *International Journal of Sports Physiology and Performance*, *18*(6), 1–9. https://doi.org/10.1123/ijspp.2022-0493

Weston, M. (2013). Difficulties in Determining the Dose-Response Nature of Competitive Football Matches. *Journal of Athletic Enhancement*, *2*(1). https://doi.org/10.4172/2324-9080.1000e107

Weston, M. (2018). Training Load Monitoring in Elite English Football: A Comparison of Practices and Perceptions between Coaches and Practitioners. *Science and Medicine in Football*, *2*(3), 216–224. https://doi.org/10.1080/24733938.2018.1427883

Weston, M., Helsen, W., MacMahon, C., and Kirkendall, D. (2004). The Impact of Specific High-Intensity Training Sessions on Football Referees' Fitness Levels. *The American Journal of Sports Medicine*, *32*(1 Suppl), 54S–61S. https://doi.org/10.1177/0363546503261421

8

WELLNESS MONITORING AND READINESS IN FOOTBALL

Jo Clubb and Amber E. Rowell

Introduction

Capturing internal and external load is only one aspect of the load monitoring process. Human physiology and responses to training are complex, whereby the response to the same training stimulus can vary greatly between individuals and within the same individual on different days. Therefore, a comprehensive monitoring system should incorporate measures that determine how athletes are coping with the demands of training and competition, in order to utilise this information to optimise future training loads.

In sports science, the terms "readiness", "wellness", and "well-being" are often used in similar contexts to refer to the overall condition of an athlete. While we may use each of these terms in the following chapter, it is worth briefly discussing the subtle differences in their definition. Readiness refers to an athlete's ability to perform at their physical best on a given day. Specifically, optimal readiness has been described as "a condition where an athlete has no impairment of physical performance, no mental fatigue or excessive psychological distress" (Ryan et al., 2020). Wellness and well-being are terms often used ubiquitously and variably in health practice. They represent a broader context than the physical focus of readiness, also encompassing mental and emotional health, as well as more esoteric aspects of life satisfaction such as happiness (McMahon et al., 2010). Interestingly, McMahon and colleagues suggest that ownership of the terms lies with the user, given they are subjective and context-specific (McMahon et al., 2010). It is therefore worth considering one athlete's perception of well-being may be different from another.

Measuring such psychosocial phenomena is a challenge given the variety of intra- and inter-individual factors that interact. Athletes represent a complex

DOI: 10.4324/9781003383475-9

Wellness Monitoring and Readiness in Football **125**

adaptive system (CAS): a non-linear, dynamic system comprised of multiple embedded complex sub-systems (Montull et al., 2022). Contemporary athlete monitoring processes have, therefore, been criticised as reductionist: based on inaccurate views of athletes as linear and deterministic (Montull et al., 2022). We must acknowledge the limitations of our approaches, yet as sports science practitioners we have a responsibility to apply current scientific understanding along with tools and technology available to support the training process of our athletes. Therefore, there is an important role for wellness and readiness monitoring in assessing how footballers are coping with training load and making suitable adjustments to their training programme. Therefore, the aims of this chapter are to present the most commonly employed methods for wellness and readiness assessment in football, briefly explore their strengths and limitations, and discuss the keys to implementing such methods in the applied environment.

Methods for Assessing Readiness

Any tool for monitoring athlete readiness should be sensitive to training load, unaffected by other factors such as diet and chronobiological rhythms, and respond to acute exercise in a manner that is distinguishable from chronic changes in adaptation (Thorpe et al., 2017). Practically, readiness tools should be quick, non-invasive, and limit any additional loading on the athlete (Thorpe et al., 2017). For the practitioner, measurement and analysis should be cost-effective and parsimonious to enable timely feedback of information to key stakeholders. Specifically for football, the context of the competition schedule, recent playing and travel demands, and the time in season should all be considered in the planning, implementation, and analysis of readiness assessments. Here we review the plethora of potential assessments available to football practitioners for wellness and readiness monitoring.

Objective Methods

Wellness and readiness assessments are frequently grouped into *objective*, those that are externally quantified, often by some form of technology, and *subjective*, those that are self-reported based on internal feelings and perceptions. Therefore, we will use these same distinctions to group the tools. Objective methods can be considered as biochemical, cardiovascular, and neuromuscular measures.

Biochemical Measures

An array of haematological, hormonal, and immunological markers, measured from the blood, urine, or saliva, may be relevant to athlete readiness given the endocrine system's role in training response and adaptation. Creatine Kinase (CK) is an enzyme that is stored inside the muscle but is often released into the bloodstream

126 Strength and Conditioning for Football

after heavy exercise, indicating muscle damage. As a blood marker, CK has been shown to be elevated 48 hours after football match play, with a return to baseline by 72 hours (Tofari et al., 2018). However, it is only an indirect measure of muscle damage and may also be influenced by factors other than muscle damage alone, and as a result, post-exercise increases may be the consequence of normal metabolic activity rather than reflecting muscle damage. In addition, large individual variability and high day-to-day variation limit its use as a regular monitoring tool.

Glutamine and glutamate are amino acids whose functions include protein synthesis and acid-base balance regulation. Reduced plasma glutamine and elevated plasma glutamate have been observed following intense training and may be associated with impaired immune function (Coutts et al., 2007). Therefore, the glutamine: glutamate ratio may be sensitive to non-functional overreaching (Coutts et al., 2007). However, evidence on glutamine and glutamate responses is conflicting and limited in football populations.

Such haematological markers require regular blood sampling via venepuncture. Given the invasive nature of this method, salivary markers have been explored as a less invasive alternative (Cormack et al., 2008). Cortisol is a glucocorticoid that is released from the adrenal cortex in response to exercise stress, with a variety of functions in metabolism, including gluconeogenesis, lipolysis, and protein degradation, and is a marker of catabolic status (Kraemer and Ratamess, 2005). It is a stress-responsive hormone and has been shown to be elevated following football match play, although substantial individual variability has been observed (Cormack et al., 2008; Rowell et al., 2017). Similarly, testosterone; an androgenic anabolic steroid hormone with a role in protein synthesis, has also shown changes in response to match play and longitudinal loads, but its response also demonstrates wide individual variation (Rowell et al., 2017). The ratio between testosterone, an anabolic hormone, and cortisol, a catabolic hormone, is intuitively appealing. A testosterone:cortisol ratio (T:C) reduced by 30% or more is suggested to be reflective of a catabolic state, yet this is unlikely in team sports athletes (Cormack et al., 2008). Both increased training loads and match-play result in a reduced T:C, yet there is a lack of association between T:C and performance (Rowell et al., 2017, 2018). Research findings appear mixed, most likely due to the high level of variability in these hormones and the complex interaction between them (Cormack et al., 2008; Rowell et al., 2018).

Other biomarkers that appear sensitive to exercise and football match play include certain cytokines, such as interleukin 6, C-reactive protein, and uric acid (Thorpe et al., 2017). However, no definitive biomarker for readiness has thus far been identified (Thorpe et al., 2017). Biochemical markers are limited in their utility in the team sport setting, due to their invasive nature and wide variability. Historically, their strict, laboratory-like collection procedures have limited their practicality to monitoring in the football environment, in which frequent sampling, fast determination of results, and cost-efficiency are key requirements. Biomarkers do however provide a benefit as part of a (less regular) comprehensive

Wellness Monitoring and Readiness in Football **127**

health assessment. As technology evolves, there may be greater potential for more practical, non-invasive biochemical evaluations for athlete readiness.

Cardiovascular Measures

Heart rate (HR) indices provide objective measures of internal load during exercise. Used as indicators of the autonomic nervous system, HR measures have also been investigated as markers of training response. HR variability (HRV) refers to the variation in time between consecutive HRs (or *R*-to-*R* intervals), which provides information on the parasympathetic and sympathetic contributions to resting and post-exercise modulation of HR (Bellenger et al., 2016). Increases in resting HRV generally represent positive adaptations to training, yet overreaching may have little effect, and there appears to be disagreement in the direction of change in vagal-related HRV indices (Bellenger et al., 2016). Moreover, the use of HRV in football as a monitoring tool can be limited by practical efficacy, given the challenge of reliably measuring HRV, particularly with large groups. However, the growing trend of athletes having access to their own HRV via personal wearable devices warrants further discussion of how practitioners may leverage such data (see *Monitoring Readiness with Wearables*).

One approach to readiness assessment that utilises HR indices is the submaximal fitness test (SMFT). Put simply, an increase in aerobic fitness is associated with a decrease in HR in response to a fixed physical demand, thus it follows that a drill with a standardised external load could be used to assess fitness. Although over 100 different team sport SMFT have been described in the literature, the SMFT Taxonomy categorises them into five distinct groups; Continuous-fixed, Continuous-incremental, Intermittent-fixed, Intermittent-incremental, and Intermittent-variable (Shushan et al., 2023). Exercise HR (HRex) is the most utilised SMFT outcome measure, generally focuses on the final 30–60 seconds of the test, and has been proposed as a marker of short-term physiological stress (Shushan et al., 2023). HR Recovery (HRR) is the assessment of the decrease in HR following the end of exercise, representing coordinated sympathetic withdrawal and parasympathetic reactivation (Bellenger et al., 2016). HRex during SMFT is a reliable and valid proxy measure of endurance performance in team sports, but HRR is associated with an inferior degree of reliability (Shushan et al., 2023). HRR may also be limited by the challenge in controlling the recovery period after a drill, although perhaps it could be used by footballers conditioning individually between training camps, seasons or school semesters, where both the training and the recovery are more controlled.

While more research is needed to better understand changes as it relates to readiness, combining HRex with an SMFT may be a low-burden approach to conducting testing in-situ. Where this is built into the training session, this provides an 'invisible monitoring' approach, whereby additional testing beyond normal training is not required. This is appealing as it can provide greater insight into athlete

128 Strength and Conditioning for Football

readiness without increasing data-collection burden on the athlete (for more see *Invisible Monitoring* at the end of the chapter). Based on research thus far, the following protocol has been recommended (Shushan et al., 2023):

- Continuous protocol using a rectangle/track course;
- Fixed intensity that is likely to elicit ~75%–85% maximum HR, generally achieved by speeds between 10 and 14 km/h, depending on age, level, and sport;
- Suitable and repeated location within a training session (e.g., integrated into the warm-up);
- 3–4 minute exercise duration;
- Calculate HRex using the mean HR over the last 30–60 s of the test;
- Use a typical error of 1–2%
- Standardised location in the micro-cycle periodisation (e.g., 72 h post-match).

Monitoring Readiness with Wearables

The increasing popularity of wearable technology across society has also influenced athletes, who now have greater access to personal devices such as smartwatches, fitness monitors, and sleep trackers. Such devices may be issued by the team, league, and/or player association, but equally may be chosen by the individual. They can help to drive engagement and support education, such as providing the athlete with personal data relating to recovery and readiness following sleep hygiene education. However, cumulative metrics that represent so-called Readiness or Recovery Scores, largely based on cardiovascular measures, have limited or unknown validity and reliability. They can also increase anxiety, with the term "orthosomnia" coined to describe the obsessive pursuit of metrics from sleep trackers (Jahrami et al., 2023). Practitioners can provide support by discussing the pros and cons of such technology with their athletes.

As wearable technology continues to evolve, football clubs and practitioners need to be aware of data privacy issues. In 2022, football bodies FIFPRO and FIFA launched the Charter of Player Data Rights based on the fundamentals of the General Data Protection Regulation. This stated that all professional footballers have the right to; be informed, access, revoke, restrict processing, data portability, rectification, complain, and erasure. These rights are relevant to data derived from wearable devices, as well as all data collected on the athletes, so require an understanding by practitioners.

Neuromuscular Measures

Neuromuscular fatigue (NMF) is a reduction in maximal voluntary force induced by exercise that can take up to 72 hours to fully resolve (Thomas et al., 2018). It can be classified based on its origin: central; attributable to the central nervous system's inability to activate muscle to the required level, or peripheral; impairments in

Wellness Monitoring and Readiness in Football **129**

muscle function (Thomas et al., 2017). While both processes contribute significantly to NMF after match play, it is the larger magnitude and slower recovery of peripheral fatigue that primarily explains the recovery of NMF (Thomas et al., 2017). 'Gold standard' assessment of NMF involves direct muscle stimulation, either throughout or immediately following voluntary isometric contractions (Collins et al., 2018). However, this is not a feasible option for regular monitoring and alternative assessments of impaired neuromuscular function are frequently utilised.

Cycling Assessments

Based on the close relationship between increased fatigue and a reduction in power output, assessing peak power in a short, maximal effort may provide a useful measure of readiness (McLean et al., 2012). Given the short turn-around time between games in many football competitions, coupled with the desire to minimise time spent on legs outside of team training, a non-fatiguing peak power cycle ergometer test may provide a useful measure of power output and fatigue status without additional loading. Peak power, measured on a cycle ergometer, is shown to be sensitive to fatigue 48 hours post-team sport match play (Wehbe et al., 2015), as well as chronic fatigue witnessed across a season, demonstrated by comparing starter and non-starter responses in female college footballers (McLean et al., 2012).

One protocol recommends athletes perform a standardised warm-up, followed by two reps of 6 seconds of maximal cycle ergometer sprint efforts, separated by 1 minute of active recovery, with peak power determined as the highest achieved across both efforts (Wehbe et al., 2015). Such a protocol may be advantageous compared to jump testing due to limited lower limb loading, reduced weight-bearing and exposure to eccentric muscle actions, and greater practicality with a large group of athletes simultaneously (Wehbe et al., 2015). Conversely, cycling may not reflect the specific movements of team sport such as running and jumping, therefore readiness assessments using these types of movement demands have also been explored.

Sprint Assessments

Practitioners can use sprint times, as well as split times (e.g., 10 and 20 m), to track changes in sprint performance as a potential indicator of readiness. One testing protocol has used 3 maximal 20 m sprint efforts with timing gates to assess the time taken at 0–10 m, 10–20 m, and 0–20 m (Gathercole et al., 2015). A reduction in sprint performance has been identified immediately post-exercise, but this assessment appears to lack the sensitivity of a longer fatigue response (i.e. >24 h post-exercise), potentially due to a lower influence reliance on the stretch-shortening cycle in sprinting (Gathercole et al., 2015). Practically, sprint testing requires athletes to perform a maximal test "on legs", thereby adding to the training load, which may not be ideal. Anecdotally, there are often concerns relating to injury risk

130 Strength and Conditioning for Football

and additional maximal sprint testing. However, where sprints are regularly built into the team training, tracking outputs from player tracking technology longitudinally may enable a form of 'invisible monitoring'.

Jump Assessments

Jump testing has become increasingly popular in team sports for both screening (see Chapter 6) and monitoring purposes. This is likely due to its appeal as a simple, reliable, and time-efficient assessment that is closely related to the movement demands of such sports (Bishop et al., 2022). Jumps can be assessed using a digital optical encoder, force plate technology, accelerometer, or contact mat. A number of different protocols can be employed, including the countermovement jump (CMJ), squat jump (SJ), drop jump (DJ), and broad jump. The CMJ and DJ may be more sensitive to changes in altered neuromuscular function, given they utilise both concentric and eccentric muscle contractions, whereas the SJ utilises concentric only (Gathercole et al., 2015). The CMJ is probably the most commonly implemented jump test, owing to its natural movement pattern for athletes and the greater technical demands in the SJ and DJ (Bishop et al., 2022). Employing jump testing as a readiness assessment requires a consistent approach to the protocol (e.g., arm swing vs no arm swing), warm-up, cueing, and location within the micro-cycle periodisation.

A key challenge for jump testing is deciding which of the abundant metrics to focus on. A meta-analysis assessing the CMJ's ability to monitor neuromuscular status found 63 different metrics used across 151 studies, with jump height and peak power the most commonly reported despite not being sensitive to fatiguing protocols (Claudino et al., 2017). It is now well established that athletes can often maintain performance (i.e., jump height) when fatigued by altering their movement patterns (Cormack et al., 2008). This may present for example, as a decrement in flight time:contraction time (FT:CT) (Cormack et al., 2008; Rowell et al., 2017). As such, monitoring metrics that represent jump strategy, as well as the outcome, is essential. Specifically, time-related variables may reveal a shift in jump strategy caused by NMF, for instance athletes may achieve the same force and jump height but by taking a longer time (Bishop et al., 2022).

Time-based metrics can be tracked to detect when NMF is present, including; FT:CT, reactive strength index modified (RSImod), time to take-off, propulsive phase duration (also known as concentric phase duration), and time to peak power (Bishop et al., 2022). With these measures, particularly any ratios, the component parts should be monitored concurrently to understand what is driving any changes. With RSImod, for example, jump height and time to take-off represent the component parts and should be tracked and interpreted alongside RSImod. It is worth noting that FT:CT and RSImod share a similar calculation and an almost perfect relationship, so practitioners do not need to monitor both. Thought should also be given as to whether the maximum or average across trials is used for between-trial analysis, although more advanced data storage and analysis techniques may now allow for both to be tracked. Although maximum CMJ height is more commonly reported, average CMJ height has been shown to be more sensitive (Claudino et al., 2017). Analysis of jump assessments may go even further by investigating the complete force-time curve through advanced techniques such as waveform analysis.

Velocity-Based Training

Velocity-Based Training (VBT) enables autoregulation of training, whereby fluctuations in performance can be accounted for by adjusting resistance training loads (Weakley et al., 2021). This method measures concentric movement velocity during traditional lifts (e.g., squats, bench press) and/or Olympic-style weightlifting, using either a linear positional transducer, an inertial measurement unit, or a camera-based tracking system. Velocity provides a suitable measurement owing to the inverse relationships with external mass, the nearly perfect linear relationship with intensity as a percentage of maximum, and the reductions in exercise velocity as fatigue accrues (Weakley et al., 2021).

The potential applications of VBT in physical preparation are extensive (Weakley et al., 2021). Athlete readiness specifically, may be assessed via a consistent exercise performed at the start of a resistance training session and/or by using velocity loss across a set. By quantifying the within-athlete standard (typical) error and tracking the typical day-to-day fluctuations in velocity, practitioners can gain regular objective insight into the effect of the training programme on performance (Weakley et al., 2021). Given the ability to assess VBT in real-time, practitioners can immediately adjust the programme (i.e., sets, repetitions, or load) based on either daily readiness or within-session fatigue accrual. Furthermore, football practitioners should consider the need to utilise valid and reliable technology to measure VBT, and the ability to implement it in a consistent and reliable method. This can include technology calibration and set-up, people and time resources to manage the data collection, and both athlete and staff familiarisation.

Muscle Strength Assessments

Recent advancements in technology permit strength testing on specific muscle groups, with hamstrings and groin musculature most commonly assessed in football. This reflects the sport's demands, with footballers required to perform repeated high-speed efforts, coupled with numerous actions requiring rapid changes in direction and/or velocity (i.e., acceleration and deceleration) often performed in confined spaces. As a result, not only do these muscle groups suffer fatigue, but they are among the most frequently injured muscle groups in professional football (Ekstrand et al., 2022; Larruskain et al., 2018). Consequently, attention has been placed on monitoring these muscle groups. It is worth noting however, that differences in injury epidemiology exist between sexes, with a higher incidence

132 Strength and Conditioning for Football

of hamstring and groin injuries in men, and conversely more quadriceps strains, anterior cruciate ligament ruptures, and ankle issues in women (Larruskain et al., 2018), and therefore this warrants considerations when selecting and implementing muscle strength assessments with a population.

The most common methods for assessing the strength of the hamstrings include isokinetic and/or handheld dynamometry, force plates, and custom instrumented devices that measure force output during specific exercises, such as the Nordic Hamstring Exercise (NHE). Assessment of the force produced by the hamstrings has become an important monitoring tool as reductions may be a precursor to injury (Opar et al., 2015; van der Horst et al., 2015). Additionally, assessment of between-limb strength asymmetry may highlight a weakness and/or a compensation favouring one side. Given the large effect of body mass on eccentric hamstring strength measured during the NHE, the following predictive equation has been proposed as a calculation for expected strength based on body mass (although it is worth noting this was based on male athletes only) (Buchheit et al., 2016):

$$\text{Expected Eccentric Strength (N)} = 4 \times \text{Body Mass (kg)} + 26.1$$

With many practitioners including the NHE routinely within the strength program, this may provide another approach of 'invisible monitoring'. However, for those unfamiliar with the exercise or not regularly employing it, the eccentric muscle action may cause muscle soreness and low compliance to the NHE has often been reported. In which case, isometric measures of hamstring strength may be preferred. One assessment uses a force plate to measure unilateral force output at the heel during a 3 second maximal isometric contraction, with the athlete lying supine and the knee flexion angle at 90° or 30° (McCall et al., 2015). The 30° knee angle maximally activates the biceps femoris muscle, whereas the 90° angle maximally activates the semi-membranosus and semi-tendinosus (McCall et al., 2015). This test has shown high reliability (coefficient of variation = 4.3%–6.3%, intraclass coefficient correlation = 0.86–0.95), as well as sensitivity to match-induced fatigue in professional football players (McCall et al., 2015). As isometric training has garnered much practical attention, leveraging this training as a monitoring tool is potentially beneficial.

Given that most groin issues tend to occur via a gradual onset and further deteriorate over time, monitoring may enable early detection and management (Wollin et al., 2018). Indeed, players with groin problems have been shown to have lower hip adduction: abduction strength ratios and eccentric adductor strength (Thorborg et al., 2014). Groin testing is most commonly conducted via sphygmomanometer, handheld dynamometry, and load cell assessment. Although handheld dynamometry enables the testing of eccentric actions, using a fixed load cell system or sphygmomanometer to conduct an adductor squeeze test is generally more commonly employed from a monitoring perspective. With the sphygmomanometer, it is

Wellness Monitoring and Readiness in Football **133**

placed between the knees with the athlete instructed to squeeze as hard as possible, with the highest pressure to 5 mmHg recorded. With different load cell devices now commercially available, these generally enable the measurement of force produced in different positions during an isometric task. These force measures are taken to represent abductor and adductor strength values, while the ratio between these two, as well as left to right asymmetries, are also of interest as monitoring measures (Wollin et al., 2018).

Monitoring the strength of the adductors may also be useful to identify if athletes have any pain upon testing. Footballers will often show a reduction in adductor squeeze strength prior to the onset of pain, with a further reduction at the onset of pain (DeLang et al., 2022). A possible explanation may be that players experience an inhibitory muscle response prior to being consciously aware of experiencing pain (DeLang et al., 2022). Tracking pain during the squeeze, either using the 0–10 Numerical Pain Rating Scale or by asking the athlete if they experience pain as a Yes/No response, is therefore worthwhile.

Standardisation of position, lever length, and joint angles are critical for making between- and within-athlete comparisons over time, which may be enhanced by using a fixed load cell adductor strength measurement system. Identifying meaningful differences relative to an individual's normative data may be a more effective way to capture individualised strength changes then using an arbitrary cut-off value (DeLang et al., 2022). It may be beneficial to perform weekly assessments of adductor strength, ideally early in the training week, so that interventions can be made in response to pain and/or reduced adductor strength.

Subjective Methods

Along with the objective markers identified above, assessing an athlete's response to training stress through subjective markers is also beneficial. Whilst self-reported measures of wellness may not necessarily reflect a linear dose-response relationship to training and match loads, they provide self-evaluated perceived physical recovery, psychological and/or social well-being, which may provide insight into the more complex nature of athlete readiness (Duignan et al., 2020; Saw et al., 2017). As a practitioner, the primary role of athlete wellness questionnaires is to gain honest feedback from the athletes on how they are coping and support communication (Saw et al., 2015).

Several questionnaires have been explored in research, including: the Profile of Mood State (POMS), the Recovery-Stress Questionnaire for athletes, Daily Analysis of Life Demands for Athletes, and the Total Recovery Scale (Halson, 2014). These questionnaires are extensive; the POMS, for example, contains 65 items measuring 6 specific mood states. Given time limitations, simplified questionnaires have become favoured in the applied setting, containing approximately three to eight questions using a Likert scale frequently ranging from 1 to 5, 1 to 7, 1 to 9, or 1 to 10. Some of the most common questions focus on ratings and location

134 Strength and Conditioning for Football

of muscle soreness, fatigue, sleep quality, stress levels, mood state, motivation to train, sleep quantity and duration, mental fatigue, energy, and perceived recovery (Duignan et al., 2020). Simple and easily understood questions are important given that athletes often face a number of demands pre-training. The questionnaires are often further customised to specific athlete groups and/or contexts. For example, questions for female athletes may also relate to the menstrual cycle, such as symptoms or phases. Student athletes may be given the opportunity to report stress relating to the additional workload of school studies. During the COVID-19 pandemic, many teams utilised daily wellness questionnaires to assess any signs/symptoms of illness to try and minimise spread of the virus.

Athletes will commonly complete their questionnaires via a smartphone app on either individual phones or shared devices that sync to a secure athlete management system (AMS). This allows for responses to be kept confidential and promote athlete honesty, with the latter being an essential component to ensure the data is both usable and actionable. Poor compliance and dishonest reporting can be an issue when buy-in is not sufficient. Practitioners need to use education, communication, and transparency to continuously share the purpose and application of subjective data collection (Saw et al., 2015).

There can be a number of summing, averaging and other statistical techniques (e.g., z-scores) used to assess self-report measures (Duignan et al., 2020). These alert the practitioner if the player "flags" on a certain area. To consider an applied example: if an athlete was to report a poor night's sleep, the relevant staff member may get a notification that this response is outside the normal individual response. Whilst one night of poor sleep may not be a major concern, if the athlete continues to report consecutive poor sleep, this may require a more in-depth enquiry and intervention. Using responses to start a conversation with athletes will promote buy-in and honest feedback.

Invisible Monitoring

Gaining insights into readiness without additional testing is an appealing prospect to practitioners and athletes alike. The idea of 'invisible monitoring', whereby the dose-response relationship is evaluated from data collected in-situ without increasing athlete burden, has gained traction in recent times (West et al., 2021). This can be a particularly effective approach in football, given the large playing group and the desire to understand individual dose-response relationships. Invisible monitoring may utilise workload measures, such as tracking the relationship between internal and external load, assessing responses to standardised drills, and understanding changes in movement patterns that may yield insight into fatigue-induced changes in movement profile. As we have highlighted throughout this chapter, certain readiness monitoring may also be considered invisible, when the information is collected as part of the training programme (on-field and/or in strength sessions).

Keys to Implementation

This chapter highlights a multitude of approaches available to assess wellness and readiness. The decision then becomes what tests to use within the program and how best to implement them. Below are some key take-home points for implementation at each stage of the data pipeline:

- *Test Selection*: Keep testing to a minimal by considering the most relevant tests and measures that can have a meaningful impact in your environment. Where suitable, use 'invisible monitoring' or measures that are already collected. For example, VBT and/or hamstring strength assessments may be performed as part of the strength programming, but can double as readiness assessments.
- *Collection*: Plan the data collection process so that it is consistent, valid, reliable, and also minimises unnecessary burden on the athlete. The worst thing to do is over-burden athletes with multiple tests and not utilise the data collected. Maintain a repeatable process, such as standardised warm-ups and cueing, calibrated equipment, and similar time of day where possible.
- *Periodisation*: Plan the timing of the tests and how this fits into the training programme (see Figure 8.1). This needs to be considered in the context of the micro-cycle and training plan, as well as the daily schedule.
- *Storage*: Consider where the data will be stored and how it will be integrated with other data streams (i.e., training and competition loads, other testing inputs). Ideally, this process should enable instantaneous display and analysis. Options include commercial AMS software or internally designed and built systems and visualisations, with popular options including Microsoft Excel,

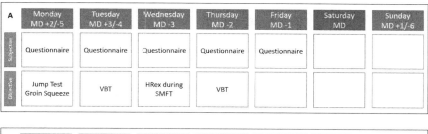

FIGURE 8.1 Example monitoring periodisation in a (A) one-game week and (B) two-game week.

136 Strength and Conditioning for Football

R Studio with associated Shiny Apps, Tableau, and Microsoft Power BI (Thornton et al., 2019).

- *Analysis*: Determining changes in athletes, monitoring data can be done so via z-scores. Practitioners should consider what range of historical data to include to calculate the z-score. Practitioners may select what change in athletes score is significant enough to identify a flag – some of the more common approaches include a z-score greater than 1 standard deviation (SD) from their mean (outside 68% of their normal variability), 1.5 or 2 SD (outside 95% of their normal variance) above their mean. Other approaches to identify a meaningful change may include typical error, effect sizes, smallest worthwhile changes, and coefficient of variation (Thornton et al., 2019). It is particularly important to identify changes that are greater than the "noise" of the test itself. This can be done by calculating the typical error within the specific athlete population you are working with. If the change in test score is greater than the typical error, the magnitude of change is greater than the testing error and therefore real.
- *Visualisation*: Given the fast-paced nature of football, coupled with the abundant amount of information already available, readiness and wellness data need to be presented in a clear and effective form with meaningful changes identified easily. This may be via colours or symbols that denote when an athlete is notably higher or lower than their usual performance. Where possible, interactive dashboards help drive engagement with the end user.
- *Communication and Buy-in*: Providing feedback to athletes and including them in the conversation is crucial for buy-in. Ensure they are educated on the purpose of all data collected and kept in the feedback loop of how information is utilised.

Practical Applications

There is a plethora of tools for today's football practitioners to consider for monitoring athlete wellness and readiness. Suitable tools should be sensitive to training load, unaffected by other factors, and respond to acute exercise. Practically, any assessment should limit additional fatigue, and efficiently accommodate the large number of athletes in a football squad. Practitioners need to plan every stage of the data pipeline so that any tool implemented provides maximum value to the programme, while minimising the unnecessary burden on both athletes and staff. A comprehensive system should include a multivariate approach in which all information is considered within the context of each individual athlete (i.e., recent training and competition load, travel demands, life stressors), and combined with training load to build an accurate picture of an athlete's dose-response relationship. By monitoring these measures, practitioners can gain insights into each individual athlete's response to training, and thereby make informed decisions about how to modify training programs to optimise performance. Finally, ongoing education and communication with athletes and other key stakeholders are essential to gain buy-in with the monitoring programme.

References

Bellenger, C. R., Fuller, J. T., Thomson, R. L., Davison, K., Robertson, E. Y., and Buckley, J. D. (2016). Monitoring athletic training status through autonomic heart rate regulation: A systematic review and meta-analysis. *Sports Medicine*, *46*, 1461–1486.

Bishop, C., Jordan, M., Torres-Ronda, L., Loturco, I., Harry, J., Virgile, A., Mundy, P., Turner, A., and Comfort, P. (2022). Selecting metrics that matter: Comparing the use of the countermovement jump for performance profiling, neuromuscular fatigue monitoring, and injury rehabilitation testing. *Strength* and *Conditioning Journal*, *45*(5), 545–553.

Buchheit, M., Cholley, Y., Nagel, M., and Poulos, N. (2016). The effect of body mass on eccentric knee-flexor strength assessed with an instrumented Nordic hamstring device (Nordbord) in football players. *International Journal of Sports Physiology and Performance*, *11*(6), 721–726. https://doi.org/10.1123/ijspp.2015-0513

Claudino, J. G., Cronin, J., Mezêncio, B., McMaster, D. T., McGuigan, M., Tricoli, V., Amadio, A. C., and Serrão, J. C. (2017). The countermovement jump to monitor neuromuscular status: A meta-analysis. *Journal of Science and Medicine in Sport*, *20*(4), 397–402. https://doi.org/10.1016/j.jsams.2016.08.011

Collins, B. W., Pearcey, G. E. P., Buckle, N. C. M., Power, K. E., and Button, D. C. (2018). Neuromuscular fatigue during repeated sprint exercise: Underlying physiology and methodological considerations. *Applied Physiology, Nutrition, and Metabolism*, *43*(11), 1166–1175. https://doi.org/10.1139/apnm-2018-0080

Cormack, S. J., Newton, R. U., McGuigan, M. R., and Cormie, P. (2008). Neuromuscular and endocrine responses of elite players during an Australian rules football season. *International Journal of Sports Physiology and Performance*, *3*(4), 439–453.

Coutts, A. J., Reaburn, P., Piva, T. J., and Rowsell, G. J. (2007). Monitoring for overreaching in rugby league players. *European Journal of Applied Physiology*, *99*(3), 313–324. https://doi.org/10.1007/s00421-006-0345-z

DeLang, M., Garrison, J. C., Hannon, J. P., Ishøi, L., and Thorborg, K. (2022). 37 weekly adductor squeeze strength monitoring in male academy football players: Is it influenced by groin pain onset? *BMJ Open Sport and Exercise Medicine*, *8*(Suppl 1). https://doi.org/10.1136/bmjsem-2022-sportskongres.10

Duignan, C., Doherty, C., Caulfield, B., and Blake, C. (2020). Single-item self-report measures of team-sport athlete wellbeing and their relationship with training load: A systematic review. *Journal of Athletic Training*, *55*(9), 944–953. https://doi.org/10.4085/1062-6050-0528.19

Ekstrand, J., Bengtsson, H., Waldén, M., Davison, M., Khan, K. M., and Hägglund, M. (2022). Hamstring injury rates have increased during recent seasons and now constitute 24% of all injuries in men's professional football: The UEFA Elite Club Injury Study from 2001/02 to 2021/22. *British Journal of Sports Medicine*, *57*(5), 292–298. https://doi.org/10.1136/bjsports-2021-105407

Gathercole, R. J., Sporer, B. C., Stellingwerff, T., and Sleivert, G. G. (2015). Comparison of the capacity of different jump and sprint field tests to detect neuromuscular fatigue. *Journal of Strength and Conditioning Research*, *29*(9), 2522–2531. https://doi.org/10.1519/JSC.0000000000000912

Halson, S. L. (2014). Monitoring training load to understand fatigue in athletes. *Sports Medicine*, *44*(Suppl 2), S139–147. https://doi.org/10.1007/s40279-014-0253-z

Jahrami, H., Trabelsi, K., Vitiello, M. V., and BaHammam, A. S. (2023). The tale of orthosomnia: I am so good at sleeping that I can do it with my eyes closed and my fitness tracker on me. *Nature and Science of Sleep*, *2023*, 13–15.

138 Strength and Conditioning for Football

Kraemer, W. J., and Ratamess, N. A. (2005). Hormonal responses and adaptations to resistance exercise and training. *Sports Medicine*, *35*, 339–361.

Larruskain, J., Lekue, J. A., Diaz, N., Odriozola, A., and Gil, S. M. (2018). A comparison of injuries in elite male and female football players: A five-season prospective study. *Scandinavian Journal of Medicine and Science in Sports*, *28*(1), 237–245. https://doi.org/10.1111/sms.12860

McCall, A., Nedelec, M., Carling, C., Le Gall, F., Berthoin, S., and Dupont, G. (2015). Reliability and sensitivity of a simple isometric posterior lower limb muscle test in professional football players. *Journal of Sports Sciences*, *33*(12), 1298–1304. https://doi.org/10.1080/02640414.2015.1022579

McLean, B. D., Petrucelli, C., and Coyle, E. F. (2012). Maximal power output and perceptual fatigue responses during a Division I female collegiate soccer season. *The Journal of Strength and Conditioning Research*, *26*(12), 3189–3196.

McMahon, A.-T., Williams, P., and Tapsell, L. (2010). Reviewing the meanings of wellness and well-being and their implications for food choice. *Perspectives in Public Health*, *130*(6), 282–286. https://doi.org/10.1177/1757913910384046

Montull, L., Slapšinskaitė-Dackevičienė, A., Kiely, J., Hristovski, R., and Balagué, N. (2022). Integrative proposals of sports monitoring: Subjective outperforms objective monitoring. *Sports Medicine - Open*, *8*(1), 41. https://doi.org/10.1186/s40798-022-00432-z

Opar, D. A., Williams, M. D., Timmins, R. G., Hickey, J., Duhig, S. J., and Shield, A. J. (2015). Eccentric hamstring strength and hamstring injury risk in Australian footballers. *Medicine and Science in Sports and Exercise*, *47*(4), 857–865. https://doi.org/10.1249/MSS.0000000000000465

Rowell, A. E., Aughey, R. J., Hopkins, W. G., Esmaeili, A., Lazarus, B. H., and Cormack, S. J. (2018). Effects of training and competition load on neuromuscular recovery, testosterone, cortisol, and match performance during a season of professional football. *Frontiers in Physiology*, *9*, 668. https://www.frontiersin.org/articles/10.3389/fphys.2018.00668

Rowell, A. E., Aughey, R. J., Hopkins, W. G., Stewart, A. M., and Cormack, S. J. (2017). Identification of sensitive measures of recovery after external load from football match play. *International Journal of Sports Physiology and Performance*, *12*(7), 969–976.

Ryan, S., Kempton, T., Impellizzeri, F. M., and Coutts, A. J. (2020). Training monitoring in professional Australian football: Theoretical basis and recommendations for coaches and scientists. *Science and Medicine in Football*, *4*(1), 52–58.

Saw, A. E., Kellmann, M., Main, L. C., and Gastin, P. B. (2017). Athlete self-report measures in research and practice: Considerations for the discerning reader and fastidious practitioner. *International Journal of Sports Physiology and Performance*, *12*(Suppl 2), S2127–S2135. https://doi.org/10.1123/ijspp.2016-0395

Saw, A. E., Main, L. C., and Gastin, P. B. (2015). Monitoring athletes through self-report: Factors influencing implementation. *Journal of Sports Science and Medicine*, *14*(1), 137–146.

Shushan, T., Lovell, R., Buchheit, M., Scott, T. J., Barrett, S., Norris, D., and McLaren, S. J. (2023). Submaximal fitness test in team sports: A systematic review and meta-analysis of exercise heart rate measurement properties. *Sports Medicine-Open*, *9*(1), 21.

Thomas, K., Brownstein, C. G., Dent, J., Parker, P., Goodall, S., and Howatson, G. (2018). Neuromuscular fatigue and recovery after heavy resistance, jump, and sprint training. *Medicine and Science in Sports and Exercise*, *50*(12), 2526–2535. https://doi.org/10.1249/MSS.0000000000001733

Thomas, K., Dent, J., Howatson, G., and Goodall, S. (2017). Etiology and recovery of neuromuscular fatigue following simulated soccer match-play. *Medicine and Science in Sports and Exercise*, *49*(5), 955–964.

Thorborg, K., Branci, S., Nielsen, M. P., Tang, L., Nielsen, M. B., and Hölmich, P. (2014). Eccentric and isometric hip adduction strength in male soccer players with and without adductor-related groin pain: An assessor-blinded comparison. *Orthopaedic Journal of Sports Medicine*, *2*(2), 2325967114521778. https://doi.org/10.1177/2325967114521778

Thornton, H. R., Delaney, J. A., Duthie, G. M., and Dascombe, B. J. (2019). Developing athlete monitoring systems in team sports: Data analysis and visualization. *International Journal of Sports Physiology and Performance*, *14*(6), 698–705. https://doi.org/10.1123/ijspp.2018-0169

Thorpe, R. T., Atkinson, G., Drust, B., and Gregson, W. (2017). Monitoring fatigue status in elite team-sport athletes: Implications for practice. *International Journal of Sports Physiology and Performance*, *12*(Suppl 2), S227–S234. https://doi.org/10.1123/ijspp.2016-0434

Tofari, P. J., Kemp, J. G., and Cormack, S. J. (2018). Self-paced team-sport match simulation results in reductions in voluntary activation and modifications to biological, perceptual, and performance measures at halftime and for up to 96 hours postmatch. *Journal of Strength and Conditioning Research*, *32*(12), 3552–3563. https://doi.org/10.1519/JSC.0000000000001875

van der Horst, N., Smits, D.-W., Petersen, J., Goedhart, E. A., and Backx, F. J. G. (2015). The preventive effect of the Nordic hamstring exercise on hamstring injuries in amateur soccer players: A randomized controlled trial. *The American Journal of Sports Medicine*, *43*(6), 1316–1323. https://doi.org/10.1177/0363546515574057

Weakley, J., Mann, B., Banyard, H., McLaren, S., Scott, T., and Garcia-Ramos, A. (2021). Velocity-based training: From theory to application. *Strength and Conditioning Journal*, *43*(2), 31–49.

Wehbe, G., Gabbett, T. J., Dwyer, D., McLellan, C., and Coad, S. (2015). Monitoring neuromuscular fatigue in team-sport athletes using a cycle-ergometer test. *International Journal of Sports Physiology and Performance*, *10*(3), 292–297. https://doi.org/10.1123/ijspp.2014-0217

West, S. W., Clubb, J., Torres-Ronda, L., Howells, D., Leng, E., Vescovi, J. D., Carmody, S., Posthumus, M., Dalen-Lorentsen, T., and Windt, J. (2021). More than a metric: How training load is used in elite sport for athlete management. *International Journal of Sports Medicine*, *42*(4), 300–306. https://doi.org/10.1055/a-1268-8791

Wollin, M., Thorborg, K., Welvaert, M., and Pizzari, T. (2018). In-season monitoring of hip and groin strength, health and function in elite youth soccer: Implementing an early detection and management strategy over two consecutive seasons. *Journal of Science and Medicine in Sport*, *21*(10), 988–993. https://doi.org/10.1016/j.jsams.2018.03.004

9

MATCH-DAY STRATEGIES TO ENHANCE FOOTBALL PERFORMANCE

Warming-Up, Priming, and Extra Time

Samuel P. Hills, Natalie Smith, Liam P. Kilduff, and Mark Russell

Introduction

Sports scientists and strength and conditioning coaches working with football teams spend much of the competitive season tailoring training and recovery plans to maximise their players' competitive performances. This primarily involves strategies that are implemented throughout the training week to optimise readiness for match day. However, notwithstanding the importance of such strategies, match day itself provides a further window of opportunity to intervene with ergogenic practices that manipulate physiological and/or hormonal responses in pursuit of enhanced football performance. Applied correctly, the use of several preparatory strategies on match day may acutely enhance performance and potentially reduce the risk of injury. This chapter will provide an overview of the current research relating to match-day preparatory strategies in team sports and provide practical recommendations for implementing likely worthwhile interventions within the context of existing football practices. Broadly speaking, match-day strategies can be categorised according to the timing of their implementation as

1 Strategies that can be adopted more than 3 h before a player's entry into the match.
2 Strategies that can be adopted within 3 h prior to a player's entry into the match.
3 Strategies that can be implemented following kick-off after a player's entry into the match, including at half-time, and before extra time.

Practitioners may choose to adopt these strategies either independently or in combination, depending on the specific circumstances in which they operate and the constraints that they face.

DOI: 10.4324/9781003383475-10

Strategies Adopted >3 h before a Player's Entry into the Match

Morning Priming Exercise

Previous research indicates that an individual's circulating testosterone concentrations may influence explosive exercise performance. For example, in trained athletes, testosterone levels have demonstrated strong positive correlations with squat strength ($r = 0.92$) and sprint ($r = 0.87$) performance (Crewther et al., 2012). Testosterone can also influence other relevant psychological or behavioural responses such as motivation, confidence, and cognitive performance. Notably for those concerned with maximising physical performance, testosterone concentrations exhibit circadian rhythmicity, peaking in the early morning and declining throughout the day (Russell et al., 2016). Given the positive correlations between testosterone concentrations and indices of exercise performance, such responses may have implications for football players wishing to optimise performance during matches that commence in the afternoon or evening. Implementing practices that offset the afternoon decline in testosterone concentrations have the potential to enhance or 'prime' performance during matches that begin later in the day (Cook et al., 2014; Harrison et al., 2019; Russell et al., 2016).

Resistance exercise can acutely increase circulating testosterone concentrations and thus, has the potential as a match-day intervention strategy that enhances muscular force production providing that hormonal elevations persist and are not outweighed by any residual fatigue at the time of exercise performance (Harrison et al., 2019). Rugby players performing morning sprints (five sprints of 40 m) and whole-body resistance training (back squats and bench press at an intensity reaching 100% of three-repetition maximum) were effective in offsetting the diurnal decline in salivary testosterone concentrations that were observed in the control trial (Cook et al., 2014). Such hormonal responses were accompanied by 1–4% greater afternoon performance when assessed 6 h following the morning exercise (Cook et al., 2014). Similarly, morning resistance training involving back squats and power cleans improved afternoon throwing performance amongst trained shot putters when compared to a rested control condition (Ekstrand et al., 2013).

High load ($\geq$85% of one-repetition maximum) resistance exercises and low load (30–40% of one-repetition maximum) ballistic exercises can each be used as a 'priming' stimulus to enhance performance in the subsequent ~6–33 h period (Harrison et al., 2019). The potential effectiveness notwithstanding, practical limitations, traditions, and preferences associated with match day means that performing whole-body exercises at near-maximal intensity may be unrealistic in many pre-competition settings. Russell et al. (2016) assessed more practically feasible modes of morning exercise for use as a match day priming stimulus, observing that sprint exercise completed in the morning (six sets of 40 m sprints each including a 180° change of direction) improved both sprinting and jumping performance by ~2–4% as well as positively affecting salivary testosterone concentrations

142 Strength and Conditioning for Football

(~22% increase) 5 h later when compared with a control condition. In this study, favourable testosterone concentrations were also observed alongside improved sprint performance following upper-body resistance exercise (bench press: five sets of ten repetitions at 75% of one-repetition maximum) whereas improved countermovement jump scores were enhanced after cycle sprints (six sets of 6 s cycle ergometer sprints against a load of 7.5% of body mass) (Russell et al., 2016). More recently, a practicable mode of sport-specific priming for cricket players involving six ~35 m sprints including a 180° change of direction was beneficial for afternoon sprinting and also cognitive performance when compared with a passive control (Nutt et al., 2022). Together, these studies highlight the potential for the possible use of more practically feasible priming stimuli when high-intensity whole-body resistance exercise is not favoured on the day of competition. Practitioners are thus afforded flexibility when designing strategies targeting a priming response and may choose exercises that are more directly relevant to sport-specific actions such as sprinting (Nutt et al., 2022; Russell et al., 2016).

Strategies Adopted <3 h before a Player's Entry into the Match

Hormonal Priming

Football players often engage in extensive pre-match talks with performance staff to outline tactics (<2 h before competition) and motivate players through verbal persuasion and encouragement (<1 h before competition). These strategies are reinforced during the pre-match warm-up and transition period between the warm-up and the match kick-off. Substitute players also receive match- and role-specific tactical information whilst awaiting pitch-entry once the match is underway, whereas half-time and in-play stoppages (including immediately before extra time in matches that require this additional period of play) offer further fleeting communication opportunities for coaches, players, and team officials. Despite such practices being widespread at all levels of football, their effectiveness and subsequent influence on a player's match-play responses remain unclear.

The environment to which a player is exposed prior to pitch-entry has the potential to influence their ability to perform thereafter. Watching videos of one's own successful skill execution ~75 min before the match kick-off, reinforced by positive verbal feedback from coaches, has been demonstrated to benefit pre-match testosterone concentrations and match-play performance ratings in professional rugby players (Cook and Crewther, 2012b). Conversely, videos of opposing player's success accompanied by cautionary feedback elicited elevated cortisol responses and worse performance ratings (Cook and Crewther, 2012b). Acute elevations in testosterone concentrations and improved back squat performance have also been observed 15 min after trained males viewed aggressive or intense training videos. There was also a positive relationship observed between an increase in three-repetition maximum strength and the acute elevation of testosterone concentrations that were triggered by visual stimulation (Cook and Crewther, 2012a). Whilst not studied directly in relation to football, such data suggests that coaches should consider the messages conveyed during the period shortly before and during competition to optimise a player's preparation for match-play. Moreover, it is possible that the acute sensory environment to which substitute players are exposed before pitch entry could influence hormonal and/or performance responses thereafter.

Active Pre-match Warm-up

Active warm-ups are universally employed pre-match as an acute preparation strategy and typically incorporate movements of varying intensities, including dynamic stretching and technical drills. The primary aim of such practices is to facilitate a transition from a state of rest to exercise, thereby improving subsequent performance and potentially reducing the risk of injury during activity performed thereafter. Numerous studies have highlighted how appropriately designed active warm-ups can benefit performance in soccer-specific tasks such as jumping, sprinting, and changing direction (Silva et al., 2018).

Although several non-temperature related mechanisms may also contribute to a warm-up's ergogenic effects (e.g., elevated oxygen consumption, post-activation performance enhancement (PAPE), and mental preparedness), the largest benefits to high-intensity exercise performance likely result from warm-up-induced increases in muscle temperature (T_m). A moderate-intensity active warm-up (at ~80–100% of an individual's lactate threshold) produces rapid increases in T_m, which reaches a relative equilibrium after ~10–20 min of exercise. Within limits, strong positive associations exist between changes in T_m and muscular power output, with a 1°C T_m increase producing performance improvements of up to ~2–10% (Sargeant, 1987). On football match days, pre-kick-off active warm-ups usually last between 20 and 45 min. These warm-ups typically initiate with low-intensity elements such as stretching and activation drills, gradually transitioning into higher intensity exercises that involve sport-specific movement patterns and technical/tactical drills. However, observations from studies conducted within and outside the domain of team sports indicate the potential opportunity to adjust warm-up intensity to optimise subsequent physical performance (Cook et al., 2013; Hills et al., 2020; Ingham et al., 2013).

Provided that an individual's tolerable limits are not surpassed, elevating the intensity of preparatory exercises can yield positive outcomes in subsequent physical performance (Cook et al., 2013; Hills et al., 2020; Ingham et al., 2013). For instance, modifying an active warm-up routine by replacing a 300 m striding segment with a combination of 100 m of striding and 200 m of race pace running led to a ~1% improvement in 800 m running performance (Ingham et al., 2013). Similarly, increasing the typical warm-up intensity of elite bob-skeleton athletes by ~30% enhanced resisted sprint performances thereafter (Cook et al., 2013). In team sports, warm-ups incorporating activities performed above the anaerobic

144 Strength and Conditioning for Football

threshold have demonstrated beneficial effects on repeated sprint ability compared to those performed below this intensity (Anderson et al., 2014). It is suggested that, for enhancing explosive physical performance in team sports players, warm-ups should encompass activities in which athletes reach approximately 90% of their maximum heart rate (Silva et al., 2018). In a football context, this may involve an active pre-match warm-up that progressively increases in intensity and concludes with near-maximal effort sports-specific movements such as jumping, sprinting, and changing direction.

In addition to these general warm-up recommendations, specific warm-up programs have gained recognition for their effectiveness. For example, the 'FIFA 11+' (Fédération Internationale de Football Association) program is a comprehensive warm-up program developed by the Fédération Internationale de Football Association (FIFA), which has the aim of reducing the risk of injuries in football players. It includes specific exercises targeting strength, balance, agility, and neuromuscular control. Implementing the FIFA 11+ warm-up program amongst men's collegiate soccer players has been shown to reduce the incidence of injuries by 46.1%, and decrease time lost to injury by 28.6% (Silvers-Granelli et al., 2015).

Protecting Warm-up Benefits

The benefits of an appropriately designed and implemented active-pre-match warm-up notwithstanding, several practical and logistical constraints exist on match day (e.g., varying match start times, lengthy transition periods between initial active warm-ups and kick-off, lack of access to equipment, and a player's media commitments) that have the potential to affect the efficacy of pre-match preparations. The end of the pre-match warm-up and the start of the match are typically separated by $\geq$10–15 min in which on-pitch warm-up activities can no longer be performed, whether this is due to practical restrictions or competition regulations (i.e., some football competitions legislate that players must clear the pitch within a certain period before the match begins). This is notable due to the fact that T_m and core temperature (T_{core}) alongside physical performance capacity decrease substantially within ~10–15 min of inactivity following initial exposure to exercise (Kilduff et al., 2013; Russell et al., 2015, 2018), declining further when the inactivity period is extended (Hills et al., 2021). Without strategies designed to mitigate such responses in cold or temperate conditions, typical pre-kick-off transition periods could thus reduce the efficacy of the preceding warm-up (Kilduff et al., 2013). Moreover, substitute players typically face much greater delays between the pre-match warm-up and their first involvement in match-play (Hills et al., 2020, 2021). This extended time period can result in all body temperature and performance benefits from the pre-match warm-up being lost by the time of a player's second-half pitch-entry (Hills et al., 2021). It may be beneficial for practitioners to consider a substitute's unique match-day demands when designing preparatory strategies aiming to optimise match-play performance for the whole playing squad.

Indeed, increasing the amount of pre-pitch-entry activity performed by professional football substitutes (i.e., during the pre-match team warm-up and whilst awaiting pitch-entry after the match kick-off) appeared to elevate match-play running responses once these players were introduced into the match (Hills et al., 2020).

Passive heat maintenance refers to the practice of applying external heat sources and/or methods of insulation (e.g., heated clothing, outdoor survival jackets, heating pads) to maintain body temperature elevations during periods of inactivity (e.g., the post–warm-up transition period, half time), with the aim of protecting performance gains that arise through temperature-mediated pathways. The development of specialised thermal clothing, such as trousers heated via electrical filaments (e.g., Signature V.1 Heated Performance Pants, Lizard Heat, UK) and survival jackets designed to reflect heat and trap air within the garment (Blizzard Survival Jacket, Blizzard Protection Systems Ltd, UK), using passive heating strategies may now provide a cost-effective and practical means through which to mitigate heat loss for football players.

Across a range of sports, using passive heat maintenance during a post-warm-up period of inactivity has increased performance outcomes. For example, in professional rugby league players, wearing a survival garment during a 15 min post-warm-up recovery period attenuated T_{core} losses by ~50% compared with when players wore normal training attire. The practice also benefitted subsequent repeated sprint performance and explosive lower body activities (Kilduff et al., 2013), with post-warm-up declines in lower-body peak power output being related ($r = 0.71$) to declines in T_{core} (Kilduff et al., 2013). Passive heat maintenance may therefore represent a valuable strategy for preserving the ergogenic effects of a pre-match warm-up if performing further warm-up activity is not possible within ~10–15 min of a player's entry into competition. Notably, with ≥75–120 min often elapsing between their initial warm-up and eventual pitch-entry, substitute players may benefit from incorporating passive heating strategies (i.e., alongside a specifically tailored active warm-up and re-warm-up strategy) into their match-day routines.

Post-Activation Performance Enhancement

Post-activation performance enhancement (PAPE) is a term commonly used to denote the notion that prior high-intensity muscle actions have the potential to transiently augment subsequent physical performance to an extent that exceeds the ergogenic benefit of warming-up (i.e., elevating body temperature) alone (Kilduff et al., 2008). This enhancement may occur through various mechanisms such as increased sensitivity of actin-myosin myofilaments to Ca^{2+}, improved motor neuron recruitment, and a more favourable input to the motor neuron from the central nervous system (Wilson et al., 2013). Whilst several factors affect a player's ability to harness the effects of PAPE, including their strength and muscle fibre composition, the volume and type of the preload stimulus, and the duration of recovery

146 Strength and Conditioning for Football

between the preload stimulus and subsequent activity (Kilduff et al., 2008; Wilson et al., 2013). Indeed, the strength of the individual may be a relevant consideration when deciding whether or not to target PAPE as a match day intervention for football players, with stronger and better trained individuals typically demonstrating greater PAPE responses than their weaker or less trained counterparts (Kilduff et al., 2008). However, this section will focus on factors that can be acutely modified with regard to the practical implementation of strategies targeted at eliciting PAPE on match day. Practitioners must determine the appropriate type, timing, and intensity with regard to such activities if they are to maximise the chances of having the desired effect.

Research into PAPE has predominantly investigated the use of moderate to heavy resistance exercise (i.e., typically 60–95% of one-repetition maximum) as the preload stimulus (Wilson et al., 2013). These studies have consistently demonstrated that performing multiple sets of such exercises yields greater enhancements in subsequent muscular performance for trained individuals (Wilson et al., 2013). However, the pre-competition constraints, traditions, and routines that exist for football players mean that it may often be unfeasible or undesirable to incorporate heavy resistance exercises shortly before a match. Consequently, there is a growing interest in identifying alternative methods that may have the potential to induce a PAPE effect yet that require minimal equipment and/or may be better tolerated by players and practitioners on the day of competition.

As weighted jumps and other ballistic exercises preferentially recruit type II motor units, they have the potential as a stimulus to induce PAPE. Whilst the specific modality used may not be feasible in the context of match-day practice, it is notable that when an 8 min recovery period was permitted, performing three sets of three repetitions of ballistic bench throws at 30% of one-repetition maximum produced improvements in upper body power output that were comparable to those observed after more traditional heavy resistance exercise (i.e., three sets of three repetitions of bench press at 87% of one-repetition maximum) (West et al., 2013b). Moreover, more practically tolerable means of inducing PAPE have also demonstrated performance improvements in tasks relevant to football. Trained men performing three sets of ten repetitions of alternate leg bounding on an indoor surface whilst wearing a weighted vest equivalent to 10% of body mass improved 10 and 20 m sprint times by 2–3% when 4 and 8 min of recovery was provided (Turner et al., 2015). Change of direction performance was also improved in women's team sports players 8 min after the same bounding exercise was completed on either a hard indoor surface or natural grass (Dann et al., 2023). Such findings suggest a potential role for using bounding or similar stretch-shortening cycle-based movements as a practically achievable pre-match or half-time preparatory strategy for football players. Moreover, whilst more research is required to develop firm guidelines, the use of low-volume flywheel eccentric overload exercises as a preconditioning stimulus has shown a potential to benefit various measures of athletic performance (Beato et al., 2020).

Match-Day Strategies to Enhance Football Performance **147**

After a high-intensity conditioning stimulus (e.g., heavy resistance exercise, alternate leg bounding), fatigue and potentiation co-exist within the targeted musculature. The balance between these two states determines whether subsequent performance capacity is either enhanced (i.e., if potentiation effects outweigh the effects of fatigue) or diminished (i.e., if fatigue outweighs potentiation). As such, the recovery time between the preload and subsequent activity is crucial in determining the performance outcome thereafter. Irrespective of the exercise modality used as the preload stimulus, a recovery period of approximately ~7–10 min appears to be optimal for maximising subsequent physical performance (Wilson et al., 2013; Kilduff et al., 2008; West et al., 2013a). The fact that performance benefits have been observed when professional rugby union players completed further upper body exercise during the recovery period following a conditioning stimulus (i.e., back squat: three repetitions at 87% one-repetition maximum) suggests that activities targeted at PAPE may be incorporated within a general pre-match warm-up without passive recovery being required (West et al., 2013a). However, considering that the time delay between the conclusion of the pre-match warm-up and the match kick-off typically exceeds 10 min, the potential to harness the effects of PAPE may be somewhat limited to the initial stages of a player's involvement in the match. It remains uncertain whether substitutes who have induced a PAPE response via targeted ballistic or isometric exercises performed pitch-side shortly prior to entering the pitch could influence markers of team performance upon pitch-entry. Additionally, the potential effectiveness of implementing PAPE as a strategic approach during halftime or other scheduled breaks in play is yet to be fully investigated in the context of football.

Strategies That Can Be Implemented after a Player's Entry into the Match Including at Half-time and before Extra time

Half-time

Half-time also represents an opportunity for practitioners working with football players to implement strategies that help optimise second-half performance. In addition to nutritional strategies (that are beyond the scope of this chapter), practitioners may be able to intervene by implementing practices targeted at maintaining body temperature over the course of a football half-time. For players who played the first half, body temperature may decline by >1°C during a passive 10–15 min half-time (Mohr et al., 2004). Such temperature responses may be at least partly responsible for the reductions in physical performance that are typical immediately after half-time relative to the first half (Mohr et al., 2004). It is therefore unsurprising that employing passive heat maintenance techniques such as wearing a survival jacket during a simulated half-time has demonstrated efficacy for preserving body temperature and maintaining physical performance capacity at the onset of the second half in professional rugby union players (Russell et al., 2015, 2018). The use

148 Strength and Conditioning for Football

of a blizzard survival jacket during a 15-min passive half-time improved repeated sprint ability and countermovement jump power output by 1.4% and 3.2% compared with a control condition in which participants wore normal clothing over the same period (Russell et al., 2015). Notably, the decline in T_{core} was approximately half that of the control trial over the 15 min (−0.6% vs −1.5%).

Positive effects on body temperature and sport-specific performance have also been observed when team sports players have performed further exercise (e.g., intermittent agility exercise, whole body vibration, small-sided games, and resistance exercises) during half-time (Mohr et al., 2004; Russell et al., 2018). In professional rugby union players, combining active half-time rewarm-ups with passive heat maintenance has demonstrated additive positive effects on both temperature and performance responses compared with when either strategy was implemented in isolation (Russell et al., 2018). Whilst active, passive, and combined heat maintenance strategies may be valuable during half-time in cold or thermoneutral conditions, the feasibility of such strategies must be considered carefully within the context of any given team and player (i.e., based on player preferences/comfort, tactical, medical, nutritional commitments). Practitioners must also be mindful of the potential for these strategies to negatively influence performance capacity in hot or humid conditions if T_{core} is substantially elevated. In such scenarios, combining lower-limb passive heat maintenance with pre-cooling strategies such as ice-slurry ingestion may allow players to preserve T_m in the legs whilst maintaining T_{core} below (or allowing T_{core} to return below) a level that could negatively affect performance (Beaven et al., 2018).

Matches That Progress to Extra time

Whilst senior football matches typically last 90 min (plus stoppage time and half-time), some tournament and cup competitions require a period of extra time to be played if the match scores are level after 90 min. Extra time typically commences 5 min after the end of normal time and consists of two 15 min periods that are separated by a 2 min break (Field et al., 2022). Given that players experience progressive fatigue over the course of a 90-min match, it is likely that exposure to a further 30 min will promote additional acute and post-match fatigue. Notably, male players cover 5–12% less distance per minute and demonstrate reduced performance in certain technical performance indicators (i.e., shot speed, number of passes, and dribbles) during extra time compared with the preceding 90 min of actual or simulated match-play (Field et al., 2022; Stevenson et al., 2017). Reductions in sprint performance have also been observed following extra time compared with during the first and second halves of soccer-specific exercise (Stevenson et al., 2017), whilst extra time has furthered the development of 'central' neuromuscular fatigue, as indicated by perturbations in voluntary activation and maximum voluntary force of the knee extensors after simulated extra time compared with before, during, and after normal time (Goodall et al., 2017).

Given the additional physical demands associated with extra time, opportunities may exist to implement interventions targeted at reducing fatigue and thus maximising performance capacity when matches are extended beyond 90 min. Whilst extra time may be perceived as a relatively infrequent occurrence generally, it is suggested that practitioners prepare players for such scenarios through the design of appropriate training sessions (Field et al., 2022). Moreover, substitutions can be used to replace those players who are experiencing acute fatigue during extra time. This practice is made more accessible in certain competitions by the availability of an additional substitution when matches progress beyond normal time (Field et al., 2022). Limited research exists to support the efficacy of nutritional interventions implemented immediately before extra time. However, fuelling strategies in the days prior to matches that could progress to extra time should be tailored to consider this potential. Similarly, reductions in blood glucose and lactate concentrations alongside increases in in plasma glycerol, non-esterified fatty acids, interleukin-6, and epinephrine during extra time compared with the initial 90 min of soccer-specific exercise (Stevenson et al., 2017), suggest a potential benefit to consuming sufficient carbohydrate on match day, including during the 5 min before extra time (Field et al., 2022). Player preferences must be taken into account, but administering caffeinated chewing gum in the 5 min before extra time may be efficacious for subsequent physical performance (Field et al., 2022), yet the effects on indices of cognitive performance remain unclear.

As professional men's players may cover an additional ~3–5 km during a 30-min extra time (Field et al., 2022; Winder et al., 2018), it may be important for practitioners to consider the post-match recovery responses when determining the best treatment for their players. Notably, professional players have demonstrated impaired subjective (i.e., wellness) and objective (i.e., countermovement jump performance) recovery markers when assessed 36 h after a match involving extra time compared with the same timepoint after 90 min of match-play (Winder et al., 2018). In addition, indices of physical performance and subsequent recovery were also reduced for some players in matches played 64 h after extra time (Winder et al., 2018). It is recommended that practitioners adopt specific nutritional strategies that replenish intramuscular and liver glycogen stores immediately following matches that involve extra time, whilst short-term reductions in training magnitude may also be warranted (Field et al., 2022). Such decisions should be made on an individual player basis and require careful consideration of the likely implications for recovery and maintaining adaptations. Strategic use of squad rotation strategies could help to minimise the effects of fatigue whilst maintaining physical adaptations across starting and non-starting players.

Practical Applications

The evidence that is currently available suggests that several opportunities exist on match day for practitioners to intervene with strategies targeted at optimising a

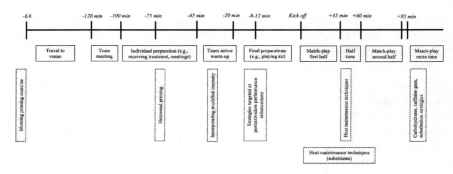

FIGURE 9.1 A timeline of typical match-day routines for football players, with the addition of suggested strategies for improving football performance.

player's performance on the pitch. Sports scientists and performance staff should consider incorporating at least some of these strategies into their players' practices on the day of competition where appropriate. Crucially, such strategies must be considered on an individual player level and within the regulatory, practical, and logistical constraints that exist. Acknowledging that different teams have their own specific routines, Figure 9.1 presents a typical competition-day timeline for professional football teams. We outline suggestions as to where the strategies discussed in this chapter could readily fit to help maximise on-pitch performance whilst minimising disruption to accepted routines. It is also suggested that these practices are trailed in training or other non-competition scenarios initially, to ensure that they are tolerated by and effective for a given player or team.

References

Anderson, P., Landers, G., and Wallman, K. (2014). Effect of warm-up on intermittent sprint performance. *Research in Sports Medicine, 22*(1), 88–99.

Beato, M., McErlain-Naylor, S. A., Halperin, I., and Iacono, A. D. (2020). Current evidence and practical applications of flywheel eccentric overload exercises as postactivation potentiation protocols: A brief review. *International Journal of Sports Physiology and Performance, 15*(2), 154–161.

Beaven, C. M., Kilduff, L. P., and Cook, C. J. (2018). Lower-limb passive heat maintenance combined with pre-cooling improves repeated sprint ability. *Frontiers in Physiology, 9*, 1064.

Cook, C., Holdcroft, D., Drawer, S., and Kilduff, L. P. (2013). Designing a warm-up protocol for elite bob-skeleton athletes. *International Journal of Sports Physiology and Performance, 8*(2), 213–215.

Cook, C. J., and Crewther, B. T. (2012a). Changes in salivary testosterone concentrations and subsequent voluntary squat performance following the presentation of short video clips. *Hormones and Behavior, 61*(1), 17–22.

Cook, C. J., and Crewther, B. T. (2012b). The effects of different pre-game motivational interventions on athlete free hormonal state and subsequent performance in professional rugby union matches. *Physiology and Behavior, 106*(5), 683–688.

Cook, C. J., Kilduff, L. P., Crewther, B. T., Beaven, M., and West, D. J. (2014). Morning based strength training improves afternoon physical performance in rugby union players. *Journal of Science and Medicine in Sport, 17*(3), 317–321.

Crewther, B. T., Cook, C. J., Gaviglio, C. M., Kilduff, L. P., and Drawer, S. (2012). Baseline strength can influence the ability of salivary free testosterone to predict squat and sprinting performance. *Journal of Strength and Conditioning Research, 26*(1), 261–268.

Dann, E., Quinn, S., Russell, M., Kilduff, L. P., Turner, A. N., and Hills, S. P. (2023). Alternate leg bounding acutely improves change of direction performance in women's team sports players irrespective of ground type. *Journal of Strength and Conditioning Research, 37*(6), 1199–1203.

Ekstrand, L. G., Battaglini, C. L., McMurray, R. G., and Shields, E. W. (2013). Assessing explosive power production using the backward overhead shot throw and the effects of morning resistance exercise on afternoon performance. *Journal of Strength and Conditioning Research, 27*(1), 101–106.

Field, A., Naughton, R. J., Haines, M., Lui, S., Corr, L. D., Russell, M., Page, R. M., and Harper, L. D. (2022). The demands of the extra-time period of soccer: A systematic review. *Journal of Sport and Health Science, 11*(3), 403–414.

Goodall, S., Thomas, K., Harper, L. D., Hunter, R., Parker, P., Stevenson, E., West, D., Russell, M., and Howatson, G. (2017). The assessment of neuromuscular fatigue during 120 min of simulated soccer exercise. *European Journal of Applied Physiology, 117*, 687–697.

Harrison, P., James, L., McGuigan, M., Jenkins, D., and Kelly, V. (2019). Resistance priming to enhance neuromuscular performance in sport: Evidence, potential mechanisms and directions for future research. *Sports Medicine, 49*(10), 1499–1514.

Hills, S. P., Aben, H. G. J., Starr, D. P., Kilduff, L. P., Arent, S. M., Barwood, M. J., Radcliffe, J. N., Cooke, C. B., and Russell, M. (2021). Body temperature and physical performance responses are not maintained at the time of pitch-entry when typical substitute-specific match-day practices are adopted before simulated soccer match-play. *Journal of Science and Medicine in Sport, 24*(5), 511–516.

Hills, S. P., Barrett, S., Hobbs, M., Barwood, M. J., Radcliffe, J. N., Cooke, C. B., and Russell, M. (2020). Modifying the pre-pitch entry practices of professional soccer substitutes may contribute towards improved movement-related performance indicators on match-day: A case study. *PloS one, 15*(5), e0232611–e0232611.

Ingham, S. A., Fudge, B. W., Pringle, J. S., and Jones, A. M. (2013). Improvement of 800-m running performance with prior high-intensity exercise. *International Journal of Sports Physiology and Performance, 8*(1), 77–83.

Kilduff, L. P., Owen, N., Bevan, H., Bennett, M., Kingsley, M. I., and Cunningham, D. (2008). Influence of recovery time on post-activation potentiation in professional rugby players. *Journal of Sports Sciences, 26*(8), 795–802.

Kilduff, L. P., West, D. J., Williams, N., and Cook, C. J. (2013). The influence of passive heat maintenance on lower body power output and repeated sprint performance in professional rugby league players. *Journal of Science and Medicine in Sport, 16*(5), 482–486.

Mohr, M., Krustrup, P., Nybo, L., Nielsen, J. J., and Bangsbo, J. (2004). Muscle temperature and sprint performance during soccer matches–beneficial effect of re-warm-up at half-time. *Scandinavian Journal of Medicine and Science in Sports, 14*(3), 156–162.

Nutt, F., Hills, S. P., Russell, M., Waldron, M., Scott, P., Norris, J., Cook, C. J., Mason, B., Ball, N., and Kilduff, L. P. (2022). Morning resistance exercise and cricket-specific repeated sprinting each improve indices of afternoon physical and cognitive performance in professional male cricketers. *Journal of Science and Medicine in Sport, 25*(2), 162–166.

152 Strength and Conditioning for Football

Russell, M., King, A., Bracken, R. M., Cook, C. J., Giroud, T., and Kilduff, L. P. (2016). A comparison of different modes of morning priming exercise on afternoon performance. *International Journal of Sports Physiology and Performance, 11*(6), 763–767.

Russell, M., Tucker, R., Cook, C. J., Giroud, T., and Kilduff, L. P. (2018). A comparison of different heat maintenance methods implemented during a simulated half-time period in professional rugby union players. *Journal of Science and Medicine in Sport, 21*(3), 327–332.

Russell, M., West, D. J., Briggs, M. A., Bracken, R. M., Cook, C. J., Giroud, T., Gill, N., and Kilduff, L. P. (2015). A passive heat maintenance strategy implemented during a simulated half-time improves lower body power output and repeated sprint ability in professional Rugby Union players. *PloS one, 10*(3), e0119374–e0119374.

Sargeant, A. J. (1987). Effect of muscle temperature on leg extension force and short-term power output in humans. *European Journal of Applied Physiology and Occupational Physiology, 56*(6), 693–698.

Silva, L. M., Neiva, H. P., Marques, M. C., Izquierdo, M., and Marinho, D. A. (2018). Effects of warm-up, post-warm-up, and re-warm-up strategies on explosive efforts in team sports: A systematic review. *Sports Medicine, 48*(10), 2285–2299.

Silvers-Granelli, H., Mandelbaum, B., Adeniji, O., Insler, S., Bizzini, M., Pohlig, R., Junge, A., Snyder-Mackler, L., and Dvorak, J. (2015). Efficacy of the FIFA 11+ Injury Prevention Program in the collegiate male soccer player. *The American Journal of Sports Medicine, 43*(11), 2628–2637.

Stevenson, E. J., Watson, A., Theis, S., Holz, A., Harper, L. D., and Russell, M. (2017). A comparison of isomaltulose versus maltodextrin ingestion during soccer-specific exercise. *European Journal of Applied Physiology, 117*, 2321–2333.

Turner, A. P., Bellhouse, S., Kilduff, L. P., and Russell, M. (2015). Postactivation potentiation of sprint acceleration performance using plyometric exercise. *Journal of Strength and Conditioning Research, 29*(2), 343–350.

West, D., Cunningham, D., Bevan, H., Crewther, B., Cook, C., and Kilduff, L. (2013a). Influence of active recovery on professional rugby union player's ability to harness postactivation potentiation. *The Journal of Sports Medicine and Physical Fitness, 53*(2), 203–208.

West, D. J., Cunningham, D. J., Crewther, B. T., Cook, C. J., and Kilduff, L. P. (2013b). Influence of ballistic bench press on upper body power output in professional rugby players. *Journal of Strength and Conditioning Research, 27*(8), 2282–2287.

Wilson, J. M., Duncan, N. M., Marin, P. J., Brown, L. E., Loenneke, J. P., Wilson, S. M., Jo, E., Lowery, R. P., and Ugrinowitsch, C. (2013). Meta-analysis of postactivation potentiation and power: effects of conditioning activity, volume, gender, rest periods, and training status. *Journal of Strength and Conditioning Research, 27*(3), 854–859.

Winder, N., Russell, M., Naughton, R. J., and Harper, L. D. (2018). The impact of 120 minutes of match-play on recovery and subsequent match performance: A case report in professional soccer players. *Sports, 6*(1), 22.

10
RECOVERY STRATEGIES AFTER MATCHES

Robin Thorpe and Robert Allan

Introduction

Every day, coaches, and athletes are challenged with the task of precisely timing and planning training periodisation to ensure optimal physiological adaptations and peak sporting performance align at the right moment (Mujika et al., 2018). Whilst some athletes may benefit from long preparation periods and short competition windows, team sports such as football experience quite the opposite; with a need to maintain frequent consistency in performance across a competition season spanning several months.

The physical and mental stress of regular training and competition can impair performance, be it through reduced quality of training or reduced competitive performance. Limited time between training sessions and competition is often experienced for elite-level players, with multiple matches regularly played in a short space of time (e.g., two to three matches in a one-week period) (Thorpe, 2021; Malone et al., 2022). These demands are further exacerbated by those players competing in leagues such as the English Premier League which does not include a winter break (Ekstrand et al., 2019). Similarly, international competitions taking place during the off-season period which typically provides players with an extensive period of rest, further increases the cumulative load experienced by those selected to represent their countries. For example, players competing in the English Premier League and also representing a nation in the European Championships 2024 likely receive only 21 days of rest between seasons. Inadequate recovery between training sessions and/or following matches may ultimately lead to fatigue; defined as the sensation of tiredness with associated decrements in muscle function and performance (Abbiss and Laursen, 2005). Ultimately, if fatigue is allowed to accumulate over time, it may lead to overreaching and overtraining, which in turn,

DOI: 10.4324/9781003383475-11

154 Strength and Conditioning for Football

increases the likelihood of illness, injury, and reduced performance (Soligard et al., 2016; Thorpe, 2021).

Recovery can be defined as the process of restoring the body's physiological and psychological function to a pre-fatigued level of performance (Versey et al., 2013) and is often considered a homeostatic rebalance (Soligard et al., 2016). Therefore, an increased emphasis on post-exercise recovery within training programs should allow the athlete to improve subsequent performance and/or quality of training, thus maintaining a suitable or improved stimulus for physiological adaptations and ability to compete. Whilst a plethora of available evidence suggests certain strategies can improve recovery in football in the short term (Haller et al., 2022), recent evidence following the use of recovery strategies over a longer period suggests an individualised and periodised approach might be more appropriate (Ihsan et al., 2021; Allan et al., 2022b; Rappelt et al., 2023). This chapter seeks to identify mechanisms underpinning recovery, whilst providing context surrounding recovery options within an elite football setting. In addition, recommendations including decision-making scenarios to inform real-world practice, led by the current scientific evidence will be proposed.

Physiological and Psychological Mechanisms Underpinning Recovery

Post-match recovery is a complex process that involves several phenomena. Some mechanisms of the recovery process have been observed and described in the scientific literature, as well as mentioned in Chapter 8. These mechanisms centre on the role of muscle damage, inflammation and regeneration, the repeated bout effect, metabolic and energetic substrates, and psychological aspects. For more detail related to the physiological and psychological demands of football, please refer to Chapters 1 and 13 respectively.

Context – Importance of Recovery for the Elite Football Player

Context is important when considering the recovery of elite players. Whilst the "physiology of recovery" is an established sub-discipline in exercise physiology and scientific research (Luttrell and Halliwill, 2015), it is important for practitioners to remember that the subsequent return to a homeostatic resting or a recovered state is a complex and multifaceted process.

Influence of Recovery and Adaptation

The importance of recovery in elite football is well established. With previous reports of professional players often being exposed to 60–80 competitive matches per season (Nédélec et al., 2012; Abaidia and Dupont, 2018), such busy schedules will require multiple games per week, over the course of a season. Whilst acute fatigue can occur after a single game (Thorpe et al., 2015, 2016), several weeks that demand multiple performances consecutively can lead to chronic fatigue. This is particularly highlighted by the time course of appropriate recovery of performance variables, which are often reported as requiring anywhere between 24 and 72 h (Abaidia and Dupont, 2018). Therefore, where multiple matches are required per week, chronic fatigue and underperformance may be experienced. The importance of this was underlined by Ekstrand et al. (2004), where players who were said to have underperformed in the 2002 World Cup in Korea/Japan had played more matches during the ten weeks leading up to the World Cup than those who performed better than expected (12.5 vs 9 games, respectively).

Beyond fatigue and underperformance, a lack of recovery may also impact football in other ways. For example, the accumulation of fatigue leading to overreaching is said to increase the risk of illness and injury (Doeven et al., 2018; Tiernan et al., 2022). Whilst the risk of injury in professional football has been well documented (Pfirrmann et al., 2016; Ekstrand et al., 2011), injuries in professional football can lead to huge implications for the clubs themselves. With fixture congestion and periods where only 2 days between matches are available, full recovery between matches is unlikely to occur (Nédélec et al., 2012) and players may be at an increased risk of injury (Bengtsson et al., 2013). The impact of injuries on a team can be extensive, particularly when 14% of the squad could be unavailable due to injury at any point during the season (Ekstrand, 2013). Data from a large study carried out over 11 seasons, suggests that elite football clubs can expect approximately 50 injuries per season, resulting in approximately two injuries per player causing playing time-loss (Ekstrand et al., 2011), with financial implications reaching >£400,000 per injured player, per month (Page et al., 2023).

Whilst the acute recovery period is vital for the restoration of energy stores and recovery from exercise-induced damage, it is also an important window for mediating adaptation to the exercise stimulus via inflammation, cell signalling, and the remodelling processes (Close et al., 2005; Howatson et al., 2009). Indeed, the external stress of completing exercise modulates important signalling networks that act as signals to "turn on or off" particular genes (e.g., mRNA levels/gene expression) that drive adaptation to the exercise stimulus (Sharples, 2017). The turning on of certain genes will ultimately lead to the production of functional proteins that create a cascade of change towards phenotypical improvements. For example, "turning on" the gene PGC-1alpha shows strong evidence for endurance-type changes in response to exercise, in an intensity-dependent manner (Sharples, 2017). PGC-1alpha regulates a number of other genes that lead to the initiation and transcription of mitochondrial DNA, and ultimately mitochondrial biogenesis (Sharples, 2017), offering endurance-related benefits. Similarly, work around the mammalian target of rapamycin (mTOR) has shown exercise that stimulates this molecular pathway, such as resistance-based exercise, promotes muscle growth and ultimately improves strength (Sharples, 2017). Thus, a greater sense of the molecular mechanisms of action involved in post-exercise adaptation allows

156 Strength and Conditioning for Football

recovery practitioners to understand the impact certain recovery modalities might have upon the adaptive processes to regular training.

In recent times, it has been suggested that the mechanistic actions of certain recovery strategies that work to reduce the post-exercise cellular stress response may inadvertently be blunting the cell signalling responses to training. Consequently, if this were to occur on a regular basis, the permanent disruption of the mechanisms of fatigue and proposed reduction of inflammatory events may actually harm an athlete's training progression and development of physical capacities (Versey et al., 2013). Recent research in cold water immersion (CWI) suggests a clear paradox is emerging. Specifically, quantification of endurance-based adaptation via cell signalling work suggests that regular post-exercise cooling does not negatively influence, and may even have a positive impact upon, mitochondrial-based adaptations (Ihsan et al., 2014; Joo et al., 2016; Allan et al., 2017, 2019, 2020). In contrast, it seems when CWI is regularly conducted after strength or resistance-based exercise sessions, the signals that drive hypertrophy-focused adaptations are somewhat dampened (Roberts et al., 2015; Fuchs et al., 2020) leading to a potential reduction in adaptations relating to improvements in muscle mass and strength (Roberts et al., 2015; Fuchs et al., 2020). Importantly, it should be noted that a dampening effect does not equal a complete removal of the training stimulus for adaptation, just somewhat less of what can be expected without post-exercise cooling. Therefore, in the case of post-exercise CWI for recovery purposes, greater individual consideration is required. However, a similar pattern assessing the dampening effect in response to other common recovery modalities has not been confirmed and therefore, this approach should not be generalised to all potential recovery strategies. This decision-making process is explored further, later in this chapter. In a conceptual model of recovery and adaptation (Figure 10.1), adequate recovery provides progression (or at least maintenance of performance), whereas inadequate recovery has the potential to be maladaptive.

Individual Considerations

The trade-off between recovery consolidation and adaptation has been discussed earlier in this chapter and, an important contextual question that ought to be considered is: *should athletes avoid post-exercise recovery strategies to protect training adaptations and avoid a dampening effect, or should recovery strategies be utilised to return the player to pre-fatigued levels, perhaps at the expense of signals for adaptations?* One intuitive factor which seems clear is that when sufficient recovery takes place, the subsequent quality of training sessions and/or performance is more likely maximised, thus providing an optimal stimulus for future adaptations. It could be argued that if recovery is not adequate, then players may return to training in a sub-standard condition, and the quality of such a session may be compromised, ultimately dampening the training stimulus for future adaptations. Our conceptual model of recovery and adaptation (Figure 10.1) outlines this approach.

Recovery Strategies after Matches **157**

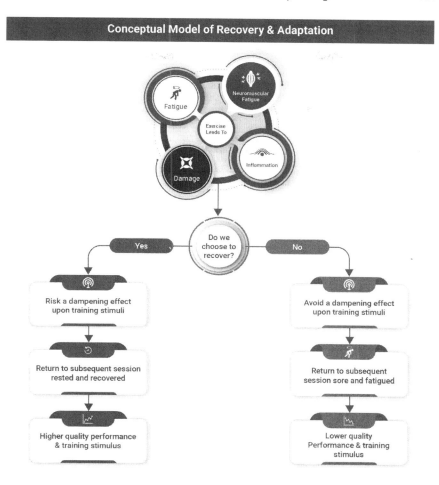

FIGURE 10.1 A conceptual model of how recovery choices might influence subsequent performances and training adaptations.

As such, current research suggests appropriate recovery should be individualised and parodied on an athlete-by-athlete basis (Moreno et al., 2015; Kellmann et al., 2018; Ihsan et al., 2021; Allan et al., 2022b; Grainger et al., 2021). To execute this, support staff and athletes should make some specific considerations on the use of post-exercise strategies including the implementation of tailor-made recovery programs for teams and players.

- **Training cycle and aim of the session**

    Post-exercise adaptations are particularly important following strength training stimuli; therefore, caution is indicated around the use of certain post-exercise recovery modalities during the pre-season or during blocks of training with a primary focus on hypertrophy-based adaptations. Importantly, recovery during these moments does not need to be ignored completely, as some evidence suggests that applying cooling methods after tactical and field-based activities (but not immediately following resistance or gym workouts) may help mitigate the observed dampening in muscle growth effects (Ihsan et al., 2021). Thus, a delayed approach after resistance-based sessions might offer an appropriate recovery, without the risk of dampening any adaptive signalling within the body.

- **Training load and frequency of sessions (training and competition)**

  High training loads and high frequency of sessions might suggest a limited amount of time for natural recovery to occur or be sufficient. For example, research shows markers of muscle damage and oxidative stress increased throughout a 72-h period after a football match (Ascensão et al., 2008; Ispirlidis et al., 2008). It could be argued that during these scenarios, any recovery modality that might allow reductions in perceived soreness or fatigue, among other things, might be advantageous; especially as this might improve the training quality (and therefore adaptive stimulus) in subsequent sessions.

- **Athletes' perception**

  Considerable attention should be given to athlete subjectivity when evaluating overall recovery strategies. Athletes often report adopting specific recovery methods based on their belief in their efficacy (Allan et al., 2022b). However, this could be due to a placebo effect. Notably, 80% of elite athletes previously surveyed, acknowledged their faith in the placebo effect (Bérdi et al., 2015). Moreover, emerging evidence suggests that a placebo component exists within recovery approaches, particularly CWI (Broatch et al., 2014; Wilson et al., 2018). Nevertheless, it remains evident that athletes perform better when they perceive less pain, fatigue, and tiredness, and if practitioners are confident that a recovery modality will have no negative effects, then an athlete's belief in it should probably be respected.

- **Consider environmental stress**

  When addressing recovery strategies, it's crucial to take into account whether the athlete is training or competing in warm environments. These conditions can pose thermoregulatory challenges, exacerbating physiological stress, thus affecting performance and overall well-being. In such scenarios, specific cryotherapy and cooling techniques may prove beneficial (Racinais et al., 2019). By reducing thermal stress, these interventions aim to restore the athlete to a pre-fatigued or homeostatic state, optimising recovery and readiness for subsequent activities.

- **Timing and proximity of the next session**

  It is widely acknowledged that warm muscles perform more effectively than cold muscles (Faulkner et al., 2013). This principle underpins the regular warm-up routines conducted by athletes. However, when planning for subsequent sessions or competitions within a short time after the previous one, thoughtful evaluation of recovery techniques becomes crucial. For instance, if performance is expected within the next few hours, it may be prudent to avoid muscle cooling methods. Instead, active recovery strategies that maintain muscle temperature and facilitate blood flow could better prepare the athlete for the upcoming demands.

Main Interventions Used to Drive the Recovery Process Following Match-play

Researchers and practitioners alike have investigated the efficacy of commonly used interventions to combat the physical and mental stress associated with football training and match-play (Nédélec et al., 2012). A recent investigation reviewing commonly used recovery strategies in the Spanish top Division (Spanish La Liga) reported that all teams utilised at least one recovery strategy following match-play (Altarriba-Bartes et al., 2020). Quality sleep and rest, nutrition, and hydration serve as the foundation of any effective recovery approach and therefore are unsurprisingly central to strategies implemented by elite clubs (Nédélec et al., 2013; Altarriba-Bartes et al., 2020; Field et al., 2021). Further to these building blocks, marked variability arises in the recovery strategies adopted following training and matches, including strategies stacked together with the nature of the protocol and timing of application across the recovery continuum (Altarriba-Bartes et al., 2020; Field et al., 2021). Extensive evaluation of the mechanisms underpinning various techniques from a recovery and physiological adaptation perspective is beyond the scope of the current chapter. Rather, in this section, we briefly review a range of recovery techniques commonly used in elite football and further highlight proposed mechanisms and utilisation recommendations (Table 10.1).

Sleep

In a survey performed on a football team participating in the Union of European Football Associations (UEFA) Europa League, 95% of the players reported poor sleep following night matches (Nédélec et al., 2015), which may be a consequence of the heightened physical and cognitive load involved during match-play (Nédélec et al., 2015). Consequently, the recovery process is likely to be detrimentally affected (Nédélec et al., 2015). In addition, poor sleep at night may accentuate muscle damage or limit muscle repair, which slows muscle performance recovery kinetics (Skein et al., 2013; Nédélec et al., 2015). Cognitive function plays a key role in fatigue perception but also in muscle function. It has been suggested that this mental aspect may also be negatively affected when the duration of sleep is insufficient (i.e., <7-h per night) or when the quality of sleep is poor (Nédélec et al., 2015). From a metabolic perspective, studies have shown a possible negative effect of a lack of sleep on glycogen resynthesis (Skein et al., 2011). Importantly, reduced sleep quality may be compensated by short napping strategies

160 Strength and Conditioning for Football

TABLE 10.1 Current Evidence of the Proposed Mechanisms of Action and Practical Applications of Commonly Used Recovery Modalities

	Proposed mechanisms of action	How?	When?
Sleep	Recovery of the neuro-metabolic costs of the exercise. Physiological restitution. Improved learning and motor memory.	Increase sleep quality and sleep quantity through sleep hygiene strategies. Such strategies are varied and inconsistent, but might include: • >7h sleep, optimally 8-9h, more when particularly fatigued • Showering (warm) • Turning off electrical devices at least 30min prior to bedtime; limit blue light exposure • Abstinence from watching TV in bed • Creating cool, dark, quiet rooms • Wearing eye masks and/or earplugs • Clean and appropriate bedding. Napping could compensate for lost sleep or benefit PM performances. Naps of 20-90mins 12h from the mid-point of the athletes usual sleep cycle.	Day-to-day, especially in-season, with greater attention before and after matches.
Nutrition	Hydrate – refuel - repair	Replace lost fluids and electrolytes following training and match play. 1.2-1.5g carbohydrate kg-1 body wt.h-1 to maximise glycogen resynthesis in the first 4 hours. ~40g protein will also assist in maximizing glycogen resynthesis and protein synthesis rates.	In most situations there is sufficient time to restore euhydration and electrolyte balance through normal eating/drinking practices. Refuel as soon as possible post-exercise and at frequent intervals (15-30mins) in the first 4 hours. Daily intakes of 6-8g kg-1 body mass of CHO and >1.5 g kg-1 body mass of protein (~20g per meal) recommended in the 24h following a game. 30-60g casein protein before sleep can enhance overnight protein synthesis.
Cooling	Analgesic effect via slowing of pain signals in peripheral nervous system and reduced activation of nociceptors through reduced swelling/oedema. Alterations in skin and muscle blood flow. Reduced core and tissue temperature. Improved subjective wellness.	Cold water immersion – 8-12mins @ 8 to 12°C. Whole-body cryotherapy – 2-4 mins @ -110 to -140°C. Phase change material/cooling garments – 3-6h @ 15°C (approx.)	Immediately post exercise preferred. Delayed at least 4h if following resistance type exercise. Immediately post exercise preferred. If not available, the following day. Immediately post exercise preferred. Often a good option during travel post-match.
Heating	Increased core and tissue temperature, increased blood flow, in turn, increasing heat shock protein release and altering gene expression. Hastens recovery of contractile function and range of motion. Protects against EIMD, soreness, swelling.	Hot water immersion – 15-40min @ 38-40°C. Sauna bathing / ~20min @ ~40°C	No evidence on best time frame in the days following metabolic based demands preferred. More often completed for recovery following training sessions than matches. Often employed prior to exercise
Active recovery	Increased muscle blood flow, promoting nutrient transport. Enhanced clearance of waste/bi-products and cell debris. Temporary analgesic effect in muscle. Does not inhibit acute anabolic response to exercise.	Incorporates dynamic, aerobic-type exercise at a low to moderate intensity. Run, bike, swim. At least 15 minutes at 30-50% VO2max.	Immediately post-exercise. Often referred to as "cool down" or "warm down". Can be used in the days following exercise.
Compression garments	Increased venous return and peak velocity via superficial compression to veins. Decreased perceived soreness and pain. Amplified sensory input and somatosensation. Reduced muscle oscillatory properties during exercise. Reductions in swelling.	Garments range from stockings, knee socks/calf sleeves, arm sleeves, whole-body garments, graduated tights and sleeved tops. Optimal duration is lacking. Research conducted wearing garments ranges from 1h to >48h. Optimal pressure is unknown. Research conducted from 7 to 30mm Hg. However, custom fitted/made to measure garments might offer greater pressure and therefore efficacy.	Sometimes during, but more often in the hours following exercise. Often employed following Away matches during return travel.
Stretching/Mobility	Improved range of motion. Decrease stiffness. Prevent future injury.	2-5 repetitions for ~30s -2min of targeted muscles/muscle groups.	Often completed prior to exercise. Meta-analyses suggest not worthwhile for reducing post-exercise muscle soreness.
Foam Rolling	Improved ROM & flexibility. Reduced perception of pain, fatigue, DOMS.	~2min per muscle/muscle group, using body weight pressure.	Following exercise. Due to positive influences on flexibility and ROM can also be considered in warm up/activation sessions.
Massage	Short term changes in flexibility. Short term reduced perception of pain, DOMS.	Tissue massage. Often completed by therapist. Percussive massage. For recovery: >3min per muscle/muscle group at low frequencies (<40Hz). For ROM & flexibility: <3min per muscle/muscle group at higher frequencies (>40Hz).	Post-exercise or following competition.

(Lastella et al., 2021). Waterhouse et al. (2007) found that napping, followed by a 30-minute recovery period, improved alertness and aspects of mental and physical performance following partial sleep loss (Waterhouse et al., 2007). The ability to nap for short periods (20–90 min) during the day (12-h from the mid-point of a regular sleep cycle) may be a useful technique for players, especially during a congested fixture schedule and when performances are required late in the evening. Additionally, recent work suggests whole-body CWI before sleep might positively influence sleep architecture, improving the quality and quantity of sleep (Chauvineau et al., 2021); implicating beneficial effects of combining strategies to improve recovery. Recommendations for sleep induction include: adopting a dark and quiet environment using eyeshades and earplugs, listening to relaxing music, and adopting regular sleep-wake schedules.

Nutrition

Match participation may induce up to a 50% decrease in muscular glycogen concentrations (Krustrup et al., 2006). Furthermore, muscle glycogen stores may not be fully replenished at 48–72 h following a football match (Jacobs et al., 1982). The reduction in muscle glycogen may impact recovery kinetics following exercise-induced muscle damage (Gavin et al., 2016). For example, reduced maximal voluntary contractions have been observed 48-h following eccentric exercise in a reduced glycogen state (Gavin et al., 2016). To counteract the deleterious effects of muscle glycogen depletion, it has been shown that an elevated muscle glycogen content through a carbohydrate intake may enhance the replenishment of glycogen stores 48-h post-match (Krustrup et al., 2011). Furthermore, it has been suggested that approximately 72 h might be required to fully replenish muscle glycogen stores, especially in type II fibres (Mohr et al., 2005, 2022; Gunnarsson et al., 2013). However, detrimental effects on recovery may arise when active recovery of long durations is performed at low intensities (Fairchild et al., 2003), leading to glycogen depletion in type 1 muscle fibers (Fairchild et al., 2003). The role of nutritional interventions including hydration, carbohydrate, and protein requirements, in relation to training and recovery is discussed in Chapter 12.

Cooling Strategies

Cryotherapy is an umbrella term describing a plethora of strategies, including, ice packs, cold water, cold air, and phase-change materials, all of which promote the withdrawal of body heat (Allan et al., 2022a). CWI or ice baths, the most applied cryotherapy technique, also represent one of the most common recovery techniques adopted in elite football (Altarriba-Bartes et al., 2020; Field et al., 2021). Cost-effectiveness, access, and greater cooling capacity of water vs other forms of cryotherapy (Mawhinney et al., 2017) explain the popularity of CWI, with recent

162 Strength and Conditioning for Football

work showing ~80% of those who used this modality found it useful for recovery (Allan et al., 2022b). The recent emergence of phase-change material, a new alternative to gel packs that provides an almost constant temperature for a longer period of time (Allan et al., 2022a), can provide a practical means of delivering prolonged post-exercise cooling which has the capacity to accelerate recovery of elite football players (Clifford et al., 2018).

Cooling strategies typically serve to reduce tissue temperature, which mediates a reduction in cell metabolism and blood flow to the exercised muscles (Mawhinney et al., 2022). This collective change in temperature and blood flow reduces clinical symptoms of inflammation such as pain and swelling, and triggers post-exercise parasympathetic activity (Al Haddad et al., 2010; Leeder et al., 2012; Roberts et al., 2014). The effects of CWI on recovery of performance are inconsistent; however, several meta-analyses have demonstrated enhanced recovery from strenuous exercise in trained athletes (Leeder et al., 2012; Poppendieck et al., 2013). Any inconsistency is likely driven by differences in the type of exercise, immersion protocol used, and performance measures evaluated. A point potentiated by difficulties in knowledge exchange, with recent work suggesting support staff (i.e. physios, S and C coaches, and sports scientists) tend to utilise methods more closely aligned to scientific research, whilst coaches and athletes often cool for too long at unnecessary temperatures (Allan et al., 2022b). This is something that a recent BASES expert statement sought to address by providing a cooling-specific decision tree for recovery (Grainger et al., 2021). Alongside its effects on acute recovery, increasing evidence has shown that post-exercise cooling, in the form of CWI, might exhibit a mode-dependant effect on training adaptation (Malta et al., 2021). In this respect, cooling could diminish adaptation to resistance training and associated strength performance but appears not to affect aerobic exercise performance (Malta et al., 2021).

Despite this, it might seem reasonable to consider that the benefits from CWI on recovery could outweigh any dampening effect upon strength. Interestingly, should cooling be delayed, or not take place immediately following a resistance-based session, it might be possible to harness the recovery benefits of cooling, whilst avoiding any negative effects upon adaptations for improvements in strength (Lindsay et al., 2016; Tavares et al., 2019; Seco-calvo et al., 2020; Tavares et al., 2020). Moreover, a recent systematic review from Grgic (2023) highlighted that a dampening effect upon strength is only seen when only the exercised limbs are cooled, whilst whole body cooling protocols (like those that are more commonly used in practice) do not actually show a dampening effect when used following resistance-based sessions. Mechanisms explaining the differential effects in localised vs whole body CWI upon the dampening effect are unclear, and further research is required to clarify. These insights infer that the decision to apply post-exercise cooling following resistance-type exercise is dependent upon the relative importance of recovery time vs the desire to maximise training adaptation, and careful attention should be placed upon the individual situation.

Heating Strategies

Heating strategies increase body temperature actively through modalities such as submaximal cycling and running (including exercise in water) or passively using external heating sources such as immersion in hot-water and sauna bathing. Active and passive heating techniques are popular in elite football with ~90% of teams in the Spanish top Division and ~70% of teams surveyed globally using such techniques (Altarriba-Bartes et al., 2020; Field et al., 2021).

Profound differences exist in the metabolic, cardiovascular, and thermoregulatory responses to active and passive heating strategies (Francisco et al., 2021). This complexity, together with a wide variation in study experimental designs, presents challenges when evaluating the influence of these techniques on exercise recovery (McGorm et al., 2018). Active and passive heating strategies increase circulation (Francisco et al., 2021), while increases in muscle temperature *per se*, directly enhance contractile function (Rodrigues et al., 2022). These physiological changes suggest heating strategies offer a plausible means through which to enhance recovery; however, evidence to date in humans remains inconclusive (Nédélec et al., 2013; McGorm et al., 2018; Rodrigues et al., 2022). Recent literature has shown positive vascular adaptations and rate of force development effects following hot water immersion post-exercise, offering a promising use case for enhancing recovery in football (Sautillet et al., 2024; Steward et al., 2024). Additionally, previous data from Jackman and colleagues (2023) suggests that whilst hot-water immersion is a viable means of maintaining intramuscular temperature post-exercise, recovery of muscle function and muscle soreness remains independent of acute changes in intramuscular temperature. Considering this recent promising work showing adaptive and recovery effects in response to hot water immersion, more research is required to investigate key contributing mechanisms associated to these outcomes following hot water immersion.

In contrast to post-exercise cooling, less attention has centred on the influence of post-exercise heating on training adaptation (McGorm et al., 2018). Horgan and colleagues (2024) have shown (albeit in elite rugby league players) that in-season use of water immersion (both hot and cold) led to improved inflammatory adaptive responses. Moreover, recent evidence from Fuchs and colleagues (2020) has shown that acute hot-water immersion following resistance-type exercise does not further increase myofibrillar protein synthesis rates, but importantly, does not dampen them like CWI might. However, more chronic evidence assessing the regular influence of hot-water immersion upon training adaptation remains to be seen.

Active Recovery

Active recovery is a process that is often termed a "cool down", or alternatively a "warm down". This is perhaps one of the more familiar methods of recovery to athletes and non-athletes alike and is one intervention that has a high affinity of "buy-in" from professional athletes (Crowther et al., 2017; Murray et al., 2018). The

164 Strength and Conditioning for Football

mechanisms of action are thought to include increases in muscle blood flow, enhancing the clearance of waste or bi-products and cell debris, whilst also having a temporary analgesic effect within the muscle (Raeder et al., 2017). However, evidence to support this is contrasting. Whilst low-intensity aerobic activity shows positive effects upon a faster clearance of by-products such as blood lactic acid concentration (McLellan et al., 1989; Monedero et al., 2000), this does not necessarily translate into improved recovery and/or performance (Bond et al., 1991). Meanwhile, with the importance of improved blood flow for recovery of performance highlighted previously (Borne et al., 2017), active recovery is more likely to prevent the post-exercise decrease in blood flow, than increase it (Vaile et al., 2010); particularly as muscle blood flow increases linearly with exercise intensity (Sjøgaard, 1988).

On the other hand, positive effects on delayed onset of muscle soreness (DOMS) (Armstrong, 1984), but not on perceived fatigue, were found in a meta-analysis (Dupuy et al., 2018); however, the influence was only significant in the initial hours after exercise (Zainuddin et al., 2006). The contrasting research is emphasised further by the work of Andersson and colleagues (2008, 2010a, 2010b) whereby up to 1 hour of active recovery seemed neutral in effect, with little beneficial or detrimental effects noted. As such, whilst player belief in active recovery seems high, contrasting data indicates its beneficial effects are questionable. What remains surprising is that no "gold standard" approach has yet to be identified, with the type, intensity, and duration of active recovery, following different modes of exercise, needing further investigation.

The utilisation of contemporary modalities such as electrical stimulation and sequential pneumatic compression devices has soared in recent times. Electrical stimulation in the form of small devices temporarily fixed to the lower limb conducting to peripheral nerves has shown increases in perceived recovery and muscle damage markers following acute treatments (Beaven et al., 2013). The suggested mechanisms for improved recovery include a mechanical involuntary contraction leading to a 'muscle pump effect' of blood flow and circulation. Moreover, pneumatic sequential compression or recovery boots as it's commonly termed, has shown efficacy in the clinical setting for increasing blood flow in patients (Feldman et al., 2012). In the exercise setting, pneumatic sequential compression has been seen to increase circulating lactate post-exercise; however, there is a lack of evidence supporting improved recovery or reduced muscle damage markers (Zelikovski et al., 1993). Given the widespread popularity of these devices, the subsequent evidence of efficacy also remains unclear. Notwithstanding that and considering the proposed mechanisms of enhancing blood flow and circulation, these modalities would logically fit under the umbrella of active recovery.

Compression Garments

Approximately 70% of teams in the Spanish top Division and clubs/national federations included in a recent global survey report use compression garments

(Altarriba-Bartes et al., 2020; Field et al., 2021). Lower limb compression garments typically apply graded external mechanical pressure to the skin which is greatest at the distal calf and lower in more proximal areas (Hill et al., 2014). Compression strategies are thought to promote several physiological changes, though evidence to date remains equivocal in many areas (Weakley et al., 2022), despite recent literature suggesting these areas as a promising landscape (O'Riordan et al., 2023). With sufficient pressure, the pressure gradient might enhance venous return through superficial compression to veins and improved capillary filtration (Partsch and Mosti, 2008; Feldman et al., 2012), whilst also increasing arterial blood flow (Dorey et al., 2018). In support of this, recent evidence has shown an increase in venous return and venous peak velocity measured by ultrasound (O'Riordan et al., 2023). Compression has also been shown to promote positive effects on muscle damage, perceived soreness and pain, sensorimotor systems, and muscle oscillatory properties (MacRae et al., 2011; Weakley et al., 2022). Despite the conflicting findings in research to date, the potential benefit of wearing compression garments seems to far outweigh the risks of any detrimental effects (MacRae et al., 2011; Brown et al., 2017; Weakley et al., 2022). Various methodological factors are likely to have contributed to the inconsistencies in experimental findings, with inter-individual variation in compression provided by commercially available compression garments representing a key limitation. This highlights the need to use individualised "made-to-measure" compression garments to ensure the desired level of compression is attained.

Range of Motion Strategies

Maintaining or improving the joint range of motion in athletes is often a key component of the work undertaken by support staff (Wilke et al., 2020). Several strategies are used to facilitate range of motion including various forms of stretching and mobility (static and dynamic), massage and self-myofascial release, or foam rolling. In elite football, self-myofascial release or foam rolling, and active and passive stretching remain popular techniques amongst elite clubs (Altarriba-Bartes et al., 2020).

Stretching has previously been reported to be the most popular recovery method undertaken by athletes of all levels, with 98% national, 79% state, 87% regional, and 77% local athletes utilising stretching to assist in post-exercise recovery (Crowther et al., 2017). The proposed mechanisms include an increase in joint range of motion and a reduction in musculotendinous stiffness, with correct application (Nédélec et al., 2013; Stojanovic and Ostojic, 2011). Teams from the English Premier League reportedly spend 40% of training time stretching with 50% of French teams in Ligue 1 using stretching for recovery purposes (Dadebo et al., 2004). Across English teams, static stretching was the most prevalent form of stretching comprising typically 30 seconds per muscle group for two to five sets per session (Nédélec et al., 2013). Although the use of stretching and particularly static stretching is widespread, there is no evidence to date to support the use of stretching in enhancing the recovery process in elite football (Kinugasa and Kilding, 2009). Indeed, a recent survey highlighted discord between science and practice, when physiotherapists, sports scientists, and coaches were questioned about the effectiveness of stretching. Ultimately, many of their positive opinions about stretching did not align with conclusions in scientific research (Warneke et al., 2024). A recent investigation of professional youth football players from an English Premier League team found no differences in muscle damage markers 24–48 hours following match-play when static stretching was performed (Pooley et al., 2017). In a similar cohort, and similar study design, active recovery and CWI improved recovery markers significantly greater than static stretching (Pooley et al., 2020). Further to this, Lund and Colleagues (1998) suggested static stretching may even hinder the recovery process following eccentric muscle damage. Thus, despite the widespread use of stretching across all levels of professional football, there is little evidence to support its effect on recovery, and under certain conditions (e.g., muscle damage), caution should be taken.

Foam rolling (self-myofascial release), is performed as a recovery strategy by 91% of Spanish La Liga teams (Altarriba-Bartes et al., 2020). Foam rolling has been likened to traditional massage; however, many investigations have shown larger improvements in the flexibility of a joint range of motion following foam rolling compared to a limited number studying traditional massage techniques (Cheatham et al., 2015; Martínez-Aranda et al., 2024). Recent investigations have found that short bouts of foam rolling (30 sec per muscle group) on soft-tissue areas may lead to a significant increase in the joint range of movement (MacDonald et al., 2013). Furthermore, the use of foam rolling as a means of self-myofascial release has shown positive effects on perceived pain, fatigue, and DOMS (Cheatham et al., 2015; Martínez-Aranda et al., 2024). Although mainly adopted in the training process as a recovery strategy, the use of foam rolling largely serves to improve joint range of motion and in some cases perceptual recovery, hence, advantageous during all periods of the training process especially following games and intense strenuous training sessions. Additionally, from a recovery perspective, foam rolling seems to show more positive evidence than stretching *per se*.

Massage

Massage, including its various forms, such as effleurage, petrissage, tapotement, friction, and vibration was used in 78% of French Ligue 1 teams. A common belief among practitioners and athletes alike has been that massage enhances muscle blood flow and subsequently the removal of disruptive metabolites from fatigued muscle regions. However, previous research has shown that massage has a limited effect on blood flow or the removal of waste products from the muscle (Fuller et al., 2015; Dakić et al., 2023). Furthermore, Wiltshire and Colleagues (2010) showed a detrimental effect of massage on blood flow by reducing the mechanical processes of muscle fibers, glycogen re-synthesis, and in turn, reducing recovery, whilst others have shown poor results following fatiguing exercise (Alonso-Calvete et al., 2022). Additionally, Viitasalo et al. (1995) observed a potentially debilitating rise in muscle damage proteins following strength exercise with the addition of immediate massage (Viitasalo et al., 1995). Small positive psychological and perceived effects have been shown in untrained individuals following tissue massage (Viitasalo et al., 1995; Dakić et al., 2023) and percussive massage (Ferreira et al., 2023; Roberts et al., 2024), with positive effects seen in perceived fatigue and DOMS (Dupuy et al., 2018). However, whilst there seems to be a small positive subjective response to massage, the physiological effect of massage remains unclear and lacks empirical support. Moreover, caution is warranted with the new popularity of handheld percussive massage guns, as anecdotal reports, and case reports (Chen et al., 2021) suggest overuse of the therapy can lead to injury.

Sequencing of Multiple Strategies

It is clear that an array of different techniques is used by professional teams and players in an attempt to accelerate recovery from football training and matches (Nédélec et al., 2013; Altarriba-Bartes et al., 2020). However, there is currently a lack of efficacy for a number of strategies in improving the multifactorial systems which underpin recovery. That being said, a selection of modalities appears to promote positive changes in recovery associated with certain systems and symptoms. Furthermore, the context, reasoning, and sequencing for use have been shown to add further promise. CWI, compression garments, joint range of motion strategies, and active or hot-water recovery appear able to promote specific physiological changes at various time points to accelerate the players' return towards their pre-training/match state. These include a reduction in tissue temperature and blood flow, together with an increase in joint range of motion, blood flow, and venous return. The difficulty of translating the science into practice is that often, in elite football, more than one recovery strategy is utilised post-exercise. Moreover, the timeframe in which they are used also differs. For example, anecdotally, nutritional strategies may be implemented almost immediately following a match; however, active recovery, range of motion techniques, and hot/cold therapies may be delayed, with massage potentially not taking place until the following day.

Whilst there are small positive influences of many of the individual recovery techniques, science is yet to provide sufficient data on the influence a combination of strategies might have, and the correct order in which they could (or should) be implemented. Indeed, the idea that one modality might have a permissive effect upon another has been demonstrated previously, with whole-body CWI improving subsequent sleep quality and quantity (Chauvineau et al., 2021). Logic might suggest multiple small wins might total a much larger win, when combining a few recovery techniques, especially when the different techniques have contrasting mechanisms of action, upon multiple physiological/psychological systems.

FIGURE 10.2 Predominant demands and reciprocal stressed physiological systems in football alongside associated typical symptoms and recovery interventions.

However, athletes' and practitioners ought to proceed with caution since multiple independent recovery modalities also elicit contraindicating effects when used simultaneously or in a short timeframe. It may be that certain modalities purported to elicit similar physiological results be stacked together in order to amplify the desired favourable outcome. Figure 10.2 illustrates this theoretical model emphasising the need for an individualised and periodised recovery programme.

Monitoring Guided Prescription of Recovery Modalities

The differences in physiological origin associated with football training and competition infer that it is illogical that a single recovery strategy and/or a generic one-size-fits-all approach would accelerate each of the systems previously discussed (Minnett and Costello, 2015). Alternatively, an approach where strategies are periodised to match the individual symptoms, organismic fatigued system, external load-type, or the response to stress may be a more preferred technique in professional football (Thorpe et al., 2017; Kellmann et al., 2018). Indeed, monitoring of recovery or the response to load may provide insights into the exact physiological stress an athlete is currently experiencing. Identifying causes of fatigue via the use of practical monitoring processes is recommended for individualisation of recovery strategy prescription and ultimately increased performance (Thorpe et al., 2017).

A recent review stated that the quantification of physiological stress via athlete response outcome measures: athlete self-report, heart rate derived autonomic nervous system, neuromuscular function protocols, biochemical, immunological, endocrine, and joint range of motion could improve practical prescription of modalities in enhancing recovery (Thorpe et al., 2017). For example, assessing changes in DOMS, joint range of motion, or the autonomic nervous system via heart rate-derived metrics (heart rate variability and/or heart rate recovery) may establish whether or not an athlete is experiencing symptoms associated with structural damage (Dupuy et al., 2018). Thus, this would provide a gateway to understanding and quantifying which strategies may be most appropriate for improving associated fatigued systems. Furthermore, attention ought to be prioritised to establish strategies which match the associated physiological stress (Figure 10.2). The decision-making process associated with this principle may likely be performed daily in professional football and possibly be more impactful on the training process in the days following competition (Figure 10.3).

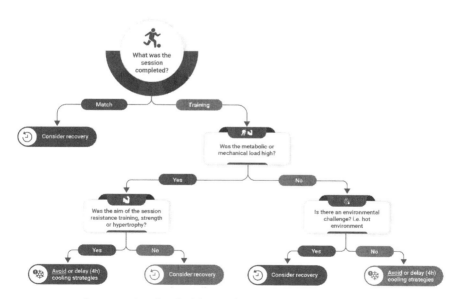

FIGURE 10.3 An example of a decision-making selection process aimed at outlining the most appropriate (adaptation-recovery) modality.

Practical Application of Recovery Strategies for Footballers

Recovery from football training and competition is a complex and multifactorial process involving physiological and psychological parameters which need to be constantly evolving to optimise individual athlete recovery and physiological adaptation. The relative importance of recovery vs adaptation will vary according to the needs of the athlete within the context of the season and within the context of the match-training sequence. This raises the idea of using recovery strategies in a manner that is periodised to mirror the current and contextual demands, and to adequately recover from the stress, but also balance the need for an adaptive response. Understanding the contextual factors which ultimately define the recovery strategy approach via the utilisation of key questions can support decision-making. A recovery strategy decision-making selection framework should serve to match a given stress with the most effective intervention to maximise the intended outcome across the stress-recovery-adaptation continuum (Figure 10.3).

A range of recovery strategies are commonly applied in the field despite limited scientific evidence to support their efficacy. Figure 10.4 illustrates an example of the timeline of recovery modality implementation in the hours and

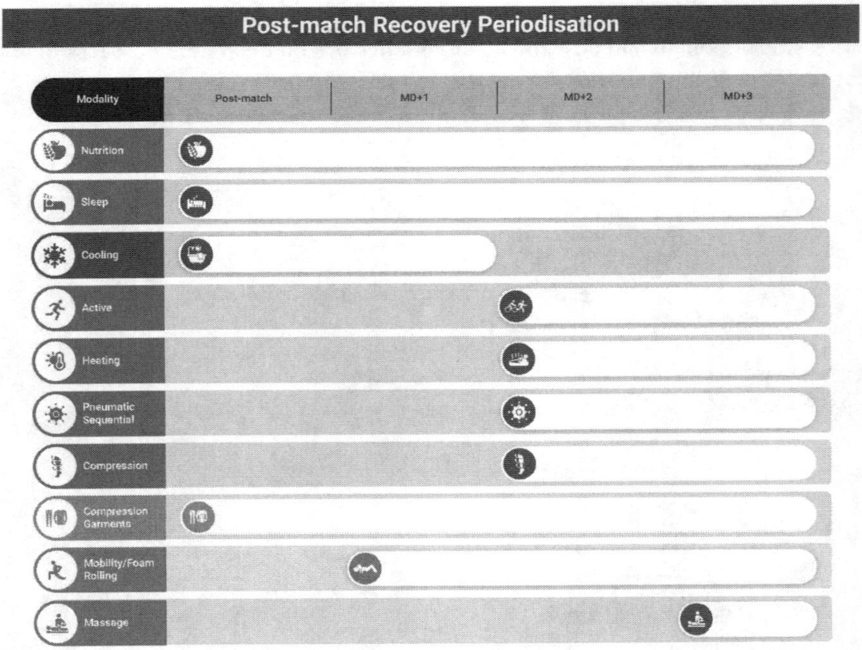

FIGURE 10.4 An example of the timeline of recovery modality selection and implementation in the hours and days post-match.

days post-match. The foundation of any intervention strategy should primarily be centered around quality sleep and rest, along with adequate nutrition factors. Beyond this, there is sufficient scientific evidence to advocate the use of effective cooling and compression techniques to further accelerate the recovery process. Range of motion strategies and heating modalities might support the recovery processes at various time points, although more research is needed to examine their targeted efficacy. Finally, an optimal recovery intervention strategy likely reflects a balance between evidence-based prescription, practitioner experience, and individual athlete preferences and response to individual interventions. Executing this balance can be achieved with decision-making approaches outlining contextual priorities.

References

Abaidia A-E, Dupont G. Recovery Strategies for Football Players. *Swiss Sports Exerc Med.* 2018; 66(4):28–36.

Abbiss CR, Laursen PB. Models to Explain Fatigue during Prolonged Endurance Cycling. *Sports Med.* 2005;35(10):865–898. https://doi.org/10.2165/00007256-200535100-00004.

Al Haddad H, Laursen PB, Ahmaidi S, Buchheit M. Influence of Cold Water Face Immersion on Post-exercise Parasympathetic Reactivation. *Eur J Appl Physiol.* 2010;108(3):599–606. https://doi.org/10.1007/s00421-009-1253-9.

Allan R, Malone J, Alexander J, Vorajee S, Ihsan M, Gregson W, Kwiecien S, Mawhinney C. Cold for Centuries: A Brief History of Cryotherapies to Improve Health, Injury and Post-exercise Recovery. *Eur J Appl Physiol.* 2022a;122(5):1153–1162. https://doi.org/10.1007/s00421-022-04915-5.

Allan R, Akin B, Sinclair J, Hurst H, Alexander J, Malone JJ, Naylor A, Mawhinney C, Gregson W, Ihsan M. Athlete, Coach and Practitioner Knowledge and Perceptions of Post-Exercise Cold-water Immersion for Recovery: A Qualitative and Quantitative Exploration. *Sport Sci Health.* 2022b;18:699–713. https://doi.org/10.1007/s11332-021-00839-3.

Allan R, Morton JP, Close GL, Drust B, Gregson W, Sharples AP. PGC-1α Alternative Promoter (Exon 1b) Controls Augmentation of Total PGC-1α Gene Expression in Response to Cold Water Immersion and Low Glycogen Availability. *Eur J Appl Physiol.* 2020;120(11):2487–2493. https://doi.org/10.1007/s00421-020-04467-6.

Allan R, Sharples AP, Close GL, Drust B, Shepherd SO, Dutton J, Morton JP, Gregson W. Postexercise Cold Water Immersion Modulates Skeletal Muscle PGC-1α mRNA Expression in Immersed and Nonimmersed Limbs: Evidence of Systemic Regulation. *J Appl Physiol (*1985). 2017;123(2):451–459. https://doi.org/10.1152/japplphysiol.00096.2017.

Allan R, Sharples AP, Cocks M, Drust B, Dutton J, Dugdale HF, Mawhinney C, Clucas A, Hawkins W, Morton JP, Gregson W. Low Pre-exercise Muscle Glycogen Availability Offsets the Effect of Post-exercise Cold Water Immersion in Augmenting PGC-1α Gene Expression. *Physiol Rep.* 2019;7(11):e14082. https://doi.org/10.14814/phy2.14082.

Alonso-Calvete A, Lorenzo-Martínez M, Padrón-Cabo A, Pérez-Ferreirós A, Kalén A, Abelairas-Gómez C, Rey E. Does Vibration Foam Roller Influence Performance and Recovery? A Systematic Review and Meta-analysis. *Sports Med Open.* 2022;8(1):32. https://doi.org/10.1186/s40798-022-00421-2.

172 Strength and Conditioning for Football

Altarriba-Bartes A, Peña J, Vicens-Bordas J, Casals M, Peirau X, Calleja-González J. The Use of Recovery Strategies by Spanish First Division Soccer Teams: A Cross-Sectional Survey. *Phys Sportsmed*. 2021;49(3):297–307. https://doi.org/10.1080/00913847.2020. 1819150.

Altarriba-Bartes A, Peña J, Vicens-Bordas J, Milà-Villaroel R, Calleja-González J. Post-competition Recovery Strategies in Elite Male Soccer Players. Effects on Performance: A Systematic Review and Meta-analysis. *PLoS One*. 2020;15(10):e0240135. https://doi. org/10.1371/journal.pone.0240135.

Andersson H, Karlsen A, Blomhoff R, Raastad T, Kadi F. Active Recovery Training Does Not Affect the Antioxidant Response to Soccer Games in Elite Female Players. *Br J Nutr*. 2010a;104(10):1492–1499. https://doi.org/10.1017/S0007114510002394.

Andersson H, Bøhn SK, Raastad T, Paulsen G, Blomhoff R, Kadi F. Differences in the Inflammatory Plasma Cytokine Response Following Two Elite Female Soccer Games Separated by a 72-h Recovery. *Scand J Med Sci Sports*. 2010b;20(5):740–747. https:// doi.org/10.1111/j.1600-0838.2009.00989.x.

Andersson H, Raastad T, Nilsson J, Paulsen G, Garthe I, Kadi F. Neuromuscular Fatigue and Recovery in Elite Female Soccer: Effects of Active Recovery. *Med Sci Sports Exerc*. 2008;40(2):372–380. https://doi.org/10.1249/mss.0b013e31815b8497.

Armstrong RB. Mechanisms of Exercise-induced Delayed Onset Muscular Soreness: A Brief Review. *Med Sci Sports Exerc*. 1984;16(6):529–538.

Ascensão A, Rebelo A, Oliveira E, Marques F, Pereira L, Magalhães J. Biochemical Impact of a Soccer Match - Analysis of Oxidative Stress and Muscle Damage Markers throughout Recovery. *Clin Biochem*. 2008;41(10–11):841–851. https://doi.org/10.1016/j.clinbiochem. 2008.04.008.

Beaven CM, Cook C, Gray D, Downes P, Murphy I, Drawer S, Ingram JR, Kilduff LP, Gill N. Electrostimulation's Enhancement of Recovery during a Rugby Preseason. *Int J Sports Physiol Perform*. 2013;8(1):92–98. https://doi.org/10.1123/ijspp.8.1.92.

Bengtsson H, Ekstrand J, Hägglund M. Muscle Injury Rates in Professional Football Increase with Fixture Congestion: An 11-year Follow-up of the UEFA Champions League Injury Study. *Br J Sports Med*. 2013;47(12):743–747. https://doi.org/10.1136/ bjsports-2013-092383.

Bérdi M, Köteles F, Hevesi K, Bárdos G, Szabo A. Elite Athletes' Attitudes towards the Use of Placebo-induced Performance Enhancement in Sports. *Eur J Sport Sci*. 2015;15(4):315–321. https://doi.org/10.1080/17461391.2014.955126.

Bond V, Adams RG, Tearney RJ, Gresham K, Ruff W. Effects of Active and Passive Recovery on Lactate Removal and Subsequent Isokinetic Muscle Function. *J Sports Med Phys Fitness*. 1991;31(3):357–361.

Borne R, Hausswirth C, Bieuzen F. Relationship Between Blood Flow and Performance Recovery: A Randomized, Placebo-Controlled Study. *Int J Sports Physiol Perform*. 2017;12(2):152–160. https://doi.org/10.1123/ijspp.2015-0779.

Broatch JR, Petersen A, Bishop DJ. Postexercise Cold Water Immersion Benefits Are Not Greater than the Placebo Effect. *Med Sci Sports Exerc*. 2014;46(11):2139–2147. https:// doi.org/10.1249/MSS.0000000000000348.

Brown F, Gissane C, Howatson G, van Someren K, Pedlar C, Hill J. Compression Garments and Recovery from Exercise: A Meta-Analysis. *Sports Med*. 2017;47(11):2245–2267. https://doi.org/10.1007/s40279-017-0728-9.

Chauvineau M, Pasquier F, Guyot V, Aloulou A, Nedelec M. Effect of the Depth of Cold Water Immersion on Sleep Architecture and Recovery among Well-Trained Male

Endurance Runners. *Front Sports Act Living*. 2021;3:659990. https://doi.org/10.3389/fspor.2021.659990.

Cheatham SW, Kolber MJ, Cain M, Lee M. The Effects of Self-Myofascial Release Using a Foam Roll or Roller Massager on Joint Range of Motion, Muscle Recovery and Performance: A Systematic Review. *Int J Sports Phys Ther*. 2015;10(6):827–838.

Chen J, Zhang F, Chen H, Pan H. Rhabdomyolysis after the Use of Percussion Massage Gun: A Case Report. *Phys Ther*. 2021;101(1):pzaa199. https://doi.org/10.1093/ptj/pzaa199.

Clifford T, Abbott W, Kwiecien SY, Howatson G, McHugh MP. Cryotherapy Reinvented: Application of Phase Change Material for Recovery in Elite Soccer. *Int J Sports Physiol Perform*. 2018;13(5):584–589. https://doi.org/10.1123/ijspp.2017-0334.

Close GL, Kayani A, Vasilaki A, McArdle A. Skeletal Muscle Damage with Exercise and Aging. *Sports Med*. 2005;35(5):413–427. https://doi.org/10.2165/00007256-200535050-00004.

Crowther F, Sealey R, Crowe M, Edwards A, Halson S. Team Sport Athletes' Perceptions and Use of Recovery Strategies: A Mixed-Methods Survey Study. *BMC Sports Sci Med Rehabil*. 2017;9:6. https://doi.org/10.1186/s13102-017-0071-3.

Dadebo B, White J, George KP. A Survey of Flexibility Training Protocols and Hamstring Strains in Professional Football Clubs in England. *Br J Sports Med*. 2004;38(4):388–394. https://doi.org/10.1136/bjsm.2002.000044.

Dakić M, Toskić L, Ilić V, Đurić S, Dopsaj M, Šimenko J. The Effects of Massage Therapy on Sport and Exercise Performance: A Systematic Review. *Sports (Basel)*. 2023;11(6):110. https://doi.org/10.3390/sports11060110.

Doeven SH, Brink MS, Kosse SJ, Lemmink KAPM. Postmatch Recovery of Physical Performance and Biochemical Markers in Team Ball Sports: A Systematic Review. *BMJ Open Sport Exerc Med*. 2018;4(1):e000264. https://doi.org/10.1136/bmjsem-2017-000264.

Dorey TW, O'Brien MW, Robinson SA, Kimmerly DS. Knee-high Compression Socks Minimize Head-Up Tilt-Induced Cerebral and Cardiovascular Responses Following Dynamic Exercise. *Scand J Med Sci Sports*. 2018;28(7):1766–1774. https://doi.org/10.1111/sms.13084.

Dupuy O, Douzi W, Theurot D, Bosquet L, Dugué B. An Evidence-Based Approach for Choosing Post-exercise Recovery Techniques to Reduce Markers of Muscle Damage, Soreness, Fatigue, and Inflammation: A Systematic Review with Meta-Analysis. *Front Physiol*. 2018;9:403. https://doi.org/10.3389/fphys.2018.00403.

Ekstrand J. Keeping Your Top Players on the Pitch: The Key to Football Medicine at a Professional Level. *Br J Sports Med*. 2013;47:723–724.

Ekstrand J, Hägglund M, Waldén M. Injury Incidence and Injury Patterns in Professional Football: The UEFA Injury Study. *Br J Sports Med*. 2011;45(7):553–558. https://doi.org/10.1136/bjsm.2009.060582.

Ekstrand J, Spreco A, Davison M. Elite Football Teams that Do Not Have a Winter Break Lose on Average 303 Player-days More per Season to Injuries than those Teams that do: A Comparison among 35 Professional European Teams. *Br J Sports Med*. 2019;53(19):1231–1235. https://doi.org/10.1136/bjsports-2018-099506.

Ekstrand J, Waldén M, Hägglund M. A Congested Football Calendar and the Wellbeing of Players: Correlation between Match Exposure of European Footballers before the World Cup 2002 and their Injuries and Performances during that World Cup. *Br J Sports Med*. 2004;38(4):493–497. https://doi.org/10.1136/bjsm.2003.009134.

Fairchild TJ, Armstrong AA, Rao A, Liu H, Lawrence S, Fournier PA. Glycogen Synthesis in Muscle Fibers during Active Recovery from Intense Exercise. *Med Sci Sports Exerc*. 2003;35(4):595–602. https://doi.org/10.1249/01.MSS.0000058436.46584.8E.

174 Strength and Conditioning for Football

Faulkner SH, Ferguson RA, Gerrett N, Hupperets M, Hodder SG, Havenith G. Reducing Muscle Temperature Drop after Warm-up Improves Sprint Cycling Performance. *Med Sci Sports Exerc.* 2013;45(2):359–365. https://doi.org/10.1249/MSS.0b013e31826fba7f.

Feldman JL, Stout NL, Wanchai A, Stewart BR, Cormier JN, Armer JM. Intermittent Pneumatic Compression Therapy: A Systematic Review. *Lymphology.* 2012;45(1):13–25.

Ferreira RM, Silva R, Vigário P, Martins PN, Casanova F, Fernandes RJ, Sampaio AR. The Effects of Massage Guns on Performance and Recovery: A Systematic Review. *J Funct Morphol Kinesiol.* 2023;8(3):138. https://doi.org/10.3390/jfmk8030138.

Field A, Harper LD, Chrismas BCR, Fowler PM, McCall A, Paul DJ, Chamari K, Taylor L. The Use of Recovery Strategies in Professional Soccer: A Worldwide Survey. *Int J Sports Physiol Perform.* 2021;16(12):1804–1815. https://doi.org/10.1123/ijspp.2020-0799.

Francisco MA, Colbert C, Larson EA, Sieck DC, Halliwill JR, Minson CT. Hemodynamics of Postexercise versus Post-Hot Water Immersion Recovery. *J Appl Physiol.* 2021;130(5):1362–1372. https://doi.org/10.1152/japplphysiol.00260.2020.

Fuchs CJ, Kouw IWK, Churchward-Venne TA, Smeets JSJ, Senden JM, Lichtenbelt WDVM, Verdijk LB, van Loon LJC. Postexercise Cooling Impairs Muscle Protein Synthesis Rates in Recreational Athletes. *J Physiol.* 2020;598(4):755–772. https://doi.org/10.1113/JP278996.

Fuchs CJ, Smeets JSJ, Senden JM, Zorenc AH, Goessens JPB, van Marken Lichtenbelt WD, Verdijk LB, van Loon LJC. Hot-Water Immersion Does Not Increase Postprandial Muscle Protein Synthesis Rates during Recovery from Resistance-type Exercise in Healthy, Young Males. *J Appl Physiol (1985).* 2020;128(4):1012–1022. https://doi.org/10.1152/japplphysiol.00836.2019.

Fuller JT, Thomson RL, Howe PR, Buckley JD. Vibration Therapy Is No More Effective Than the Standard Practice of Massage and Stretching for Promoting Recovery from Muscle Damage After Eccentric Exercise. *Clin J Sport Med.* 2015;25(4):332–337. https://doi.org/10.1097/JSM.0000000000000149.

Gavin JP, Myers SD, Willems ME. Effect of Eccentric Exercise with Reduced Muscle Glycogen on Plasma Interleukin-6 and Neuromuscular Responses of Musculus Quadriceps Femoris. *J Appl Physiol (1985).* 2016;121(1):173–184.

Grainger A, Malone J, Costello JT, Bleakley CM, Allan R. The BASES Expert Statement on the Use of Cooling Therapies for Post Exercise Recovery. *Sport Exerc Sci.* 2021(70). https://www.bases.org.uk/imgs/9193_bas_bases_tses_winter_2021_online_expert_statement736.pdf.

Grgic J. Effects of Post-Exercise Cold-Water Immersion on Resistance Training-Induced Gains in Muscular Strength: A Meta-analysis. *Eur J Sport Sci.* 2023;23(3):372–380. https://doi.org/10.1080/17461391.2022.2033851.

Gunnarsson TP, Bendiksen M, Bischoff R, Christensen PM, Lesivig B, Madsen K, Stephens F, Greenhaff P, Krustrup P, Bangsbo J. Effect of Whey Protein- and Carbohydrate-Enriched Diet on Glycogen resynthesis during the First 48 h after a Soccer Game. *Scand J Med Sci Sports.* 2013;23(4):508–515. https://doi.org/10.1111/j.1600-0838.2011.01418.x.

Haller N, Hübler E, Stöggl T, Simon P. Evidence-Based Recovery in Soccer - Low-Effort Approaches for Practitioners. *J Hum Kinet.* 2022;82:75–99.

Hill J, Howatson G, van Someren K, Leeder J, Pedlar C. Compression Garments and Recovery from Exercise-induced Muscle Damage: A Meta-analysis. *Br J Sports Med.* 2014;48(18):1340–1346. https://doi.org/10.1136/bjsports-2013-092456.

Horgan BG, West NP, Tee N, Halson SL, Drinkwater EJ, Chapman DW, Haff GG. Effect of Repeated Post-resistance Exercise Cold or Hot Water Immersion on in-season

Inflammatory Responses in Academy Rugby Players: A Randomised Controlled Crossover Design. *Eur J Appl Physiol*. 2024;124(9):2615–2628. https://doi.org/10.1007/s00421-024-05424-3.

Howatson G, Goodall S, van Someren KA. The Influence of Cold Water Immersions on Adaptation Following a Single Bout of Damaging Exercise. *Eur J Appl Physiol*. 2009;105(4):615–621. https://doi.org/10.1007/s00421-008-0941-1.

Ihsan M, Abbiss CR, Allan R. Adaptations to Post-exercise Cold Water Immersion: Friend, Foe, or Futile? *Front Sports Act Living*. 2021;3:714148. https://doi.org/10.3389/fspor.2021.714148.

Ihsan M, Watson G, Choo HC, Lewandowski P, Papazzo A, Cameron-Smith D, Abbiss CR. Postexercise Muscle Cooling Enhances Gene Expression of PGC-1α. *Med Sci Sports Exerc*. 2014;46(10):1900–1907. https://doi.org/10.1249/MSS.0000000000000308.

Ispirlidis I, Fatouros IG, Jamurtas AZ, Nikolaidis MG, Michailidis I, Douroudos I, Margonis K, Chatzinikolaou A, Kalistratos E, Katrabasas I, Alexiou V, Taxildaris K. Time-course of Changes in Inflammatory and Performance Responses Following a Soccer Game. *Clin J Sport Med*. 2008;18(5):423–431. https://doi.org/10.1097/JSM.0b013e3181818e0b.

Jackman JS, Bell PG, Van Someren K, Gondek MB, Hills FA, Wilson LJ, Cockburn E. Effect of Hot Water Immersion on Acute Physiological Responses Following Resistance Exercise. *Front Physiol*. 2023;14:1213733. https://doi.org/10.3389/fphys.2023.1213733.

Jacobs I, Westlin N, Karlsson J, Rasmusson M, Houghton B. Muscle Glycogen and Diet in Elite Soccer Players. *Eur J Appl Physiol Occup Physiol*. 1982;48(3):297–302. https://doi.org/10.1007/BF00430219.

Joo CH, Allan R, Drust B, Close GL, Jeong TS, Bartlett JD, Mawhinney C, Louhelainen J, Morton JP, Gregson W. Passive and Post-exercise Cold-Water Immersion Augments PGC-1α and VEGF Expression in Human Skeletal Muscle. *Eur J Appl Physiol*. 2016;116(11–12):2315–2326. https://doi.org/10.1007/s00421-016-3480-1.

Kellmann M, Bertollo M, Bosquet L, Brink M, Coutts AJ, Duffield R, Erlacher D, Halson SL, Hecksteden A, Heidari J, Kallus KW, Meeusen R, Mujika I, Robazza C, Skorski S, Venter R, Beckmann J. Recovery and Performance in Sport: Consensus Statement. *Int J Sports Physiol Perform*. 2018;13(2):240–245.

Kinugasa T, Kilding AE. A Comparison of Post-match Recovery Strategies in Youth Soccer Players. *J Strength Cond Res*. 2009;23(5):1402–1407. https://doi.org/10.1519/JSC.0b013e3181a0226a.

Krustrup P, Mohr M, Steensberg A, Bencke J, Kjaer M, Bangsbo J. Muscle and Blood Metabolites during a Soccer Game: Implications for Sprint Performance. *Med Sci Sports Exerc*. 2006;38(6):1165–1174. https://doi.org/10.1249/01.mss.0000222845.89262.cd.

Krustrup P, Ortenblad N, Nielsen J, Nybo L, Gunnarsson TP, Iaia FM, Madsen K, Stephens F, Greenhaff P, Bangsbo J. Maximal Voluntary Contraction Force, SR Function and Glycogen Resynthesis during the First 72 h after a High-level Competitive Soccer Game. *Eur J Appl Physiol*. 2011;111(12):2987–2995. https://doi.org/10.1007/s00421-011-1919-y.

Lastella M, Halson SL, Vitale JA, Memon AR, Vincent GE. To Nap or Not to Nap? A Systematic Review Evaluating Napping Behavior in Athletes and the Impact on Various Measures of Athletic Performance. *Nat Sci Sleep*. 2021;13:841–862. https://doi.org/10.2147/NSS.S315556.

Leeder J, Gissane C, van Someren K, Gregson W, Howatson G. Cold Water Immersion and Recovery from Strenuous Exercise: A Meta-analysis. *Br J Sports Med*. 2012;46(4):233–240. https://doi.org/10.1136/bjsports-2011-090061.

Lindsay A, Othman MI, Prebble H, Davies S, Gieseg SP. Repetitive Cryotherapy Attenuates the In vitro and In vivo Mononuclear Cell Activation Response. *Exp Physiol.* 2016;101(7):851–865. https://doi.org/10.1113/EP085795.

Lund H, Vestergaard-Poulsen P, Kanstrup IL, Sejrsen P. The Effect of Passive Stretching on Delayed Onset Muscle Soreness, and Other Detrimental Effects Following Eccentric Exercise. *Scand J Med Sci Sports.* 1998;8(4):216–221. https://doi.org/10.1111/j.1600-0838.1998.tb00195.x.

Luttrell MJ, Halliwill JR. Recovery from Exercise: Vulnerable State, Window of Opportunity, or Crystal Ball? *Front Physiol.* 2015;6:204. https://doi.org/10.3389/fphys.2015.00204.

MacDonald GZ, Penney MD, Mullaley ME, Cuconato AL, Drake CD, Behm DG, Button DC. An Acute Bout of Self-myofascial Release Increases Range of Motion Without a Subsequent Decrease in Muscle Activation or Force. *J Strength Cond Res.* 2013;27(3):812–821. https://doi.org/10.1519/JSC.0b013e31825c2bc1.

MacRae BA, Cotter JD, Laing RM. Compression Garments and Exercise: Garment Considerations, Physiology and Performance. *Sports Med.* 2011;41(10):815–843. https://doi.org/10.2165/11591420-000000000-00000.

Malone JJ, Hodges D, Roberts C, Sinclair JK, Page RM, Allan R. Effect of Alterations in Whole-Body Cryotherapy (WBC) Exposure on Post-match Recovery Markers in Elite Premier League Soccer Players. *Biol Sport.* 2022;39(1):31–36. https://doi.org/10.5114/biolsport.2021.102931.

Malta ES, Dutra YM, Broatch JR, Bishop DJ, Zagatto AM. The Effects of Regular Cold-Water Immersion Use on Training-Induced Changes in Strength and Endurance Performance: A Systematic Review with Meta-Analysis. *Sports Med.* 2021;51(1):161–174. https://doi.org/10.1007/s40279-020-01362-0.

Martínez-Aranda LM, Sanz-Matesanz M, García-Mantilla ED, González-Fernández FT. Effects of Self-Myofascial Release on Athletes' Physical Performance: A Systematic Review. *J Funct Morphol Kinesiol.* 2024;9(1):20. https://doi.org/10.3390/jfmk9010020.

Mawhinney C, Heinonen I, Low DA, Han C, Jones H, Kalliokoski KK, Kirjavainen A, Kemppainen J, Di Salvo V, Lolli L, Cable NT, Gregson W. Cool-Water Immersion Reduces Postexercise Quadriceps Femoris Muscle Perfusion More than Cold-Water Immersion. *Med Sci Sports Exerc.* 2022;54(7):1085–1094. https://doi.org/10.1249/MSS.0000000000002898.

Mawhinney C, Low DA, Jones H, Green DJ, Costello JT, Gregson W. Cold Water Mediates Greater Reductions in Limb Blood Flow than Whole Body Cryotherapy. *Med Sci Sports Exerc.* 2017;49(6):1252–1260. https://doi.org/10.1249/MSS.0000000000001223.

McGorm H, Roberts LA, Coombes JS, Peake JM. Turning Up the Heat: An Evaluation of the Evidence for Heating to Promote Exercise Recovery, Muscle Rehabilitation and Adaptation. *Sports Med.* 2018;48(6):1311–1328. https://doi.org/10.1007/s40279-018-0876-6.

McLellan TM, Jacobs I. Active Recovery, Endurance Training, and the Calculation of the Individual Anaerobic Threshold. *Med Sci Sports Exerc.* 1989;21(5):586–592.

Minett GM, Costello JT. Specificity and Context in Post-Exercise Recovery: It Is Not a One-Size-Fits-All Approach. *Front Physiol.* 2015;6:130. https://doi.org/10.3389/fphys.2015.00130.

Mohr M, Krustrup P, Bangsbo J. Fatigue in Soccer: A Brief Review. *J Sports Sci.* 2005;23(6):593–599. https://doi.org/10.1080/02640410400021286.

Mohr M, Vigh-Larsen JF, Krustrup P. Muscle Glycogen in Elite Soccer - A Perspective on the Implication for Performance, Fatigue, and Recovery. *Front Sports Act Living.* 2022;4:876534. https://doi.org/10.3389/fspor.2022.876534.

Monedero J, Donne B. Effect of Recovery Interventions on Lactate Removal and Subsequent Performance. *Int J Sports Med.* 2000;21(8):593–597. https://doi.org/10.1055/s-2000-8488.

Moreno J, Ramos-Castro J, Rodas G, Tarragó JR, Capdevila L. Individual Recovery Profiles in Basketball Players. *Span J Psychol.* 2015;18:E24. https://doi.org/10.1017/sjp.2015.23.

Mujika I, Halson S, Burke LM, Balagué G, Farrow D. An Integrated, Multifactorial Approach to Periodization for Optimal Performance in Individual and Team Sports. *Int J Sports Physiol Perform.* 2018;13(5):538–561. https://doi.org/10.1123/ijspp.2018-0093.

Murray A, Fullagar H, Turner AP, Sproule J. Recovery Practices in Division 1 Collegiate Athletes in North America. *Phys Ther Sport.* 2018;32:67–73. https://doi.org/10.1016/j.ptsp.2018.05.004.

Nédélec M, Halson S, Delecroix B, Abaidia AE, Ahmaidi S, Dupont G. Sleep Hygiene and Recovery Strategies in Elite Soccer Players. *Sports Med.* 2015;45(11):1547–1559. https://doi.org/10.1007/s40279-015-0377-9.

Nédélec M, McCall A, Carling C, Legall F, Berthoin S, Dupont G. Recovery in Soccer: Part I - Post-match Fatigue and Time Course of Recovery. *Sports Med.* 2012;42(12):997–1015. https://doi.org/10.2165/11635270-000000000-00000.

Nédélec M, McCall A, Carling C, Legall F, Berthoin S, Dupont G. Recovery in Soccer: Part II-Recovery Strategies. *Sports Med.* 2013;43(1):9–22. https://doi.org/10.1007/s40279-012-0002-0.

O'Riordan SF, McGregor R, Halson SL, Bishop DJ, Broatch JR. Sports Compression Garments Improve Resting Markers of Venous Return and Muscle Blood Flow in Male Basketball Players. *J Sport Health Sci.* 2023;12(4):513–522. https://doi.org/10.1016/j.jshs.2021.07.010.

Page RM, Field A, Langley B, Harper LD, Julian R. The Effects of Fixture Congestion on Injury in Professional Male Soccer: A Systematic Review. *Sports Med.* 2023;53(3):667–685. https://doi.org/10.1007/s40279-022-01799-5.

Partsch H, Mosti G. Thigh Compression. *Phlebology.* 2008;23(6):252–258. https://doi.org/10.1258/phleb.2008.008053.

Pfirrmann D, Herbst M, Ingelfinger P, Simon P, Tug S. Analysis of Injury Incidences in Male Professional Adult and Elite Youth Soccer Players: A Systematic Review. *J Athl Train.* 2016;51(5):410–424. https://doi.org/10.4085/1062-6050-51.6.03.

Pooley S, Spendiff O, Allen M, Moir HJ. Comparative Efficacy of Active Recovery and Cold Water Immersion as Post-match Recovery Interventions in Elite Youth Soccer. *J Sports Sci.* 2020;38(11–12):1423–1431. https://doi.org/10.1080/02640414.2019.1660448.

Pooley S, Spendiff O, Allen M, Moir HJ. Static Stretching Does Not Enhance Recovery in Elite Youth Soccer Players. *BMJ Open Sport Exerc Med.* 2017;3(1):e000202. https://doi.org/10.1136/bmjsem-2016-000202.

Poppendieck W, Faude O, Wegmann M, Meyer T. Cooling and Performance Recovery of Trained Athletes: A Meta-analytical Review. *Int J Sports Physiol Perform.* 2013;8(3):227–242. https://doi.org/10.1123/ijspp.8.3.227.

Racinais S, Casa D, Brocherie F, Ihsan M. Translating Science into Practice: The Perspective of the Doha 2019 IAAF World Championships in the Heat. *Front Sports Act Living.* 2019;1:39. https://doi.org/10.3389/fspor.2019.00039.

Raeder C, Wiewelhove T, Schneider C, Doweling A, Kellmann M, Meyer TF, Pfieffer M, Ferrauti A. Effects of Active Recovery on Muscle Function Following High-intensity Training Sessions in Elite Olympic Weightlifters. *ASMFA.* 2017;1(1):3–12.

Rappelt L, Javanmardi S, Heinke L, Baumgart C, Freiwald J. The Multifaceted Nature of Recovery after Exercise: A Need for Individualisation. *Sports Orthop Traumatol.* 2023;39(4):359–367. https://doi.org/10.1016/j.orthtr.2023.10.006.

178 Strength and Conditioning for Football

Roberts LA, Nosaka K, Coombes JS, Peake JM. Cold Water Immersion Enhances Recovery of Submaximal Muscle Function after Resistance Exercise. *Am J Physiol Regul Integr Comp Physiol*. 2014;307(8):R998–R1008. https://doi.org/10.1152/ajpregu.00180.2014.

Roberts LA, Raastad T, Markworth JF, Figueiredo VC, Egner IM, Shield A, Cameron-Smith D, Coombes JS, Peake JM. Post-exercise Cold Water Immersion Attenuates Acute Anabolic Signalling and Long-term Adaptations in Muscle to Strength Training. *J Physiol*. 2015;593(18):4285–4301. https://doi.org/10.1113/JP270570.

Roberts TD, Costa PB, Lynn SK, Coburn JW. Effects of Percussive Massage Treatments on Symptoms Associated with Eccentric Exercise-Induced Muscle Damage. *J Sports Sci Med*. 2024;23(1):126–135. https://doi.org/10.52082/jssm.2024.126.

Rodrigues P, Trajano GS, Stewart IB, Minett GM. Potential Role of Passively Increased Muscle Temperature on Contractile Function. *Eur J Appl Physiol*. 2022;122(10):2153–2162. https://doi.org/10.1007/s00421-022-04991-7.

Sautillet B, Bourdillon N, Millet GP, Billaut F, Hassar A, Moufti H, Ahmaïdi S, Costalat G. Hot but Not Cold Water Immersion Mitigates the Decline in Rate of Force Development following Exercise-Induced Muscle Damage. *Med Sci Sports Exerc*. 2024. https://doi.org/10.1249/MSS.0000000000003513.

Seco-Calvo J, Mielgo-Ayuso J, Calvo-Lobo C, Córdova A. Cold Water Immersion as a Strategy for Muscle Recovery in Professional Basketball Players during the Competitive Season. *J Sport Rehabil*. 2020;29(3):301–309. https://doi.org/10.1123/jsr.2018-0301.

Sharples A. Cellular and Molecular Exercise Physiology: A Historical Perspective for the Discovery of Mechanisms Contributing to Skeletal Muscle Adaptation. *Cell Mol Exerc Physiol*. 2017;5:e10. https://doi.org/10.7457/cmep.v5i1.e10

Sjøgaard G, Savard G, Juel C. Muscle Blood Flow during Isometric Activity and Its Relation to Muscle Fatigue. *Eur J Appl Physiol Occup Physiol*. 1988;57(3):327–335. https://doi.org/10.1007/BF00635992.

Skein M, Duffield R, Edge J, Short MJ, Mündel T. Intermittent-Sprint Performance and Muscle Glycogen after 30 h of Sleep Deprivation. *Med Sci Sports Exerc*. 2011;43(7):1301–1311. https://doi.org/10.1249/MSS.0b013e31820abc5a.

Skein M, Duffield R, Minett GM, Snape A, Murphy A. The Effect of Overnight Sleep Deprivation after Competitive Rugby League Matches on Postmatch Physiological and Perceptual Recovery. *Int J Sports Physiol Perform*. 2013;8(5):556–564. https://doi.org/10.1123/ijspp.8.5.556.

Soligard T, Schwellnus M, Alonso JM, Bahr R, Clarsen B, Dijkstra HP, Gabbett T, Gleeson M, Hägglund M, Hutchinson MR, Janse van Rensburg C, Khan KM, Meeusen R, Orchard JW, Pluim BM, Raftery M, Budgett R, Engebretsen L. How Much Is Too Much? (Part 1) International Olympic Committee Consensus Statement on Load in Sport and Risk of Injury. *Br J Sports Med*. 2016;50(17):1030–1041. https://doi.org/10.1136/bjsports-2016-096581.

Steward CJ, Hill M, Menzies C, Bailey SJ, Rahman M, Thake CD, Pugh CJA, Cullen T. Post Exercise Hot Water Immersion and Hot Water Immersion in Isolation Enhance Vascular, Blood Marker, and Perceptual Responses When Compared to Exercise Alone. *Scand J Med Sci Sports*. 2024;34(3):e14600. https://doi.org/10.1111/sms.14600.

Stojanovic MD, Ostojic SM. Stretching and Injury Prevention in Football: Current Perspectives. *Res Sports Med*. 2011;19(2):73–91. https://doi.org/10.1080/15438627.2011.556476.

Tavares F, Beaven M, Teles J, Baker D, Healey P, Smith TB, Driller M. Effects of Chronic Cold-Water Immersion in Elite Rugby Players. *Int J Sports Physiol Perform*. 2019;14(2):156–162. https://doi.org/10.1123/ijspp.2018-0313.

Tavares F, Simões M, Matos B, Smith TB, Driller M. The Acute and Longer-Term Effects of Cold Water Immersion in Highly-Trained Volleyball Athletes during an Intense Training Block. *Front Sports Act Living*. 2020;2:568420. https://doi.org/10.3389/fspor.2020.568420.

Thorpe RT. Post-exercise Recovery: Cooling and Heating, a Periodized Approach. *Front Sports Act Living*. 2021;3:707503. https://doi.org/10.3389/fspor.2021.707503.

Thorpe RT, Strudwick AJ, Buchheit M, Atkinson G, Drust B, Gregson W. Monitoring Fatigue During the In-Season Competitive Phase in Elite Soccer Players. *Int J Sports Physiol Perform*. 2015;10(8):958–964. https://doi.org/10.1123/ijspp.2015-0004.

Thorpe RT, Strudwick AJ, Buchheit M, Atkinson G, Drust B, Gregson W. Tracking Morning Fatigue Status across In-Season Training Weeks in Elite Soccer Players. *Int J Sports Physiol Perform*. 2016;11(7):947–952. https://doi.org/10.1123/ijspp.2015-0490.

Thorpe RT, Strudwick AJ, Buchheit M, Atkinson G, Drust B, Gregson W. The Influence of Changes in Acute Training Load on Daily Sensitivity of Morning-Measured Fatigue Variables in Elite Soccer Players. *Int J Sports Physiol Perform*. 2017;12(Suppl 2):S2107–S2113. https://doi.org/10.1123/ijspp.2016-0433.

Tiernan C, Comyns T, Lyons M, Nevill AM, Warrington G. The Association between Training Load Indices and Injuries in Elite Soccer Players. *J Strength Cond Res*. 2022;36(11):3143–3150. https://doi.org/10.1519/JSC.0000000000003914.

Vaile J, O'Hagan C, Stefanovic B, Walker M, Gill N, Askew CD. Effect of Cold Water Immersion on Repeated Cycling Performance and Limb Blood Flow. *Br J Sports Med*. 2011;45(10):825–829. https://doi.org/10.1136/bjsm.2009.067272.

Versey NG, Halson SL, Dawson BT. Water Immersion Recovery for Athletes: Effect on Exercise Performance and Practical Recommendations. *Sports Med*. 2013;43(11):1101–1130. https://doi.org/10.1007/s40279-013-0063-8.

Viitasalo JT, Niemelä K, Kaappola R, Korjus T, Levola M, Mononen HV, Rusko HK, Takala TE. Warm Underwater Water-Jet Massage Improves Recovery from Intense Physical Exercise. *Eur J Appl Physiol Occup Physiol*. 1995;71(5):431–438. https://doi.org/10.1007/BF00635877.

Warneke K, Konrad A, Wilke J. The Knowledge of Movement Experts about Stretching Effects: Does the Science Reach Practice? *PLoS One*. 2024;19(1):e0295571. https://doi.org/10.1371/journal.pone.0295571.

Waterhouse J, Atkinson G, Edwards B, Reilly T. The Role of a Short Post-Lunch Nap in Improving Cognitive, Motor, and Sprint Performance in Participants with Partial Sleep Deprivation. *J Sports Sci*. 2007;25(14):1557–1566. https://doi.org/10.1080/02640410701244983.

Weakley J, Broatch J, O'Riordan S, Morrison M, Maniar N, Halson SL. Putting the Squeeze on Compression Garments: Current Evidence and Recommendations for Future Research: A Systematic Scoping Review. *Sports Med*. 2022;52(5):1141–1160. https://doi.org/10.1007/s40279-021-01604-9.

Wilke J, Müller AL, Giesche F, Power G, Ahmedi H, Behm DG. Acute Effects of Foam Rolling on Range of Motion in Healthy Adults: A Systematic Review with Multilevel Meta-analysis. *Sports Med*. 2020;50(2):387–402. https://doi.org/10.1007/s40279-019-01205-7.

Wilson LJ, Cockburn E, Paice K, Sinclair S, Faki T, Hills FA, Gondek MB, Wood A, Dimitriou L. Recovery Following a Marathon: A Comparison of Cold Water Immersion, Whole Body Cryotherapy and a Placebo Control. *Eur J Appl Physiol*. 2018;118(1):153–163. https://doi.org/10.1007/s00421-017-3757-z.

Wiltshire EV, Poitras V, Pak M, Horg T, Rayner J, Tschakovsky ME. Massage Impairs Postexercise Muscle Blood Flow and "Lactic Acid" Removal. *Med Sci Sports Exerc*. 2010;42(6):1062–1071. https://doi.org/10.1249/MSS.0b013e3181c9214f.

Zainuddin Z, Sacco P, Newton M, Nosaka K. Light Concentric Exercise Has a Temporarily Analgesic Effect on Delayed-Onset Muscle Soreness, but No Effect on Recovery from Eccentric Exercise. *Appl Physiol Nutr Metab*. 2006;31(2):126–134. https://doi.org/10.1139/h05-010.

Zelikovski A, Kaye CL, Fink G, Spitzer SA, Shapiro Y. The Effects of the Modified Intermittent Sequential Pneumatic Device (MISPD) on Exercise Performance Following an Exhaustive Exercise Bout. *Br J Sports Med*. 1993;27(4):255–259.

11

OPTIMIZING RETURN TO PERFORMANCE FOLLOWING INJURY

Luca Maestroni and Paul Read

Introduction

Injuries in football have a detrimental impact on team and individual performance, with increased player availability improving the chances of success [1]. The available data suggest an interaction between injury, performance, physical outputs, and success at both a team and individual level in the professional game [2, 3]. Furthermore, several studies have reported that a previous injury may increase the risk for subsequent injuries in male football players [4, 5]. This raises the question of whether persistent deficits have been fully assessed and targeted before athletes return to play (RTP), and if a greater emphasis should be placed on a return to performance strategy as a means of tertiary prevention [6]. Despite variability in RTP definitions [7], a consensus statement [8] agreed to include three elements in the RTP continuum. "Return to participation" refers to an athlete participating in rehabilitation, modified or unrestricted training, or in sport, but at a level lower than his or her RTP goal. "Return to sport" is used when a player has returned to competition but is not performing at his or her desired performance level. Ultimately, "return to performance" indicates a return to preinjury levels (inclusive of physical capacity and match performance).

Incidence data suggest the upper leg (predominantly hamstrings) is the most frequently reported injury in soccer [9]. However, the number of days soccer players are typically absent is ~18, with knee ligament injuries resulting in substantially greater time loss [10], of which anterior cruciate ligament (ACL) injuries carry the greatest burden to teams (due to financial costs and a long duration absence of ~210 days) [10]. In spite of their relatively low season prevalence (about 1.5%) in elite-level male European football [11], and high RTP rates [12], only two-thirds compete at the same pre-injury level three years after ACL rupture [11].

DOI: 10.4324/9781003383475-12

Performance indicators (i.e., the number of passes, dribbles, scoring points, and minutes played) and career survival are reduced in ACL-reconstructed players in comparison with uninjured matched controls (median professional career length of 3.4 years following return to training). Cumulatively, this highlights the need to develop highly effective rehabilitation and return to sports programs that target residual deficits following injury. Here we discuss a contemporary, multidimensional approach to optimize recovery [8] and facilitate a return to performance. In this chapter, we use ACL rehabilitation as an illustration of the process, but it should be considered that the approach can be adapted to a range of other soccer injuries that result in substantial time loss from training and competition (e.g., hamstrings).

Criteria-Based Progression

Current guidelines suggest temporal and criterion-based rehabilitation progressions for RTS, where each step is built upon in sequence (see Figure 11.1). For example, following ACL reconstruction, recovering knee extension range of motion (ROM) is deemed essential to normalize gait in the first few weeks following surgery. Not achieving this first milestone has been associated with poorer long-term outcomes [13]. Similarly, not recovering knee extensor strength is associated with a lower level of function and a higher risk of re-injury [14], which may result in maladaptive movement strategies. Restoration to pre-injury levels or those of teammates is not guaranteed with time only. This chapter is focused on optimizing soccer-relevant

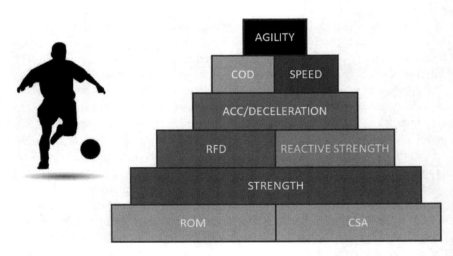

FIGURE 11.1 Return to play progression scheme. Each rehabilitation emphasis is decided according to a targeted test-training integration process. CSA = cross sectional area, ROM = range of motion, RFD = rate of force development, ACC = acceleration, COD = change of direction.

physical capacities to enhance return to performance following injury; however, it is recommended that the importance of early-stage rehabilitation is not overlooked, and injured players are recommended to follow a rehabilitation program aimed at restoring knee extension ROM and strength capacity in a periodized manner before returning to more dynamic sport-specific activities and full soccer participation. Accelerating rehabilitation phases too quickly and missing important fundamentals may compromise performance gains and robustness to load, and ultimately on-field performance at the time of RTS.

Assessment and Re-development of Physical Capacities Following Injury to Optimize Return to Performance

Following the occurrence of injury or pain onset, deficits in strength [15–17], strength ratios [18], rate of force development [19–21], reactive strength [22, 23], leg stiffness [24, 25], and peak power [26, 27], have all been shown. Equally, these same attributes are considered important physical performance determinants in soccer [28]. Pain interference might reduce maximal voluntary contraction [29] and thus, should be taken into consideration when interpreting physical outputs. Optimal loading strategies within an incremental rehabilitation programme encourage early recovery of the histological and mechanical properties of injured tissue [30]. This section will outline important physical characteristics to assess in soccer players and recovery strategies to aid in their re-development, enhancing readiness to re-perform following injury.

Strength Assessment

Dynamic and isometric muscle actions are two common modalities used to measure muscle strength. Isometric strength can be used to quantify peak force values at specific joint angles whereas dynamic strength assessment examines muscular performance throughout the entire ROM. One-repetition maximum (1RM) testing, or multiple RM (i.e., 2 to 10RM) can be used as a measure of dynamic muscular strength. However, when using multiple RM to estimate 1RM, it must be acknowledged that prediction accuracy remains high only within 5RM [31].

During the soccer player's return to sports journey, both multi-joint and single-joint strength assessment should be included to provide information about the status of the global system and isolated structures within the kinetic chain. Single-joint strength assessment is important to highlight specific strength deficits within the kinetic chain. However, it is important to note that single-joint strength capacities are not strongly associated with athletic performance, functional activity outcomes, and pain levels, whereas, strong associations between multi-joint strength levels and functional/athletic performance have been consistently reported [31].

The majority of studies which have examined strength in athletic populations post ACL reconstruction, have included an isokinetic dynamometer at a variety of

184 Strength and Conditioning for Football

test speeds (60°/s,120°/s,180°/s, and 300°/s) for both the quadriceps and hamstring muscles [32–34]. Other testing modes included isometric maximal voluntary isometric contraction on a dynamometer [35–37], or uniaxial load cells [36]. However, peak torque values alone have been shown to mask angle-specific moment generation capacity, and additional angle-specific analysis are recommended to more accurately identify residual deficits [38]. In particular, deficits in knee extension strength appear more pronounced in angles between 50 and 80 degrees of knee flexion in male soccer players [38], owing to reduced quadriceps voluntary activation, spinal-reflexive and corticospinal excitability, and smaller muscle volumes [39]. Longer rehabilitation periods (≥9 months) may also be needed to recover knee extensor torque deficits [40].

Re-developing Strength

From a rehabilitation perspective, players should gradually progress to heavier loads in a periodized manner. From a neurobiological perspective, it may also reverse alterations to intra-cortical inhibitory networks in individuals with persistent musculoskeletal pain [41, 42]. Current evidence indicates that prescription of maximal strength training should involve a load (or intensity) of 80–100% of the participant's 1RM, utilizing approximately 1–6 repetitions, across 3–5 sets, with rest periods of 3–5 minutes and a frequency of 2–3 times per week [43]. To improve maximal force during the relevant phases of rehabilitation, players should progressively work towards this volume load prescription. However, in the initial stages when heavy loads are not tolerated, lower intensities may be employed in multiple high volume sets until momentary failure, in order to recruit the highest threshold motor units and increase Cross-Sectional Area (CSA) [44]. Alternatively, blood flow restriction training can be used to provide an effective stimulus during rehabilitation for players who are load-compromised due to a reduction in mechanical loading and high metabolic stress [45]. Cross-education (i.e., heavy resistance training of the unaffected limb) is also a viable option to reduce corticospinal inhibition [46], increase contralateral limb strength [47], and induce hypoalgesia [48]. A potential progression based on the rehabilitation phase post-ACL reconstruction might be (1) bodyweight single leg squat performed at high volume sets focusing on technique mastery and cross-education, (2) single leg squat with a light load and high volume sets until failure (with/without blood flow restriction), (3) split squat with progressive loading in a traditional periodization scheme until reaching the recommended prescription for maximal strength, and (4) split squat performed accordingly with maximal strength recommendations.

Assessing Power and Rate of Force Development

The ability to express high power outputs is important to increase athletic performance [28]. Given the components of power, it appears intuitive that strength

Optimizing Return to Performance Following Injury **185**

(indicating high levels of force production) and speed are the main physical determinants of game-related activities, such as jumping, landing (given the need for braking force), accelerating, and changing direction [28, 49]. In ACL literature, power has been calculated primarily during bilateral [50] and unilateral countermovement jumps (CMJ) [26]. The synchronization of kinetic and kinematic data has also been used to assess single-joint power contribution, highlighting intra-limb compensation strategies commonly documented in ACL reconstructed cohorts [51].

Rate of force development (RFD) is defined as the ability of the neuromuscular system to produce a high rate in the rise of muscle force in the first 0–250 milliseconds [52], calculated as ΔForce/ΔTime, and is determined from the slope of the force-time curve (generally between 0 and 250 milliseconds) [53]. RFD is typically assessed during single (e.g., knee extension/flexion and seated plantarflexion) and/or multi-joint (isometric mid-thigh pull, isometric squat) tasks, although particular caution should be used when interpreting RFD values owing to its poor reliability scores in comparison to other metrics such as peak force. Impaired knee extension rate of torque development and leg extension RFD [19] has been reported following ACL reconstruction [19, 54]. Assessment of RFD in a dynamic task during the eccentric phase of a CMJ has also been investigated in soccer players showing residual deficits in braking characteristics [50].

Recovering Explosiveness

Maximal strength production occurs under high loads and low velocities with periods of ~0.6–0.8 seconds necessary to develop peak force [49]. Given that a range of soccer-based game actions occur in <0.3 seconds, players are generally required to execute their motor skills and to generate a high level of force as quickly as possible [49]. Pertinent to rehabilitation and performance outcomes, deficits in RFD have been observed in several musculoskeletal disorders and specifically in soccer players following ACL reconstruction [50]. Heavy strength training, plyometrics, ballistic exercises, Olympic weightlifting, and their derivatives with the intention of rapid force production (i.e., moving weights and objects as quickly as possible) are considered effective strategies to improve RFD [53, 55]. Targeted exercise prescription to enhance rapid braking force production abilities should also form part of a return to performance program including altitude landing drills, loaded drop catches, and augmented eccentric loading.

Assessment of Reactive Strength

Maximal strength underpins reactive-strength ability, allowing efficient storage and reutilization of elastic energy during stretch-shortening cycle (SSC) activities involved in soccer such as running, jumping, and changing direction. Quantification is typically done via the reactive strength index (RSI) = jump height (m)/ground contact time (sec), during a drop vertical jump task [56]. In long

186 Strength and Conditioning for Football

SSC actions (>250 ms) such as a CMJ, this is commonly assessed using the RSI modified (RSI-mod) (calculated by dividing jump height by contraction time) [57]. Measurements of CMJ height and RSI-mod are obtainable using a variety of measurement tools (e.g., force place, OptoJump, and smartphone applications). Lower RSI [58], and RSI-mod [59] scores have been shown in male soccer players with ACL reconstruction compared to healthy controls, indicating these qualities should be targeted as part of a player's return to performance program.

Targeting Improvements in Reactive Strength

Between-limb differences in single leg drop jump (SLDJ) performance, kinetics, and kinematics are present in the later stages of rehabilitation following ACL reconstruction [59–61]. These deficits are more apparent in soccer players who display lower isokinetic knee extension torque and SLDJ RSI [59]. The involved limb displays a "stiff" knee movement strategy, characterised by lower thigh angular velocity, reduced centre of mass displacement, and peak landing force occurring in the earlier stages of ground contact, which is associated with a higher risk of re-injury [51].

Plyometric training is widely adopted to optimize the modulation of the SSC. Variables such as a player's strength level, fatigue, technique competency, and training phase should be considered before progressing plyometric training. Flanagan et al. [56] suggested a 4-step progression focusing on the eccentric jumping action while landing (phase 1); rebound spring-like actions with short ground contact times (e.g., pogos) (phase 2); hurdle jumps with an emphasis on short ground contact while increasing intensity of the eccentric stimulus (phase 3); and finally, depth jumps in order to maximize jump height while maintaining minimal ground contact times (phase 4). Plyometrics can also be subdivided into 'extensive' and 'intensive' based on the magnitude of the ground reaction forces and eccentric velocity during the ground contact phase. Extensive plyometrics are sub-maximal in nature, focus on sustainable effort and rhythm, and therefore, are prescribed earlier during rehabilitation. Intensive plyometrics require maximal output and non-sustainable effort, with a focus on reactive strength appearing in the later phases of a return to sports conditioning plan. Drills in each classification can also be categorized as short or long coupled based on the ground contact time, to elicit either fast or slow SSC adaptations, respectively.

A recent meta-analysis [62] showed that plyometric training can elicit large improvements in COD performance. Progressive plyometric training should be performed both bilaterally and unilaterally in vertical, horizontal, and lateral directions, to match the braking, propulsive, and medio-lateral forces which are typical of COD tasks and sprinting actions that frequently occur in soccer. Understanding and manipulating how players generate and dissipate forces during SSC activities is therefore essential for an effective transfer to game-related activities.

Late Phase Rehabilitation – Restoring Soccer-Specific Capacities

Acceleration and Maximal Running Speed

Sprint acceleration is defined as the rate of change in running velocity, whereas maximal running speed is defined as a period after acceleration in which peak sprint velocity is reached [63]. In soccer, the ability to accelerate over short distances is more important than maximal velocity, with the majority of sprints being <30 m and many <10 m before a change in angle, velocity, or movement pattern. Furthermore, it has been reported that sprint acceleration and top-speed running were the common injury mechanisms in around 70% of hamstring injuries among soccer players [64], further highlighting the importance of re-developing these physical characteristics prior to RTP.

One of the main determinants of sprint performance is the technical ability to apply Ground Reaction Force (GRF) in a more horizontal direction. This specific ability has been shown to be impaired in soccer following hamstring injury [65]. Effective force application onto the ground has been described by the ratio of forces (RF), which is the net horizontal component over the resultant (horizontal and vertical force vectors) GRF. Maximal horizontal power output and sprint performance over short distances exhibit a very strong relationship, but the degree of this association decreases over longer distances [66]. During the first phase of acceleration, large contact times are used to develop and apply high levels of propulsive force into the ground to displace the centre of mass forward. In the second phase of acceleration, the achievement of maximal stride frequency, concomitant with increased stride length, and shorter ground contact times gradually increase running velocity and decrease the body's forward lean [67]. Overall, this decreases RF linearly with increasing velocity [63]. Once the top speed is reached, the vertical component of the total force becomes more important [68].

Vertical stiffness is a significant determinant of sprint speed [69]. This quality aids the lower limbs' ability to withstand large displacements of the COM during the landing (eccentric) phase (allowing shorter ground contact times, and a more efficient running strategy reducing energy cost), while also increasing the RFD during the propulsive (concentric) phase. It appears that faster sprint times are attained by applying greater vertical GRF in shorter ground contact times. This reinforces the need for players to display lower limb stiffness characteristics during fast ground contact-based actions (sprinting, changing direction), further supported by near-perfect relationships ($r = -0.99$) between contact time and vertical stiffness at maximal speed [70].

Re-developing Speed

From a pragmatic perspective, these theoretical notions suggest that rehabilitation programs would aim to enhance: (a) higher levels of horizontal force applications to improve acceleration ability, (b) technical aspects such as a more forward

188 Strength and Conditioning for Football

lean to facilitate effective horizontal force application in the first sprint phase, and (c) short contact times and higher vertical stiffness, which are critical in attaining high maximal velocity. Given such requirements, it is not surprising that plyometric training appears to be an effective method to improve sprint performance, with programs incorporating greater horizontal force vectors being recommended to maximize sprint improvements [71], and to restore optimal horizontal force production capability.

Equally, in highly trained soccer players, increments of 15.8% in 1RM half squat resulted in 1.9% average improvements in 40-m sprint time [72]. Several studies showed the beneficial effect of strength training on sprint performance in soccer [73–75]. With regard to hamstring injuries, the Nordic Hamstring exercise has been shown to improve critical physical qualities such as strength and muscle architecture [76]. In addition, current evidence [77] indicates that increases in lower-body strength positively transfer to sprint performance. For example, large statistically significant correlations between squat and sprint ($r = -0.77$; $r^2 = 0.60$; $p \leq 0.001$; 95% confidence interval (CI) -0.85 to -0.67) have been demonstrated and exercises such as the hip thrust may be implemented in rehabilitation to improve qualities related to the first acceleration phase [78, 79].

Furthermore, sprint drills such as hurdle drills, walking high knees, running high knees, skips, and straight leg bounding are commonly used to target key technical elements and specific physical qualities (e.g., ankle stiffness) that ensure positive training transfer to sprint performance. Preparatory running drills (e.g., A-march exercise) can be introduced early in rehabilitation to restore abnormal sagittal sprint mechanics commonly found at RTP [80]. These can then be progressed (e.g., A-skip and A-run, scissor runs, and bounding) according to the players' recovery journey.

Finally, resisted sled sprint training is a popular method aimed to maximize the transfer of physical training to sprint performance. The use of a sled device increases trunk lean angle, thus, generating a greater application of force in the horizontal direction when compared with an unresisted sled sprint. This methodology can be used to restore horizontal force production under a variety of loads and speeds. Recommended resisted sprint training loads are moderate (10–20% BM) or "very heavy" (>30% BM). "Light" (<10% BM), "very heavy" (43% BM) [63], and un-resisted sprinting appears equally effective in the improvement of acceleration for individuals without prior sprint or strength training experience, whereas un-resisted sprinting displays greater benefits for maximal sprint velocity. Sled sprint training blocks are effective when adopted ≥6 weeks, with a frequency of two to three sessions per week of 5–35 m sprints, totalling 60–340 m, per session [63].

Deceleration

The ability to produce eccentric braking forces is a fundamental component of a return to a performance rehabilitation program, as they underpin effective deceleration mechanics. Individuals who have undergone ACL reconstruction tend to adopt inter-limb and intra-limb "offloading" strategies characterized by reductions

Optimizing Return to Performance Following Injury **189**

in GRF and power contribution at the ACL reconstructed knee [51]. This is often accompanied by a reduction in knee ROM concomitant with greater trunk flexion as a compensatory mechanism for decreased knee extension strength. This strategy is considered an important risk factor for subsequent ACL injury [51]. Deceleration requires a reduction in a velocity of the body's centre of mass before a COD or after a jump. To accomplish this, the body's momentum (mass × velocity) needs to be decreased by applying high levels of braking force, dissipated over as many joints as possible, during the preceding steps prior to stopping or changing direction. Eccentric loading capacity has been found reduced following ACL reconstruction [50]. These strategies are particularly evident in COD of angles ≥60° (e.g., side step cutting) where optimal braking strategies in the penultimate foot contact (PFC) and final foot contact (FFC) are necessary for effective COD performance [81].

Re-developing Deceleration

The body's ability to absorb high eccentric forces is underpinned by maximal strength capacity. In particular, eccentric strength has been identified as a key determinant in female soccer players [82]. Not surprisingly, effective strategies to improve such physical qualities involve accentuated eccentric loading and plyometric training with specific directional components. Technical strategies include a sequence of progressive deceleration drills using first low velocity and wide base of support exercises (e.g., bilateral to unilateral snap downs). These can be progressed to higher velocity braking actions with increasing loads (e.g. using a trap bar) or over increasing distances and smaller base of support (e.g. lunge positions/variations and horizontal deceleration tasks).

Change of Direction

A typical end goal of rehabilitation augmenting a return for a soccer player would be the demonstration of a high level of COD ability. The ability to perform sudden COD is crucial for performance in field sports [83]. In-effective COD has also been identified as a situational mechanism in non-contact ACL injuries [84]. It is worth noting that the types of COD vary according to the task, environment, and the individual. However, general technical model principles exist to provide effective foundations for movement execution. These consist of manipulating the base of support and the centre of mass to ensure that the force application is outside the COM to propel into the desired direction of travel. In doing so, the COM should be lowered and the shin leans towards the desired direction, thus, generating positive shin angles. Such efficient movement strategies appear compromised in ACLR [85, 86]; thus, requiring targeted rehabilitation strategies.

It is important to underline that the biomechanical demands of COD are angle and velocity-dependent [87]. In directional changes <45°, velocity maintenance is a key determinant with braking requirements reduced. A COD angle of 45°–60° occurs frequently in soccer [88] and involves fast approach and exit velocities with moderate

190 Strength and Conditioning for Football

braking forces evenly distributed across the PFC and FFC. In more extreme COD actions of 60°–180°, greater braking forces in the anti, penultimate, and FFC are needed to reduce approach velocity. Posterior GRF appears greater in the PFC, which influences total knee joint loading (also expressed as knee abduction moment and frequently associated with knee injury risk). Adopting a strategy of greater braking force in the anti, and PFCs during larger angular changes is advantageous for reducing injury risk due to more favourable lower limb alignment compared to the FFC where substantial rotational forces and moments will be present.

Re-developing COD Ability

Physical factors associated with faster COD performance are related to technical ability and lower limb strength characteristics such as maximum strength, eccentric strength, RFD, and reactive strength [82]. Applying these qualities efficiently over greater horizontally directed force vectors in a short GCT is associated with improved performance outcomes in sharper COD angles (60°–180°) [89]. Whole body anticipatory adjustments in the PFC can alter kinematic and kinetic variables in foot placement and trunk lean and rotation. This highlights the importance of technical factors such as stride adjustment, final and PFC placement, trunk alignment, and rotation towards the intended direction in performance and biomechanical variables in COD [89]. In athletes returning to soccer following ACL reconstruction, it is also important to consider how reductions in knee extension strength may affect injury risk on the contralateral limb. Specifically, lower braking forces applied by the ACL reconstructed limb during the PFC will result in greater forces and moments during the turn step on the un-involved limb to reduce the forward momentum of the body and re-direct movement into a new direction. Therefore, assessment and monitoring of limb capacity (i.e., concentric/eccentric strength, RFD, and RSI) during this phase of rehabilitation is recommended. Furthermore, we also suggest the integration of effective braking mechanics (considering there is both a capacity and skill demand) into COD drills at different angles and speeds to optimize whole body mechanics prior to RTS. The appropriate level in a progressive sequence of technical COD drills is selected for each player. In addition, resistance training, plyometrics, and the use of small-sided games [90] have all been shown to improve COD performance; thus, multimodal interventions are recommended. Once a high level of COD ability is demonstrated, it appears logical that perceptual and fast decision-making challenges can be gradually introduced to replicate the game demands and situational patterns of soccer match-play.

Agility

Agility is defined as "skills and abilities needed to change direction, velocity, or mode in response to a stimulus" [91]. In soccer, this is dictated by ball possession and the repetitive transitioning from defence to attack phases. Agility is underpinned by both cognitive (i.e., perceptual and fast decision-making abilities) and physical elements typical of COD ability. A recent review [92] of studies assessing the correlation between agility and COD tests, showed a variance below 50% indicating that agility and COD are largely independent skills. It is not surprising that agility is more closely linked to performance levels than pre-planned COD considering the importance of perceptual and decision-making elements. Indeed, Young et al. [93] found a high correlation ($r = 0.77$, $p = 0.001$) between decision-making time and total time, in a reactive agility test – although it should be noted this was in Australian Rules athletes.

Although pattern recognition, anticipation, and decision-making time in response to a game situation are of primary importance, producing a faster response to a stimulus is underpinned by several trainable determinants such as increased muscle pre-activation, greater early RFD, and muscular stiffness [94]. These enable a more effective impulse to be applied to the required movement. Therefore, a multicomponent training program encompassing physical, technical, and cognitive qualities appears recommended to develop agility. Small-sided games and 1 vs 1, 2 vs 2 situations can also be used as they contain soccer-specific skills and tactics, providing an ecologically valid stimulus.

Decision-Making

Owing to the multidimensional nature of return to soccer preparation, there is no consensus on when a player is ready or the optimal testing procedures. Current practice following ACL reconstruction involves passing a battery of strength and hop tests, with a limb symmetry index of 90% recommended as the cut-off point [95]. However, there is a reduction in the probability of passing when multiple tests across several domains are added to a battery. In addition, there is a potential for performance decrements in the uninvolved limb after an injury and surgery and using four horizontal hops will test similar constructs [96]. Cumulatively, this limits the utility of this approach for the purpose of augmenting RTS decision-making.

We have recently proposed an alternative method via the use of the Total Score of Athleticism (TSA) in soccer players, who returned to sports following ACL reconstruction [97]. Using the TSA to determine physical preparedness may overcome some of the aforementioned limitations. Firstly, the TSA avoids the need for passing tests using symmetry alone, reducing overestimation of recovery (using the potentially deteriorated contralateral limb), by including comparative data from healthy players. Furthermore, this approach avoids the normal reduction in pass probability when there is a requirement to obtain a specific score across multiple tests. Importantly, the TSA allows judgement of single test scores within a measure of general performance level, instead of binary "pass" or "fail" criteria. This allows contextualization of a single player's data in relation to their teammates and can be used to set benchmarks and rehabilitation goals which are realistic during

192 Strength and Conditioning for Football

rehabilitation for restoration of physical performance to a level no lesser than uninjured players and are reflective of the RTS demands [97].

Recent data indicate the TSA was substantially lower in male soccer players with a history of ACL reconstruction at the time of RTS compared to healthy matched controls ($d = 0.84$, 95% CI [0.40, 1.27]) [95]. Although the optimal testing procedure to determine return to soccer readiness remains unclear, these data confirm the utility of an overall measure of contextualized physical preparedness before RTS to differentiate between injured and un-injured players. To understand which specific component of the total score needs specific attention, each physical characteristic can be broken down and further analysed, by using z-scores and respective threshold values (Table 11.1).

Data visualization using a simple figure schematic (see, for example, Figures 11.2–11.4) can be a logical and simple way to understand the weaknesses and strengths of each individual player (i.e., scores below or above zero indicating an athlete being worse or better than average), and can be used to identify one or multiple components to be targeted to collectively increase the TSA during specific rehabilitation and training cycles [97]. Bars below zero represent opportunities for improvement that should be targeted during rehabilitation before RTS to achieve important, safe, and specific physical quality thresholds and to increase the TSA overall. It should be noted that an optimal TSA assessment battery will include a range of tests to examine the relevant physical capacities for soccer selected following a comprehensive needs analysis and only consider variables which display acceptable reliability.

For example, player 14 (18th percentile, TSA $= -0.91$, 30 years old, 166 cm, 58 kg, hamstring graft, 9.5 months post-surgery) (see Figure 11.2), displayed lower power (CMJ relative power $= 41.2$ W/kg, jump height $= 25.4$ cm) and reactive strength (CMJ RSImod $= 0.30$) characteristics within his cohort. Also, jump height and relative power did not meet currently available reference values (i.e., jump height $= 34.5 \pm 4.0$ cm and relative power $= 50.4 \pm 4.9$ W/kg) [50]. In addition, he showed lower relative peak knee flexion strength (1.70 Nm/kg) of the ACL reconstructed limb when compared to the rest of the group. At about two months following RTS, he was diagnosed with an involved knee-deep chondral fissure and distal biceps femoris myotendinous junction strain injury. Maladaptive functioning of the dampening mechanisms has been demonstrated following ACL reconstruction. This can impair force attenuation during fast sporting actions such as jumping, landing, and change of direction, exposing athletes to large impact forces, which have been associated with more deleterious compositional changes in the articular cartilage of the tibiofemoral compartment Similarly, players with a history of ACL reconstruction and lower knee flexor strength have higher probability of future hamstring strain injury than stronger players and knee flexor strength deficits are more pronounced in those who elect for a hamstring graft. For this player, it seems reasonable to suggest that targeted interventions prior to RTS may have been warranted to improve maximal strength, power, and plyometric ability to enhance the modulation of the SSC and to improve general strength as well as knee flexion force generation capacity before RTS.

TABLE 11.1 Physical Characteristics Threshold of a Cohort of Professional Soccer Players Returned to Sports Following ACL Reconstruction in Each Tertile

Tertile	CMJ Jump Height (cm)	CMJ Rel Peak Power (W/kg)	CMJ RSImod (m/s)	SLCMJ height UNINV (cm)	SLCMJ Rel Peak Power UNINV (W/kg)	SLCMJ RSImod UNINV (m/s)	SLCMJ height INV (cm)	SLCMJ Rel Peak Power INV (W/kg)	SLCMJ RSImod INV (m/s)	Rel Knee Extension Strength UNINV (Nm/kg)	Rel Knee Extension Strength INV (Nm/kg)	Rel Knee Flexion Strength UNINV (Nm/kg)	Rel Knee Flexion Strength INV (Nm/kg)	TSA
First	< 33.5	< 47.4	< 0.39	< 16.1	< 29.3	< 0.18	< 14.0	< 27.5	< 0.16	< 3.0	< 2.8	< 1.6	< 1.6	< -0.20
Second	33.5 to 36.3	47.4 to 52.6	0.39 to 0.47	16.1 to 19.2	29.3 to 33.0	0.18 to 0.24	14.0 to 17.5	27.5 to 30.6	0.16 to 0.21	3.0 to 3.4	2.8 to 3.1	1.6 to 1.9	1.6 to 1.9	-0.20 to 0.39
Third	> 36.3	> 52.6	> 0.47	> 19.2	> 33.0	> 0.24	> 17.5	> 30.6	> 0.21	> 3.4	> 3.1	> 1.9	> 1.9	> 0.39

194 Strength and Conditioning for Football

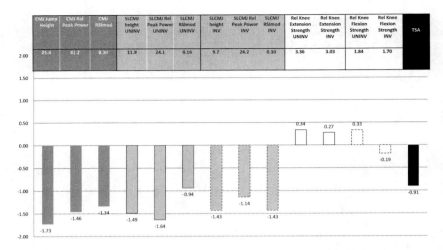

FIGURE 11.2 Strength, power and reactive strength values and standardized scores for a hypothetical, individual player.

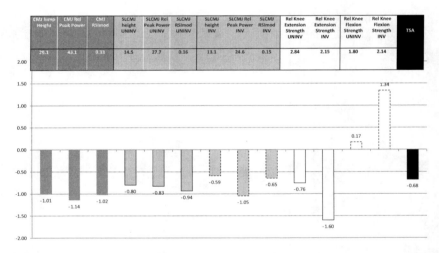

FIGURE 11.3 Strength, power and reactive strength values and standardized scores for a hypothetical, individual player.

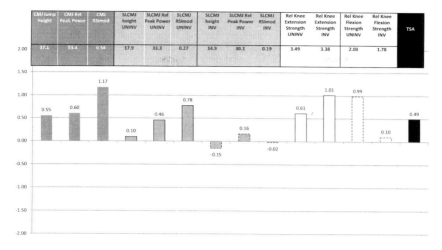

FIGURE 11.4 Strength, power and reactive strength values and standardized scores for a hypothetical, individual player.

Summary

The concepts expressed in this chapter highlight how the re-development of fundamental physical qualities are necessary for soccer players to compete at their fullest athletic potential and 'return to performance'. Rehabilitation programs contain specific milestones and should be supported by regular testing and monitoring using an assessment guided approach to individualize and optimize test-training integration. It should also be considered that while specific methods may vary, rehabilitation and return to performance conditioning programs should be principal driven and adaptation led.

References

1. Drew, M.K., B.P. Raysmith, and P.C. Charlton, Injuries Impair the Chance of Successful Performance by Sportspeople: A Systematic Review. *Br J Sports Med*, 2017. **51**(16): pp. 1209–1214.
2. Hagglund, M., et al., Injuries Affect Team Performance Negatively in Professional Football: An 11-year Follow-up of the UEFA Champions League Injury Study. *Br J Sports Med*, 2013. **47**(12): pp. 738–742.
3. Windt, J., et al., Does Player Unavailability Affect Football Teams' Match Physical Outputs? A Two-Season Study of the UEFA Champions League. *J Sci Med Sport*, 2018. **21**(5): pp. 525–532.
4. Esteve, E., et al., Preseason Adductor Squeeze Strength in 303 Spanish Male Soccer Athletes: A Cross-sectional Study. *Orthop J Sports Med*, 2018. **6**(1): p. 2325967117747275.
5. Hägglund, M., M. Waldén, and J. Ekstrand, Risk Factors for Lower Extremity Muscle Injury in Professional Soccer: The UEFA Injury Study. *Am J Sports Med*, 2012. **41**(2): pp. 327–335.

6. Jacobsson, J., and T. Timpka, Classification of Prevention in Sports Medicine and Epidemiology. *Sports Med*, 2015. **45**(11): pp. 1483–1487.
7. Doege, J., et al., Defining Return to Sport: A Systematic Review. *Orthop J Sports Med*, 2021. **9**(7): p. 23259671211009589.
8. Ardern, C.L., et al., 2016 Consensus Statement on Return to Sport from the First World Congress in Sports Physical Therapy, Bern. *Br J Sports Med*, 2016. **50**(14): p. 853.
9. Pfirrmann, D., et al., Analysis of Injury Incidences in Male Professional Adult and Elite Youth Soccer Players: A Systematic Review. *J Athl Train*, 2016. **51**(5): pp. 410–424.
10. Ekstrand J, Krutsch W, Spreco A, van Zoest W, Roberts C, Meyer T, Bengtsson H. Time before return to play for the most common injuries in professional football: a 16-year follow-up of the UEFA Elite Club Injury Study. Br J Sports Med. 2020 Apr;54(7):421-426. doi: 10.1136/bjsports-2019-100666. Epub 2019 Jun 10. PMID: 31182429; PMCID: PMC7146935.
11. Niederer, D., et al., Return to Play, Performance and Career Duration after ACL Rupture: A Case-Control Study in in the Five Biggest Football Nations in Europe. *Scand J Med Sci Sports*, 2018. **28**(10): pp. 2226–2233.
12. Della Villa, F., et al., High Rate of Second ACL Injury Following ACL Reconstruction in Male Professional Footballers: An Updated Longitudinal Analysis from 118 Players in the UEFA Elite Club Injury Study. *Br J Sports Med*, 2021. 55(23).
13. Delaloye, J.R., et al., Knee Extension Deficit in the Early Postoperative Period Predisposes to Cyclops Syndrome After Anterior Cruciate Ligament Reconstruction: A Risk Factor Analysis in 3633 Patients from the SANTI Study Group Database. *Am J Sports Med*, 2020. **48**(3): pp. 565–572.
14. Grindem, H., et al., Simple Decision Rules Reduce Reinjury Risk after Anterior Cruciate Ligament Reconstruction: The Delaware-Oslo ACL Cohort Study. *Br J Sports Med*, 2016. **50**(13): pp. 804–808.
15. Bourne MN, Timmins RG, Opar DA, Pizzari T, Ruddy JD, Sims C, Williams MD, Shield AJ. An Evidence-Based Framework for Strengthening Exercises to Prevent Hamstring Injury. Sports Med. 2018 Feb;48(2):251-267. doi: 10.1007/s40279-017-0796-x. PMID: 29116573.
16. O'Neill, S., P.J. Watson, and S. Barry., A Delphi Study of Risk Factors for Achillies Tendinopathy-Opinions of World Tendon Experts. *Int J Sports Phys Ther*, 2016. **11**(5): pp. 684–697.
17. Anderson, M.J., et al., A Systematic Summary of Systematic Reviews on the Topic of the Anterior Cruciate Ligament. *Orthop J Sports Med*, 2016. **4**(3): p. 2325967116634074.
18. Thorborg, K., et al., *Eccentric and Isometric Hip Adduction Strength in Male Soccer Players with and without Adductor-Related Groin Pain: An Assessor-Blinded Comparison.* Orthop J Sports Med, 2014. **2**(2): p. 2325967114521778.
19. Angelozzi, M., et al., Rate of Force Development as an Adjunctive Outcome Measure for Return-to-Sport Decisions after Anterior Cruciate Ligament Reconstruction. *J Orthop Sports Phys Ther*, 2012. **42**(9): pp. 772–780.
20. Wang, H.K., et al., Evoked Spinal Reflexes and Force Development in Elite Athletes with Middle-Portion Achilles Tendinopathy. *J Orthop Sports Phys Ther*, 2011. **41**(10): pp. 785–794.
21. Opar, D.A., et al., Rate of Torque and Electromyographic Development during Anticipated Eccentric Contraction Is Lower in Previously Strained Hamstrings. *Am J Sports Med*, 2013. **41**(1): pp. 116–125.
22. Doherty, C., et al., Recovery from a First-Time Lateral Ankle Sprain and the Predictors of Chronic Ankle Instability: A Prospective Cohort Analysis. *Am J Sports Med*, 2016. **44**(4): pp. 995–1003.

23. King E, Richter C, Franklyn-Miller A, Daniels K, Wadey R, Moran R, Strike S. Whole-body biomechanical differences between limbs exist 9 months after ACL reconstruction across jump/landing tasks. Scand J Med Sci Sports. 2018 Dec;28(12):2567-2578. doi: 10.1111/sms.13259. Epub 2018 Aug 6. Erratum in: Scand J Med Sci Sports. 2020 Aug;30(8):1551-1565. doi: 10.1111/sms.13699. PMID: 29972874.
24. Gore, S.J. and A. Franklyn-Miller, Is Stiffness Related to Athletic Groin Pain? *Scand J Med Sci Sports*, 2018. **28**(6): pp. 1681–1690.
25. Debenham, J.R., et al., Achilles Tendinopathy Alters Stretch Shortening Cycle Behaviour during a Sub-maximal Hopping Task. *J Sci Med Sport*, 2016. **19**(1): pp. 69–73.
26. O'Malley, E., et al., Countermovement Jump and Isokinetic Dynamometry as Measures of Rehabilitation Status after Anterior Cruciate Ligament Reconstruction. *J Athl Train*, 2018. **53**(7): pp. 687–695.
27. Pratt KA, Sigward SM. Detection of Knee Power Deficits Following Anterior Cruciate Ligament Reconstruction Using Wearable Sensors. J Orthop Sports Phys Ther. 2018 Nov;48(11):895-902. doi: 10.2519/jospt.2018.7995. Epub 2018 Jul 11. PMID: 29996735.
28. Haff, G.G. and M.H. Stone, Methods of Developing Power With Special Reference to Football Players. *Strength Cond J*, 2015. **37**(6): pp. 2–16.
29. Graven-Nielsen, T. and L. Arendt-Nielsen, Impact of Clinical and Experimental Pain on Muscle Strength and Activity. *Curr Rheumatol Rep*, 2008. **10**(6): pp. 475–481.
30. Bleakley, C., P. Glasgow, and D. MacAuley, *PRICE Needs Updating, Should We Call the POLICE?* BMJ Publishing Group Ltd and British Association of Sport and Exercise Medicine. 2012. pp. 220–221.
31. Verdini, E., et al., Do People with Musculoskeletal Pain Differ from Healthy Cohorts in Terms of Global Measures of Strength? A Systematic Review and Meta-analysis. *Clin Rehabil*, 2023. **37**(2): pp. 244–260.
32. Mohammadi, F., et al., Comparison of Functional Outcome Measures after ACL Reconstruction in Competitive Soccer Players: A Randomized Trial. *J Bone Joint Surg Am*, 2013. **95**(14): pp. 1271–1277.
33. Welling, W., et al., Progressive Strength Training Restores Quadriceps and Hamstring Muscle Strength within 7 months after ACL Reconstruction in Amateur Male Soccer Players. *Phys Ther Sport*, 2019. **40**: pp. 10–18.
34. Almeida, A.M., et al., Aerobic Fitness in Professional Soccer Players after Anterior Cruciate Ligament Reconstruction. *PLoS One*, 2018. **13**(3): p. e0194432.
35. Holsgaard-Larsen, A., et al., Concurrent Assessments of Lower Limb Loading Patterns, Mechanical Muscle Strength and Functional Performance in ACL-Patients--A Cross-Sectional Study. *Knee*, 2014. **21**(1): pp. 66–73.
36. Timmins, R.G., et al., Biceps Femoris Architecture and Strength in Athletes with a Previous Anterior Cruciate Ligament Reconstruction. *Med Sci Sports Exerc*, 2016. **48**(3): pp. 337–345.
37. Ward, S.H., et al., Quadriceps Neuromuscular Function and Jump-Landing Sagittal-Plane Knee Biomechanics after Anterior Cruciate Ligament Reconstruction. *J Athl Train*, 2018. **53**(2): pp. 135–143.
38. Read PJ, Trama R, Racinais S, McAuliffe S, Klauznicer J, Alhammoud M. Angle specific analysis of hamstrings and quadriceps isokinetic torque identify residual deficits in soccer players following ACL reconstruction: a longitudinal investigation. J Sports Sci. 2022 Apr;40(8):871-877. doi: 10.1080/02640414.2021.2022275. Epub 2022 Jan 5. PMID: 34983321.
39. Lepley, A.S., et al., Contributions of Neural Excitability and Voluntary Activation to Quadriceps Muscle Strength Following Anterior Cruciate Ligament Reconstruction. *The Knee*, 2014. **21**(3): pp. 736–742.

198 Strength and Conditioning for Football

40. Bodkin, S.G., et al., How Much Time Is Needed Between Serial "Return to Play" Assessments to Achieve Clinically Important Strength Gains in Patients Recovering From Anterior Cruciate Ligament Reconstruction? *Am J Sports Med*, 2020. **48**(1): pp. 70–77.

41. Roy, J.S., et al., Beyond the Joint: The Role of Central Nervous System Reorganizations in Chronic Musculoskeletal Disorders. *J Orthop Sports Phys Ther*, 2017. **47**(11): pp. 817–821.

42. Chang, W.J., et al., Altered Primary Motor Cortex Structure, Organization, and Function in Chronic Pain: A Systematic Review and Meta-Analysis. *J Pain*, 2018. **19**(4): pp. 341–359.

43. American College of Sports Medicine Position Stand. Progression Models in Resistance Training for Healthy Adults. *Med Sci Sports Exerc*, 2009. **41**(3): pp. 687–708.

44. Schoenfeld, B.J., et al., Strength and Hypertrophy Adaptations between Low- vs. High-Load Resistance Training: A Systematic Review and Meta-analysis. *J Strength Cond Res*, 2017. **31**(12): pp. 3508–3523.

45. Hughes, L., et al., Blood Flow Restriction Training in Clinical Musculoskeletal Rehabilitation: A Systematic Review and Meta-analysis. *Br J Sports Med*, 2017. **51**(13): p. 1003.

46. Kidgell, D.J., et al., Increased Cross-education of Muscle Strength and Reduced Corticospinal Inhibition Following Eccentric Strength Training. *Neuroscience*, 2015. **300**: pp. 566–575.

47. Cirer-Sastre, R., J.V. Beltrán-Garrido, and F. Corbi, Contralateral Effects After Unilateral Strength Training: A Meta-Analysis Comparing Training Loads. *J Sports Sci Med*, 2017. **16**(2): pp. 180–186.

48. Vaegter, H.B., Exercising Non-painful Muscles Can Induce Hypoalgesia in Individuals with Chronic Pain. *Scand J Pain*, 2017. **15**: pp. 60–61.

49. Turner, A.N., et al., Developing Powerful Athletes, Part 1: Mechanical Underpinnings. *Strength Cond J*, 2020. 42(3): p. 1.

50. Read PJ, Michael Auliffe S, Wilson MG, Graham-Smith P. Lower Limb Kinetic Asymmetries in Professional Soccer Players With and Without Anterior Cruciate Ligament Reconstruction: Nine Months Is Not Enough Time to Restore "Functional" Symmetry or Return to Performance. Am J Sports Med. 2020 May;48(6):1365-1373. doi: 10.1177/0363546520912218. Epub 2020 Apr 15. PMID: 32293904.

51. Maestroni, L., et al., Relationships between Physical Capacities and Biomechanical Variables during Movement Tasks in Athletic Populations Following Anterior Cruciate Ligament Reconstruction. *Phys Ther Sport*, 2021. **48**: pp. 209–218.

52. Taber, C., et al., *Roles of Maximal Strength and Rate of Force Development in Maximizing Muscular Power. Stren Cond J*, 2016. **38**(1): pp. 71–78.

53. Maffiuletti, N.A., et al., Rate of Force Development: Physiological and Methodological Considerations. *Eur J Appl Physiol*, 2016. **116**(6): pp. 1091–116.

54. Turpeinen JT, Freitas TT, Rubio-Arias JÁ, Jordan MJ, Aagaard P. Contractile rate of force development after anterior cruciate ligament reconstruction-a comprehensive review and meta-analysis. Scand J Med Sci Sports. 2020 Sep;30(9):1572-1585. doi: 10.1111/sms.13733. Epub 2020 Jun 18. PMID: 32478931.

55. Blazevich, A.J., C.J. Wilson, and P.E. Alcaraz, Effects of Resistance Training Movement Pattern and Velocity on Isometric Muscular Rate of Force Development: A Systematic Review with Meta-analysis and Meta-regression. *Sports Med*, 2020. **50**(5): pp. 943–963.

56. Flanagan, E.P. and T.M. Comyns, The Use of Contact Time and the Reactive Strength Index to Optimize Fast Stretch-Shortening Cycle Training. *Stren Cond J*, 2008. **30**(5): pp. 32–38.

57. Suchomel, T.J., et al., Using Reactive Strength Index-modified as an Explosive Performance Measurement tool in Division I Athletes. *J Strength Cond Res*, 2015. **29**(4): pp. 899–904.
58. Read, P.J., et al., Residual Deficits in Reactive Strength After Anterior Cruciate Ligament Reconstruction in Soccer Players. *J Athl Train*, 2023. **58**(5): pp. 423–429.
59. Maestroni L, Turner A, Papadopoulos K, Pedley J, Sideris V, Read P. Single leg drop jump is affected by physical capacities in male soccer players following ACL reconstruction. Sci Med Footb. 2024 Aug;8(3):201-211. doi: 10.1080/24733938.2023.2225481. Epub 2023 Jun 20. PMID: 37314868.
60. Read PJ, Davies WT, Bishop C, Mc Auliffe S, Wilson MG, Turner AN. Residual deficits in reactive strength indicate incomplete restoration of athletic qualities following anterior cruciate ligament reconstruction in professional soccer players. J Athl Train. 2020 Nov 5. doi: 10.4085/169-20. Epub ahead of print. PMID: 33150442.
61. Read, P.J., et al., Impaired Stretch-Shortening Cycle Function Persists Despite Improvements in Reactive Strength after Anterior Cruciate Ligament Reconstruction. *J Stren Cond Res*, 2022. **36**(5): pp. 1238–1244.
62. Nygaard Falch, H., H. Guldteig Rædergård, and R. van den Tillaar, Effect of Different Physical Training Forms on Change of Direction Ability: A Systematic Review and Meta-Analysis. *Sports Med*, 2019. **5**(1): p. 53.
63. Petrakos, G., J.B. Morin, and B. Egan, Resisted Sled Sprint Training to Improve Sprint Performance: A Systematic Review. *Sports Med*, 2016. **46**(3): pp. 381–400.
64. Ekstrand, J., et al., Hamstring Muscle Injuries in Professional Football: The Correlation of MRI Findings with Return to Play. *Br J Sports Med*, 2012. **46**(2): pp. 112–117.
65. Mendiguchia, J., et al., Field Monitoring of Sprinting Power-force-velocity Profile before, during and after Hamstring Injury: Two Case Reports. *J Sports Sci*, 2016. **34**(6): pp. 535–41.
66. Haugen, T., et al., The Training and Development of Elite Sprint Performance: an Integration of Scientific and Best Practice Literature. *Sports Med Open*, 2019. **5**(1): p. 44.
67. Nagahara, R., et al., Association of Acceleration with Spatiotemporal Variables in Maximal Sprinting. *Int J Sports Med*, 2014. **35**(9): pp. 755–761.
68. Clark, K.P. and P.G. Weyand, Are Running Speeds Maximized with Simple-Spring Stance Mechanics? *J Appl Physiol (*1985), 2014. **117**(6): pp. 604–615.
69. Brughelli, M. and J. Cronin, Influence of Running Velocity on Vertical, Leg and Joint Stiffness. *Sports Med*, 2008. **38**(8): pp. 647–657.
70. Douglas, J., et al., Reactive and Eccentric Strength Contribute to Stiffness Regulation during Maximum Velocity Sprinting in Team Sport Athletes and Highly Trained Sprinters. *J Sports Sci*, 2020. **38**(1): pp. 29–37.
71. Sáez de Villarreal, E., B. Requena, and J.B. Cronin, The Effects of Plyometric Training on Sprint Performance: A Meta-Analysis. *J Strength Cond Res*, 2012. **26**(2): pp. 575–584.
72. Silva, J.R., G.P. Nassis, and A. Rebelo, Strength Training in Soccer with a Specific Focus on Highly Trained Players. *Sports Med Open*, 2015. **1**(1): p. 17.
73. Chelly, M.S., et al., Effects of a Back Squat Training Program on Leg Power, Jump, and Sprint Performances in Junior Soccer Players. *J Strength Cond Res*, 2009. **23**(8): pp. 2241–2249.
74. Styles, William J.; Matthews, Martyn J.; Comfort, Paul. Effects of Strength Training on Squat and Sprint Performance in Soccer Players. Journal of Strength and Conditioning Research 30(6):p 1534-1539, June 2016. | DOI: 10.1519/JSC.0000000000001243

200 Strength and Conditioning for Football

75. Rønnestad, B.R., B.S. Nymark, and T. Raastad, Effects of In-season Strength Maintenance Training Frequency in Professional Soccer Players. *J Strength Cond Res*, 2011. **25**(10): pp. 2653–2660.
76. Cuthbert M, Ripley N, McMahon JJ, Evans M, Haff GG, Comfort P. The Effect of Nordic Hamstring Exercise Intervention Volume on Eccentric Strength and Muscle Architecture Adaptations: A Systematic Review and Meta-analyses. Sports Med. 2020 Jan;50(1):83–99. doi: 10.1007/s40279-019-01178-7. Erratum in: Sports Med. 2020 Jan;50(1):101–102. doi: 10.1007/s40279-019-01208-4. PMID: 31502142; PMCID: PMC6942028.
77. Seitz, L.B., et al., Increases in Lower-body Strength Transfer Positively to Sprint Performance: A Systematic Review with Meta-analysis. *Sports Med*, 2014. **44**(12): pp. 1693–1702.
78. Loturco, I., et al., Vertically and Horizontally Directed Muscle Power Exercises: Relationships with Top-level Sprint Performance. *PLOS ONE*, 2018. **13**(7): p. e0201475.
79. Contreras, B., et al., Effects of a Six-Week Hip Thrust vs. Front Squat Resistance Training Program on Performance in Adolescent Males: A Randomized Controlled Trial. *J Strength Cond Res*, 2017. **31**(4): pp. 999–1008.
80. Pairot-de-Fontenay, B., et al., Running Biomechanics in Individuals with Anterior Cruciate Ligament Reconstruction: A Systematic Review. *Sports Med*, 2019. **49**(9): pp. 1411–1424.
81. Dos'Santos, T., et al., Role of the Penultimate Foot Contact During Change of Direction: Implications on Performance and Risk of Injury. *Strength Cond J*, 2019. **41**(1): pp. 87–104.
82. Jones PA, Thomas C, Dos'Santos T, McMahon JJ, Graham-Smith P. The Role of Eccentric Strength in 180° Turns in Female Soccer Players. Sports (Basel). 2017 Jun 17;5(2):42. doi: 10.3390/sports5020042. PMID: 29910402; PMCID: PMC5968983.
83. Brughelli, M., et al., Understanding Change of Direction Ability in Sport: A Review of Resistance Training Studies. *Sports Med*, 2008. **38**(12): pp. 1045–1063.
84. Marques JB, Paul DJ, Graham-Smith P, Read PJ. Change of Direction Assessment Following Anterior Cruciate Ligament Reconstruction: A Review of Current Practice and Considerations to Enhance Practical Application. Sports Med. 2020 Jan;50(1):55-72. doi: 10.1007/s40279-019-01189-4. PMID: 31531768; PMCID: PMC6942029.
85. King, E., et al., Biomechanical but Not Timed Performance Asymmetries Persist between Limbs 9 months after ACL Reconstruction during Planned and Unplanned Change of Direction. *J Biomech*, 2018. **81**: pp. 93–103.
86. King, E., et al., Back to Normal Symmetry? Biomechanical Variables Remain More Asymmetrical Than Normal During Jump and Change-of-Direction Testing 9 Months After Anterior Cruciate Ligament Reconstruction. *Am J Sports Med*, 2019. **47**(5): pp. 1175–1185.
87. Dos'Santos, T., et al., The Effect of Angle and Velocity on Change of Direction Biomechanics: An Angle-Velocity Trade-Off. *Sports Med*, 2018. **48**(10): pp. 2235–2253.
88. Barnes C, Archer DT, Hogg B, Bush M, Bradley PS. The evolution of physical and technical performance parameters in the English Premier League. *Int J Sports Med*. 2014 Dec;35(13):1095-100. doi: 10.1055/s-0034-1375695. Epub 2014 Jul 10. PMID: 25009969.
89. Dos'Santos T, McBurnie A, Thomas C, Comfort P, Jones PA. Biomechanical Determinants of the Modified and Traditional 505 Change of Direction Speed Test. *J Strength Cond Res*. 2020 May;34(5):1285-1296. doi: 10.1519/JSC.0000000000003439. PMID: 31868815.

90. Bujalance-Moreno, P., F. García-Pinillos, and P. Latorre-Román, Effects of a Small-sided Game-based Training Program on Repeated Sprint and Change of Direction Abilities in Recreationally-trained Soccer Players. *J Sports Med Phys Fitness*, 2018. **58**(7–8): pp. 1021–1028.
91. Nimphius, Sophia PhD1,2; Callaghan, Samuel J. BSc (Honours)1; Bezodis, Neil E. PhD3; Lockie, Robert G. PhD4. Change of Direction and Agility Tests: Challenging Our Current Measures of Performance. *Strength and Conditioning Journal* 40(1):p 26-38, February 2018. | DOI: 10.1519/SSC.0000000000000309
92. Young, W.B., B. Dawson, and G.J. Henry, Agility and Change-of-Direction Speed are Independent Skills: Implications for Training for Agility in Invasion Sports. *Int J Sports Sci Coach*, 2015. **10**(1): pp. 159–169.
93. Young, W.B. and B. Willey, Analysis of a Reactive Agility Field Test. *J Sci Med Sport*, 2010. **13**(3): pp. 376–378.
94. Spiteri, T., R.U. Newton, and S. Nimphius, Neuromuscular Strategies Contributing to Faster Multidirectional Agility Performance. *J Electromyogr Kinesiol*, 2015. **25**(4): pp. 629–636.
95. Maestroni, L., et al., Total Score of Athleticism: Profiling Strength and Power Characteristics in Professional Soccer Players after Anterior Cruciate Ligament Reconstruction to Assess Readiness to Return to Sport. *Am J Sports Med*, 2023. **51**(12): pp. 3121–3130.
96. Read, P., et al., Better Reporting Standards Are Needed to Enhance the Quality of Hop Testing in the Setting of ACL Return to Sport Decisions: A Narrative Review. *Br J Sports Med*, 2021. **55**(1): pp. 23–29.
97. Turner, A.N., et al., Total Score of Athleticism: Holistic Athlete Profiling to Enhance Decision-making. *Strength Cond J*, 2019. **41**(6): pp. 91–101.

12

NUTRITION AND SOCCER

Andrew T. Hulton and Don P.M. MacLaren

Introduction

Soccer is a high-intensity intermittent sport that places a significant stress upon both the aerobic and anaerobic energy systems, with constant fluctuations between low and high-intensity exercise. Male soccer players, at an elite level, typically cover around 11–13 km per match. In addition, the total distance covered is position-dependent, with central midfielders typically covering the highest and central defenders the lowest distances (Bradley et al., 2009). Having said that, distances covered at higher intensities may be more relevant and related to key match activities than total distance. Distances covered at speeds greater than 20 km·h⁻¹ are observed to be approximately 1,150 m, with around 60 sprints performed per match. Furthermore, within the match players perform utility and game-specific movements with more than 1,200 unpredictable changes in activity, which also comprises ~700 turns and 30–40 tackles and jumps (Bloomfield et al., 2007).

As such the energy demands placed on players during competition places a significant requirement on both the aerobic and anaerobic systems in order to perform at an elite level. Soccer match-play elicits average and peak heart rates of ~85% and ~98% of maximal values, respectively (Krustrup et al., 2005), and such data suggests that the average oxygen uptake is around ~70% $\dot{V}O_{2max}$. The physical and physiological demands of match play represent a high-volume and high-intensity sport, placing a significant need to utilise the body's limited glycogen stores as the primary energy source due to anaerobic glycolysis and carbohydrate (CHO) oxidation. The depletion of glycogen stores during competition has been reported to be around 43% of pre-match levels and remains significantly reduced up to and beyond 24 hours post-match (Krustrup et al., 2011). This highlights the need for soccer players to adequately prepare and recover from both a training and

DOI: 10.4324/9781003383475-13

competitive perspective to fully meet the nutritional and energy requirements to maintain performance.

This chapter highlights some of the key available scientific literature concerning the energy demands of both soccer training and match-play and thereafter examines energy requirements with a view to suggesting practical guidelines. The objective is to provide evidence-based nutritional strategies for practitioners to implement in order to optimise soccer performance. Consequently, exploration of the energy expenditure (EE) as well as the metabolic changes that take place during training and matches is examined before attention is given to the nutritional needs of players.

Fatigue, Soccer, and Carbohydrates

Fatigue, which can be described as an inability to sustain the necessary speed or power output, has received much interest within the literature due to its potential links to the outcome of matches. Though there are many potential mechanisms responsible, two of the main explanations which have a nutritional implication are (i) a depletion of muscle glycogen and (ii) hypoglycaemia (Mujika and Burke, 2010). The first investigation into glycogen and soccer was led by Prof Bengt Saltin in the early 1970s (Saltin, 1972), when it was demonstrated that players starting a match with low muscle glycogen content ultimately fully depleted these limited stores by the end of the match. Moreover, results showed that an early onset of fatigue ensued, which was characterised by a significant increase in time spent at low-intensity movements such as walking (50% vs 27% of total distance), and an inability to complete sprinting activities (15% vs 24% of total distance) compared to those who started the match with 'normal' glycogen availability. Similar work has since been conducted within a detailed field-based investigation by Krustrup and colleagues (2006) who also observed gradual reductions in muscle glycogen throughout the duration of a friendly match with Danish fourth-division players. The authors observed that approximately 47% of all muscle fibres were 'depleted or almost depleted of glycogen'. Further analysis of the fibre type identified that depletion was apparent within type IIa (intermediate) and type IIx (fast) fibres. These are the fibres responsible for high-intensity actions, and as such, the investigation also observed a significant reduction in sprint ability (reflected in slower times for 30 m sprints) throughout the match (see Figure 12.1). However, it would be prudent to consider the level of players employed in this investigation, as they may be labelled more of a sub-elite population. Within soccer, it has been shown that the volume and intensity of the game increase at the elite level with greater engagement in high-intensity activities, and as a result, no formal investigation with an elite soccer population has been conducted, although we could hypothesise a greater glycogen depletion could occur.

The second likely fatigue factor with regard to soccer is that of hypoglycaemia (low blood glucose concentration, <4 mmol/L). Currently, there is no direct

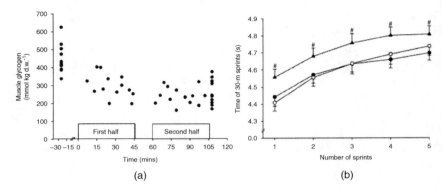

FIGURE 12.1 (A) Muscle glycogen use throughout a football match (B) Time of five 30 m sprints before the game (●), after the first half (○), and after the game (▲) with Danish fourth-division players (Krustrup et al., 2006).

evidence illustrating that hypoglycaemia occurs in soccer (i.e., no data showing blood glucose is below 4 mM), although indirect evidence suggests that any decrements in skill or running performance could be attributed to hypoglycaemia rather than muscle glycogen depletion. For example, soccer skills such as dribbling ability (Currell et al., 2009) and shooting (Ali et al., 2007) during simulated soccer activity are improved when consuming CHO beverages compared to a placebo. These findings demonstrate that CHO availability within the blood is an important factor of performance (notably in the last 15–20 minutes of a match). Further, Backhouse et al. (2007) suggested that the consumption of CHO during a high-intensity intermittent protocol elicited an enhanced perceived activation profile in soccer players that may support task persistence and performance, in addition to the physiological benefits of an exogenous supply of energy. Although there is a lack of direct evidence with regard to hypoglycaemia during soccer, the fact that CHO feeding during simulated play improves skill, speed, and decision-making tasks, implies that players should ensure liver glycogen stores are full before a match or training.

The evidence concerning the importance of CHO as a fuel for soccer performance is considerable. Within some of the forthcoming sections, suggestions are made regarding how, what, and when to ingest CHO for maximal benefit. Furthermore, as training loads vary throughout the weekly microcycle in a periodised manner, we also need to consider a periodised approach to the CHO intake to support training. Figure 12.2 provides the recommendations for CHO consumption linked to training and competition.

Relevance of Protein

Proteins are an essential macronutrient without which a human is unable to survive for prolonged periods of time. There is a general agreement among nutritionists

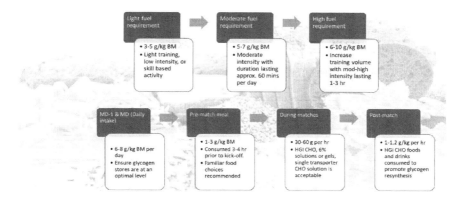

FIGURE 12.2 CHO requirements for varying fuelling requirements and around MD.

that an average protein intake of 0.8 g/kg body mass (BM)/day is suitable for sedentary persons. However, for athletic populations, 1.3–1.7 g/kg BM/day is advised (Thomas et al., 2016), with such a range resulting in a daily amount of 97.5–127.5 g for a 75 kg player. An inevitable consequence of undertaking any form of exercise such as soccer (training or match play) is that muscle protein breakdown (MPB) ensues and that muscle protein synthesis (MPS) is attenuated (Phillips, 2014). It is also well established that feeding protein in the hours prior to engaging in such bouts of activity and in the 1–2 hours afterwards, results in an increase in net protein balance, whereas failure to consume protein at such times causes a deficit in net protein balance (Tipton et al., 2007). Consuming a pre-match meal with some protein 3-h before is advisable as is the consumption of protein in the changing room and/or in a post-match meal. For those players who find it difficult to eat after a match, whey protein drinks should be considered. If protein is to be consumed before and after exertion, how much is required? Data from a number of studies suggests that the maximum amount of protein for any meal should be 0.3–0.4 g/kg BM (Witard et al., 2014), which equates to 22.5–30 g for a 75 kg player per meal. A lower intake may not result in complete recovery, whilst a higher intake is wasteful since no additional elevation of MPS occurs (Egan, 2016). If meals were to contain 0.3–0.4 g/kg of protein, then a 4-meal per day strategy would result in 1.2–1.6 g/kg BM/day of protein and thereby meet the required daily intake.

A further element of thought is to recognise that there are some periods where a reduced CHO intake may be deemed desirable – such as when injured, during days of light training, or when body fat is raised. If CHO foods are to be reduced, then protein foods may be used as alternates. Under such circumstances, a higher daily protein intake should be considered – such as 1-8–2.0 g/kg BM/day. In order to attain this level of daily protein, players would likely require five or even six meals per day.

206 Strength and Conditioning for Football

Fluid Considerations

As a consequence of the energy demands of soccer match play, metabolic heat production increases body temperature. The rise in body temperature results in evaporation of sweat in an attempt to reduce core temperature and may lead to a sweat loss in excess of 2 litres. When the sweat loss accounts for a decrease in body mass of >2%, there is invariably impaired performance such as reduced sprint capacity and soccer dribbling ability (Judelson et al., 2007). Most players find it difficult to drink sufficient fluids during a match due to the limited opportunities for a break (although this is not the case during training) with the consequence that some degree of dehydration ensues. Consequently, players need to ensure they start the match euhydrated. Evidence-based on the assessment of urinary parameters demonstrates that a large proportion of players may start competition in a relatively dehydrated state (Maughan and Shirreffs, 2007). It is good practice to assess the urine osmolality of players prior to training and potentially on MD if logistics allow, in order to ascertain hydration status on an individual basis, and if some degree of dehydration is evident then there may be some time to rectify the situation. Therefore, to ensure players are well prepared with regards to their fluid status, they should slowly drink between 5 and 7 ml·kg^{-1} at least 4 hours prior to the match and to consider a further 3–5 ml/kg in the intervening 2 hours if required (ACSM, 2007).

Rehydration following a match or training should adhere to the various findings from Evans et al. (2017) where they observed that the ideal means to rehydrate are: (1) to ingest ~ 1.5× the body mass loss due to sweat in litres of fluid, and (2) to ensure that there is sodium in the ingested fluid in order to prevent further fluid loss via urine. The addition of CHO or protein or other electrolytes to the ingested drink does not impair rehydration and may be welcome. CHO-electrolyte drinks are preferable to plain water as indeed are drinks such as milk or soups (both of which contain sodium).

Energy Expenditure: Training and Match Day

In order to gain an understanding of the nutritional demands of the sport, an appreciation for the EE during training and matches is necessary. Early methods to calculate EE have utilised HR data and estimated EE based on the HR-$\dot{V}O_2$ regression during incremental treadmill running. This may limit the accuracy of the data, although more robust measures may not be possible due to the limited time frame needed for a match and data collection process. Nevertheless, a physiological review of the literature by Iaia et al. (2009) provided an approximation of EE during match play to be between 1,519 and 1,772 kcal.

Daily total EE, which can be measured over a number of consecutive days employing the doubly labelled water technique, has observed a value of approximately 3,566 kcal/day in male senior soccer players in the English Premier League (Anderson et al., 2017) Similarly, Brinkmans et al. (2019) revealed group average

EE data of 3,285 kcal/day, which included goalkeepers and outfield players from the Netherlands.

Data from a recent review (Hulton et al., 2022) highlighted that investigations that have directly compared energy balance through energy intake (EI) and EE, show a negative energy balance of around ~200–500 kcal/day across training and match-play. A potential explanation for this imbalance may be due to a fear of adding excessive body weight or body fat during the competitive season, which is seen as a negative consequence of excessive EI by both players and coaching staff. However, it is clear that this is not the case, and in fact players' intake can be increased to support the demands of both training and MD.

Nutrition for Pre-Match Day (MD-1)

As previously indicated, the high-intensity intermittent nature of soccer relies heavily on CHO to fuel activity. Therefore, the emphasis for an increase in CHO intake typically between 6 and 8 g/kg BM (i.e., 450–600 g of CHO in absolute terms for a 75 kg player) is required prior to competition. The day before competition (MD-1) is potentially the most important day when preparing nutritional needs. It is difficult to replenish significant losses of muscle glycogen on MD due to the limited time prior to kick off. Furthermore, as players may have trained the day before (MD-2), not only are they attempting to replenish glycogen from previous training, but MD-1 is primed to ensure that both muscle and liver glycogen stores are optimally elevated in preparation for the forthcoming MD. With regards to the actual training that may take place during MD-1, typically the session would focus on light tactical work and brief activity at high-intensity to maintain 'sharpness'.

CHO is required at every opportunity throughout the day to achieve the desired intake. Table 12.1 provides an example of what may be consumed throughout MD-1 in order to attain such a goal for a 75 kg player, whereby a minimum of 450 g of CHO is recommended i.e., 6 g/kg BM (Hulton et al., 2022). This example is a traditional format of three main meals, although alternative strategies to include a four or five-meal strategy may be applicable (i.e., breakfast, lunch, mid-afternoon snack, dinner, and supper). This strategy may support players who prefer to eat smaller portions, but more frequently. Further, the use of CHO drinks and juices may be appropriate as it is well known that glycogen is stored with water, thus fluid consumption with each meal/snack is necessary.

CHO can be classified into low and high glycaemic index (HGI) foods based on their glucose response and speed of digestion. Therefore, as players are encouraged to eat greater amounts of CHO on MD-1, it would be appropriate to consider consuming foods which have an HGI as these are digested and absorbed more quickly than the low glycaemic index (LGI) alternatives. Examples of HGI foods from Table 12.1 include CHO-electrolyte drinks, mashed potato, and white rice, whereas LGI foods include carrots, broccoli, green beans, and apple juice. It must be noted that more research is required in relation to GI CHO intake during MD-1. Using an

208 Strength and Conditioning for Football

TABLE 12.1 Example from Hulton et al. (2022) Demonstrating a Nutritional Plan to Attain a CHO Intake of 6 g/kg BM for a 75 kg Player on MD-1

Meal	Food Source	Amount	Amount of CHO
Breakfast	Cereal – Weetabix	37 g (135 ml)	31.6 g
Total – 88.1 g	(with milk)	60 g (14 g)	31.0 g
(1.2 g/kg CHO)	Toast – Two slices	100 g	11.7 g
	(with flora light)	160 ml	14.1 g
	Fruit cocktail (in juice)	100 g	0 g
	Fresh orange (glass)		
	Poached eggs × 2		
Lunch	*Rice*	160 g	50.4 g
Total – 156.6 g	Sweet and sour	160 g	9.4 g
(2.1 g/kg CHO)	chicken	85 g	3 g
	Broccoli	60 g	2.3 g
	Green beans	150 g 100 g	68.4 g
	Apple crumble and custard	300 ml	23.1 g
	Fresh apple juice (tall tumbler)		
Dinner	Mashed potato	300 g	41.4 g
Total – 152 g	Salmon (white wine	210 g (121 g)	6.4 g
(2 g/kg CHO)	sauce)	90 g	5.2 g
	Carrots	85 g	3 g
	Broccoli	80 g	7.4 g
	Peas	160 g/32 g	39.1 g
	Strawberry (1 cup)	35 g	7.4 g
	and meringue (×2)	500 ml	31.5 g
	Ice cream		
	CHO-electrolyte drink		
Drinks/Snacks	Slice of fruit cake/	77 g	40.8 g
Total – 72.3 g	loaf	500 ml	31.5 g
(0.96 g/kg CHO)	CHO-electrolyte drink		
Total CHO Intake	459 g (6.1 g/kg CHO)		

Data analysed with nutritional management software Nutritics (Dublin, Ireland).

HGI feeding strategy during recovery results in rapid glycogen replenishment, so it may be prudent to allow players to consume all CHO sources they enjoy during MD-1 as long as there are sufficient amounts to achieve ~6 g/kg BM.

Nutrition for Match-Day: Pre-Match

If the high CHO strategy has been followed successfully during MD-1, then the MD itself should be more of a 'top up' of liver glycogen whilst enabling muscles to retain glycogen. It is important to note that liver glycogen stores can be significantly depleted following overnight sleep whereas muscle glycogen is hardly diminished. Thankfully, liver glycogen is rapidly restored following a CHO-based meal, so the need for a good CHO-based breakfast and pre-match meal is encouraged.

An important consideration to bear in mind is that of variation in kick-off times. Within the UK, kick-off times can start as early as 12:00 or 12:30 and be as late as 20:00, although the common kick-off time remains 15:00. Therefore, kick-off times will dictate the feeding strategy prior to matches. For a midday kick off, a single-meal strategy fed in the hours beforehand is appropriate, whereas, for 15:00 and 20:00 starts, it is more desirable to follow a two and three-meal strategy, respectively. For the earlier start times, the importance of a sufficient CHO intake during MD-1 is paramount, whilst marginally less so for evening matches as there are further timepoints to store glycogen throughout the MD prior to kick-off.

A relatively high amount of CHO is recommended approximately 3–4 hours before kick-off, with the general consensus suggesting between 1 and 4 g/kg BM (Mujika and Burke, 2010). LGI meals are recommended above HGI meals as they maintain a more stable blood glucose and insulin profile that facilitates a greater endurance capacity, potentially due to a glycogen-sparing effect. An HGI meal has been observed (in some individuals) to result in so-called rebound hypoglycae-mia, and consequently may not be desirable for those susceptible players. How-ever, when soccer specific investigations have examined the GI comparison for pre-match feeding, no difference between HGI and LGI pre-match foods (Little et al., 2009) or meals (Hulton et al., 2012) has been found. Even though significant differences in postprandial glucose responses were observed, no metabolic or per-formance difference was evident, and glucose remained stable between conditions during the soccer activity (Hulton et al., 2012; see Figure 12.3). Further, Little and colleagues (2009) identified no glycogen-sparing effect between the HGI or LGI foods, with only a significant difference observed between the control trial (fasted) and both HGI and LGI.

As there appears to be no great benefit of consuming either an LGI or HGI meal prior to competition, an investigation into the potential use of an isocaloric high fat meal compared to an LGI high CHO meal was conducted prior to a soccer-specific simulation (Hulton et al., 2013). Although differences were observed between fat metabolites and substrate oxidation rates that increased in line with the meal type (i.e. high fat meal increase fat metabolites, fat oxidation, and reduced CHO oxida-tion, and vice versa with the CHO meal for oxidation rates), in addition to differ-ences between subjective ratings of fullness (increased with CHO meal) and hunger (increased with fat meal), no transferable effect on performance or subjective rat-ing of perceived exertion were highlighted. These results indicated that as long as players are prepared optimally in the days leading into a match, the MD itself may provide more flexibility and a more personalised approach for the pre-match meal. Such a personalised approach is particularly suitable for players based on their food preferences, cultural differences, habits, rituals, and/or superstitions.

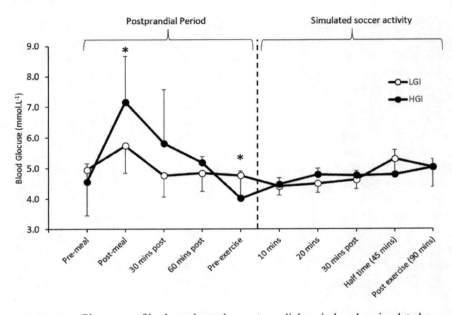

FIGURE 12.3 Glucose profile throughout the postprandial period and a simulated soccer protocol. *significant differences between HGI and LGI (Hulton et al., 2012).

The importance of fluid and protein for soccer players has been discussed previously, and both are key within the pre-match preparations. Consumption of water is advised following the pre-match meal and the start of the warm-up to avoid any disruption of glucose concentrations that may occur due to CHO-containing beverages that may result in rebound hypoglycaemia. CHO may be re-introduced after the warm-up and in the 5–10 minute period before kick-off. Including protein (~20–30 g) within the pre-match meal is advised, and although not commonly followed, the consumption of protein within the hour before kick-off may also be beneficial due to a potential increase in net protein balance (Tipton et al., 2007). While there is a lack of specific scientific evidence associated with this suggested pre-match protein feeding, theoretically the ingestion of a protein bar, shake, or gel may be a valuable consideration and help reduce MPB during the match.

Nutrition for Match-Day: During Matches

In order to maintain adequate hydration, muscle glycogen, and blood glucose concentrations, sufficient intake of CHO and fluid are the main nutritional considerations during match-play. Data from laboratory-based studies show that CHO ingestion during soccer-specific exercise augments plasma glucose availability and maintains rates of CHO oxidation (Clarke et al., 2008). However, given the acyclic nature of activity in soccer, with no scheduled breaks until half-time when fluid can be consumed, it may be difficult to consume adequate fluids. In addition, gastric tolerance and the perception of gut fullness do not allow for suitable rehydration for soccer players, where it has been demonstrated that the intensity corresponding to that of a soccer match is sufficient to slow gastric emptying. Therefore, due to the continuous nature of play, with infrequent, unscheduled stoppages, the only two occasions that a player is guaranteed to be able to consume fluid are before the game and at half-time. It is therefore prudent that players take onboard fluid during additional breaks in play, wherever possible (e.g., injury stoppages).

The intensity of exercise associated with a competitive match is sufficient to induce appreciable heat load, causing players to lose up to 3 litres of sweat during a match (even in temperate conditions). Therefore, as a guide, players should aim to drink sufficient fluids to prevent a deficit of no more than 2%–3% of pre-match euhydrated body mass (ACSM, 2007). It is considered unlikely that athletes in any sport would ingest more than 1 litre/hour due to gastric discomfort. In the case of soccer, consuming anywhere close to 1 litre/hour is highly unlikely. The addition of CHO to ingested fluid can further improve exercise capacity, possibly due to the aforementioned prevention of hypoglycaemia, maintenance of high CHO oxidation rates, glycogen sparing, and effects on the central nervous system, delaying the onset of fatigue. Consequently, a CHO intake at a rate of 30–60 g/h has been associated with a consistent beneficial effect on performance in soccer (Baker et al., 2015). However, players in the English Premier League report a CHO intake of 32 g/h just before and during a match (Anderson et al., 2017).

The ingestion of CHO has frequently resulted in improvements in exercise capacity during the performance of exercise protocols that simulate the work rate of soccer and actual match-play, although sprint performance is less consistent. However, soccer performance is not only dependent on physical performance since motor skills and cognitive performance also play a crucial role, and there is a tendency for skills and cognitive performance to decline during the latter stages of a match. CHO has been shown to attenuate, or even eliminate, this detrimental effect over the course of a match. For example, Harper and colleagues reported that a CHO–electrolyte gel improved dribbling speed during the later stages of a soccer match simulation. Furthermore, CHO supplementation has been demonstrated to attenuate the decrements in shooting and passing accuracy during simulated soccer match-play. This exogenous CHO may not be sparing the endogenous glycogen stores per se, but instead providing an additional CHO fuel to maintain oxidation.

Caffeine may have ergogenic appeal for soccer players. The co-ingestion of a 6% CHO solution and caffeine (3.7 mg/kg BM) has been reported to improve sprint performance in the second half by approximately 4%, with a 2.2% increase in countermovement jumping (Gant et al., 2010). Similarly, the addition of caffeine (5 mg/kg BM) to a high CHO feeding strategy reduced perceived exertion throughout a simulated soccer protocol (Hulton et al., 2020). It is interesting to note that caffeinated gum containing 200 mg of caffeine (2 × 100 mg pieces of gum) prior to

212 Strength and Conditioning for Football

soccer-specific tests has been reported to enhance the Yo-Yo intermittent recovery test level 1 (YIRT1) well as countermovement jumping performance by approximately 2% (Ranchordas et al., 2018), although only small effect sizes were reported and the result for the YIRT1 is within the co-efficient of variation for test-retest (Krustrup et al., 2003). This method of caffeine delivery may be advantageous due to the speed of delivery, and offers a potential to utilise at the half-time period to support second-half performance, although further research is required. Caffeine found in coffee may be more ecological, although a standard coffee contains low doses of caffeine that would not meet the recommended amount (3–6 mg/kg BM) to induce ergogenic effects. Research that has observed improved performance in strength and endurance has used larger volumes of coffee to offset the low dose, which may not a recommended to soccer players and well-tolerated.

Matches can extend to extra time and penalty shoot-outs, and as previously mentioned, ingestion of a CHO– electrolyte gel before a simulated extra-time period has been shown to be beneficial. Finally, the use of CHO mouth rinse has been shown to increase self-selected jogging speed with likely benefits for repeated 15 m sprint performance. Therefore, CHO consumption and mouth rinsing prior to extra-time or penalty shootout could potentially enhance performance in situations where CHO consumption is limited by gastrointestinal concerns.

Nutrition for Match-Day: Post-Match

Due to the depletion of muscle and liver glycogen during match play, the main focus for recovery is to replenish these stores in addition to rehydration and ensuring muscle protein is recovered. Normally, this should be achieved within a 2-h window after a match and is especially important if fixtures are congested (i.e., within 2–3 days). This limited time frame for glycogen resynthesis is due to exercise-induced glycogen depletion promoting activation of glycogen synthase, exercise-induced increases in insulin sensitivity, and exercise sensitisation of muscle cell membranes to glucose delivery. Therefore, the sooner the CHO intake after exercise the better. Those players who are unable to consume adequate CHO following a match, due to suppression of appetite following exercise for example, risk a reduced ability to re-synthesise glycogen by approximately 50% throughout a 4-h period, although over a 24-h time frame, there does not appear to be a difference when the nutritional goal is to maximise glycogen synthesis. High glycaemic index CHO sources are the variety of choice compared with an LGI equivalent, at least in the short term (over 24-h there is no difference in overall glycogen replenishment). A recommended intake of approximately 1.0–1.2 g/kg BM/h in the first 4–6 hours is suggested (Burke et al., 2004). If sufficient CHO cannot be ingested in the immediate post-match period, there is some evidence that additional protein may help glycogen resynthesis. Thereby, if the recommended intake of 1.2 g/kg BM/h is unable to be attained, then an additional amount of 0.4g /kg BM/h of protein could ensure adequate rates of glycogen storage (van Loon et al., 2000).

A vital component of nutritional recovery is to replenish muscle protein. Many reported investigations into the optimal amount of protein to ingest after exercise recommend 20–40 g (McGlory et al., 2016). Further, MacNaughton and colleagues (2016) conducted an investigation following a bout of whole body resistance exercise and found that 40 g of protein stimulates a 16% greater myofibrillar protein synthesis response than 20 g in young resistance-trained men, irrespective of their lean body mass. Solid or whole foods rich in protein would generally be recommended, but whey protein shakes are often favoured as a more expedient way to consume protein, especially when appetite maybe suppressed following exercise. Whey protein is recommended over casein and soy protein due to its rapid absorption, and importantly its high proportion of leucine, which is a key amino acid that at high doses can stimulate MPS. Nonetheless, there is still a role for casein protein. It would be advantageous to consume casein in the evening, as consuming 30–60 g of casein prior to sleep can result in a prolonged and sustained overnight protein synthesis (Trommelen and van Loon, 2016). Rather than employ casein as a supplement per se, casein can be consumed via milk products such as yogurt and cottage cheese before bed.

Another important aspect of recovery from match play is rehydration. Players can be hyperthermic at the final whistle and sweat losses can exceed 3–4 litres. Therefore, it is important to replace any fluid and electrolyte deficit. After a match, it is usual for players to consume foods that contain sodium, and under these circumstances drinking plain water would suffice (ACSM, 2007). However, if sodium is not present or insufficient due to the type of food eaten there is likely to be a delay in return to a euhydrated state. This is because sodium is considered crucial for the retention of any fluid ingested. To be on the safe side, it is advisable for a player to eat food and drink an electrolyte drink containing sodium.

As to the volume of fluid needed for rehydration, 150% of weight loss or 1.5 litres per 1 kg of weight loss is suggested. Such a volume is required to support the fluid loss from ensuing urination, although consideration should be made regarding hyperhydration following evening matches, as sleep disturbances have been attributed to waking throughout the night to urinate. After an evening match and prior to bed, milk may be a drink of choice, not only for the protein/casein, but also due to its good sodium content.

Due to the nature of the game at professional levels, many substitutes are available for selection at various times. These players are required to load up on fluid and CHO in the same manner as those starting the match. However, if they play only a few minutes or not at all, then it is strongly advisable not to engage in the high CHO eating strategies outlined above. Rather, these players should focus on low-CHO, high-protein foods both in the changing room and for their post-match meal. Failure to do so over repetitive matches is likely to lead to increases in body fat due to the conversion of the excess CHO ingested into fat. Table 12.2 provides some suggestions for foods and drinks to consume post-match.

TABLE 12.2 Suggestions for Nutritional Support in the Changing Room after a Match and for a Post-match Meal

	Changing Room		*Post-Match Meal*	
	Player	*Substitute*	*Player*	*Substitute*
Fluids	1 litre CHO-electrolyte OR 1 litre CHO-protein shake	300 ml protein shake (no CHO) Water	Fresh fruit juice	Water
Main Meal	Baked wedges Pizza slices Sushi Chicken goujons and dip Prawn goujons and dip Sliced frittata	Chicken goujons + dip Prawn goujons and dip Sliced omelette Chicken Kebab	Pasta meal Curry, rice, and naan Sweet and sour meal Chicken kebab and rice Paella Cottage pie Salmon and mashed potato Frittata and fries Jerk chicken, rice, and peas	Chicken or beef salad Prawn stir fry Chicken kebab with salad Bolognaise and Courgetti Omelette and beans Roast meat and vegetables Salmon and roasted vegetables
Dessert	Meringue Fresh pineapple slices	Apple slices	Sticky toffee pudding Banoffee pie Fruit crumble Eton mess	No Dessert

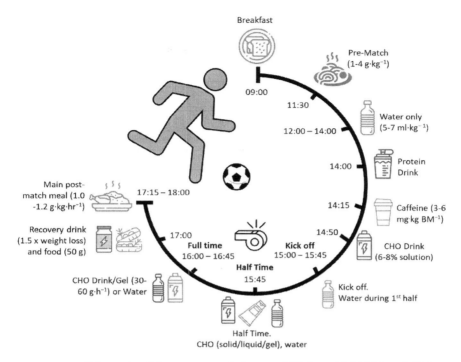

FIGURE 12.4 Schematic of the recommendations on MD for a 15:00 kick-off (Hulton et al., 2022).

Practical Applications

The physical demands imposed by soccer training and competition emphasise the reliance on CHO for fuel. In light of this, recommendations that focus on an increased CHO intake are clear but also allow for CHO intake to be manipulated or periodised in line with the physical demands of training, or proximity of competition. Therefore, light training days may require only 3–5 g/kg BM, whereas the CHO consumption increases to 6–8 g/kg BM during training days with enhanced volume and intensity and around MD-1, in preparation for competition. Further, an augmented protein intake (1.3–1.7 g/kg BM) is required to support muscular adaptation and recovery, with fluid intake also key to maintain hydration. Figure 12.4 summarises the nutritional requirements of MD, suggesting the timing and quantities of CHO, protein, and fluid required to provide more practical application.

References

Ali, A., Williams, C., Nicholas, C.W., and Foskett, A. (2007). The influence of carbohydrate-electrolyte ingestion on soccer skill performance. *Med Sci Sports Exerc*, 39(11), 1969–1976. https://doi.org/10.1249/mss.0b013e31814fb3e3

216 Strength and Conditioning for Football

American College of Sports Medicine, Sawka, M.N., Burke, L.M., Eichner, E.R., Maughan, R.J., Montain, S.J., and Stachenfeld, N.S. (2007). American College of Sports Medicine position stand. Exercise and fluid replacement. *Med Sci Sports Exerc*, 39(2), 377–390. https://doi.org/10.1249/mss.0b013e31802ca597

Anderson, L., Orme, P., Naughton, R.J., Close, G.L., Milsom, J., Rydings, D., O'Boyle, A., Di Michele, R., Louis, J., Hambly, C., Speakman J.R., Morgans R., Drust B., and Morton J.P. (2017). Energy intake and expenditure of professional soccer players of the English Premier League: Evidence of carbohydrate periodization. *Int J Sport Nutr Exerc Metab*, 27(3), 228–238. https://doi.org/10.1123/ijsnem.2016-0259

Backhouse, S.H., Ali, A., Biddle, S.J.H., and Williams, C. (2007). Carbohydrate ingestion during prolonged high-intensity intermittent exercise: Impact on affect and perceived exertion. *Scand J Med Sci Sports*, 17(5), 605–610. https://doi.org/10.1111/j.1600-0838.2006.00613.x

Baker, L.B., Rollo, I., Stein, K.W., and Jeukendrup, A.E. (2015). Acute effects of carbohydrate supplementation on intermittent sports performance. *Nutrients*, 14(7), 5733–5763. https://doi.org/10.3390/nu7075249

Bloomfield, J., Polman, R., and O'Donoghue, P. (2007). Physical demands of different positions in FA Premier League soccer. *J Sport Sci Med*, 6(1), 63–70.

Bradley, P.S., Sheldon, W., Wooster, B., Olsen, P., Boanas, P., and Krustrup, P. (2009). High-intensity running in English FA Premier League soccer matches. *J Sports Sci*, 27(2), 159–168. https://doi.org/10.1080/02640410802512775

Brinkmans, N.Y.J., Iedema, N., Plasqui, G., Wouters, L., Saris, W.H.M., van Loon, L.J.C., and van Dijk, J.W. (2019). Energy expenditure and dietary intake in professional football players in the Dutch Premier League: Implications for nutritional counselling. *J Sports Sci*, 37(24), 2759–2767. https://doi.org/10.1080/02640414.2019.1576256

Burke, L.M., Kiens, B., and Ivy, J.L. (2004). Carbohydrates and fat for training and recovery. *J Sports Sci*, 22(1), 15–30. https://doi.org/10.1080/0264041031000140527

Clarke, N.D., Drust, B., Maclaren, D.P., and Reilly, T. (2008). Fluid provision and metabolic responses to soccer-specific exercise. *Eur J Appl Physiol*, 104(6), 1069–1077. https://doi.org/10.1007/s00421-008-0864-x

Currell, K., Conway, S., and Jeukendrup, A.E. (2009). Carbohydrate ingestion improves performance of a new reliable test of soccer performance. *Int J Sport Nutr Exerc Metab*, 19(1), 34–46. https://doi.org/10.1123/ijsnem.19.1.34

Egan, B. (2016) Protein intake for athletes and active adults: Current concepts and controversies. *Nutr Bull*, 41(3), 202–213. https://doi.org/10.1111/nbu.12215

Evans, G.H., James, L.J., Shirreffs, S.M., and Maughan, R.J. (2017). Optimizing the restoration and maintenance of fluid balance after exercise-induced dehydration. *J Appl Physiol*, 122(4), 945–951. https://doi.org/10.1152/japplphysiol.00745.2016

Gant, N., Ali, A., and Foskett, A. (2010). The influence of caffeine and carbohydrate coingestion on simulated soccer performance. *Int J Sport Nutr Exerc Metab*, 20(3), 191–197. https://doi.org/10.1123/ijsnem.20.3.191

Harper, L.D., Stevenson, E.J., Rollo, I., and Russell, M. (2017). The influence of a 12% carbohydrate-electrolyte beverage on self-paced soccer-specific exercise performance. *J Sci Med Sport*, 20(12), 1123–1129. https://doi.org/10.1016/j.jsams.2017.04.015

Hulton, A.T., Edwards, J.P., Gregson, W., Maclaren, D., and Doran, D.A. (2013). Effect of fat and CHO meals on intermittent exercise in soccer players. *Int J Sports Med*, 34(2), 165–169. https://doi.org/10.1055/s-0032-1321798

Hulton, A.T., Gregson, W., Maclaren, D., and Doran, D.A. (2012). Effects of GI meals on intermittent exercise. *Int J Sports Med*, 33(9), 756–762. https://doi.org/10.1055/s-0031-1299754

Hulton, A.T., Malone, J.J., Clarke, N.D., and MacLaren, D.P.M. (2022). Energy requirements and nutritional strategies for male soccer players: A review and suggestions for practice. *Nutrients*, 14(3), 657. https://doi.org/10.3390/nu14030657

Hulton, A.T., Vitzel, K., Doran, D.A., and MacLaren, D.P.M. (2020). Addition of caffeine to a carbohydrate feeding strategy prior to intermittent exercise. *Int J Sports Med*, 41(9), 603–609. https://doi.org/10.1055/a-1121-7817

Iaia, F.M., Rampinini, E., and Bangsbo, J. (2009). High-intensity training in football. *Int J Sports Physiol Perform*, 4(3), 291–306. https://doi.org/10.1123/ijspp.4.3.291

Judelson, D.A., Maresh, C.M., Anderson, J.M., Armstrong, L.E., Casa, D.J., Kraemer, W.J., and Volek J.S. (2007). Hydration and muscular performance: Does fluid balance affect strength, power and high-intensity endurance? *Sports Med*, 37(10), 907–921. https://doi.org/10.2165/00007256-200737100-00006

Krustrup, P., Mohr, M., Amstrup, T., Rysgaard, T., Johansen, J., Steensberg, A., Pedersen, P.K., and Bangsbo, J. (2003). The yo-yo intermittent recovery test: Physiological response, reliability, and validity. *Med Sci Sports Exerc*, 35(4), 697–705. https://doi.org/10.1249/01.MSS.0000058441.94520.32

Krustrup, P., Mohr, M., Ellingsgaard, H., and Bangsbo, J. (2005). Physical demands during an elite female soccer game: Importance of training status. *Med Sci Sports Exerc*, 37(7), 1242–1248. https://doi.org/10.1249/01.mss.0000170062.73981.94

Krustrup, P., Mohr, M., Steensberg, A., Bencke, J., Klær, M., and Bangsbo, J. (2006). Muscle and blood metabolites during a soccer game: Implications for sprint performance. *Med Sci Sports Exerc*, 38(6), 1165–1174. https://doi.org/10.1249/01.mss.0000222845.89262.cd

Krustrup, P., Ortenblad, N., Nielsen, J., Nybo, L., Gunnarsson, T.P., Iaia, F.M., Madsen, K., Stephens, F., Greenhaff, P., and Bangsbo, J. (2011). Maximal voluntary contraction force, SR function and glycogen resynthesis during the first 72 h after a high-level competitive soccer game. *Eur J Appl Physiol*, 111(12), 2987–2995. https://doi.org/10.1007/s00421-011-1919-y

Little, J.P., Chilibeck, P.D., Ciona, D., Vandenberg, A., and Zello, G.A. (2009). The effects of low- and high-glycemic index foods on high-intensity intermittent exercise. *Int J Sports Physiol Perform*, 4(3), 367–380. https://doi.org/10.1123/ijspp.4.3.367

Macnaughton, L.S., Wardle, S.L., Witard, O.C., McGlory, C., Hamilton, D.L., Jeromson, S., Lawrence, C.E., Wallis, G.A., and Tipton, K.D. (2016). The response of muscle protein synthesis following whole-body resistance exercise is greater following 40 g than 20 g of ingested whey protein. *Physiol Rep*, 4(15), e12893. https://doi.org/10.14814/phy2.12893

Maughan, R.J., and Shirreffs, S.M. (2007). Nutrition for soccer players. *Curr Sports Med Rep*, 6(5), 279–280. https://doi.org/10.1097/01.CSMR.0000306487.30777.2f

McGlory, C., Devries, M.C., and Phillips, S.M. (2016). Skeletal muscle and resistance exercise training; the role of protein synthesis in recovery and remodeling. *J Appl Physiol*, 122(3), 541–548. https://doi.org/10.1152/japplphysiol.00613.2016

Mujika, I., and Burke, L.M. (2010). Nutrition in team sports. *Ann Nutr Metab*, 57(Suppl. 2), 26–35. https://doi.org/10.1159/000322700

Phillips, S.M. (2014). A brief review of critical processes in exercise-induced muscular hypertrophy. *Sports Med*, 44(Suppl. 1), 71–77. https://doi.org/10.1007/s40279-014-0152-3

Ranchordas, M.K., King, G., Russell, M., Lynn, A., and Russell, M. (2018). Effects of caffeinated gum on a battery of soccer-specific tests in trained university-standard male soccer players. *Int J Sport Nutr Exerc Metab*, 28(6), 629–634. https://doi.org/10.1123/ijsnem.2017-0405

Saltin, B. (1972). Substrate metabolism of the skeletal musculature during exercise. 5. Muscle glycogen. *Lakartidningen*, 69(14), 1637–1640.

Thomas, D.T., Erdman, K.A., and Burke, L.M. (2016). Position of the academy of nutrition and dietetics, dietitians of Canada, and the American College of Sports Medicine: Nutrition and athletic performance. *Med Sci Sports Exerc*, 48, 543–568.

Tipton, K.D., Elliott, T.A., Cree, M.G., Aarsland, A.A., Sanford, A.P., and Wolfe, R.R. (2007). Stimulation of net muscle protein synthesis by whey protein ingestion before and after exercise. *Am J Physiol Endocrinol Metab*, 292, E71–E76. https://doi.org/10.1152/ajpendo.00166.2006

Trommelen, J., and van Loon, L.J. (2016). Pre-sleep protein ingestion to improve the skeletal muscle adaptive response to exercise training. *Nutrients*, 8(12), 763. https://doi.org/10.3390/nu8120763

van Loon, L.J., Kruijshoop, M., Verhagen, H., Saris, W.H., and Wagenmakers, A.J. (2000). Ingestion of protein hydrolysate and amino acid-carbohydrate mixtures increases postexercise plasma insulin responses in men. *J Nutr*, 130(10), 2508–2513. https://doi.org/10.1093/jn/130.10.2508

Witard, O.C., Jackman, S.R., Breen, L., Smith, K., Selby, A., and Tipton, K.D. (2014). Myofibrillar muscle protein synthesis rates subsequent to a meal in response to increasing doses of whey protein at rest and after resistance exercise. *Am J Clin Nutr*, 99(1), 86–95. https://doi.org/10.3945/ajcn.112.055517

13
BASIC PSYCHOLOGY FOR COACHES IN TALENT DEVELOPMENT AND ELITE FOOTBALL

Alexander T. Latinjak and Eduardo Morelló Tomás

Introduction

Sport, Exercise, and Performance Psychology (SEPP) constitutes an integral component of sports science, offering essential insights for professionals in this profession. SEPP is twofold in its objectives: firstly, it seeks to investigate and comprehend the psychological descriptors (e.g., emotions), skills (e.g., emotion regulation), and external factors (e.g., stressors) that significantly influence individuals or groups in sports and physical activities. This understanding is pivotal for explaining their participation, enjoyment, and performance levels (Latinjak and Hatzigeorgiadis, 2021). Secondly, SEPP is committed to the development and application of evidence-based practices, including therapeutic interventions and professional training aimed at enhancing the interplay between psychological factors and external influences to improve sports performance and overall well-being.

While sports coaches, strength and conditioning coaches, and physiotherapists are among those who receive foundational training in SEPP, it is crucial to distinguish between possessing knowledge of SEPP and practicing as a sport, exercise, and performance psychologist (SEPPist). The latter involves a professional application of SEPP principles, which requires specialized training and expertise. The distinction highlights a concerning issue within the field: the gap between theoretical knowledge and its practical application. Many practitioners identify as SEPPists without a deep understanding of the field's complexities, prompting professional organizations to advocate for a more rigorous, science-based approach to practice (Schinke et al., 2023).

In the dynamic environment of sports, particularly in team settings like football clubs, psychological factors play a continuous role, irrespective of a SEPPist's presence or expertise level. Coaches and support staff must have a foundational

DOI: 10.4324/9781003383475-14

220 Strength and Conditioning for Football

understanding of SEPP to recognize and address the psychological needs of athletes effectively (Fletcher and Sarkar, 2012). Players often face challenges such as regaining confidence post-injury or managing anxiety before significant matches, exacerbated by external pressures, discriminatory practices, and adverse environments (Bean et al., 2014). These issues underscore the need for basic SEPP literacy among coaches and staff to provide adequate support and foster resilience in athletes.

This chapter aims to bridge the gap between SEPP theoretical knowledge and its practical application in the context of talent development and performance enhancement in professional football. It leverages the interdisciplinary and holistic #PsychMapping model of SEPP (Latinjak and Hatzigeorgiadis, 2021) to outline practical strategies. These strategies are designed to enable coaches and staff to apply psychological insights effectively, enhancing player development and performance through a nuanced understanding of their psychological characteristics, environmental perceptions, emotional and behavioural responses, and self-regulatory capabilities.

The following five sequences (Figures 13.1–13.3) demonstrate how coaches can significantly impact players by influencing their worldview, stable traits, performance-related states, self-regulation, and ultimately, their outcomes on the field. These sequences delve into key areas where coaches can shape team culture and motivational climate, collaborate with multidisciplinary teams, manage psychological loads during training, provide constructive feedback to players, and deliver effective halftime talks during competitive games. By understanding these sequences, coaches can better appreciate their role in not only developing individual players but also in building a cohesive and successful team environment.

Sequence 13.1: From Club Culture and Motivational Climate to Effort Expenditure and Fair-Play

Club culture (Figure 13.1, Point 1A), comprising explicit and implicit values, norms, and expectations, significantly shapes players' perceptions and behaviours over time (Wagstaff and Burton-Wylie, 2018). This culture, with values ranging from the rational ("fight to the end") to the less rational ("win or die"), influences players' integration of these values into their personal philosophies. While altering a club's entrenched culture may be challenging, exceptions like Pep Guardiola's time at Barcelona demonstrate the potential for transformative leadership (Maitland et al., 2015).

The motivational climate within a team (Figure 13.1, Point 1B), a concept distinct yet influenced by club culture, plays a critical role in defining success and guiding player behaviour. According to Iwasaki and Fry (2016), climates are categorized as task-oriented, emphasizing personal growth and collective effort, or ego-oriented, prioritizing victory and individual superiority. The internalization

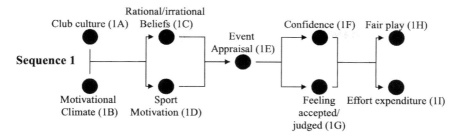

FIGURE 13.1 Sequence 1, from a club's culture and a team's motivational climate to fair play and effort expenditure.

of these climates shapes players' beliefs (Figure 13.1, Point 1C), and motivations (Figure 13.1, Point 1D; Harwood et al., 2015).

The distinction between rational beliefs ("I want to win") encouraged by a performance-oriented climate and irrational beliefs ("I must win") fostered by an ego-oriented climate is crucial (Turner, 2016). The latter can lead to unhealthy emotions and suboptimal performance, highlighting the importance of promoting intrinsic motivation and rational beliefs for healthier emotional responses and improved performance (King et al., 2023).

Players' appraisals of specific external events (Figure 13.1, Point 1E) within the sporting context—namely the fluctuations and pressures inherent in game situations, the nature and tone of feedback provided by coaches, and the accomplishments or progress of fellow teammates—are intricately influenced by their deeply held beliefs and motivational drives. According to research by Kavussanu et al. (2014), these interpretations are not direct reflections of the events themselves but are significantly coloured by the athletes' internal psychological frameworks.

In environments dominated by an ego-oriented climate, where the focus is predominantly on outperforming others, securing victories, and gaining external recognition, athletes are more inclined to view such external events through a lens of threat. For instance, falling behind during a match, receiving critical feedback from a coach, or witnessing a teammate's standout performance might be perceived as direct challenges to their status, competence, or value within the team. This threat-oriented interpretation can erode an athlete's self-confidence and diminish their sense of integration and value within the team fabric. Contrastingly, a task-oriented climate, which prioritizes personal mastery, collective effort, and intrinsic enjoyment of the sport, encourages athletes to interpret these same external events as opportunities for growth and learning. A deficit in the scoreboard becomes a chance to demonstrate resilience and teamwork, constructive criticism from a coach is seen as valuable guidance for skill improvement, and a teammate's success serves as inspiration and proof of the team's collective potential. Through this lens of challenge rather than threat, athletes experience enhanced self-efficacy—belief in

222 Strength and Conditioning for Football

their abilities to meet the demands of the task at hand—and feel a stronger sense of camaraderie and support within the team environment.

The lens through which players view events critically shapes their reactions, thereby influencing key psychological states such as self-confidence (or self-efficacy; Figure 13.1, Point 1F) and their sense of belonging within the team (Meijen et al., 2020; Figure 13.1, Point 1G). Negative interpretations, such as viewing falling behind in a game, receiving coach criticism, or witnessing a teammate's success as threats, can erode self-confidence and foster feelings of judgment (Jones and Harwood, 2008). In contrast, perceiving these same events as challenges to overcome can bolster self-confidence and reinforce a player's sense of acceptance and support within the team. For instance, when coach feedback, often misconstrued as criticism, is seen as constructive and a sign of the coach's investment in the player's development, it can significantly enhance the player's confidence. Similarly, viewing a teammate's achievements as a benchmark for personal growth, rather than a threat, encourages a collaborative and supportive team environment (Ramis et al., 2017).

The psychological state of players during performance crucially dictates their on-field behaviour and overall performance (Weinberg and Gould, 2018). A confident player, perceiving less external pressure, is more likely to engage in ethical play (Figure 13.1, Point 1H) and focus on collective success rather than individual accolades. Conversely, a player grappling with self-doubt may succumb to unethical behaviours under the guise of competitive pressure. Additionally, the sense of acceptance or judgment players feel within their team context directly influences their willingness to exert effort (Figure 13.1, Point 1I) not just for personal gain but for the team's benefit. Thus, fostering an environment where players feel valued and supported is paramount for optimal team cohesion and performance (Jowett and Cockerill, 2003).

Coaches wield considerable influence over the team's cultural and motivational landscape through mindful practices and reflective leadership. Transitioning from a win-at-all-costs mentality to embracing the journey and striving for continuous improvement can profoundly affect the team's ethos. Utilizing inclusive language, such as shifting from "you" to "we," reinforces team unity and collective responsibility (Fransen et al., 2012). Thoughtful allocation of individual attention, a precious resource in coaching, can affirm each player's value to the team, especially in a task-oriented climate that prioritizes equitable engagement. Moreover, coaches must strive for a balanced evaluation of performances, acknowledging both strengths and areas for improvement, to avoid the pitfalls of complacency or demotivation (Côté and Gilbert, 2009).

In essence, the interplay between players' interpretations of events and the broader team culture and motivational climate set by coaches significantly impacts individual and team dynamics. Through strategic interventions and a commitment to fostering a positive, growth-oriented environment, coaches can enhance players' psychological resilience, promote fair play, and drive performance excellence.

Sequence 2: From Home Environment and Coaching Staff's Multidisciplinary Mindset to Action Accuracy

Two critical factors profoundly influence athletes' lifestyles and their journey in talent development: their home environment and the guidance they receive from their coaches. The home environment (Figure 13.2, Point 2A) encompasses more than just the physical space where an athlete resides, including sleeping arrangements. It extends to the cultural atmosphere shaped by familial traditions and values, as well as the influence exerted by family members' behaviours, such as parental discipline (Strandbu et al., 2020). This environment plays a pivotal role in establishing an athlete's foundational habits concerning nutrition, recreation, and rest—elements crucial to their overall development and performance.

On the other hand, coaches are instrumental in refining athletes' physical capabilities and instilling discipline in their training routines, which significantly affect their health and fitness. Coaches' expertise should not be limited to sports-specific knowledge but should also include a comprehensive understanding of exercise science, encompassing sports nutrition, strength and conditioning, and biomechanics. In an ideal setting, coaches would collaborate within a multidisciplinary team (Figure 13.2, Point 2B), bringing together experts from various fields of sports science to offer a holistic development approach (Till and Baker, 2020). While coaches can directly influence athletes' physical conditioning through targeted exercises and drills, fostering lasting healthy habits poses a greater challenge, requiring a nuanced and consistent approach.

Healthy habits (Figure 13.2, Point 2C) are the bedrock of an athlete's daily routine, encompassing crucial aspects like nutrition and sleep (Fältström et al., 2022). The objective is to cultivate in athletes the capacity for making independent, health-conscious choices regarding their diet and sleep patterns. This development is facilitated by a supportive home environment and constructive coaching strategies, employing a blend of modelling, positive reinforcement, and educational outreach. *Modelling* involves athletes observing and emulating the positive behaviours

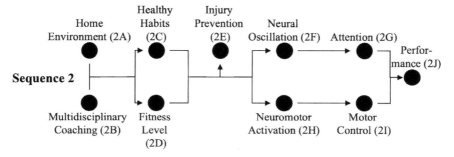

FIGURE 13.2   Sequence 2, from players' home environment and multidisciplinary coaching to in-game performance.

224 Strength and Conditioning for Football

demonstrated by influential figures such as family members and coaches. *Positive reinforcement* encourages desirable behaviours through rewards, fostering a motivational climate without resorting to punitive measures, which can lead to resistance and negative attitudes (Leeder, 2022). *Educational efforts* aim to equip athletes with knowledge about the benefits and drawbacks of various lifestyle choices, empowering them to make informed decisions.

Maintaining optimal fitness (Figure 13.2, Point 2D)—characterized by strength, speed, agility, and endurance—and adhering to healthy habits are beneficial both in the immediate and long term. Over time, these practices serve as safeguards against injuries (Figure 13.2, Point 2E) and as catalysts for the holistic development of athletes, enhancing their physical, mental, and cognitive capacities (Fältström et al., 2022). In the short term, they contribute significantly to improved neural function, manifesting in enhanced neural oscillations and neuromotor coordination. Neural oscillations (Figure 13.2, Point 2F), or the rhythmic electrical patterns in the brain, are crucial for synchronizing information processing across different regions, impacting sensory perception, focus, and motor skills (di Fronso et al., 2017). Optimal physical condition and lifestyle choices enhance the frequencies of alpha and beta waves, associated with efficient decision-making and stress management. Conversely, negative habits can increase theta wave frequencies, indicative of reduced vigilance and attention (Figure 13.2, Point 2G), ultimately impairing athletic performance (Harmony, 2013). By fostering a culture that values healthful living and physical preparedness, athletes can maximize their performance potential and resilience in the face of challenges.

Neuromotor activation (Figure 13.2, Point 2H) serves as the foundational neurophysiological mechanism underlying all motor actions in athletes (Figure 13.2, Point 2I). Coaches dedicate considerable effort to nurturing players' technical abilities, recognizing that skill acquisition is not merely about learning movements but involves significant neural adaptations. This includes enhanced connectivity within the brain's white matter tracts linked to the learned skill, which facilitates more efficient neural communication (Taubert et al., 2010). Yet, mastering a skill transcends mere acquisition; it demands precise neuromotor execution during performance (Yarrow et al., 2009). This execution relies on the seamless activation of specific motor neurons, signal transmission to muscles, and the meticulous coordination of muscle contractions. Optimal physical condition, balanced nutrition, and sufficient rest are crucial for consistent neuromotor activation, enabling athletes to realize their full potential (Figure 13.2, Point 2J). Conversely, fatigue, poor dietary habits, and inadequate sleep can disrupt this delicate neuromotor balance, leading to performance errors that are not typical of the athlete's true capabilities (Beato et al., 2024).

In light of these insights, it seems imperative for coaches to embrace a holistic, multidisciplinary approach to athlete development. Collaborating with experts across various domains can enrich the training regime with comprehensive strategies that encompass fitness, nutrition, and cognitive well-being. Moreover, engaging with the athletes' family members to reinforce the importance of healthy lifestyle choices at home can amplify these efforts. For instance, minimizing exposure to blue light before bedtime can be more effective if it is a shared family practice, thus promoting better sleep hygiene among athletes. Positive reinforcement strategies, such as acknowledging good practices or rewarding health-oriented achievements, can be highly motivating for athletes. Conversely, punitive measures for failing to meet health or fitness goals should be avoided to maintain a positive coach-athlete relationship and prevent resistance. Instead, education about the benefits of certain health behaviours, like the advantages of a protein-rich diet for muscle development or the protective effects of antioxidants found in foods like spinach, can empower athletes to make informed choices. Understanding the rationale behind these lifestyle recommendations can significantly increase the likelihood of their integration into daily routines, setting a solid foundation for both personal well-being and athletic excellence.

Sequence 3: From Psychological Loads in Training Designs to Emotion Expression and Performance

In contemporary football training, while the emphasis on physical training load is prevalent, the significance of psychological load management remains underexplored (Fletcher and Sarkar, 2012). This oversight partly stems from the challenge of quantifying psychological loads — the mental and emotional stressors induced by training — as opposed to the more tangible physical loads. Psychological load (Figure 13.3, Point 3A) encompasses the mental resilience and focus demanded by various training activities, from the concentration needed in rapidly changing drills to the motivation required for longer, predictable exercises. Mellalieu et al. (2021) highlight the inherent presence and influence of psychological loads, despite the absence of precise measurement tools.

Psychological loads affect the state of players, which includes physical states (Figure 13.3, Point 3B) such as fatigue or pain, psychological states (Figure 13.3, Point 3C) such as frustration, and social experiences such as envy. Fatigue and pain are common in football training and players must learn to manage them in order to avoid injury and maintain high levels of performance despite their presence. Frustration is almost a necessary state for development, although short-term frustration can lead to self-centred decision-making and aggressive behaviour (Skinner and Brewer, 2004). Envy is part of any team sport, especially during the talent development phase, and can negatively impact decision-making, teamwork, and fair play (Dore et al., 2020). Each player is able to cope with a certain amount of these internal challenges based on their everyday life experiences. However, when the psychological load in training and even most games is low, players become mentally lazy (Figure 13.3, Point 3D) and unprepared for challenging moments (Sarkar and Page, 2022). When the psychological load in training and most games is too high and uncontrollable, players become mentally overtrained or "injured" (Figure

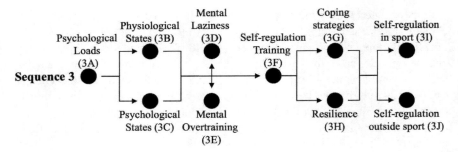

FIGURE 13.3 Sequence 3, from psychological loads in training to players' self-regulation within and outside sport.

13.3, Point 3E), resulting in aggressive behaviour, burnout, depression, eating and sleeping disorders, addictive behaviours, and even suicidal tendencies (Mellalieu et al., 2021). However, when the psychological loads in training and most games are challenging and manageable, players have an ideal environment to develop their self-regulation skills and prepare for more challenging moments in the future (Figure 13.3, Point 3F).

Recognizing psychological loads as internal challenges, such as fatigue, pain, frustration, or envy, marks the beginning of an athlete's attempt at self-regulation. This process, however, is not without its pitfalls. Athletes may occasionally adopt counterproductive coping mechanisms, such as making excuses to avoid facing challenges directly. These strategies, while offering temporary relief, ultimately hinder long-term development and resilience. Coaches play a pivotal role in identifying and redirecting these negative coping strategies towards more constructive ones (Figure 13.3, Point 3G). The objective is to cultivate positive coping strategies that empower players to manage their psychological states effectively (Crocker et al., 2015). For instance, athletes can learn to mitigate pain through techniques like focused muscle relaxation, which not only addresses the physical sensation of pain but also reduces the psychological burden associated with it (Mosley et al., 2023). Furthermore, encouraging self-talk can be a powerful tool for boosting energy levels and fostering a positive mindset that fuels performance. Visualization techniques, where athletes picture themselves successfully overcoming a challenge, can significantly diminish feelings of frustration, replacing them with motivation and confidence (Short et al., 2005). Similarly, by shifting focus from individual achievements to collective team goals, athletes can transform envy into a constructive force that promotes unity and team success (Filho et al., 2014). These strategies not only aid in immediate performance enhancement but also contribute to the development of robust psychological resilience (Figure 13.3, Point 3H), equipping athletes with the skills needed to navigate the complexities of competitive sports and personal challenges alike.

Repeated practice in managing psychological loads not only hones self-regulation skills within athletes but also ensures these skills are adaptable to both competitive contexts (Figure 13.3, Point 3I) and broader life scenarios (Figure 13.3, Point 3J). For instance, the process of confronting and mastering pain and fatigue during training instils a robust sense of confidence in athletes, assuring them of their ability to navigate similar challenges in competitive environments. This resilience transcends physical endurance, extending to emotional and social resilience (Fletcher and Sarkar, 2012). Athletes who regularly engage in exercises that challenge their emotional coping mechanisms and social interactions are better equipped to handle the psychological demands of competition. Such preparedness positively influences their emotional responses under pressure, contributing significantly to enhanced performance outcomes. Moreover, the benefits of self-regulation skills developed through sports extend far beyond the playing field. The challenges encountered in sports—pain, fatigue, frustration, envy—are microcosms of life's broader challenges. The ability to manage these states within the controlled environment of sports training provides a valuable framework for navigating similar experiences in everyday life. As noted by Pierce et al. (2017), discipline, emotional control, and resilience cultivated through sports are universally applicable skills, offering profound benefits across various life domains.

Coaches play a pivotal role in carefully designing drills and their variations to introduce appropriate psychological challenges to players (Mellalieu et al., 2021). It is crucial for coaches to understand that initial struggles are part of the learning process and resist the urge to directly intervene in resolving players' challenges. For instance, in the case of a conflict between players, the coach's role is to facilitate a constructive dialogue, guiding the players toward resolving their disputes independently (Sarkar and Page, 2022). This approach not only empowers players but also fosters essential life skills such as conflict resolution and emotional intelligence. Ensuring that challenges are perceived as manageable is fundamental (Pierce et al., 2017). Coaches must be adept at adjusting the difficulty of tasks to prevent any player from feeling overwhelmed, thereby minimizing the risk of mental health issues. Simultaneously, it is important for coaches to stay vigilant about the coping strategies adopted by players. Recognizing and addressing negative coping mechanisms early can prevent them from undermining the benefits of self-regulation training and leading to adverse outcomes (Latinjak and Hatzigeorgiadis, 2021). Moreover, acknowledging and celebrating players' efforts in mastering self-regulation is vital. Recognition from coaches can significantly boost players' motivation and confidence, encouraging them to assume greater responsibility for their mental state and performance. This positive reinforcement helps cultivate an environment where players feel valued and supported in their journey toward self-improvement and team contribution. In summary, coaches must strategically balance the psychological load within training, providing a supportive framework that encourages independent problem-solving, while being mindful of the challenges' impact on players. Through attentive guidance and positive acknowledgment, coaches can significantly enhance players' ability to self-regulate, laying a foundation for both sports and life success.

Sequence 4: From Coach Feedback to Self-Talk, Self-Control, and Performance

Coaches play a pivotal role as external influencers for athletes, shaping their development through both direct interactions and their impact on other elements within the athletes' environments, such as practice routines or game strategies. The behaviour of coaches encompasses the feedback they provide (Figure 13.4, Point 4A), which can be understood as any action, verbal or non-verbal, offering athletes insights into the effectiveness of their performance. Non-verbal feedback may include actions like substituting a player, as well as gestures and facial expressions, all of which communicate performance evaluations without words. Verbal feedback, as detailed by Mason et al. (2020), spans a range from evaluative—where a coach assesses the quality of an athlete's action (e.g., "well done")—to informative, offering a detailed comparison between an athlete's actual action and potential alternatives (e.g., "you opted for the safe pass instead of seeking a deeper pass"). Furthermore, verbal feedback can adopt an interrogative form, where coaches pose strategic questions to prompt athletes into deeper self-reflection about their decisions and actions (e.g., "why do you think your passes are falling short?").

The influence of coach feedback on athlete development and the coach-athlete relationship (Yang and Jowett, 2013) is significant yet indirect, leading to varied effects on players. The personal evaluation of feedback (Figure 13.4, Point 4B) by each player determines its impact, where feedback can be perceived as either a positive challenge or a threat (Dixon et al., 2017). This perception affects how a player reacts; some may find criticism motivating, while others view it as a harbinger of negative consequences. Furthermore, the relevance of the feedback (Figure 13.4, Point 4C) to the player plays a crucial role; feedback deemed irrelevant by the player will have a lesser impact compared to feedback considered relevant.

In the realm of stable player characteristics, coach feedback significantly influences two key aspects pivotal to peak performance in elite sports: competitive know-how and self-knowledge. Merely accumulating game experiences (Figure 13.4, Point 4D) does not confer an advantage. Instead, the value of game

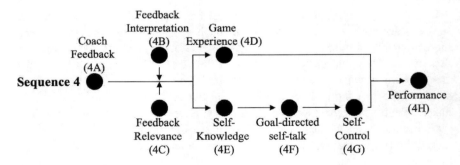

FIGURE 13.4 Sequence 4, from coach feedback to in-game performance.

Basic Psychology for Coaches in Talent Development **229**

experience lies in learning from past occurrences, a process frequently facilitated by coaches through their interpretation of events and the posing of questions to players via interrogative feedback (McCardle et al., 2019). To enhance players' development, it is essential for coaches to provide feedback that is not only informative but also focuses on elements of the game that players can control (Rascle et al., 2015). For instance, advice such as "We need to adopt simpler strategies during high-pressure situations" is far more constructive than blaming external factors like "The referee's error cost us the match." When players attribute the outcomes of a game to factors beyond their control, such as the performance of opponents or referee decisions, coaches can employ interrogative feedback to encourage players to reflect on controllable aspects and consider alternative approaches they could have undertaken.

Coach feedback is crucial for the development of players' self-knowledge (Figure 13.4, Point 4E; Latinjak and Hatzigeorgiadis, 2021). Athletes with a high degree of self-knowledge are aware of how they respond to specific situations and understand what actions are appropriate, inappropriate, or impossible for them in those contexts. For example, they may recognize their tension in the closing minutes of a tight game, know that concentrating on the ball can help distract them from worrying about the game's outcome, realize they are unable to relax and play as they normally would, and acknowledge that avoiding key positions to shirk responsibility is not a solution. However, it is common for players to form a biased view of their capabilities, often overestimating their strengths and blaming others or external factors like bad luck for unfavourable results, as part of a self-protective strategy (Allen et al., 2020). Coaches can leverage their feedback, especially through questioning methods, to encourage players to critically examine the controllable aspects of their behaviour and performance, thus fostering a more accurate and helpful form of self-knowledge.

Self-regulation is deeply interconnected with self-knowledge, enabling enhanced foresight of potential internal challenges, which often proves simpler to manage than actual obstacles. This understanding facilitates the selection of more effective coping mechanisms, such as adopting acceptance-oriented approaches over more exhausting change-oriented tactics (Birrer and Morgan, 2010). Additionally, a crucial benefit of self-knowledge is the practice of goal-directed self-talk by athletes (Figure 13.4, Point 4F), where they engage in self-coaching or self-apply sport psychology techniques (Latinjak et al., 2023). This intentional goal-directed self-dialogue empowers athletes to control themselves (Figure 13.4, Point 4G), soothe their nerves, intensify their efforts, elevate their confidence, make logical choices, and, as a result, enhance their performance (Figure 13.4, Point 4H).

To enhance players' self-coaching and effective self-talk, coaches should focus on nurturing the athletes' self-knowledge and shaping their internal dialogue. It is beneficial when players phrase their self-talk as suggestions rather than demands and use inclusive language, such as "we should try harder" instead of "I must try harder". Emphasizing collaborative language, like using "we" over "I", fosters a team-oriented mindset (Son et al., 2011). Coaches should mirror this approach in their feedback, promote trust in the players' inner voice, and guide them towards refining the content of their self-messages, without dismissing their intuition. Encouraging persistence and adaptive strategies in the face of setbacks is key.

Sequence 5: From Half-Time Analysis to Coping Strategy Selection

A pivotal opportunity for coaches to shape their players' performance lies in the halftime team talk (Figure 13.5, Point 5A) within the locker room, primarily focusing on tactical and psychological strategies. Psychological elements typically revolve around attitudes and motivation, focus and concentration, and emotional regulation. The effectiveness of coaching interventions is significantly influenced by the players' preexisting perceptions of the coach and the nature of their relationship with them (Figure 13.5, Point 5B; Jowett, 2017), which subsequently affects how players interpret the coach's directives (Figure 13.5, Point 5C). When coaches are regarded as proficient and supportive figures, their guidance is more likely to be embraced positively. Conversely, coaches viewed as lacking competence or support tend to have their advice dismissed as irrelevant or even perceived as hostile. Hence, cultivating a robust coach-player relationship, underpinned by transparency, integrity, and mutual respect, is crucial for making a meaningful impact during moments like halftime conversations (Côté and Gilbert, 2009).

During halftime talks, coaches have the prime opportunity to address the specific challenges their players are encountering. While some coaches may choose to ignore or minimize these issues, such an approach seldom yields beneficial outcomes (Olsen et al., 2020). Acknowledging difficulties directly—whether they pertain to distraction, fatigue, frustration, jealousy, or anxiety—enables players to actively address them. Coaching interventions are pivotal in heightening players' consciousness of their personal hurdles (Figure 13.5, Point 5D), with coaches often stepping in to mitigate these challenges, be it through motivational support or

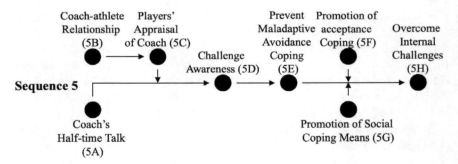

FIGURE 13.5 Sequence 5, from coaches' half-time talks to players' in-game coping with challenges.

Basic Psychology for Coaches in Talent Development **231**

strategic adjustments to aid performance on the field. While these efforts can sometimes lead to success, their effectiveness is typically limited. Solving problems for players can inadvertently foster a dependency on the coach, which is not ideal for player development. Therefore, coaches should aim to empower players towards self-regulation whenever feasible (Ansell and Spencer, 2022). This involves guiding players to recognize their own regulatory needs, selecting effective coping mechanisms, and steering clear of detrimental ones (Latinjak and Hatzigeorgiadis, 2021).

Coping strategies in the realm of sports psychology are diverse, underscoring the principle that no single approach is universally applicable (Nicholls and Polman, 2007). More effective strategies often fall into categories such as change-oriented coping, where players transform a negative emotional state (like anger) into a positive one (such as motivation). Perception-oriented strategies involve altering the interpretation of external events (for example, viewing the last 5 minutes of a game as ample time for a comeback), and acceptance-oriented strategies (Cunningham and Turner, 2016), where athletes cease to view certain conditions as insurmountable personal challenges, instead maintaining optimal performance despite them (acknowledging, for instance, that nervousness is a natural response in high-stakes scenarios and choosing to press on). Conversely, some tactics, while occasionally beneficial, can predominantly lead to negative outcomes. Avoidance strategies, such as feigning an injury to dodge the stress of competition, compensation mechanisms like using alcohol to deal with career challenges, or indulging in self-pity to garner sympathy from others, typically serve as impediments to personal and professional growth (Kaiseler et al., 2009). Recognizing and guiding athletes towards employing constructive coping mechanisms, while steering clear of counterproductive ones, is a critical aspect of effective coaching.

Coaches often observe players resorting to negative coping mechanisms during games, which may include behaviours like expecting defeat, assigning blame to others or to luck, simulating injuries, and giving up. These actions fall under avoidance coping strategies (Figure 13.5, Point 5E). During halftime discussions, coaches have the opportunity to address these observed or potential behaviours without imposing penalties on players. This is crucial because the adoption of negative coping mechanisms usually arises from a lack of knowledge on how to cope more effectively or an inability to do so (Batmaz et al., 2021). Coaches should, therefore, offer constructive alternatives, focusing on strategies that promote change and adjust perceptions. For instance, a coach might encourage self-awareness and proactive coping by saying,

I see that you're exhausted, and it might seem easier to shy away from challenging situations. However, this approach won't lead us to victory. Instead, let's enhance our communication and support each other, especially when one

232 Strength and Conditioning for Football

of us needs a moment to regroup. This strategy not only helps us cope but also strengthens our team dynamic.

At times, the issue emerges when players unsuccessfully attempt to employ change or perception-oriented strategies. For instance, a player might try to handle frustration or reinterpret a negative outcome in a more positive light, only to find the situation remains equally challenging and frustrating. Consequently, the player may revert to avoidance coping, such as attributing blame to others or diminishing the significance of the game. In such cases, prompting them to continue with change or perception-oriented strategies may prove ineffective. Instead, coaches could recommend acceptance-oriented strategies (Figure 13.5, Point 5F), which have been recognized for their value in elite sports, where athletes frequently face an overwhelming number of difficult situations (Gledhill et al., 2017). Effective acceptance-based coping involves ceasing to fret over managing an internal challenge, such as fatigue or anger, and concentrating on how to persist in spite of these difficulties. For example, a coach might advise frustrated players to acknowledge the irritation of the moment and channel the energy from their anger into intensifying pressure on the opposing team, while avoiding aggressive fouls. Promoting acceptance-based coping also has the beneficial effect of teaching players that perfection is not the goal; rather, learning to navigate their imperfections is key.

Beyond the mental strategies we've discussed for coping, there are various means through which these strategies can be enacted, moving beyond solely mental or cognitive approaches. These include utilizing social interactions, objects, and even substances. Social means (Figure 13.5, Point 5G), in particular, hold significant importance in team sports like football, where collective support and interaction among players can play a crucial role in overcoming internal challenges such as fatigue, frustration, and emotional management (Tamminen et al., 2022). This communal support can also reignite motivation, highlighting the power of teamwork not just in strategy but in mental and emotional resilience. Coaches, therefore, have a unique opportunity during halftime talks to encourage players to lean on one another for support, emphasizing the value of collective coping over isolated self-regulation (Eckardt and Tamminen, 2023). This approach underscores the notion that overcoming obstacles (Figure 13.5, Point 5H) can be a shared endeavour, enhancing team cohesion and individual resilience.

Practical Applications

Coaches and their staff might not be SEPPists, unless one specifically has that qualification. Nonetheless, the psychological aspect of players is an integral part of their performance and development, necessitating coaches and their teams to facilitate players' growth and self-regulation. Throughout this chapter, we have explored five interconnected factors, all of which relate to common coaching behaviours that naturally influence player development and performance significantly. Firstly, every action a coach takes is filtered through the player's perception, making it crucial for the formation of a positive coach-player relationship. Such a relationship should be grounded in honesty, integrity, and respect, ensuring that the coach's actions are perceived as relevant and supportive rather than inconsequential or adversarial. Furthermore, beyond establishing a strong individual relationship, coaches have the opportunity to cultivate a positive club culture and motivational climate. This broader environment significantly affects interactions within the team, reinforcing the importance of a supportive, cohesive atmosphere in promoting optimal performance and personal growth.

A recurring theme in this discussion is the importance of communication style in coaching. Key communication strategies include striking the right balance between offering criticism and praise, adopting a suggestive rather than a directive tone, and employing inclusive language by using plural first-person pronouns ("we", "us") instead of isolating individuals. These approaches foster a more positive team atmosphere, enrich game experiences, enhance players' self-awareness, and strengthen their ability to engage in constructive self-dialogue. Self-awareness and effective self-talk are pivotal for self-regulation, a vital component of talent development. Players who can self-regulate are better equipped to solve problems independently, thus lightening the coach's workload. Moreover, the skills associated with efficient self-regulation extend beyond the sports arena, offering benefits in various life situations. This underscores the value of nurturing these abilities not only for the sake of athletic performance but also for broader personal development and adaptability across life's domains.

Football offers a unique platform for players to cultivate healthy fitness and lifestyle routines, underscoring the importance of a holistic approach to player development. To facilitate these lifelong benefits, coaches should either collaborate within multidisciplinary teams or draw upon interdisciplinary knowledge. This approach enables them to educate players on the importance of making healthy choices, particularly in areas such as leisure activities, nutrition, and sleep. Additionally, the presence of positive role models in the players' home environments plays a pivotal role in reinforcing these healthy habits. The broader perspective highlighted here showcases the necessity for talent development and elite football to adopt a comprehensive approach to players, rather than focusing solely on the sport-specific context. Players grow and perform not just as athletes but as individuals, with both internal and external life events influencing their development and performance. While coaches cannot control these external events, they must remain cognizant of them, working in coordination with others in the players' lives, such as parents and teachers. This awareness and collaboration underscore the recognition that players' lives extend far beyond the football field, emphasizing the need for respect and support for their overall well-being.

234 Strength and Conditioning for Football

In summary, the following five practical considerations can be drawn from this chapter's lessons learned: (1) create a positive club culture and motivational climate by emphasizing personal growth, teamwork, and intrinsic motivation; (2) encourage constructive communication and feedback by avoiding evaluative terminology and focusing on informative and inclusive language; (3) manage psychological loads in training by finding a balance between challenging athletes and maintaining a supportive environment to foster self-regulation skills; (4) promote self-regulation and coping strategies, including positive self-talk, visualization, and acceptance-oriented techniques to boost emotional regulation and resilience; and (5) foster coach-athlete relationships built on trust and respect, creating an environment where athletes are open to feedback and guidance, ultimately encouraging growth and high performance.

References

Allen, M. S., Robson, D. A., Martin, L. J., and Laborde, S. (2020). Systematic review and meta-analysis of self-serving attribution biases in the competitive context of organized sport. *Personality and Social Psychology Bulletin, 46*(7), 1027–1043.

Ansell, D. B., and Spencer, N. L. (2022). "Think about what you're doing and why you're doing it": Coach feedback, athlete self-regulation, and male youth hockey players. *Journal of Applied Sport Psychology, 34*(3), 459–478.

Batmaz, S., Altinoz, A. E., and Sonkurt, H. O. (2021). Cognitive attentional syndrome and metacognitive beliefs as potential treatment targets for metacognitive therapy in bipolar disorder. *World Journal of Psychiatry, 11*(9), 589.

Bean, C. N., Fortier, M., Post, C., and Chima, K. (2014). Understanding how organized youth sport may be harming individual players within the family unit: A literature review. *International Journal of Environmental Research and Public Health, 11*(10), 10226–10268.

Beato, M., Madsen, E. E., Clubb, J., Emmonds, S., and Krustrup, P. (2024). Monitoring readiness to train and perform in female football: Current evidence and recommendations for practitioners. *International Journal of Sports Physiology and Performance, 19*(3), 223–231.

Birrer, D., and Morgan, G. (2010). Psychological skills training as a way to enhance an athlete's performance in high-intensity sports. *Scandinavian Journal of Medicine and Science in Sports, 20*, 78–87.

Côté, J., and Gilbert, W. (2009). An integrative definition of coaching effectiveness and expertise. *International Journal of Sports Science and Coaching, 4*(3), 307–323.

Crocker, P. R., Tamminen, K. A., and Gaudreau, P. (2015). Coping in sport. In S. Mellalieu and S. Hanton (Eds.), *Contemporary Advances in Sport Psychology* (pp. 28–67). Routledge.

Cunningham, R., and Turner, M. J. (2016). Using Rational Emotive Behavior Therapy (REBT) with Mixed Martial Arts (MMA) athletes to reduce irrational beliefs and increase unconditional self-acceptance. *Journal of Rational-Emotive and Cognitive-Behavior Therapy, 34*, 289–309.

di Fronso, S., Robazza, C., Bortoli, L., and Bertollo, M. (2017). Performance optimization in sport: A psychophysiological approach. *Motriz: Revista de Educação Física, 23*, e1017138.

Dixon, M., Turner, M. J., and Gillman, J. (2017). Examining the relationships between challenge and threat cognitive appraisals and coaching behaviours in football coaches. *Journal of Sports Sciences, 35*(24), 2446–2452.

Dore, I., Pila, E., Gilchrist, J., and Sabiston, C. (2020). Investigating the association between social identity and group-based self-conscious emotions and with sport commitment among adolescent female athletes. *International Journal of Sport Psychology, 51*(4), 297–319.

Eckardt, V. C., and Tamminen, K. A. (2023). A scoping review on interpersonal coping in sports. *International Review of Sport and Exercise Psychology, 6*, 1–27.

Fältström, A., Skillgate, E., Weiss, N., Källberg, H., Lyberg, V., Waldén, M., Hägglund, M., Asker, M., and Tranaeus, U. (2022). Lifestyle characteristics in adolescent female football players: Data from the Karolinska football Injury Cohort. *BMC Sports Science, Medicine and Rehabilitation, 14*(1), 1–13.

Filho, E., Dobersek, U., Gershgoren, L., Becker, B., and Tenenbaum, G. (2014). The cohesion–performance relationship in sport: A 10-year retrospective meta-analysis. *Sport Sciences for Health, 10*, 165–177.

Fletcher, D., and Sarkar, M. (2012). A grounded theory of psychological resilience in Olympic champions. *Psychology of Sport and Exercise, 13*(5), 669–678.

Fransen, K., Vanbeselaere, N., Exadaktylos, V., Vande Broek, G., De Cuyper, B., Berckmans, D., . . . Boen, F. (2012). "Yes, we can!": Perceptions of collective efficacy sources in volleyball. *Journal of Sports Sciences, 30*(7), 641–649.

Gledhill, A., Harwood, C., and Forsdyke, D. (2017). Psychosocial factors associated with talent development in football: A systematic review. *Psychology of Sport and Exercise, 31*, 93–112.

Harmony, T. (2013). The functional significance of delta oscillations in cognitive processing. *Frontiers in Integrative Neuroscience, 7*, 83.

Harwood, C. G., Keegan, R. J., Smith, J. M., and Raine, A. S. (2015). A systematic review of the intrapersonal correlates of motivational climate perceptions in sport and physical activity. *Psychology of Sport and Exercise, 18*, 9–25.

Iwasaki, S., and Fry, M. D. (2016). Female adolescent soccer players' perceived motivational climate, goal orientations, and mindful engagement. *Psychology of Sport and Exercise, 27*, 222–231.

Jones, M. I., and Harwood, C. (2008). Psychological momentum within competitive soccer: Players' perspectives. *Journal of Applied Sport Psychology, 20*(1), 57–72.

Jowett, S. (2017). Coaching effectiveness: The coach–athlete relationship at its heart. *Current Opinion in Psychology, 16*, 154–158.

Jowett, S., and Cockerill, I. M. (2003). Olympic medallists' perspective of the althlete–coach relationship. *Psychology of Sport and Exercise, 4*(4), 313–331.

Kaiseler, M., Polman, R., and Nicholls, A. (2009). Mental toughness, stress, stress appraisal, coping and coping effectiveness in sport. *Personality and Individual Differences, 47*(7), 728–733.

Kavussanu, M., Dewar, A. J., and Boardley, I. D. (2014). Achievement goals and emotions in athletes: The mediating role of challenge and threat appraisals. *Motivation and Emotion, 38*, 589–599.

King, A. M., Turner, M. J., Plateau, C. R., and Barker, J. B. (2023). The socialisation of athlete irrational beliefs. *Journal of Rational-Emotive and Cognitive-Behavior Therapy, 41*(2), 290–313.

Latinjak, A. T., and Hatzigeorgiadis, A. (2021). The knowledge map of sport and exercise psychology: An integrative perspective. *Frontiers in Psychology, 12*, 661824.

Latinjak, A. T., Morin, A., Brinthaupt, T. M., Hardy, J., Hatzigeorgiadis, A., Kendall, P. C., Neck, C., Oliver, E. J., Puchalska-Wasyl, M. M., Tovares, A., and Winsler, A. (2023). Self-talk: An interdisciplinary review and transdisciplinary model. *Review of General Psychology, 27*, 355–386.

Leeder, T. M. (2022). Behaviorism, skinner, and operant conditioning: Considerations for sport coaching practice. *Strategies, 35*(3), 27–32.

Maitland, A., Hills, L. A., and Rhind, D. J. (2015). Organisational culture in sport–A systematic review. *Sport Management Review, 18*(4), 501–516.

Mason, R. J., Farrow, D., and Hattie, J. A. (2020). An analysis of in-game feedback provided by coaches in an Australian Football League competition. *Physical Education and Sport Pedagogy, 25*(5), 464–477.

McCardle, L., Young, B. W., and Baker, J. (2019). Self-regulated learning and expertise development in sport: Current status, challenges, and future opportunities. *International Review of Sport and Exercise Psychology, 12*(1), 112–138.

Meijen, C., Turner, M., Jones, M. V., Sheffield, D., and McCarthy, P. (2020). A theory of challenge and threat states in athletes: A revised conceptualization. *Frontiers in Psychology, 11*, 126.

Mellalieu, S., Jones, C., Wagstaff, C., Kemp, S., and Cross, M. J. (2021). Measuring psychological load in sport. *International Journal of Sports Medicine, 42*(9), 782–788.

Mosley, E., Duncan, S., Jones, K., Herklots, H., Kavanagh, E., & Laborde, S. (2023). A Smartphone Enabled Slow-Paced Breathing Intervention in Dual Career Athletes. *Journal of Sport Psychology in Action, 15*(3), 149–164. https://doi.org/10.1080/21520704.2 023.2194256

Nicholls, A. R., and Polman, R. C. (2007). Coping in sport: A systematic review. *Journal of Sports Sciences, 25*(1), 11–31.

Olsen, M. G., Haugan, J. A., Hrozanova, M., and Moen, F. (2020). Coping amongst elite-level sports coaches: A systematic review. *International Sport Coaching Journal, 8*(1), 34–47.

Pierce, S., Gould, D., and Camiré, M. (2017). Definition and model of life skills transfer. *International Review of Sport and Exercise Psychology, 10*(1), 186–211.

Ramis, Y., Torregrosa, M., Viladrich, C., and Cruz, J. (2017). The effect of coaches' controlling style on the competitive anxiety of young athletes. *Frontiers in Psychology, 8*, 572.

Rascle, O., Le Foll, D., Charrier, M., Higgins, N. C., Rees, T., and Coffee, P. (2015). Durability and generalization of attribution-based feedback following failure: Effects on expectations and behavioral persistence. *Psychology of Sport and Exercise, 18*, 68–74.

Sarkar, M., and Page, A. E. (2022). Developing individual and team resilience in elite sport: Research to practice. *Journal of Sport Psychology in Action, 13*(1), 40–53.

Schinke, R., Wylleman, P., Henriksen, K., Si, G., Wagstaff, C. R., Zhang, L., Tshepang, T., Noce, F., and Li, Y. (2023). International Society of Sport Psychology position stand: Scientist practitioners. *International Journal of Sport and Exercise Psychology, 22*(2), 1–23.

Short, S. E., Tenute, A., and Feltz, D. L. (2005). Imagery use in sport: Mediational effects for efficacy. *Journal of Sports Sciences, 23*(9), 951–960.

Skinner, N., and Brewer, N. (2004). Adaptive approaches to competition: Challenge appraisals and positive emotion. *Journal of Sport and Exercise Psychology, 26*(2), 283–305.

Son, V., Jackson, B., Grove, J. R., and Feltz, D. L. (2011). "I am" versus "we are": Effects of distinctive variants of self-talk on efficacy beliefs and motor performance. *Journal of Sports Sciences, 29*(13), 1417–1424.

Strandbu, Å., Bakken, A., and Stefansen, K. (2020). The continued importance of family sport culture for sport participation during the teenage years. *Sport, Education and Society, 25*(8), 931–945.

Tamminen, K., Wolf, S. A., Dunn, R., and Bissett, J. E. (2022). A review of the interpersonal experience, expression, and regulation of emotions in sport. *International Review of Sport and Exercise Psychology, 17*(2), 1132–1169.

Taubert, M., Draganski, B., Anwander, A., Müller, K., Horstmann, A., Villringer, A., and Ragert, P. (2010). Dynamic properties of human brain structure: Learning-related changes in cortical areas and associated fiber connections. *Journal of Neuroscience, 30*(35), 11670–11677.

Till, K., and Baker, J. (2020). Challenges and [possible] solutions to optimizing talent identification and development in sport. *Frontiers in Psychology, 11*, 664.

Turner, M. J. (2016). Rational emotive behavior therapy (REBT), irrational and rational beliefs, and the mental health of athletes. *Frontiers in Psychology, 7*, 1423.

Wagstaff, C. R., and Burton-Wylie, S. (2018). Organizational culture in sport: A conceptual, definitional, and methodological review. *Sport and Exercise Psychology Review, 14*(1), 32–52.

Weinberg, R. S., and Gould, D. (2018). *Foundations of Sport and Exercise Psychology* (7th ed.). Human Kinetics.

Yang, S. X., and Jowett, S. (2013). Conceptual and measurement issues of the complementarity dimension of the coach–athlete relationship across cultures. *Psychology of Sport and Exercise, 14*(6), 830–841.

Yarrow, K., Brown, P., and Krakauer, J. W. (2009). Inside the brain of an elite athlete: The neural processes that support high achievement in sports. *Nature Reviews Neuroscience, 10*(8), 585–596.

14

CONSIDERATIONS FOR WORKING WITH FEMALE PLAYERS

Stacey Emmonds, Ric Lovell, Dawn Scott, Georgie Bruinvels, and Jo Clubb

Introduction

Women's football has seen rapid recent growth, demonstrated by increased media attention (Fédération Internationale de Football Association [FIFA], 2019), professionalism (many players are now full-time professionals), and recognition by international bodies in the form of new governing strategies (Kryger et al., 2021). This growth looks set to continue with FIFA targeting an increase in female participation worldwide from 13.3 million in 2019 to 60 million by 2026 (FIFA, 2019). Whilst research into the women's game has also intensified, there remains substantial disparity, and the application of knowledge generated from the men's game to the women's game is questionable (Emmonds et al., 2019; Kryger et al., 2021). It is not known and is often questioned whether applying what is known from men's football to the women's game can provide an accurate and comprehensive understanding of the women's side of the game. Given the magnitude of growth in women's football, along with the continued commitment of investment and increasing participation, there is a need to accelerate high-quality research and disseminate knowledge of practical applications that benefit the health, injury, and performance outcomes of female footballers. Therefore, there are two main aims of this chapter: (1) briefly outline the between-sex differences in match demands, physiology, injury epidemiology, maturation, and health considerations within the context of football and (2) provide practical strength and conditioning recommendations when working with female players.

Match Demands

Understanding the physical requirements of match-play is necessary to inform athletic preparation. This presents a particular challenge in women's game given

DOI: 10.4324/9781003383475-15

Considerations for Working with Female Players **239**

its rapid evolution, since a 21% increase in high-speed ($\geq$19 km/h) running was observed from the 2015 to 2019 FIFA Women's World Cups (FIFA, 2019). Although there are a few recent studies profiling the physical match demands of women's football (Harkness-Armstrong et al., 2021; Scott et al., 2020), there remains a dearth of information and a need for further research in women's game. In the only direct sex comparison of match demands, Bradley et al. (2014) also observed similar total distance covered (<4% difference), but female players covered less distances at high speed (>18 km/h: 718 vs 986 m) and sprinting (>25 km/h: 59 vs 200 m). However, this study was undertaken nearly a decade ago (Bradley et al., 2014), and therefore, this data should be viewed with caution given the increased professionalism and associated improvement in athletic qualities of female players. Additionally, the use of the same velocity thresholds to define high-speed running and sprinting for men's and women's football may be questioned. For example, when considering sprint speed, male players have been reported to be ~8% faster over 10 m and ~11% faster over 40 m; Haugen et al., 2020; Cardoso de Araújo et al., 2020). Therefore, transposing male velocity thresholds to the women's game may not accurately reflect female match demands. As such, female-specific velocity thresholds derived from retrospective data-mining have been proposed as $\geq$12.5 km/h, $\geq$19.0 km/h, and $\geq$22.5 km/h for high speed, very-high speed, and sprinting categories, respectively (Park et al., 2018; Harkness-Armstrong et al., 2021). Furthermore, to our knowledge, adjustment in thresholds to quantify energetically taxing acceleration and deceleration actions has also yet to be examined in the research literature, which may be warranted considering sex-based differences in explosive lower-limb power (Cardoso de Araújo et al., 2020) and its relevance to football (Harper et al., 2021). Whilst it is challenging to empirically test the utility of different velocity thresholds proposed, consensus and a consistent application of female-specific thresholds across both research and applied practice will contribute to a more relevant understanding of match physical characteristics. Overall, a more comprehensive understanding of female match demands (e.g., within-match characteristics, effects of fixture congestion, influence of contextual match factors), with particular emphasis on the interaction with physical and physiological attributes, is required to inform contemporary athletic development practice.

Differences in Physiology

On average, males have a greater quantity of skeletal muscle mass, which alongside larger segment lengths, contribute to the major performance differences, such as ~40% higher peak power and 30% greater mean power during sprinting (Billaut and Bishop, 2009). Furthermore, females have a greater proportion of type I muscle fibres (Ansdell et al., 2020). Accordingly, female players likely have greater muscle oxidative capacity and lower reliance on glycolytic pathways following all-out exercise, owing to accelerated oxygen uptake kinetics (moderate intensity), enhanced mitochondrial function, and higher capillary density per unit of skeletal muscle (Ansdell et al., 2020). Therefore, although females have greater central limitations to the performance of high-intensity whole body exercise (i.e., smaller lungs, airways, less alveoli, and haemoglobin), higher blood flow during maximal contractions perhaps reduces inhibition to activate muscle (lower H^+ accumulation and ion disturbances), providing fatigue-resistance to contractile elements and faster recovery between repeated exhaustive efforts (Ansdell et al., 2020; Hunter, 2014). However, there is a superficial understanding of the origins of the sex differences in fatigability under different task conditions, and the responsible physiological mechanisms. This is in part due to the predominance of male-only studies in the physiology, fatigability, and exercise training literature. Notwithstanding, these sex-based physiological differences highlight why it may be erroneous to use training strategies predicated on male physiology and may suggest differences in periodisation strategies between sexes. Figure 14.1 displays the proposed differences in fatigability between men and women, however further research specific to the demands of football is undoubtedly required.

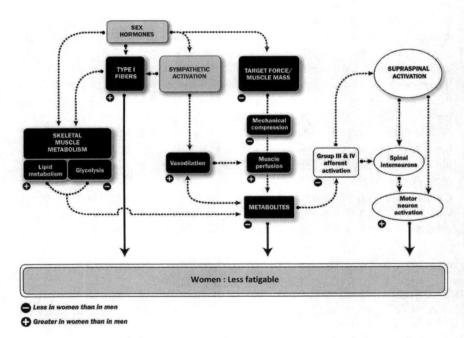

FIGURE 14.1 Potential physiological mechanisms for the sex difference in muscle fatigability (or time to task failure). The figure shows those potential mechanisms that can contribute to women being more fatigue-resistant than men (Hunter et al., 2014).

Since female players likely require less metabolic recovery between high-intensity repeated efforts, training program recommendations derived predominantly from research in males may provide sub-optimal stimuli for adaptation. However, translating research observations from studies is challenging since: (1) most studies are underpowered and often recruit untrained individuals; (2) there is a high degree of variability in training parameters (mode, duration, intensity, etc.); and (3) the confounding influence of the hormonal profile (e.g., menstrual cycle phase, use of hormonal contraception, and hormonal changes through the female lifecycle) is rarely considered. Therefore, training recommendations made in the following sections should be considered with a degree of caution, since rigorous chronic training studies in high-level team-sport players are not currently available in the women's game.

Differences in Training Responses

Whilst less muscle metabolic disruption may confer some performance advantages for the female player in a prolonged high-intensity intermittent sport like football, it may also provide a diminished adaptive stimulus for an equivalent training 'dose'. For example, females have been reported to have a blunted performance response to high-intensity interval training (HIIT) (Schmitz et al., 2020) where sufficient recovery time is permitted (1:4 work:rest ratio; Schmitz et al., 2020). Alternatively, a 1:1 work:rest ratio for repeated high-intensity bursts (30 secs) induced a positive performance response over a short-term HIIT program (four weeks; Schmitz et al., 2020). Whilst the physiological response to work may be exacerbated in females (i.e., higher relative heart rate, oxygen consumption, RPE; Laurent et al., 2014), the greater predisposition to aerobic metabolism accelerates recovery during relief intervals, potentially diminishing the adaptive stimulus (e.g., mitochondrial biogenesis). Indeed, trained females also demonstrate less reduction in muscle contractility following a heavy lower-limb resistance exercise session. Theoretically at least, programming parameters such as relief intensity and duration, and inter-set recovery periods might be reconsidered to account for the accelerated recovery of female players in many football training modalities (i.e., small-sided games), resistance training, and high-intensity interval training. However, extensive research is required to understand how female-specific training methods impact physical capacities, as well as performance and injury outcomes. Clearly, more research is needed regarding the patterns of high-intensity and sprinting actions, and the contribution of football-specific movements to the overall metabolic load and fatigue pattern for a better understanding of the women's game.

Differences in Recovery

Owing to the sex-specific physiology outlined above in this chapter, the recovery time-course post-matches may also differ for female players. A meta-analysis in women's football (Goulart et al., 2020) observed a slightly faster time-course

242 Strength and Conditioning for Football

recovery (~72 hours) for physical performance measures (i.e., countermovement jump, sprint performance) versus male players (Silva et al., 2018). Indeed, the lower acute post-match fatigue observed might reflect a combination of the slightly lower high-intensity nature of match-play in the women's game combined with greater fatigue resistance of female players. This may have implications for micro-cycle scheduling and may permit the female player to return to full physical training 48 hours post-match. However, female players' self-reported ratings of wellness (e.g., muscle soreness, fatigue) have been reported to be 'not recovered' two days following the match (Scott et al., 2020), and there may be some residual muscle damage. Moreover, the physiological consequences of fluctuating sex-hormone levels during the menstrual cycle may further delay the recovery of wellness, muscle damage, and physical performance in certain phases for some individuals. In contrast, it has been reported that oestrogen may have a positive antioxidant and anti-inflammation effect, albeit definitive evidence is still lacking in football. Although more evidence is necessary to make robust inferences about training practices, preliminary information would suggest that the female players may be able to recover from matches quicker, which may facilitate additional opportunities to enhance physical qualities during the typical in-season micro-cycle, particularly an increase in load on Match Day +2 with a view to enhancing both physical performance and resilience to injury.

Differences in Injury Epidemiology

Identifying conclusive sex-based differences in injuries is problematic given the wide array of contextual factors that may underpin epidemiological findings (i.e., playing standard, fixture density, increasing game intensity, season length, playing conditions, hormonal changes). At the time of writing, data suggests women's football has a lower incidence of injury overall (Larruskain et al., 2017; López-Valenciano et al., 2021). However, there are differences in injury patterns between male and female players. Female players tend to incur a greater propensity of anterior cruciate ligament (ACL) rupture, quadriceps strains, and ankle ligament injuries, but fewer hip/groin and hamstring injuries (Larruskain et al., 2017). For example, it has been reported that female players are two to ten times more likely to suffer an ACL injury compared with men practising the same sport. Anatomical and hormonal aspects may contribute to the high incidence of ACL injuries in female players, including joint laxity, limb alignment, intercondylar notch proportions, ligament size, and hormonal fluctuations (Harmon and Ireland, 2000). Research demonstrates that females have reduced knee flexion angles and coronal plane knee control (ligament dominance), increased knee valgus, increased quadriceps activation, decreased hamstring activation, and core dysfunction (trunk dominance) compared with male athletes (Myer et al., 2005; Harmon and Ireland, 2000). Such altered motor control strategies may lead to an increased load on the ACL, which could contribute to the increased risk of injury in female athletes. These neuromuscular deficits are linked with the potential inability to efficiently dissipate ground reaction forces and the reduced control of their centre of mass. Noteworthy, most ACL injuries have been reported to come from non-contact mechanisms (i.e., deceleration, change of direction, and unplanned landing) (Dos'Santos and Jones, 2023). Therefore, it is important that resistance training, plyometrics, and the development of athletic motor skill competencies are integrated into training programmes for female players. The greater incidence of severe injuries (e.g., ACL, ankle ligament) may contribute to the higher injury burden (days lost to injury) in women's football compared to men's (Larruskain et al., 2017). The higher injury burden, however, may reflect comparatively lower access to professionalised medical support for injury risk reduction, diagnostics, treatment, and rehabilitation (Geertsema et al., 2021). Accordingly, to reduce injuries in the women's game, the priority focus may be to equalise the medical resourcing available to elite players. At a minimum, injury rates should be tracked, ideally alongside the evolving physical demands of the women's game and appropriate levels of strength and conditioning provision should be provided to players.

Given the potential sex-based differences in injury epidemiology, burden, and aetiological risk factors (i.e., anatomy, neuromuscular control, and fatiguability), practitioners within the women's game might consider tailoring features of available exercise-based injury risk reduction programmes (e.g., exercises, programming parameters, and scheduling) to further enhance athletic preparation and resilience for football. However, to date, there is very little evidence available regarding the efficacy of injury-risk reduction programs in the elite women's game, and its rapidly evolving nature requires a dynamic approach to stakeholder education and applied practice. In addition, as injury risk factors become better understood, and injury epidemiology and risk reduction programmes are developed, they should be considered within the context of female health considerations, which are discussed below.

Differences in Growth and Maturation

There is an abundance of research in youth male football reporting the impact growth and maturation may have on athletic development (summarised by Towlson et al., 2021). Research has shown boys of advanced maturity display better athleticism than maturation-matched girls (Morris et al., 2018). However, findings from youth male studies may not be transferable to females, especially during maturation, given the differences in the timing and tempo of maturation coupled with differences between the sexes in physical and physiological characteristics from the onset of puberty.

In contrast to males, whereby hormonal and morphological changes associated with maturation are advantageous to athletic development, girls experience different hormonal changes, such as an increase in oestrogen and progesterone which may also be associated with widening of the hips and an increase in non-functional mass (see Figure 14.2; Emmonds and Beech, unpublished). Such hormonal and morphological changes may not be advantageous to athletic performance and this

244 Strength and Conditioning for Football

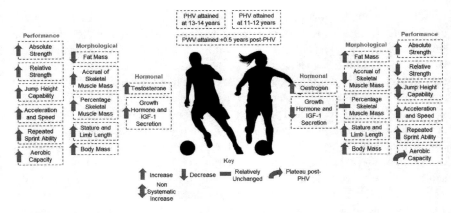

FIGURE 14.2 Summary of hormonal, morphological, and performance measures change during the adolescent growth spurt for boys and girls (Emmonds and Beech, unpublished).

may have implications for the athletic development of youth female players. For example, when compared to boys, a clear plateau in the ability to apply force (e.g., standing broad jump, 10 × 5 m change of direction speed, and hand grip strength) is observed around the age of peak height velocity (PHV) circa aged 12–14 years. Furthermore, cross-sectional and longitudinal research on girls' football players in U.K. development pathways has shown progression in sprinting-related physical qualities after PHV (Emmonds et al., 2017). However, rapid (100 ms) lower body force application, relative to body weight, showed marked reductions in players after PHV (Emmonds et al., 2017). This may be explained by a potential increase in fat mass associated with peak weight velocity that occurs in females 3.5–10.5 months after PHV. This is important for both performance and injury prevention because serious knee injuries, such as ACL ruptures, tend to occur within the first 50 ms of ground contact (Krosshaug et al., 2007). Improving the ability to apply force quickly to stabilise the knee is proven to reduce injury incidence and a recommended strategy before PHV. Resistance training has been shown to enhance holistic fundamental movement skills competence, including the product (or outcome) of the movement and the process (how the skill was performed) in children. Therefore, there is a need to facilitate S and C practices not only at a youth level for girls both in talent development environments but also at a grassroots level.

Furthermore, in contrast to boys, girls have been reported to have a plateau in aerobic performance post-PHV. Emmonds et al. (2020) illustrated increases in total distance covered during the Yo-Yo intermittent endurance test (level 1) around PHV in elite youth female football players, however unclear differences are observed between circa PHV-post-PHV maturation groups. This trend of increasing aerobic capacity around PHV with plateaus and/or small decreases thereafter is in contrast to the increase observed in boys and suggests that girls may need to

Considerations for Working with Female Players **245**

follow a structured conditioning programme (i.e., maximal aerobic speed training) to continue developing their aerobic capacity and high-intensity running capabilities post-PHV. A plateau in aerobic capacity post-PHV may be explained by gains in fat mass post-PHV, which is an important factor for the variation of aerobic fitness in this cohort (Emmonds et al., 2020).

Differences in Health Considerations

There are clear sex differences in primary reproductive hormones between the sexes. From, approximately, 11–50 years of age, females experience a circa-mensal rhythm called the menstrual cycle (MC), whereby large fluctuations in oestrogen and progesterone are observed (Hackney, 2021). A typical, eumenorrheic MC lasts an average of 28 days (ranging from 21 to 35 days) and consists of two main phases: the follicular and luteal phases, separated by ovulation. The changes in concentrations of endogenous female sex hormones (primarily oestrogen and progesterone) can impact a myriad of physiological and psychological factors, which can ultimately affect readiness to perform (Hackney, 2021). Over 90% of female athletes experience unwanted symptoms in response to these hormonal changes (Bruinvels et al., 2020). The primary windows for symptoms are during menstruation (the beginning of the follicular phase), and in the 4–5 days prior to the onset of menstruation. Therefore, the menstrual and premenstrual phases are key time windows which should be monitored and a proactive approach to symptom management may be warranted. Significant inter-individual variation in the menstrual cycle means that tracking it is important at an individual level. Research suggests that 60%–70% of female athletes feel menstrual cycle symptoms (e.g., menstrual cramps, lower back pain, mood changes, heavy bleeding) affect their training and performance, therefore identifying and proactively supporting athletes with management is important. Tracking MC can also identify menstrual dysfunction (e.g., infrequent or irregular menstruation) that can indicate a state of low energy availability or an underlying gynaecological issue, both of which warrant further investigation by medical practitioners. Furthermore, tracking the MC as part of wellness monitoring practices with youth players will allow the early identification of primary amenorrhoea and the player can be referred to a medical practitioner.

Approximately 33%–50% of elite female athletes have been reported to use hormonal contraception (Clarke et al., 2021), which will alter their endogenous hormonal profile and can affect systemic physiology. Again, there is a significant inter-individual variation in response to exogenous hormones, so monitoring is advisable. While the research to date has shown no influence or only trivial-small influences of the menstrual cycle on performance and there is insufficient evidence to modify training based on menstrual cycle phase, it is important that individual monitoring is still integrated into standard wellness tracking practices given the perceived influence of symptoms on performance by players (Parker et al., 2022).

It is recommended that players and practitioners track MCs and symptoms to improve awareness of any phase-related effects on individual performance, aiming

246 Strength and Conditioning for Football

to reduce the impact of such symptoms through the implementation of individual MC cycle mitigation plans, and most specifically with support from the Multi-Disciplinary Team. Furthermore, female players should be integral in decision-making when managing individual MC symptoms to minimise negative impacts and maximise performance outcomes, education is essential to help with tracking and behaviour change (McNulty et al., 2020). It is recommended that MC questions are incorporated into existing daily wellness monitoring tools commonly used within football and, if developed and implemented appropriately, would provide an appropriate method of tracking and monitoring.

Aside from the MC, there are a number of other considerations that must be appreciated when working with female athletes, such as pelvic floor health, pregnancy, return to play post-partum, and breast health, all of which should be considered in their own right. Each of these female-specific contexts, added to the fluctuating hormonal milieu of the MC, warrants applied consideration and further research in the women's game to inform training strategies.

Given the potential sex differences discussed above, practitioners involved in the athletic development of female players should be cautious of traditional research and practices that have been adopted according to the typical white 70 kg reference male. Instead, a critical assessment of female physiology, endocrinology, social, and other health considerations within the context of physical football preparation, and the individual athlete in question, is necessary. The building of a collaborative environment between universities, member associations, clubs, practitioners, coaches, and ultimately players is key to success. Knowledge implementation and adoption should be facilitated in order to achieve results that will improve the health and performance of female players.

Practical Applications

With the increase in professionalisation and funding in women's football, further research is necessary to improve our understanding of how to train women for both optimal health and performance. Based on the findings in this chapter and the research, there is some evidence to suggest that there are specific considerations for women regarding training; however, overall, there are more similarities than differences between men and women regarding training.

The principles of training and training modalities are consistent between training male and female players. However, given the sex differences discussed above, practitioners involved in athletic development and preparation of female players should be considerate of these when transforming knowledge generated within male cohorts to the women's game. Therefore, it is proposed that when practitioners and coaches are reviewing research and training practices for female players, they should consider the current evidence base, determine if there are likely to be differences for female players, and the female-specific context (Figure 14.3).

Table 14.1 summarises some considerations for both research and practice when working with female players:

Considerations for Working with Female Players 247

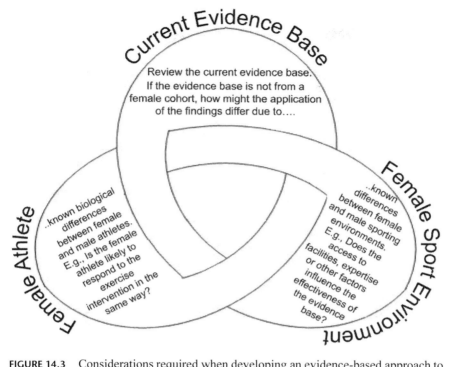

FIGURE 14.3 Considerations required when developing an evidence-based approach to practice in female sport (Emmonds et al., 2019).

TABLE 14.1 Suggestions for Closing the Gender Data Gap in Football Physical Preparation across Research and Applied Practice

	Potential Research Directions	*Applied Practice Implications*
Match Demands	• Consensus on appropriate Women's velocity thresholds using tracking data from multiple teams during competitive tournaments • Rigorous development and evaluation of appropriate acceleration and deceleration thresholds • Examine and refine techniques to integrate velocity and acceleration data in external load monitoring • Re-explore the interaction between physical match demands and physical qualities in the modern game	• Routine tracking of physical match demands to inform training considering the rapid evolution • Apply female-specific thresholds to your own dataset to facilitate interpretation and benchmarking • Development of athletic qualities to reduce the physical burden of match-play • Consideration of non-football occupational loads for amateur players • Consider individual factors in the evaluation of match demands (e.g., positional role, match context, physical qualities, fixture congestion)

(Continued)

248 Strength and Conditioning for Football

TABLE 14.1 (Continued)

	Potential Research Directions	Applied Practice Implications
Physiology	• Evaluation of within-match physical demands • Determine the impact of fixture congestion upon match demands • Examine the implications of enhanced female fatigue-resistance upon acute and chronic training responses • Recruitment of high-level players for training research studies • Consider hormonal profile in study design • Explore the implications of altered physiology upon match and training recovery kinetics, and potential implications for scheduling	• Development of optimal athletic development guidelines for youth female football players. • Reconsider programming parameters for the female player (i.e., frequency, volume, work/relief intensity and duration, and inter-set recovery periods) • Engage with research stakeholders to bridge the data gap on female training physiology • Track responses to training and matches to understand physiological state • Re-evaluate micro-cycle scheduling considering female physiology and recovery kinetics
Injury	• Evaluate the impact of injury on economic and performance outcomes • Investigate the potential role of the menstrual cycle and hormonal contraception on injury • Explore the timing of injuries and the aetiological role of fatigue • Evaluate the efficacy of injury risk reduction programmes in the elite female population • Examine the role of external injury risk factors upon injury (e.g., medical support, fixture congestion, training load) • Examine sex-specific considerations in return-to-play	• Implement injury surveillance methods in your own setting to inform practice • Equalise medical resourcing to facilitate rigorous surveillance and return to play systems • Tailor injury risk reduction exercise programs to address female injury epidemiology • Consider the female anatomy and its implication for biomechanics and neuromuscular control in injury risk reduction programmes (e.g., posterior chain activation)
Maturation	• Training intervention studies to examine the influence of growth and maturation on training strategies with youth female players (i.e., high-intensity running capability, strength development)	• It is important to monitor the maturity status of female players alongside physical development to identify periods of plateau and decrease in performance • Improvements in relative strength should be targeted circa PHV and post-PHV

(Continued)

Considerations for Working with Female Players **249**

TABLE 14.1 (Continued)

	Potential Research Directions	Applied Practice Implications
		• Training strategies to develop high-intensity running capabilities should be introduced in post-PHV players
Health	• Control for oral contraceptive and menstrual cycle phase when researching sex hormone perturbations • Investigate the potential role of the menstrual cycle and hormonal contraception on training response and performance • Explore the impact of pelvic floor health, pregnancy, return to play post-partum, and breast health on performance, injury, and health outcomes in female footballers	• Implement screening and tracking of menstrual cycle, symptoms, and hormonal contraception use, if granted permission by players. Align with training load and response data to assess individual patterns • Refer players demonstrating menstrual dysfunction to medical practitioners for further investigation • Provide education, communication, self-management strategies, and sanitary products

References

Ansdell, P., Thomas, K., Hicks, K. M., Hunter, S. K., Howatson, G., and Goodall, S. (2020). Physiological sex differences affect the integrative response to exercise: Acute and chronic implications. *Experimental Physiology*, *105*(12), 2007–2021. https://doi.org/10.1113/EP088548

Billaut, F., and Bishop, D. (2009). Muscle fatigue in males and females during multiple-sprint exercise. *Sports Medicine*, *39*(4), 257–278. https://doi.org/10.2165/00007256-200939040-00001

Bradley, P. S., Dellal, A., Mohr, M., Castellano, J., and Wilkie, A., (2014). Gender differences in match performance characteristics of soccer players competing in the UEFA Champions League. *Human Movement Science*, *33*, 159–171.

Bruinvels, G., Goldsmith, E., Blagrove, R., et al. (2020). Prevalence and frequency of menstrual cycle symptoms are associated with availability to train and compete: A study of 6812 exercising women recruited using the Strava exercise app. *British Journal of Sports Medicine*, *55*(8). https://doi.org/10.1136/bjsports-2020-102792

Cardoso de Araújo, M., Baumgart, C., Jansen, C. T., Freiwald, J., and Hoppe, M. W. (2020). Sex differences in physical capacities of German Bundesliga Soccer Players. *Journal of Strength and Conditioning Research*, *34*(8), 2329–2337. https://doi.org/10.1519/JSC.0000000000002662

Clarke, A. C., Bruinvels, G., Julian, R., Inge, P., Pedlar, C. R., and Govus, A. D. (2021). Hormonal contraceptive use in football codes in Australia. *Frontiers in Sports and Active Living*, *3*, 634866. https://doi.org/10.3389/fspor.2021.634866

Jones, P., & Dos'Santos, T. (Eds.). (2023). Multidirectional Speed in Sport: Research to Application (1st ed.). Routledge. https://doi.org/10.4324/9781003267881

250 Strength and Conditioning for Football

Emmonds, S., Heyward, O., and Jones, B. (2019). The challenge of applying and undertaking research in female sport. *Sports Medicine*, *5*(1), 1–4.

Emmonds, S., Morris, R., Murray, E., Robinson, C., Turner, L., and Jones, B. (2017). The influence of age and maturity status on the maximum and explosive strength characteristics of elite youth female soccer players. *Science and Medicine in Football*, *1*(3), 209–215.

Emmonds, S., Scantlebury, S., Murray, E., Turner, L., Robsinon, C., and Jones, B. (2020). Physical characteristics of elite youth female soccer players characterized by maturity status. *The Journal of Strength and Conditioning Research*, *34*(8), 2321–2328.

FIFA (2019). Physical analysis of the FIFA Women's World Cup France 2019™. https://img.fifa.com/image/upload/zijqly4oednqa5gffgaz.pdf

Geertsema, C., Geertsema, L., Farooq, A., Harøy, J., Oester, C., Weber, A., and Bahr, R. (2021). Injury prevention knowledge, beliefs and strategies in elite female footballers at the FIFA Women's World Cup France 2019. *British Journal of Sports Medicine*, *55*(14), 801–806.

Goulart, K.N.O., Coimbra, C.C., Campos, H.O. et al. (2022). Fatigue and recovery time course after female soccer matches: A systematic review and meta-analysis. *Sports Medicine - Open 8*, 72. https://doi.org/10.1186/s40798-022-00466-3

Hackney, A. C. (2021). Menstrual cycle hormonal changes and energy substrate metabolism in exercising women: A perspective. *International Journal of Environmental Research and Public Health*, *18*(19), 10024.

Hagglund, M., Walden, M., and Ekstrand, J. (2009). Injuries among male and female elite football players. *Scandinavian Journal of Medicine and Science in Sports*, *19*(6), 819–827. https://doi.org/10.1111/j.1600-0838.2008.00861.x

Harkness-Armstrong, A., Till, K., Datson, N., and Emmonds, S. (2021). Whole and peak physical characteristics of elite youth female soccer match-play. *Journal of Sports Sciences*, *39*(12), 1320–1329.

Harmon, K. G., and Ireland, M. L. (2000). Gender differences in noncontact anterior cruciate ligament injuries. *Clinics in Sports Medicine*, *19*(2), 287–302.

Harper, D. J., Sandford, G. N., Clubb, J., et al. (2021). Elite football of 2030 will not be the same as that of 2020: What has evolved and what needs to evolve?. *Scandinavian Journal of Medicine and Science in Sports*, *31*(2), 493–494. https://doi.org/10.1111/sms.13876

Haugen, T., Tønnessen, E., Hem, E., Seiler, S., and Leirstein, S. (2014). VO_{2max} characteristics of elite female soccer players, 1989–2007. International Journal of Sports Physiology and Performance, *9*(3), 515–521. https://doi.org/10.1123/ijspp.2012-0150

Haugen, T. A., Breitschädel, F., and Seiler, S. (2020). Sprint mechanical properties in soccer players according to playing standard, position, age and sex. *Journal of Sports Sciences*, *38*(9), 1070–1076.

Hunter, S. K. (2014). Sex differences in human fatigability: Mechanisms and insight to physiological responses. *Acta Physiologica*, *210*, 768–789. https://doi.org/10.1111/apha.12234

Krosshaug, T., Nakamae, A., Boden, B. P., Engebretsen, L., Smith, G., Slauterbeck, J. R., Hewett, T. E., Bahr, R. (2007). Mechanisms of anterior cruciate ligament injury in basketball: video analysis of 39 cases. *The American Journal of Sports Medicine*, *5*(3), 359–367.

Kryger, K., Wang, A., Mehta, R., Impellizzeri, F. M., Massey, A., an McCall, A. (2021). Research on women's football: A scoping review. *Science and Medicine in Football*, *6*(5), 1–10. https://doi.org/10.1080/24733938.2020.1868560

Larruskain, J., Lekue, J. A., Diaz, N., Odriozola, A., and Gil, S. M. (2017). A comparison of injuries in elite male and female football players: A five-season prospective study. *Scandinavian Journal of Medicine and Science in Sports*, *28*(1), 237–245. https://doi.org/10.1111/sms.12860

Laurent, C. M., Vervaecke, L. S., Kutz, M. R., and Green, J. M. (2014). Sex-specific responses to self-paced, high-intensity interval training with variable recovery periods. *Journal of Strength and Conditioning Research*, *28*, 920–927. https://doi.org/10.1519/JSC.0b013e3182a1f574

López-Valenciano, A., Raya-González, J., Garcia-Gómez, J. A., Aparicio-Sarmiento, A., de Baranda, P. S., De Ste Croix, M., and Ayala, F. (2021). Injury profile in women's football: A systematic review and meta-analysis. *Sports Medicine*, *51*(3), 423–442. https://doi.org/10.1007/s40279-020-01401-w

McNulty, K. L., Elliott-Sale, K. J., Dolan, E., et al. (2020). The effects of menstrual cycle phase on exercise performance in eumenorrheic women: A systematic review and meta-analysis. *Sports Medicine*, *50*, 1813–1827.

Morris, R., Emmonds, S., Jones, B., et al. (2018). Seasonal changes in physical qualities of elite youth soccer players according to maturity status: Comparisons with aged matched controls. *Science and Medicine in Football*, *2*(4), 272–280.

Myer, G. D., Ford, K. R., and Hewett, T. E. (2005). The effects of gender on quadriceps muscle activation strategies during a maneuver that mimics a high ACL injury risk position. *Journal of Electromyography and Kinesiology*, *15*(2), 181–189.

Nassis, G. P., Brito, J., Tomás, R., Heiner-Møller, K., Harder, P., Kryger, K. O., and Krustrup, P. (2021). Elite women's football: Evolution and challenges for the years ahead. *Scandinavian Journal of Medicine and Science in Sports*, *32*(S1), 7–11. https://doi.org/10.1111/sms.14094

Park, L. A. F., Scott, D., and Lovell, R. (2018). Velocity zone classification in elite women's football: Where do we draw the lines? *Science and Medicine in Football*, *3*, 21–28.

Parker, L. J., Elliott-Sale, K. J., Hannon, M. P., Morton, J. P., and Close, G. L. (2022). An audit of hormonal contraceptive use in Women's Super League soccer players; implications on symptomology. *Science and Medicine in Football*, *6*(2), 153–158.

Schmitz, B., Niehues, H., Thorwesten, L., Klose, A., Krüger, M., and Brand, S.-M. (2020). Sex Differences in high-intensity interval training – Are HIIT protocols interchangeable between females and males? *Frontiers in Physiology*, *11*, 38. https://doi.org/10.3389/fphys.2020.00038

Scott, D., Haigh, J., and Lovell, R. (2020). Physical characteristics and match performances in women's international versus domestic-level football players: A 2-year, league-wide study. *Science and Medicine in Football*, *4*(3), 211–215.

Scott, D., Norris, D., and Lovell, R. (2020). Dose-response relationship between external load and wellness in elite women's soccer matches: Do customized velocity thresholds add value? *International Journal of Sports Physiology and Performance*, *15*(9), 1–7. https://doi.org/10.1123/ijspp.2019-0660

Towlson, C., Salter, J., Ade, J. D., Enright, K., Harper, L. D., Page, R. M., and Malone, J. J. (2021). Maturity-associated considerations for training load, injury risk, and physical performance in youth soccer: One size does not fit all. *Journal of Sport and Health Science*, *10*(4), 403–412.

15

STRENGTH AND CONDITIONING FOR YOUTH FOOTBALL

Perry Stewart, Thomas John, and Charlie Norton-Sherwood

Introduction

In the pursuit of competitive advantage, many elite sports organisations are investing in sophisticated systems that strategically develop athletes to compete at the highest level (de Bosscher et al., 2015). Consequently, the systematic identification and development of youth athletes has received much attention, with many young athletes now being introduced to formal training and competition environments at increasingly younger ages. An example of such a system is the Elite Player Performance Plan, which is a long-term strategy within English football aimed at developing more and better home-grown players. Within such youth training environments, strength and conditioning (S and C) has become a recognised and integral discipline intended to help optimise athletic potential and mitigate injury risk. The overarching objective of youth S and C is "to foster a supportive learning environment that provides an appropriate balance between challenge and fun, which helps young athletes develop robust levels of athleticism, reduce injury risk and enhance health and wellbeing" (Lloyd et al., 2019a, p.77). In addition, the International Olympic Committee states that training youth athletes should help develop both multiple physical qualities and reduce training monotony to keep them motivated and engaged in training (Bergeron et al., 2015). As such, S and C within youth populations is considered multifaceted and requires more than the mere knowledge and application of adult-like interventions. Youth S and C coaches must possess an awareness of how growth, maturation, and psychosocial development can impact training-induced adaptations, skill acquisition, recovery rates, and healing processes from injury (Lloyd et al., 2019a). Possessing and appropriately applying such knowledge must be used to effectively facilitate appropriate training programmes from childhood, through adolescence, and into adulthood. Therefore,

DOI: 10.4324/9781003383475-16

the aim of this chapter is to (1) discuss the implications of growth and maturation on injury prevalence and athletic development, and (2) provide practical guidance for S and C coaches working with young football players.

Implications of Growth and Maturation

Possessing the appropriate knowledge and understanding of growth and maturation has been proven valuable for S and C coaches within youth football (Towlson et al., 2021). This is due to factors such as the guidance it can provide when designing both development and injury prevention programmes. Within youth football, biological maturation has been defined as the timing and tempo of a player's progress to their estimated adult stature (Malina et al., 2004). The term growth within youth football is simply the process of increasing in stature (i.e., becoming taller). During the period of adolescence, the timing and tempo of growth is highly individual and is independent of the chronological age of the players (Philippaerts et al., 2006). Therefore, within a single age group squad (i.e., U14 male team or U12 female team), it should be expected that there will be a large variance of biological maturation and growth rates amongst players. Although growth and maturation processes occur over the first two decades of life, adolescence has been identified as a key stage due to the accelerated period of growth that occurs (Malina et al., 2015). This accelerated period of growth is often referred to as peak height velocity (PHV) or the adolescent growth spurt, and various studies have demonstrated that individuals can grow at velocities of 8.2–11.2 cm per year (Malina et al., 2012; Philippaerts et al., 2006). During the adolescent growth spurt, the individual experiences one of the most rapid periods of post-natal growth, which is subsequently followed by epiphyseal fusion (closure of the growth plates) and final adult height (Bogin et al., 2018; Boeyer et al., 2020). Due to variations in timing and tempo of development between individuals, players are often classified within the maturity statuses of pre-PHV, circa-PHV, and post-PHV within football academies and research. Understanding a player's growth and maturity is particularly important for S and C coaches as it has the potential to influence the rate of development, physical performance, injury, and talent identification (Hill et al., 2020; Kemper et al., 2015).

Injury Prevalence

Youth football players are increasingly exposed to bouts of high-intensity activity during training and match play, which inherently presents a risk of attaining sports-related injuries (Hewett et al., 2005). Players within the earlier stages of maturity (i.e., pre-PHV) have been shown to have a reduced risk of injury incidence (frequency of injuries) and burden (severity of injury) compared to later stages (i.e., circa-PHV and post-PHV) (Van Der Sluis et al., 2013). Similar to the pattern of growth itself, growth-related injuries typically follow a distal to proximal pattern. Therefore, it is unsurprising to see injuries occur at the ankle (i.e., Sever's disease),

254 Strength and Conditioning for Football

followed by the knee (i.e., Osgood-Schlatter's disease), and then around the hip and spine (i.e., spondylolysis) (Monasterio et al., 2021, 2023a). The development of connective tissue and bone density occurs after the rapid changes to skeletal stature, meaning that tendons, ligaments, and cartilage are particularly vulnerable during the adolescent growth spurt (Van der Sluis et al., 2013; Cohen and Sala, 2010; Blimkie et al., 1993). As a player matures and progresses into post-PHV, there is a higher risk of muscular injuries occurring. This is likely caused by the hormonally driven changes to muscle morphology combined with an increase in training and match demands (Monasterio et al., 2021). Understanding the prevalence, type, and site of injuries during different stages of development may aid the S and C coach in developing injury mitigation programmes and strategies. Such programmes are likely to encourage: (1) a functional range of movement through the use of flexibility and mobility interventions and (2) target balance, coordination and joint stability to maintain or increase motor control. Other strategies to mitigate the risk of injury include minimising a player's exposure to monotonous and repetitive exercise and acute increases in training load.

Athletic Development

Development of an athletic development program within the context of a football academy or club should be guided by paediatric exercise science principles and long-term athletic development (LTAD) models (Côté and Hay, 2002; Balyi and Hamilton, 2004; Ford et al., 2011; Lloyd and Oliver, 2012; Lloyd et al., 2013; Meylan et al., 2014a; Harrison et al., 2015; Pichardo et al., 2018). Typically, LTAD programs have been designed with the purpose of appropriately preparing children and adolescents for not only successful sporting careers but also to allow for an active lifestyle during adulthood (Lloyd et al., 2016). Such models have provided useful insights into optimal trainability periods for different physical capacities based on factors such as growth, maturation, and age (Lloyd and Oliver, 2012). In an attempt to consolidate the multitude of LTAD principles, Pichardo et al. (2018) developed a composite model that includes developmental guidance such as, participation aims, optimal periods of trainability, session structure, and the impact of growth and maturation.

As demonstrated within the composite LTAD model, physiological capabilities and athletic development are highly influenced by the biological maturity and growth of the player (Philippaerts et al., 2006; Ford et al., 2011). It is therefore advised that an individual approach to athletic development is executed for players of different maturity statuses. During the early years (i.e., pre-PHV) it is widely accepted that children experience an accelerated adaptation to their neuromuscular system, with neural pathways becoming established and less flexibility to adapt thereafter (Rabinowicz, 1986; Borms, 1986). Thus, this period is crucial for the development of fundamental movement skills (FMS) (i.e., running, jumping, and falling), as well as specific sports skills (i.e., kicking, catching, and tackling), which should serve as a useful foundation for the movement patterns players are exposed to in the sport (Higgs et al., 2008). When aiming to develop these fundamental motor skills, it has been proven beneficial to allow the player to sample a variety of sports in an unstructured manor (Côté, 1999; Lloyd and Oliver, 2012). This could be achieved through the use of multi-sports within the athletic development framework, which has been demonstrated to increase the chances of sporting success during adulthood (Barth et al., 2022; Cupples et al., 2018; Güllich et al., 2022). Within the context of a youth football program, this could be the use of sports such as parkour, tennis, or basketball to develop specific physical and psychological attributes of the players. Hypothetically, when trying to develop the jumping and landing ability of the players, it may be beneficial to include a parkour session where the players are required to move through a specific route set out by the S and C coach. The S and C coach should then add minor rules or constraints to the game to promote the desired outcomes of the session and ensure that the appropriate number of jump and land actions is being executed by the players. If done correctly, there should be a large variety of movement strategies, high volume of social interactions, and little coach interventions. As the player progresses in age and maturation, the adaptation to training and the opportunity to develop different physical capacities changes (Balyi and Hamilton, 2004).

A key influence that should be considered when developing physical capacities is the adolescent growth spurt. Throughout the adolescent growth spurt, it has been shown that some children experience regressions in several sensorimotor functions which subsequently have a negative impact on perceived performance (Quatman-Yates et al., 2012; Hill et al., 2023). Due to the changing of stature and centre of mass during this period, motor skills such as change of direction (COD) ability and sport-specific movements should be continuously developed to allow the player to maintain efficient motor patterns and establish new movement solutions. This period is also categorised as the period in which the players will start specialising within football, which would allow for additional time to be spent developing football-specific actions as the player is growing. Throughout the development journey from pre- to post-PHV there are additional changes occurring within the athlete such as puberty and their progression towards sexual maturity. During this period, both male and female players will experience an increased production of growth hormone, which usually occurs around the time of circa-PHV onwards (Clark and Rogol, 1996). It has been suggested that this increased secretion of hormones within the body can be taken advantage of, and significant improvements in strength, power, and speed can be achieved (Meylan et al., 2014b). Whilst resistance training is effective in developing strength and power throughout all stages of development, such training is likely to elicit changes to cross-sectional area and pennation angle. In subsequent sections, speed, agility, strength, and power and endurance are considered within the context of developing youth football players.

256 Strength and Conditioning for Football

Speed

Sprinting ability is an integral component of successful match play and can often be the decisive action that determines the outcome of a match. The importance of speed for football players has considerably increased over the past couple of decades with both high-speed running (HSR) and sprinting demands increasing within match play (Reynolds et al., 2021). Within the English Premier League, it has been demonstrated that central midfield players are now expected to be able to run between 500–900 m and 100–190 m of HSR (speed ranging from 19.8 km/h to 25.2 km/h) and sprinting (speed above 25.2 km/h), respectively (Gregson, 2010). In addition to performance benefits, the inclusion of sprinting within the weekly training schedule has been suggested to reduce the likelihood of lower limb muscle (e.g. hamstrings) injuries, and the quantity of sprinting prescribed to the player should be individualised based on their starting status (e.g. starters and non-starters) in order to allow for optimal recovery and peaking for match day (Beato et al., 2021). Both acceleration (associated with longer ground contact times and higher net impulse) and maximal speed (associated with shorter periods of ground contact time and higher rates of force development), need to be developed for optimal football performance. Biomechanically, youth athletes' stride length increases with age, whereas stride frequency decreases slightly in late childhood before stabilising during adolescence (Froehle et al., 2013). The underpinning aim of any speed-related training programme should be to increase the rate and magnitude of force applied during ground contact while also aiming to reduce ground contact time (Lloyd, 2014). Although it's accepted that all physical parameters are trainable throughout childhood and adolescence, there are opportunities to develop specific qualities at different times through the process of 'synergistic adaptations'. This refers to the targeting of physical qualities that will also be naturally developing. In 1999, Viru et al., reported critical periods for development, with a pre-adolescent spurt in speed between 5 and 9 years old, followed by a second spurt which appears to coincide with the onset of the adolescent growth spurt between the ages of 12 and 15 years old. The pre-pubertal spurt is attributed to rapid central nervous system development, with the adolescent spurt being predominantly attributed to the rise in hormone levels with maturity. It is pertinent to note that whilst male and female players' sprint ability during childhood is comparable, the result of increased testosterone in males during adolescence means development rates diverge from this point.

S and C coaches should consider how different modes of training can influence speed development as well as how growth, maturation, and training age can affect the training response. As seen in Table 15.1, it is suggested that as age and stage of development increase, speed development training should advance from FMS, with an emphasis of games in early childhood, to formal technical drills at pre-PHV, with the addition of maximal sprints at circa-PHV and a greater emphasis on maximal sprints at post-PHV. During a meta-analysis by Moran et al. (2017), it

Strength and Conditioning for Youth Football **257**

TABLE 15.1 Speed Development Considerations for Youth Football

	Early Childhood 0–7 years old	Prepubertal Male: 7–12 Female: 7–11	Circumpubertal Male: 12–15 Female: 11–15	Postpubertal Male: 16+ Female: 15+
Speed Development	FMS	Sprint Technique	Sprint Technique and Maximal Sprints	Maximal Sprints
Complimentary Training	Physical literacy and strength training	Strength and plyometric training	Strength, hypertrophy and plyometric training	Strength, hypertrophy and plyometric training
Coaching Focus	Active play and games that encourage good running technique	Prescriptive drills that focus on technical execution	Emphasis on coordination and technique during PHV	More complex and novel methods such as resisted sprints can be used

Oliver et al. (2013).

FMS = Fundamental movement skills; PHV = Peak height velocity.

was reported that maximal speed training resulted in more favourable adaptations for athletes who were circa-PHV and post-PHV, compared to those who were pre-PHV. This accelerated adaptation during circa-PHV and post-PHV compared to pre-PHV players has been attributed to the development of the stretch-shortening cycle activity caused by the increasing leg stiffness from pre- to post-PHV (Rumpf et al., 2013). In addition to the specific speed development training youth players are exposed to, the S and C should coordinate concurrent complimentary training activities. Low-level resistance training in combination with plyometric and speed exercises over a six-week period can result in positive sprinting improvements in pre-PHV adolescents (Rodríguez-Rosell et al., 2016). Plyometric training would seem to target positive adaptations in musculotendinous stiffness and neurological factors such as neural firing rates, pre-activation, and the stretch reflex, which are all known to be naturally developing during this time. It has been suggested that during post-PHV, combining strength, plyometric, and speed training may be the most effective training method to enhance sprint performance. It is also suggested that as movement competency improves and the player increases in training experience, the S and C coach can introduce resisted sprint modalities which can be an effective tool to increase speed performance. In accordance with existing research, sprint-specific training sessions are most effective when they comprise of up to 16 sprints between 10 and 30 m, with a work-to-rest ratio of 1:25, and conducted two to three times per week (Rumpf et al., 2012; Moran et al., 2017). The suggested work to rest ratio allows for full recovery to ensure a maximal effort in each sprint. However, it should be noted that less mature athletes will likely require less

258 Strength and Conditioning for Football

rest to recover. While training speed in isolation will help develop the underpinning physical capacities, it inherently neglects the perceptual and cognitive skills required for effective football performance. Therefore, as athletes age and the stage of development increases an attempt to integrate speed training with the technical coaches should be made to improve on-field performance (Table 15.2).

Agility

Agility can be described as a fast whole-body movement involving COD or speed in response to a given stimulus (Sheppard and Young, 2006). The two key sub-components highlighted from this definition are COD-speed, and the perceptual and decision-making processes. Like speed, COD-speed does improve naturally throughout childhood and adolescence owing to synergistic adaptation, but in a non-linear fashion. Jeffreys (2017), proposes the implementation of the agility development pyramid, whereby the *foundation* is concerned with developing broad effective movement capabilities, followed by *development* where the emphasis is to increase movement challenge via increasing degrees of freedom, and then finally *performance* where S and C coaches are challenged to improve context-specific agility.

In relation to developing agility during different stages of development, Lloyd et al. (2013) propose a framework for training agility, which includes the development of fundamental movement patterns (FMS), COD-speed, and reactive agility training (RAT) (Table 15.3). All three proponents are present in a player's agility programme, albeit in different proportions. It has been proposed that for younger players (i.e., pre-PHV), where neural plasticity is heightened, FMS development is vital to ensure that the correct movement patterns are mastered in a safe and fun environment, before these movements are tested in more complex, open-skilled, sport-specific situations. COD-speed development builds upon FMS and focuses on the player's ability to rapidly accelerate, decelerate, and then reaccelerate, but in a controlled and pre-planned environment, with prior knowledge of the direction and magnitude of the COD. When coaching movements such as deceleration, side-shuffling, backpedalling, curvilinear running, cutting, cross-stepping, and drop stepping, the S and C coach should focus on optimising the base of support, controlling centre of mass, body weight transfer, and foot placement for maximal force-production (Jeffreys, 2006). It is advisable that FMS and COD skills are revisited with players experiencing rapid bouts of growth as *adolescent awkwardness* may lead to temporal disruption of motor control and COD patterns. Force producing capabilities such as relative strength and reactive strength positively impact COD-speed (Nimphius, 2010). Therefore, it is recommended that strength and plyometric training should be factored into the players' development programme throughout childhood and adolescence. As players move through into post-puberty (post-PHV), the emphasis of agility training shifts towards RAT (providing sound COD-speed mechanics have been learned). This allows the players to practice their

TABLE 15.2 Sample Speed Sessions

Sample Speed Sessions

Age Group	PRE-PHV	CIRCA-PHV	POST-PHV
1, Movement and Mechanics	**(A1) Knee Drive and Balance Challenge** The player stands on 1 leg whilst balancing a sandbag on their knee in a 90° position. After balancing for 5-seconds they quickly switch legs and attempt to catch the sandbag on the opposite knee in the same balanced position.	**(A1) Dynamic Hurdle Mobility** The player must get through, over, or around the hurdle maze. Hurdles are set at a variety of heights and directions to promote hip flexion and extension. Different rules and constraints can be added such as, "You must pass the hurdle differently to the player ahead of you" to promote variation of movement. **(A2) Running Mechanics** >A-March (2 × 15 m) >A-Skip (2 × 15 m) >B-Skip (2 × 15 m) >High Knee Bounds (2 × 25 m) >Straight Leg Bounds (2 × 25 m)	**(A1) Floor based mobility** Mobility and activation focused around lumbo-pelvic area, hamstrings, and quadriceps/hip flexors. **(A2) Dynamic Mobility** >SL RDL (2 × 10 m) >Reverse Lunge (2 × 10 m) >Carioca (2 × 15 m) >Leg Swings (2 ×15 m) **(A3) Running Mechanics** >Band Resisted A-March (2 × 15 m) >Band Resisted A-Skip (2 × 15 m) >B-Skip (2 × 15 m)
2, Plyometrics/ Jumping	**(B1) Hop Challenge** The player aims to hop across the "lily pads" to get to the other side of the pond. If they are on the "lily pad" for over 3-seconds they sink, but if they're on it less than 1 second it breaks.	**(B1)** >Linear Double Leg Pogos (2 × 15 ground contacts) >Double Leg Broad Jumps (3 × 2) >Small Distance Single Leg Hops (2 × 10 ground contacts each leg)	**(B1)** >Linear Double Leg Pogos (2 × 15 Ground Contacts) >Single Leg Hops (2 × 15 m) (emphasising short GCT, large distances, and cyclical action of lower limb shank) >Bounds (2 × 25 m) >Straight Leg Bounds (2 × 25 m) >Straight Leg Bounds into High Bounds (2 × 30 m)

(Continued)

TABLE 15.2 (Continued)

Sample Speed Sessions

Age Group	PRE-PHV	CIRCA-PHV	POST-PHV
3, Sprints	**(C1) What's the time Mr Wolf (Red light/Green light)** The player aims to get to the opposite side of the box without getting captured by the "wolf" (Teammate). The quicker the player runs, the more chance they have of winning.	**(C1) Escape Race** Two players are attached via an evasion belt separated by 2-metres. One player is the "evader", and the other player is the "pursuer". The evader must try to escape up a 30 m narrow channel and break the connection with the pursuer. The pursuer must try to stay within the 2 m belt range and not allow the belt to break. The evader initiates the race by sprinting forward in the channel. Each player gets two efforts as the evader.	**(C1)** >Floating Wicket Runs - 15 m Build – 15 m Wickets – 10 m Maintain × 2 >Competitive Sprints - 2 × 20 m, 2 × 30 m (with live feedback) - Ensure adequate rest between efforts
4, Context	**(D1) Tag Rugby** Small-sided tag rugby matches with large spaces to allow for high amounts of straight and curved sprints.	**(D1) 3-vs-2 American Football** The attacking team has a centre, quarter back, and a wide receiver. The defensive team has a middle line-backer and a cornerback. The pitch is 40m in length and the objective is to get from one side to the other. Each player rotates positions after every attempted play.	**(D1) Contextual Drill** Two teams of three (one attacking, one defending) line up 10 m behind the halfway line. On a coach's whistle, each player has to get up to the halfway line and around a pole. Once around halfway pole and running back towards goal, a coach will play a ball through for the attacking team to run onto. The attacking team must be as quick as they can to score, will defending team is also running back to try and prevent a goal.

PHV – Peak Height Velocity; SL – Single Leg; RDL – Romanian Deadlift.

Strength and Conditioning for Youth Football **261**

TABLE 15.3 Agility Development Considerations for Youth Football

Pre-Pubertal (Pre-PHV) (%)	Circum-Pubertal (Circa-PHV) (%)	Post Pubertal (Post-PHV) (%)
FMS: 60	FMS: 30	FMS: 20
COD: 25	COD: 40	COD: 20
RAT: 15	RAT: 30	RAT: 60
Training Structure: Low	Training Structure: Moderate	Training Structure: High

Adapted from Lloyd et al. (2013).

COD-speed in relation to sport-specific scenarios and therefore, develop perceptual and decision-making processes as well. It is recommended that the youth S and C coach work collaboratively with the technical coach to design specific drills which relate to aspects of the games and positional demands to enhance the transferability of agility training. The structure of training in this framework increases as the stages of development progress and should in turn become more challenging and football-specific (Table 15.4).

Strength and Power

Muscular strength is defined as the ability to exert force against an external resistance (Stone, 1993). The nature of football is such that athletes must be able to manipulate their own mass against gravity (e.g., sprinting), against the opponent's mass (e.g., body contact, tackling), and against an external object (e.g., football) (Stewart et al., 2019). For the purpose of this chapter 'strength training' encompasses the relevant sub-qualities of strength that are likely to form a part of the training process (i.e. hypertrophy, strength, power). Youth strength and power training has been shown to improve general motor skills and sport-specific skills, running velocity, changes of direction (CODS), aerobic endurance, and mobility and has a potential injury-reducing benefit (Faigenbaum et al., 2019). Young players will naturally develop strength and power without a structured training programme through the physiological process of maturation. However, maximising synergistic adaptation where the stimulus of strength and power training complements the naturally occurring adaptions throughout childhood and adolescence is recommended. Myer et al. (2013) suggest that appropriate strength and plyometric training initiated during pre-PHV and maintained into adolescence will maximise training age and the potential to achieve neuromuscular potential in adulthood. Further to this, additional research has shown that elite adolescent football players who participated in regular resistance training in addition to their football training showed greater improvements in a 1RM (rep max) back squat and linear sprint speed compared to teammates who only participated in football training (Sander et al., 2013).

TABLE 15.4 Sample Agility Sessions

Sample COD Sessions

Age Group	*PRE-PHV*	*CIRCA-PHV*	*POST-PHV*
1, Movement and Mechanics	**(A1) Lateral Hop and Catch** Two players stand on one leg balancing with a ball in their hands. They must coordinate throwing and catching both of the balls whilst simultaneously hopping laterally onto their other leg 0.25 m to the side. No player is allowed to have more than one ball at any time. The winning pair is the duo that can perform the most catches within 30-seconds.	**(A1) Laser-Beam Mobility** The player must get through the "laser-beam" zone without touching the lasers. The arena should be set up to promote external rotation at the hip and disassociation of the upper and lower body. **(A2) Running Mechanics** >Lateral Shuffle (2 × 15 m) >Lateral A-March (2 × 15 m) >Lateral A-Skip (2 × 15 m) >Cross-Over Runs (2 × 15 m)	**(A1) Floor based mobility** Mobility and activation focused around lumbo-pelvic area and groin. **(A2) Dynamic Mobility** >SL RDL (2 × 10 m) >Lateral Lunge (2 × 10 m) >Carioca (2 × 15 m) >Shuffle (2 × 15 m) >Forward and Backward Jockey (2 × 15 m) **(A3) Running Mechanics** >Lateral Shuffle (2 ×15 m) >Lateral A-March (2 ×15 m) >Lateral A-Skip (2 × 15 m) >Cross-Over and Hold (2 × 15 m) >Cross-Over Skip (2 × 15 m)
2, Plyometrics/ Jumping	**(B1) Parkour Obstacle Course** The player aims to hop, jump, and bounce through the obstacle course. The coach can add points for creativity or speed of movement.	**(B1)** >Lateral Broad Jump (3 × 2 each side) >Single Leg Lateral Hops (2 ×10 each leg) >Diagonal Alternate Single Leg Hops (2 × 12)	**(B1)** >SL Lateral and Medial Hops (2 × 10 each leg) (emphasising short GCT) >Rotational SL Pogo Variations (2 × 8) >Lateral Bounds >Diagonal Bounds

Strength and Conditioning for Youth Football

3, COD	**(C1) Parkour Tag** The player aims to get to survive within the parkour arena for 30 seconds without getting tagged by the defender.	**(C1) Bulldog 5-v-2** Create a 15 × 30 pitch area. Two players are in the centre of the rectangle as defenders. The remaining five players aim to sprint around the defenders and make it to the opposite side of the rectangle. If a player is tagged or tackled, they swap places with the defender.	**(C1)** >Lateral Shuffle to Acceleration (2 × 15 m) >Crossover Step to Acceleration (2 × 15 m) >Pre-Planned Cuts (2 × 15 m – minimum 1 cut for each foot) >Pre-Planned Cuts Races (2 × 15 m – minimum 1 cut for each foot)
4, Context	**(D1) Soft Tennis** 1-vs-1 tennis match with an emphasis on hitting the ball to the side of the opponent to promote cut step movements.	**(D1) 1-vs-1 Football Drill** The attacking players must get away from the defender in order to create space and become an available option to receive the ball. If the defender stays with the attacker, the outside player shouldn't play the ball into the area.	**(D1) 1-vs-1 Wave Football Drill** In a 10 × 6 m area, with mini goals on either end, players stand behind both mini goals. A player from one goal accelerates out to play into the opposite goal. Once he has played into the goal, a player from behind that goal accelerates out to try to score in the other goal. The player who just shot becomes the defender. The drills keep going, player who attacks then transitions to defend straight away until everyone has gone three to four times.

264 Strength and Conditioning for Football

To capitalise on synergistic adaptation, the S and C coach must understand associated physiological developments. Owing to the plasticity of the neuromuscular system during early development, there is an unparalleled opportunity to develop athletic motor skill competencies (AMSC), which include lower body exercises (bilateral and unilateral), upper body pushing and pulling (vertical and horizontal), anti-rotation and core bracing, jumping, landing, and rebounding, throwing, catching and grasping. During the early stages of development these movements should be coached in a fun and engaging manner. Lloyd et al. (2019b) suggest a model for ensuring movement quality and ideas for progressing movements: (1) can the player demonstrate a competent shape (e.g., upright torso with heels on the floor at the bottom of a squat), (2) can the player hold the shape (e.g., hold the bottom position of the squat for 5–10 s), (3) can the player move in and out of the shape competently (e.g., descend and ascend into and out of a squat position multiple times), and (4) make it more challenging through increasing resistance, increasing movement complexity and/or increasing the movement velocity. Whilst appearing to be fun, game orientated and of low structure to the young player, the S and C coach must ensure that the session is purposefully planned with key session objectives met.

Once players are circumpubertal, training-induced adaptations shift to being a combination of neural, hormonal, muscular, and tendinous. This shift is caused by the increase of circulating androgens (accentuated more within male athletes). Providing adolescents have built technical proficiency in the requisite movement patterns, the structure and loading paradigm of resistance training can exponentially increase. As players progress through chronological age and stage of development, the individualisation and sport specificity of strength and power programmes should also increase. As such, training prescription may partially be determined by the player profile and positional demands which could require collaboration and input from the technical coach. Lloyd et al. (2012) suggest that prescription should be based according to biological status, training age, motor skill competency, technical proficiency, existing strength levels, and psychosocial maturity. Table 15.5 offers practical guidance on resistance training for youth athletes (Table 15.6).

Endurance

There are innumerable differences between children and adults in how energy metabolises during activity. In comparison to adults, children rely more on aerobic energy production and less on anaerobic glycolysis, meaning that they work at lower intensities, fatigue slower, and recover quicker. Growth and maturation influence energy metabolism through physiological changes such as increase size of the heart, blood volume, and haemoglobin content, higher proportion of type II muscle fibres, and greater anaerobic enzyme activity (Rowland, 2005; Harrison et al., 2015). Whilst there is conflicting evidence, it is suggested that the rate of improvement to absolute peak oxygen uptake and anaerobic energy system activity

Strength and Conditioning for Youth Football **265**

TABLE 15.5 Suggested Resistance Training Guidance Youth Football Players

	Beginner	*Intermediate*	*Experienced*	*Advanced*
Volume (sets × reps)	1–2 × 8–12	2–4 × 6–10	2–4 × 5–8	2–5 × 2–5
Total number of exercises per session	6–10	3–6	3–6	2–5
Estimated Intensity (% 1RM)	Body weight or 50–70	60–80	70–85	85–100
Rest Intervals (minutes)	1	1–2	2–3	2–5
Frequency (sessions per week)	2–3	2–3	2–4	2–5
Recovery (hours between sessions)	72–48	72–48	48	48–24

Adapted from Lloyd et al. (2012).

peaks around PHV. Therefore, a natural consequence of maturing means adolescents can work at higher intensities and perform better in endurance activities than before. However, this comes at the cost of higher rates of fatigue and taking longer to recover (Oliver and Harrison, 2019).

Although peak oxygen uptake and lactate threshold are trainable throughout childhood and adolescence, the high volume of football-specific training, competition, and training in different sports, means that developing endurance should be a relatively low priority in most youth S and C programmes, especially those pre-PHV. During such time, strength, and plyometric training should be prioritised in an attempt to improve the running economy. Furthermore, developing adequate strength in skeletal, muscular, and connective tissues will enhance a player's ability to tolerate the loadings experienced during aerobic or anaerobic activities. Players who are circa or post-PHV, may want to improve their endurance (i.e., peak oxygen uptake and lactate threshold) to improve their football performance. Whilst both continuous and intermittent exercise can stimulate improvements in young players, it may be prudent to limit the amount of continuous training exposure in maturing football players. A more time-efficient approach is suggested, with intermittent methods such as interval training, repeated sprints, and small-sided games (SSG) being effective for improving aerobic and anaerobic capabilities. In addition, intermittent training is likely to be more engaging and enjoyable as it is likely to be more representative of football and it can be designed to encourage competition. In particular, Harrison et al. (2015) suggest that youth team players from the age of 13 should participate in high-intensity intermittent work (90–95% HRmax), 2–3 times a week for 8–28 min. Such training should be comprised of high-intensity interval training (HIIT), sided games, and supplemented with repeated sprint training (4–6 maximal efforts with 20–120 s between repetitions). Tactical periodisation

266 Strength and Conditioning for Football

TABLE 15.6 Sample Strength and Power Sessions

Sample Strength and Power Sessions

Age Group	PRE-PHV	CIRCA-PHV	POST-PHV
	A1) Running Through the Jungle	**Foundation movements**	**Lower Body Strength and Power Session**
	Through storytelling, the players will aim to follow along by replicating the animals and actions that are within the story. E.g. "The frogs jumped across the stream" and the player will perform rebound jumps into a low squat position.	**(A1)** Partner Squat (3 × 12)	**(A1)** Trap Bar Jump 3 × 3
		(B1) Aqua-Bag Reverse Lunge (3 × 8 each leg)	**(A2)** Repeat Hurdle Jumps 3 × 4
		(C1) SL Assisted Hinge (3 × 8 each leg)	**(B1)** Rear Foot Elevated Split Squat 3 × 5
		(D1) Overhead Step-Up (3 × 6 each leg)	**(B2)** Single Leg Box Jump 3 × 3
	A2) Multi-Sport	**(E1)** Kneeling Pallof Press (3 × 12 each side)	**(C1)** SL RDL 3 × 5
	The use of gymnastics allows the players to explore different movements and challenges. You can base your exercise selection around fundamental movements such as rolling, swinging, and jumping.	**(F1)** Elevated Press-Up (3 × 12)	**(D1)** Lateral Slide Board Squat 2 × 6
		(G1) Assisted Pull-Ups (3 × 8)	**(D2)** Eccentric Slide Board Hamstring Curls 2 × 5
			(E1) Seated Calf Raise 2 × 12

models (i.e., using SSG, medium-sided games [MSG], and large-sided games [LSD]) have become popular in football training and are an effective tool in simultaneously developing the players capacity and skill (Gualtieri et al., 2023). However, for the stimuli to be of adequate intensity, the S and C and technical coach must effectively design pitch dimensions, number of players, and rules to evoke a physiological response. For example, the use of LSG have been shown to demand a greater distance per minute compared to SSG, whereas MSG affords increased accelerations compared to LSG (Beato et al., 2023). Although SSG formats may result in lesser distance per minute compared to larger formats, they have been shown to induce ~90% of max heart rate due to the metabolic demands of the intermittent activity (Owen et al., 2011). When you consider that training intensities of 90–95% of max heart rate can lead to improvements in aerobic fitness and subsequently improve football performance, it highlights the importance of monitoring the demands of the football drill formats within training sessions (Impellizzeri et al., 2006). It should also be considered that SSG formats have been demonstrated to achieve far less HSR and sprinting compared to LSG variations (Beato et al., 2023[2]). Therefore, if the adaptation desired within the training session aligns with the players performing specific actions such as high quantities of HSR or repeated accelerations, it is critical for the S and C coach to influence the session format and collaborate with the technical coach. As players mature, the structure of training increases and so too does the individualisation and specialisation of endurance training. At this point the S and C coach will need to consider the players' physical profile, training history, and positional demands before implementing appropriate strategies (Beato et al., 2024).

Practical Applications

To be successful, S and C coaches working with youth football players must be able to understand the practical implications of growth and maturation and long-term athletic development. Without said knowledge, it is unlikely that the S and C coach will be able to effectively optimise athleticism and/or mitigate the risk of certain injuries. When considering programme design there are some recommended principles. First, younger athletes should be exposed to a highly diverse programme designed to primarily develop FMS with low training structure and formality. This is followed by an exponential increase in training structure designed to refine FMS and develop specific and specialised physical qualities in late adolescence and early adulthood. Second, youth athletes will only adapt and develop when repeatedly exposed to relevant and desired stimuli. Therefore, using our understanding of natural physiological developments in youth players can help determine what adaptation is being targeted (i.e., pre-PHV – neural, circa and post-PHV – combination of morphological and neural).

References

Balyi, I., and Hamilton, A. (2004). Long-term athlete development: Trainability in childhood and adolescence. *Olympic Coach*, 16(1), 4–9.

Barth, M., Güllich, A., Macnamara, B. N., and Hambrick, D. Z. (2022). Predictors of junior versus senior elite performance are opposite: A systematic review and meta-analysis of participation patterns. *Sports Medicine*, 52(6), 1399–1416.

Beato, M., de Keijzer, K. L., and Costin, A. J. (2023). External and internal training load comparison between sided-game drills in professional soccer. *Frontiers in Sports and Active Living*, 5, 1150461.

Beato, M., Drust, B., and Iacono, A. D. (2021). Implementing high-speed running and sprinting training in professional soccer. *International Journal of Sports Medicine*, 42(4), 295–299.

Beato, M., Vicens-Bordas, J., Peña, J., and Costin, A. J. (2023). Training load comparison between small, medium, and large-sided games in professional football. *Frontiers in Sports and Active Living*, 5, 1165242.

268 Strength and Conditioning for Football

Beato, M., Youngs, A., and Costin, A. J. (2024). The analysis of physical performance during official competitions in professional English football: Do positions, game locations, and results influence players' Game demands?. *The Journal of Strength and Conditioning Research*, 38(5), e226–e234.

Bergeron, M. F., Mountjoy, M., Armstrong, N., Chia, M., Côté, J., Emery, C. A., . . . and Engebretsen, L. (2015). International Olympic Committee consensus statement on youth athletic development. *British Journal of Sports Medicine*, 49(13), 843–851.

Blimkie, C. J., Lefevre, J., Beunen, G. P., Renson, R. O. L. A. N. D., Dequeker, J., and Van Damme, P. (1993). Fractures, physical activity, and growth velocity in adolescent Belgian boys. *Medicine and Science in Sports and Exercise*, 25(7), 801–808.

Boeyer, M. E., Middleton, K. M., Duren, D. L., and Leary, E. V. (2020). Estimating peak height velocity in individuals: A comparison of statistical methods. *Annals of Human Biology*, 47(5), 434–445.

Bogin, B., Varea, C., Hermanussen, M., and Scheffler, C. (2018). Human life course biology: A centennial perspective of scholarship on the human pattern of physical growth and its place in human biocultural evolution.

Borms, J. (1986). The child and exercise: An overview. *Journal of Sports Sciences*, 4(1), 3–20.

Clark, P. A., and Rogol, A. D. (1996). Growth hormones and sex steroid interactions at puberty. *Endocrinology and Metabolism Clinics*, 25(3), 665–681.

Cohen, E., and Sala, D. A. (2010). Rehabilitation of pediatric musculoskeletal sport-related injuries: A review of the literature. *European Journal of Physical and Rehabilitation Medicine*, 46(2), 133–145.

Côté, J. (1999). The influence of the family in the development of talent in sport. *The Sport Psychologist*, 13(4), 395–417.

Côté, J., and Hay, J. (2002). Children's involvement in sport: A developmental perspective, 484–502.

Cupples, B., O'Connor, D., and Cobley, S. (2018). Distinct trajectories of athlete development: A retrospective analysis of professional rugby league players. *Journal of Sports Sciences*, 36(22), 2558–2566.

De Bosscher, V., Sotiriadou, P., Brouwers, J., and Truyens, J. (2015). Systems and athletes: Integrating the micro-and meso-level approaches to athlete development and success. In *Managing Elite Sport Systems* (pp. 155–173). Routledge.

Faigenbaum, A. D., French, D. N., Lloyd, R. S., and Kraemer, W. J. (2019). Strength and power training for young athletes. In *Strength and Conditioning for Young Athletes* (pp. 131–154). Routledge

Ford, P., De Ste Croix, M., Lloyd, R., Meyers, R., Moosavi, M., Oliver, J., . . . and Williams, C. (2011). The long-term athlete development model: Physiological evidence and application. *Journal of Sports Sciences*, 29(4), 389–402.

Froehle, A. W., Nahhas, R. W., Sherwood, R. J., and Duren, D. L. (2013). Age-related changes in spatiotemporal characteristics of gait accompany ongoing lower limb linear growth in late childhood and early adolescence. *Gait and Posture*, 38(1), 14–19.

Gregson, W., Drust, B., Atkinson, G., and Salvo, V. D. (2010). Match-to-match variability of high-speed activities in premier league soccer. *International Journal of Sports Medicine*, 31(04), 237–242.

Gualtieri, A., Rampinini, E., Dello Iacono, A., and Beato, M. (2023). High-speed running and sprinting in professional adult soccer: Curret thresholds definition, match demands and training strategies. A systematic review. *Frontiers in Sports and Active Living*, 5, 1116293.

Güllich, A., Macnamara, B. N., and Hambrick, D. Z. (2022). What makes a champion? Early multidisciplinary practice, not early specialization, predicts world-class performance. *Perspectives on Psychological Science*, 17(1), 6–29.

Harrison, C. B., Gill, N. D., Kinugasa, T., and Kilding, A. E. (2015). Development of aerobic fitness in young team sport athletes. *Sports Medicine*, 45, 969–983.

Hewett, T. E., Myer, G. D., Ford, K. R., Heidt Jr, R. S., Colosimo, A. J., McLean, S. G., ... and Succop, P. (2005). Biomechanical measures of neuromuscular control and valgus loading of the knee predict anterior cruciate ligament injury risk in female athletes: A prospective study. *The American Journal of Sports Medicine*, 33(4), 492–501.

Higgs, C., Balyi, I., Way, R., Cardinal, C., Norris, S., and Bluechardt, M. (2008). *Developing Physical Literacy: A Guide for Parents of Children Ages 0 to 12*. Vancouver, BC: Canadian Sports Centres.

Hill, M., John, T., McGee, D., and Cumming, S. P. (2023). 'He's got growth': Coaches understanding and management of the growth spurt in male academy football. *International Journal of Sports Science and Coaching*, 18(1), 24–37.

Hill, M., Scott, S., McGee, D., and Cumming, S. (2020). Coaches' evaluations of match performance in academy soccer players in relation to the adolescent growth spurt. *Journal of Science in Sport and Exercise*, 2, 359–366.

Impellizzeri, F. M., Marcora, S. M., Castagna, C., Reilly, T., Sassi, A., Iaia, F. M., and Rampinini, E. (2006). Physiological and performance effects of generic versus specific aerobic training in soccer players. *International Journal of Sports Medicine*, 27(6), 483–492.

Jeffreys, I. (2006). Motor learning-applications for agility, Part 1. *Strength and Conditioning Journal*, 28(5), 72–76.

Jeffreys, I. (2017). *Gamespeed: Movement Training for Superior Sports Performance*. Coaches Choice.

Kemper, G. L. J., Van Der Sluis, A., Brink, M. S., Visscher, C., Frencken, W. G. P., and Elferink-Gemser, M. T. (2015). Anthropometric injury risk factors in elite-standard youth soccer. *International Journal of Sports Medicine*, 36(13), 1112–1117.

Lloyd, R. S., Cronin, J. B., Faigenbaum, A. D., Haff, G. G., Howard, R., Kraemer, W. J., ... and Oliver, J. L. (2016). National Strength and Conditioning Association position statement on long-term athletic development. *Journal of Strength and Conditioning Research*, 30(6), 1491–1509.

Lloyd, R. S., Faigenbaum, A. D., Myer, G. D., Stone, M., Oliver, J., Jeffreys, I., and Pierce, K. J. (2012). UKSCA position statement: Youth resistance training. *Professional Strength and Conditioning*, 26, 26–39.

Lloyd, R. S., Moeskops, S., and Granacher, U. (2019a). Coaching young athletes. In *Strength and Conditioning for Young Athletes* (pp. 103–130).

Lloyd, R. S., Moeskops, S., and Granacher, U. (2019b). Motor skill training in young athletes. In *Strength and Conditioning for Young Athletes* (pp. 103–130). Routledge.

Lloyd, R. S., and Oliver, J. L. (2012). The youth physical development model: A new approach to long-term athletic development. *Strength and Conditioning Journal*, 34(3), 61–72.

Lloyd, R. S., Oliver, J. L., and Cumming, S., eds. (2014). Working with younger athletes. In *High-Performance Training for Sports*. Human Kinetics.

Lloyd, R. S., Read, P., Oliver, J. L., Meyers, R. W., Nimphius, S., and Jeffreys, I. (2013). Considerations for the development of agility during childhood and adolescence. *Strength and Conditioning Journal*, 35(3), 2–11.

Malina, R. M., Coelho, E., Silva, M. J., Figueiredo, A. J., Carling, C., and Beunen, G. P. (2012). Interrelationships among invasive and non-invasive indicators of biological maturation in adolescent male soccer players. *Journal of Sports Sciences*, 30(15), 1705–1717.

Malina, R. M., Eisenmann, J. C., Cumming, S. P., Ribeiro, B., and Aroso, J. (2004). Maturity-associated variation in the growth and functional capacities of youth football (soccer) players 13–15 years. *European Journal of Applied Physiology*, 91, 555–562.

Malina, R. M., Rogol, A. D., Cumming, S. P., e Silva, M. J. C., and Figueiredo, A. J. (2015). Biological maturation of youth athletes: Assessment and implications. *British Journal of Sports Medicine*, 49(13), 852–859.

Meylan, C. M. P., Cronin, J. B., Oliver, J. L., Hopkins, W. G., and Contreras, B. (2014a). The effect of maturation on adaptations to strength training and detraining in 11–15-year-olds. *Scandinavian Journal of Medicine and Science in Sports*, 24(3), 156–164.

Meylan, C. M., Cronin, J. B., Oliver, J. L., Hughes, M. G., and Manson, S. (2014b). An evidence-based model of power development in youth soccer. *International Journal of Sports Science and Coaching*, 9(5), 1241–1264.

Monasterio, X., Gil, S. M., Bidaurrazaga-Letona, I., Lekue, J. A., Santisteban, J., Diaz-Beitia, G., . . . and Larruskain, J. (2021). Injuries according to the percentage of adult height in an elite soccer academy. *Journal of Science and Medicine in Sport*, 24(3), 218–223.

Monasterio, X., Gil, S. M., Bidaurrazaga-Letona, I., Lekue, J. A., Santisteban, J. M., Diaz-Beitia, G., . . . and Larruskain, J. (2023a). The burden of injuries according to maturity status and timing: A two-decade study with 110 growth curves in an elite football academy. *European Journal of Sport Science*, 23(2), 267–277.

Moran, J., Sandercock, G., Rumpf, M. C., and Parry, D. A. (2017). Variation in responses to sprint training in male youth athletes: A meta-analysis. *International Journal of Sports Medicine*, 38(1), 1–11.

Myer, G. D., Lloyd, R. S., Brent, J. L., and Faigenbaum, A. D. (2013). How young is "too young" to start training? *ACSM's Health and Fitness Journal*, 17(5), 14.

Nimphius, S., McGuigan, M. R., and Newton, R. U. (2010). Relationship between strength, speed, and change of direction performance of female softball players. *Journal of Strength and Conditioning Research*, 24, 885–895.

Oliver, J. L., and Harrison, C. B. (2019). Aerobic and anaerobic training for young athletes. In *Strength and Conditioning for Young Athletes: Science and Application* (pp. 248–278). Routledge.

Oliver, J. L., Lloyd, R. S., and Rumpf, M. C. (2013). Developing speed throughout childhood and adolescence: The role of growth, maturation and training. *Strength and Conditioning Journal*, 35(3), 42–48.

Owen, A. L., Wong, D. P., McKenna, M., and Dellal, A. (2011). Heart rate responses and technical comparison between small-vs. large-sided games in elite professional soccer. *The Journal of Strength and Conditioning Research*, 25(8), 2104–2110.

Philippaerts, R. M., Vaeyens, R., Janssens, M., Van Renterghem, B., Matthys, D., Craen, R., . . . and Malina, R. M. (2006). The relationship between peak height velocity and physical performance in youth soccer players. *Journal of Sports Sciences*, 24(3), 221–230.

Pichardo, A. W., Oliver, J. L., Harrison, C. B., Maulder, P. S., and Lloyd, R. S. (2018). Integrating models of long-term athletic development to maximize the physical development of youth. *International Journal of Sports Science and Coaching*, 13(6), 1189–1199.

Quatman-Yates, C. C., Quatman, C. E., Meszaros, A. J., Paterno, M. V., and Hewett, T. E. (2012). A systematic review of sensorimotor function during adolescence: A developmental stage of increased motor awkwardness? *British Journal of Sports Medicine*, 46(9), 649–655.

Rabinowicz, T. (1986). The differentiated maturation of the cerebral cortex. In *Postnatal Growth Neurobiology* (pp. 385–410). Boston, MA: Springer US.

Reynolds, J., Connor, M., Jamil, M., and Beato, M. (2021). Quantifying and comparing the match demands of U18, U23, and 1ST team English professional soccer players. *Frontiers in Physiology*, 12, 706451.

Rodríguez-Rosell, D., Franco-Márquez, F., Pareja-Blanco, F., Mora-Custodio, R., Yáñez-García, J. M., González-Suárez, J. M., and González-Badillo, J. J. (2016). Effects of 6 weeks resistance training combined with plyometric and speed exercises on physical performance of pre-peak-height-velocity soccer players. *International Journal of Sports Physiology and Performance*, 11(2), 240–246.

Rowland, T. (2005). *Children's Exercise Physiology*. Champaign: Human Kinetics.

Rumpf, M. C., Cronin, J. B., Oliver, J. L., and Hughes, M. G. (2013). Vertical and leg stiffness and stretch-shortening cycle changes across maturation during maximal sprint running. *Human Movement Science*, 32(4), 668–676.

Rumpf, M. C., Cronin, J. B., Pinder, S. D., Oliver, J., and Hughes, M. (2012). Effect of different training methods on running sprint times in male youth. *Pediatric Exercise Science*, 24(2), 170–186.

Sander, A., Keiner, M., Wirth, K., and Schmidtbleicher, D. (2013). Influence of a 2-year strength training programme on power performance in elite youth soccer players. *European Journal of Sport Science*, 13(5), 445–451.

Sheppard, J. M., and Young, W. B. (2006). Agility literature review: Classifications, training and testing. *Journal of Sport Science*, 24, 919–932.

Stewart, P. F., Carroll, N. P., and Turner, A. N. (2019) Strength, power, speed, and agility in soccer. In *Elite Soccer Players: Maximizing Performance and Safety* (p. 175–198). Routledge.

Stone, M. H. (1993). Position statement: Explosive exercise and training. *Strength and Conditioning Journal*, 15(3), 7–15.

Towlson, C., Salter, J., Ade, J. D., Enright, K., Harper, L. D., Page, R. M., and Malone, J. J. (2021). Maturity-associated considerations for training load, injury risk, and physical performance in youth soccer: One size does not fit all. *Journal of Sport and Health Science*, 10(4), 403–412.

Van Der Sluis, A., Elferink-Gemser, M. T., Coelho-e-Silva, M. J., Nijboer, J. A., Brink, M. S., and Visscher, C. (2013). Sport injuries aligned to peak height velocity in talented pubertal soccer players. *International Journal of Sports Medicine*, 35(04), 351–355.

Viru, A., Loko, J., Harro, M., Volver, A., Laaneots, L., and Viru, M. (1999). Critical periods in the development of performance capacity during childhood and adolescence. *European Journal of Physical Education*, 4(1), 75–119.

16

CONSIDERATIONS FOR DISABILITY FOOTBALL

Dave Sims

Introduction

Impairment football is adapted football formats that allow people with physical and sensory impairments to participant in footballing activities between grassroots and elite levels. 'Para football' is a term used to describe the footballing activities of people with impairments that run 'parallel' to mainstream, able-bodied formats. There are currently a host of different Para football formats that are available to people with physical and sensory impairments, of which The English Football Association currently oversees the provision of five specific formats: (i) blind, (ii) partially sighted, (iii) deaf, (iv) cerebral palsy (CP), and (v) powerchair whilst also including amputee football within their annual Disability Cup. These formats are not exhaustive to Para football but will be the focus of this chapter. For more information on other formats, such as Down syndrome, frame, and dwarf football, the reader is encouraged to visit www.parafootball.com.

Para football is gaining more global recognition, due in part to the Paralympics, but more so due to the governing bodies of individual countries providing greater opportunities, finance, and support for players with impairments to play. Para football encompasses the ethos of football in that 'anyone can play' but differs to the able-bodied 11-a-side game, in respect to the formats and adapted rules available for different impairments. The game is modified to suit the impairment to ensure it is physically demanding but also fair for all players in each respective format (see Table 16.1 for a description of impairment-specific formats). Men's blind football is currently the only Para football format included in the Paralympic games after CP football was removed following Rio 2016. However, all formats have their respective world and continental major championships.

DOI: 10.4324/9781003383475-17

Considerations for Disability Football **273**

Formats of Para Football

Blind and Partially Sighted Football

Blind football uses a 5-a-side format (outdoor pitch dimensions of 40 × 20 m) over 2 × 20-minute stop clock halves, following futsal rules, where the four outfield players are blind (B1 classification [IBSA, 2017]). In contrast, goalkeepers are fully sighted (able-bodied) and are only allowed to work in a 2 × 6 m area. Blind football also has 1.2 m high sideboards that act as an echo rebounding soundboard but also to aid in keeping the ball in play for longer. A major rule modification is that defending players must say 'voy' when an attacking player is close by so that attacking players have an audible cue as to the location of the defender. Naturally, this is also an attempt to lower the incidence of injury by mitigating the risk of players running into each other. The ball is also adapted for blind players in that it contains six hollow metal panels containing metal ball bearings within them which make the ball audible for players to detect. The ball is also heavier than a standard futsal ball allowing the ball to stay on the floor for longer. This makes the ball more audible due to the ball bearings moving more frequently when the ball is in contact with the floor. Similarly, partially sighted football uses a 5-a-side format (indoor pitch dimensions of 40 × 20 m) over 2 × 20-minute stop clock halves, following futsal rules with the four outfield players being partially sighted (B2 and B3 classification). Goalkeepers are fully sighted (able-bodied) and are only allowed to work within the D-shaped area of the futsal court. There are no other adaptions to this format of the game compared to able-bodied futsal.

Cerebral Palsy Football

CP football uses a 7-a-side format (outdoor pitch dimensions between 70 and 75 × 50 and 55 m) over 2 × 30-minute halves, where all players are impacted by their impairment to greater or lesser extents than others on the pitch (Football (FT), one to three classifications, respectively, IFCPF (2018)). There must be at least 1 × FT1 on the pitch at any one time and teams are only allowed to field 1 × FT3 at any one time. If teams fail to field an FT1, they can replace this player with an FT2 but must play with six players. Major rule adaptions for this format are that there are no offsides and players can roll the ball back into play instead of a 'throw in' as some players do not have the shoulder mobility or range of motion to perform a traditional able-bodied throw in.

Amputee Football

Amputee football also uses a 7-a-side format (outdoor pitch dimensions of between 70 and 75 × 50 and 55 m) over 2 × 30-minute halves. Outfield players have a single leg amputation above or below their knee and use two crutches for mobility.

274 Strength and Conditioning for Football

Goalkeepers have a single arm amputation above or below the elbow and their amputated arm must be strapped to their side when in goal. The major rule changes in this format are that a 'hand ball' is committed when the ball hits any part of the players' crutch and that 'throw ins' are performed as 'kick ins' from where the ball exited the pitch dimensions.

Powerchair Football

Powerchair football is a 4-a-sdie format (indoor pitch dimension of 29 × 15 m) played over 2 × 20 min halves. All players play in modified, motorised chairs with a foot plate that is used to 'kick' the ball by manipulating the chair through fine motor skills. The ball is a large, 33 cm diameter ball. Players are classified as powerchair football (PF) 1 and 2 and teams must always field at least two PF1s.

Deaf Football

There are no modifications to deaf football or deaf futsal, compared to able-bodied formats. The only adaption to this format is that referees and assistants must use flags instead of whistles when stopping/starting play. For this chapter, only deaf 11-a-side football is being discussed.

Classification

Para athletes must show their impairment is of a significant severity to be allowed to compete locally, nationally, and/or internationally. The process by which Para footballers are given their impairment severity is called 'classification' and works in the same manner as other Para sports. Classification is a tiered system whereby the impairment is given a letter code, whilst the severity of the impairment is given a number, with smaller numbers indicating a more severe impairment. For example, within visually impairment football, athletes are classified as 'B' with the severity ranging from B1 (visual acuity <2.60 LogMAR) to B5 (visual acuity >0.6 - ≤0.48 LogMAR) (IBSA, 2017). However, in Para football, only B2 and B3 players classify to play partially sighted football, whilst only B1 classifications can play blind football. Note, in blind football, players must also wear eye patches and shades to eliminate any light perception some players may have.

Classification within Para football can be both subjective (technical) and objective (clinical) observation of how their impairment effects them to perform physical and technical elements of the respective formats. For most impairments, there can be up to three classifications a player may fall under (see Table 16.1) and are assessed in several ways to ensure that those participating in sanctioned events are competing at a fair and equal level. In most impairments, there are multiple classifications playing amongst outfield and goalkeeper positions, and in the majority of cases, this does not deter from the ability of players to compete between

TABLE 16.1 Para Football Formats, Rules and Key

Impairment	Classification	Classification Assessment	Classification Eligibility	Format	Dimensions	Substitutions	Offside	Adapted Rules
Blind	B1	- Ophthalmologist assessment alongside medical notes	- Visual acuity poorer than LogMAR 2.60	5-a-side	~40 × ~25 m	Rolling	No	- All outfield players must wear adhesive patches over both eyes as well as conforming eye mask to eliminate any light perception players may have - The ball is a size 4 and contains 6 × metal panels with ball bearings to make the ball audible for players - Side boards to keep ball in play and act as a echo rebound - Goal keepers are fully sighted and are only allowed to work in a 2 × 6 m area - Defenders to say "voy" to allow attackers an audible location of them

(Continued)

TABLE 16.1 (Continued)

Impairment	Classification	Classification Assessment	Classification Eligibility	Format	Dimensions	Substitutions	Offside	Adapted Rules
Cerebral Palsy	FT1	All CP players are assessed clinically and technically. The subtle differences between classifications are provided below: – Difficulty making turns, pivoting, or stopping – Run shorter distances and are slower over known distances – Reduced step length – Limited upper body range of motion – Increased muscle tone and reduced range of motion in affected leg – Reduced balance in affected leg(s)	– Diplegia – Asymmetric diplegia – Double hemiplegia – Dystonia	7-a-side	~70 × ~60 m	3	No	– Teams can field no more than 1 FT3 at any one time – There are no offsides – Players are allowed to roll balls back into play as well as performing a traditional throw in
	FT2	– Difficulty making turns, pivoting, or stopping – Run shorter distances and are slower over known distances – Obvious and pronounced limp	– Athetosis – Ataxia – Mixed cerebral palsy – Hemiplegia					

	FT3	– Reduced step length on affected leg(s) – Limited upper body range of motion in affected arm(s) – Increased muscle tone and reduced range of motion in affected leg(s) – Reduced balance in affected leg(s) – Relatively 'normal' gait when walking, jogging and running, compared to FT1 and FT2 – Will have some spasticity in affected leg(s) but is not detrimental to performance – Passing and finishing can be impaired in athletes with athetosis or ataxia – Athletes may walk with a slight limp	– Asymmetric diplegia or diplegia – Double hemiplegia – Dystonia – Spastic hemiplegia grade 1–2 – Monoplegia with spasticity to a greater degree – Athetosis – Ataxia or mixed cerebral palsy					
Powerchair	PF1	All CP players are assessed clinically and technically. The subtle differences between classifications are provided below:	- Cerebral palsy, traumatic brain injury, stroke, Friedreich's ataxia, progressive neurological conditions	5-a-side	~30 × ~18 m	Rolling	Yes	– The ball is 33 cm in diameter

(*Continued*)

TABLE 16.1 (Continued)

Impairment Classification	Classification Assessment	Classification Eligibility	Format	Dimensions	Substitutions	Offside	Adapted Rules
	This denotes a player who has moderate to mild levels of physical difficulty which affects their overall performance. These include - Reflex activity - Fine motor control - Gross motor movement pattern - Fluency of motor skill movements	- Orthopaedic disorders such as arthritis – all four extremities, arthrogryposis, some types of dwarfism, brittle bone disease (Osteogenesis-Imperfecta) - Amputations, congenital or acquired, where there is three or four limb involvement above the knee and elbow, or double upper limb amputation above the elbow - Myopathies such as muscular dystrophies, spinal muscular atrophy, amyotonia congenita - Spinal cord injury such as polio, Guillain-Barre, tetraplegia					- Chairs are motorised with a modified front bumber to 'kick' the ball
PF2	This denotes a player who has moderate to mild levels of physical difficulty which affects their overall performance. These include - Reflex activity - Fine motor control	- Cerebral palsy, traumatic brain injury, stroke, Frederic's ataxia, progressive neurological conditions - Orthopaedic disorders such as arthritis – all four extremities, arthrogryposis, some types of dwarfism, BRITTLE bone disease (Osteogenesis-Imperfecta)					

Disability	Class	Assessment	Criteria	Team	Pitch	Subs		Notes
		- Gross motor movement pattern - Fluency of motor skill movements These criteria can combine to affect the performance of a player but it is evident that they are more functionally effective as athletes in the category of PF1	- Amputations, congenital or acquired, where there is three or four limb involvement above the knee and elbow, or double upper limb amputation above the elbow - Myopathies such as muscular dystrophies, spinal muscular atrophy, amyotonia congenita - Spinal cord injury such as polio, Guillain-Barre, tetraplegia					
Partially Sighted	B2	- Ophthalmologist assessment alongside medical notes	- Visual acuity ranging from LogMAR 1.50 to 2.60 - Visual field constricted to a diameter of less than 10 degrees	5	~40 × ~25 m	Rolling	No	- Goal keepers are fully sighted and are only allowed to work in The standard futsal Goal keeping area
	B3		- Visual acuity ranging from LogMAR 1.40 to 1 (inclusive) - Visual field constricted to a diameter of less than 40 degrees					
Deaf	Deaf	- Determined through audiologist assessment	- Hearing loss of <55 dB in dominant hearing ear - 3 tone frequency average of 500, 1,000 and 2,000 Hz, ANSI 1969 standard	11-a-side	~100-~50 m	3	Yes	- Players must not play with any hearing aid device during match play - Referees must use flags as well as whistles to stop play

(*Continued*)

TABLE 16.1 (Continued)

Impairment	Classification	Classification Assessment	Classification Eligibility	Format	Dimensions	Substitutions	Offside	Adapted Rules
Amputee	A2	- Confirmed via physical assessment and through medical notes	- Unilateral below the knee (proximally) lower limb amputations - Play can only play as an outfield player - Player must use standard, unmodifiable crutches	7-a-side	~70 × ~60 m	Rolling	No	- If the ball touches a crutch at any point, it is considered 'handball' - Players kick the ball back into play instead of a throw in
	A4		- Unilateral above the knee (distally) lower limb amputations - Play can only play as an outfield player - Player must use standard, unmodifiable crutches					
	A6		- Unilateral below the elbow (proximally) upper limb amputations - Play can only play as a goalkeeper - Players must have their amputated arm strapped to their side, inside their playing shirt					
	A8		- Unilateral above the elbow (distally) upper limb amputations - Play can only play as a goalkeeper - Players must have their amputated arm strapped to their side, inside their playing shirt					

Considerations for Disability Football **281**

classifications within their impairment. However, where physical impairments exist (e.g., within CP football), the severity of impairment appears to impact the outcome of matches due to the more dominant physical characteristics of the less impaired players (FT3) compared to the more impaired players (FT1) (Gamonales, Muñoz-Jiménez, Gómez-Carmona, and Ibáñez, 2022; Reina et al., 2021); see Table 16.2 and section titled *Impairment Specific Formats* in the current chapter, for a more detailed overview of the topic.

Para Football vs Able Bodied Football

Major international tournaments for Para football are typically shorter in duration (i.e., time from opening game to final) and have fewer competitive matches than able-bodied equivalents due to a lower number of national entrants/qualifiers. However, Para teams are required to play matches beyond the group stage to 'classify' the position a team has finished in the tournament. This is important as it contributes to the team/nation's national, continental, and/or world ranking. Group stage and classification matches are often played without rest days or with only one rest day between fixtures. For example, in the 2019 and 2022 CP World Cup, teams played every other day until the classification matches, where two rest days were permitted, whereas in the 2022 Blind European Championships, teams were expvected to play every other day during a 14-day tournament.

In able-bodied football, it is well established that following match play activity, players have increased levels of neuromuscular fatigue, loss of power, increased levels of muscle damage (Beattie, Fahey, Pullinger, Edwards, and Robertson, 2020), which are also position dependent (Schuth et al., 2021), and observe a depletion in glycogen levels meaning that recovery can take up to three days (Nédélec et al., 2012). Increased muscle damage can lead to reduced power output and force production, knee flexion range of motion (a criterion of impairment classification in CP football) and aerobic performance (Howatson and Milak, 2009; Hunkin, Fahrner, and Gastin, 2014; Beattie, Fahey, Pullinger, Edwards, and Robertson, 2020; Mohr, Krustrup, and Bangsbo, 2003) with peak power output correlating negatively ($r = -0.349$ to -0.390, $p \leq 0.05$) and muscle damage correlating positively ($r = 0.363–0.433$, $p \leq 0.05$) with game related movements, such as number of sprints and high intensity running in able-bodied football (Russell et al., 2016; Thorpe and Sunderland, 2012). Importantly, muscle damage measures, such as creatine kinase, peak on the second day of recovery following match play in able-bodied footballers (Baird, Graham, Baker, and Bickerstaff, 2012; Mohr, Krustrup, and Bangsbo, 2003). Thus, having equal to, or fewer than, two rest days between matches, as is the case in international Para football tournaments, is only likely to increase neuromuscular fatigue, muscle damage, and psychological stress in the Para players through a tournament.

When considering impairments such as CP, there is already an exacerbation of strength and power loss of paretic limbs compared to non-paretic limbs and to able-bodied individuals (Hussain, Onambélé, Williams, and Morse, 2014, 2017).

TABLE 16.2 Global Positioning System Characteristics of Para Football and Able-Bodied Formats Found in the Literature. Key Variables Stated as Mean (SD) or Median [IQR]

Reference	Impairment	No. of Players	Level of Play	Duration	Total Distance (m)	Low Walking (m)	Walking (m)	Jogging (m)	ISR (m)	HSR (m)	Sprinting (m)	Ave. Speed (kph)	Max Speed (kph)	Ave. HR (bpm)	Ave. HR (%)
Gamonales et al. (2021a)[d]	Blind	28	International	40[f]	1,654 (182)					2.72 (2.03)	0.02 (0.11)	3.01 (0.18)	15.06 (0.91)	143 (4)	71 (2)
Gamonales et al. (2021b)[d]	Blind	50	International	40[f]						2.64 (2.37)	0.05 (0.16)			143 (4)	
Papadopoulos et al. (2022)	Blind	6	National	40[f]	1,820 (342)							2.03 (0.48)		159 (10)	
Boyd et al. (2014)[e]	Cerebral Palsy	40	International	60	5,839 (668)					13 (2)	13 (4)		25.74 (1.62)	163 (13)	
Yanci et al. (2018)[d, e]	Cerebral Palsy	42	International	60	92.6 (13.5)	1.11 (0.68)	8.30 (4.94)	40.02 (4.84)	27.87 (9.18)	12.0 (4.52)	3.27 (1.96)		22.8 (2.3)		
Yanci et al. (2019)[e]	Cerebral Palsy	31	International	60	4,342 (1,808)	56.6 (49.3)	408.7 (363.9)	1,920.0 (821.1)	1,270.3 (600.0)	537.6 (283.4)	148 (97)		22.7 (2.3)		
Gamonales et al. (2022)[d]	Cerebral Palsy FT1	5	International	60	60.55 (23.62)	38.06 (8.72)	16.72 (12.90)	5.40 (5.95)	0.96 (1.76)	0.06 (0.18)	0.00 (0.00)				
	Cerebral Palsy FT2	5	International	60	84.24 (17.27)	41.97 (3.21)	29.54 (10.28)	23.49 (6.26)	3.85 (3.6)	0.54 (0.76)	0.11 (0.25)				
	Cerebral Palsy FT3	2	International	60	106.42 (9.59)	39.80 (5.08)	36.50 (4.43)	23.49 (6.26)	9.87 (3.65)	1.79 (1.14)	0.32 (0.23)				
Henríquez et al. (2021)[d]	Cerebral Palsy	14	National	30	99.43 (9.48)	14.79 (1.90)	41.56 (4.84)	30.41 (8.33)	9.64 (3.01)	2.47 (1.37)	0.64 (0.55)		22.59 (1.87)	159 (14)	
Peña-Gónzalez et al. (2021)	Cerebral Palsy	10	National	60	3,891 (2,133)					475.8 (355.8)				154 (22)	
Reina et al. (2021)[d]	Cerebral Palsy	259	International	60	84.51 (16.50)	2.68 (1.21)	10.16 (5.03)	42.33 (8.52)	19.38 (25.45)	9.47 (5.46)	3.05 (2.79)	5.07 (0.99)	22.58 (3.18)		
	Cerebral Palsy FT1	42	International	60	81.26 (15.35)	2.03 (0.85)	12.21 (8.32)	39.45 (9.14)	17.21 (7.32)	8.08 (4.97)	2.04 (2.09)	4.87 (0.93)	21.28 (2.86)		

Study	Group	n	Level													
Yanci et al. (2022)[d]	Cerebral Palsy FT2	177	International	60	85.23 (17.05)	1.69 (0.99)	9.92 (4.11)	42.54 (8.17)	20.33 (30.42)	9.81 (5.59)	3.18 (2.82)	5.12 (1.02)	22.74 (3.05)		
	Cerebral Palsy FT3	40	International	60	84.75 (5.13)	1.78 (1.11)	9.10 (3.54)	44.40 (8.78)	17.47 (6.26)	9.45 (5.30)	3.56 (3.11)	5.09 (0.91)	23.22 (3.75)		
	Cerebral Palsy	170	International	60	84.94 (15.99)	3.16 (18.54)	10.39 (5.29)	41.86 (7.71)	18.05 (7.49)	9.56 (5.52)	3.17 (2.99)	5.10 (0.96)	22.50 (3.04)		
Maehana et al. (2018)	Amputee	12	National	50	2,984 (562)									177 (8)	96 (5)
Panagiotopoulou et al. (2020)	Amputee	10	National	50	3,388 (638)	1,608.5 (246.1)	1,418.7 (424.9)	594.1 (276.6)	82.2 (68.5)	1.28 (1.86)	0 (0)			153 (11)	83 (6)
Esatbeyoglu et al. (2022)[d]	Amputee	5	National	50	102.62 (7.24)	73.86 (0.57)	16.97 (1.20)	9.04 (0.21)	2.46 (0.23)	0.24 (0.04)		11.46 (0.80)	35.25 (0.50)	152 (16)	
Ravé (2020)	Male Football		Professional	90	10,690.5 (924.5)					705.0 (183.6)	342.0 (72.5)				
Ingebrigsten et al. (2015)[b]	Male Football	59	Professional	90	10,896 (950)	3,953 (291)	4,691 (662)	1,577 (421)		686 (248)	160 (76)				
Ingebrigsten et al. (2015)[c]	Male Football	42	Professional	90	11,699 (858)	3,868 (234)	4,732 (515)	2,014 (399)		1,084 (288)	287 (211)				
Bueno et al. (2014)	Male Futsal (AB)	93	Professional	40	*3,133 [2,249]*						*7.75 [2.4]*				
Serrano et al. (2020)[d, a]	Male Futsal (AB)	14	Professional	37.1 (13.6)	3,375 (1,139)						15	6.18			
Beato et al. (2017)	Female Futsal (AB)	16	National	40	2,737 (207)					50 (33)	4.02 (0.30)				83 (3)

ISR = Intermittent Speed Running; HSR = High Speed Running; AB = Able-bodied; [a] Positional data is reported in this paper, the means of the positions were averaged and inputted into this table, hence why there is no (SD); [b] Central playing positions included only here; [c] Wide playing positions included here only; [d] data presented per min of activity; [e] data collected before a classification rule change; [f] time recorded on a stop clock.

284 Strength and Conditioning for Football

Therefore, the effects of tournament football on neuromuscular fatigue and muscle damage may be even more pronounced in this impairment but likely occur in other Para football impairments too. This may provoke acute and/or chronic central fatigue and increases in psychological stress associated with match play demands as observed in able-bodied football (Nédélec et al., 2012). Combined, this may ultimately lead to a reduction in technical performance, increases in injuries, and athlete burnout, as has been observed in able-bodied football (Ekstand, Walden, and Haqqlund, 2004) and other team sports (Hunkin, Fahrner, and Gastin, 2014).

Programming physical performance and/or strength and conditioning programmes for any athlete is a complex, dynamic, and challenging task, but is much easier when working with able-bodied footballers given the wealth and depth of research available in the respective sport. For Para footballers, there is still the same complexity when programming, but with the added complications of the athlete's impairment, the format they play, and the lack of available data surrounding the format(s). At present, there are no available guidelines to better prepare Para footballers leading into major tournaments. This is in part due to the lack of data available in each format to objectively build a programme that will combat the physical effects of an intense tournament schedule. For the practitioner, it is advised that considerations are made when designing and developing a strength and conditioning programme, that incorporates player benchmarking and monitoring, match analysis, ideally through global positioning systems (GPS), to identify and replicate movement patterns and a clear periodised programme that emphasises the huge demand that tournament play elicits on the players. There should also be an emphasis on a structured strength programme to help mitigate injury risk, however, there will be scenarios whereby exercise selection is critical due to the players' ability, or inability, to complete the exercise with correct form due to their impairment. The following sections will outline the major components of strength and conditioning programming for the Para footballer with regards to the demands of the formats, exercise selection, and modification for those athletes that require it. These are predominantly based on anecdotal evidence from the author's >10 years' experience with these populations, as well as using the available literature to guide the reader.

Practical Applications: Strength and Conditioning in Para Footballers

When working with any new athlete, a strength and conditioning practitioner will ultimately use the available literature for guidance around what the athletes' needs are during competition. This will ultimately determine a periodised programme leading into a major tournament or event so the athlete can cope with the demands of the event and allow them to perform at their maximum physical capability with a planned reduced risk of non-contact injury. This section provides an overview of the available literature to describe the match and training demands of each of the Para football formats before then providing some recommendations around programming and exercise selection for specific impairments.

Match and Training Load Analysis in Para Football

Impairment Specific Formats

The introduction of GPS within individual and team sports has brought about a huge technological advance in sport, by providing data analytics of movement patterns, conditioning strategies, and aiding session design (Beato et al., 2017). While able-bodied football has a plethora of in-house and published GPS research, there appears to be little transfer to Para football. An extensive literature review for this chapter demonstrated that there are no publicly available data describing the kinematic movements of visually impaired and deaf football (male and female), nor of electric wheelchairs. Given that deaf football is predominantly 11-a-side and futsal based, while partially sighted football is a futsal format, it is recommended that practitioners refer to the available able-bodied literature of those formats when planning programmes for these impairments (some reference data is provided in Table 16.2), although data on these impairments is still necessary to truly programme effectively.

Of the available literature, blind (Gamonales, Muñoz Jiménez, Mancha-Triguero, and Ibáñez, 2021b; Gamonales, León, Rojas-Valverde, Sánchez-Ureña, and Muñoz-Jiménez, 2021a; Papadopoulos et al., 2022), CP (Boyd et al., 2016; Gamonales, Muñoz-Jiménez, Gómez-Carmona, and Ibáñez, 2022; González, Marin, Triguero, Ramon, and Puerto, 2021; Henríquez et al., 2021; Reina et al., 2021; Yanci, Castillo, Iturricastillo, Urbán, and Reina, 2018; Yanci, Castillo, Iturricastillo, and Reina, 2019; Yanci, Iturricastillo, Henríquez, Roldan, and Reina, 2022) and amputee (Maehana, Suzuki, Koshiyama, and Yoshimura, 2018; Panagiotopoulo, 2020; Esatbeyoglu, Hazir, and İsler, 2022) seem to be the most prevalent in GPS match descriptions, although this is still limited and some descriptions of the game within the available articles are sparse. It is worth noting here that there was a significant rule change within CP football in 2018, where classification moved from a four-tier system (FT5-8), with more severe presentations of CP receiving an FT5 classification and the least severe presentations receiving an FT8 classification, to a three-tier system as it is now (FT1-3) (IFCPF, 2018). Effectively, the least impaired players (FT8) were removed from the sport as they were perceived to be more effective in matches compared to their more impaired counterparts, which was supported empirically with time-motion data (Boyd et al., 2016). For the readers' reference, data from both the old and new classification systems is included in Table 16.2, but the discussion is concentrated around the new system.

Given the differences in rules and formats of Para football, it is unsurprising that there are clear differences in key GPS metrics of the formats. For example, the average (standard deviation) distance travelled during blind football is the lowest at 1,737 (117.4) m, with amputee football at 3,834.3 (1,141.0) m and CP being the highest at 4,549.2 (1,183.8) m. However, the formats are 40, 50, and 60 min in duration, respectively, which could explain the relatively larger distances covered in each format. When made relative to per min played ($m \times min^{-1}$), CP and amputee football are much more similar with ~8 $m \times min^{-1}$ difference at 82.9 (17.6) and

76.7 (22.8) respectively, whereas blind football is ~48% lower than CP football at 43.4 (2.9) m×min^{-1}. Even CP football, at the highest coverage, is ~30% lower than 11-a-side professional football at 118.8 (10.03) m×min^{-1} (Ravé, Granacher, Boullosa, Hackney, and Zouhal, 2020), which shows there is a clear physical difference between formats and able-bodied football meaning that data from 11-a-side could not, and should not, be used as reference data for Para football formats where the rules are vastly different.

Total distance is one of many key variables to consider when conducting a physical performance analysis of a multi-directional sport such as football. However, the variable does not tell the practitioner about the movement patterns within the distance covered. Breaking total distance down to speed zones and directions is critical to devise individual sessions, micro- and/or mesocycles (Ravé, Granacher, Boullosa, Hackney, and Zouhal, 2020). There is a general consensus in 11-a-side football literature that speed is broken down into five to six zones and qualitatively described as standing/arbitrary, walking, jogging or intermittent speed running, running or moderate speed running, high-speed running and sprinting (Rago et al., 2020). There seems to be a better consensus when observing the faster speed zones though, with running (~14.4 – ~20.0 km·h^{-1}), high-speed running (~20.0 – ~25.0 km·h^{-1}), and sprinting (>25.0 km·h^{-1}) being defined throughout the literature (Gualtieri, Rampinini, Dello Iacono, and Beato, 2023). GPS manufacturers set their default settings to these zones too and are described quantitatively in Table 16.3. Within manufacturers' software set-up, users can determine the speed zones of their athletes. In Para football, it appears that many authors have chosen this latter route as there are subtle, but important, differences between speed zones within and between formats of the game. For example, Yanci et al. (2018 and 2019) class intermittent speed running as 9.0–13.0 km·h^{-1}, while Henríquez et al. (2021) use 13.0–15.9 km·h^{-1}, all of which were used within CP football. The results show that the distance covered at intermittent speed running in Henríquez's population is far lower than Yanci's data and largely incomparable; the same data in Henríquez's population more closely aligns with Yanci's high-speed running. This observation is consistent amongst other Para football formats, see Table 16.2 and use Table 16.4 to show each authors' selected speed bands for their GPS comparisons. As such, it is very difficult to compare the distances covered by players

TABLE 16.3 GPS Speed Zone Metrics between Manufactures. Zones Given in km/h

	Statsports™	*Catapult™*	*Polar Team Pro™*
Zone 1	0–5.4	0.0–7.9	3.0–6.9
Zone 2	5.4–10.8	8.0–12.9	7.0–10.9
Zone 3	10.8–14.4	13.0–15.9	11.0–14.9
Zone 4	14.4–19.8	16.0–19.9	15.0–18.9
Zone 5	19.8–25.2	19.0–21.9	>19.0
Zone 6	>25.2	>22.0	

TABLE 16.4 Definitions of Speed Zones to Analyse Movement Patterns of Para Football Formats

Reference	Low Walking (m)	Walking (m)	Jogging (m)	ISR (m)	HSR (m)	Sprinting (m)
Gamonales et al. (2021a)					>15.0 kph	21.0–24.0 kph
Gamonales et al. (2021b)					>15.0 kph	21.0–24.0 kph
Boyd et al. (2014)					17.6–23.0 kph	>23 kph
Yanci et al. (2018)	<0.4 kph	0.4–3.0 kph	3.0–9.0 kph	9.0–13.0 kph	13.0–18.0 kph	>18.0 kph
Yanci et al. (2019)	<0.4 kph	0.4–3.0 kph	3.0–9.0 kph	9.0–13.0 kph	13.0–18.0 kph	>18.0 kph
Reina et al. (2021)	<0.4 kph	0.4–3.0 kph	3.0–9.0 kph	9.0–13.0 kph	13.0–18.0 kph	>18.0 kph
Gamonales et al. (2022)		0.6–6.0 kph	6.0–12.0 kph	12.0–18.0 kph	18.0–21.0 kph	21.0–24.0 kph
Henríquez et al. (2021)	<6.9 kph	7.0–9.9 kph	10.0–12.9 kph	13.0–15.9 kph	16.0–17.9 kph	>18.0 kph
Peña-Gónzalez et al. (2021)					>16.0 kph	
Yanci et al. (2022)	<0.4 kph	0.4–3.0 kph	3.0–9.0 kph	9.0–13.0 kph	13.0–18.0 kph	>18.0 kph
Panagiotopoulou et al. (2020)	<0.4 kph	0.4–5.0 kph	5.0–8.0 kph	8.0–13.0 kph	13.0–18.0 kph	>18.0 kph
Esatbeyoglu et al. (2022)	0–7 kph	7.1–9.5 kph	9.6–13.2 koh	13.3–16.8 kph	>16.9 kph	
Ravé (2020)					19.8–25.2 kph	>25.2 kph
Ingebrigsten et al. (2015)		0–7.1 kph	7.2–14.3 kph	14.4–19.7 kph	19.8–25.2 kph	
Bueno et al. (2014)		<6.0 kph	6.1–12.0 kph	12.1–15.4 kph	15.5–18.3 kph	>18.4 kph
Beato et al. (2017)					>14.4 kph	
Serrano et al. (2020)		0–10 kph		10.1–15.0 kph	15.1–18.0 kph	>18.1 kph

ISR = Intermittent Speed Running; HSR = High Speed Running.

288 Strength and Conditioning for Football

when moving at different speeds within and between impairments. Therefore, it is challenging for practitioners to understand the needs of the players when working with them; a useful example of this is within CP football.

As mentioned earlier in this chapter, CP has classifications within the impairment and is made up of FT1, 2, and 3s, with a lower number denoting a more impaired player. Given the CP classification rule change in 2018, there are only a few papers that have commented on the differences in GPS metrics between the current classification profiles. Notably, Reina et al. (2021) described the GPS profiles of >250 CP players and showed that there are clear kinematic differences between FT1, 2, and 3s during international match play, most notably, these were between FT1s compared to FT2 and 3s, whereas there were similarities between FT2 and FT3s (Table 16.2). Specifically, FT1s appear to conduct slower movement patterns compared to other classifications, this though is likely to be due to the maximum speed of more impaired players being slower than more able players (Reina et al., 2021; Henriquez, Kokaly, Herrera, and Reina, 2020), although this has not been measured empirically in the new classification system. It would mean though, that the physical characteristics of FT1s are missed due to the relatively high-speed boundaries of the GPS units for these players that are based on more able impaired and unimpaired football players. Therefore, where possible, practitioners should collect GPS data from their athletes to ensure: (i) the speed zones are known and potentially personalised relative to max speed of the athlete, and (ii) in order to understand the movement patterns of your athlete(s) in the format of the game they participate in from which guidance around loading during micro- and mesocycles can be adopted. Caution should be made though, that using relative values of training load may differ largely between impairments and within a squad and so the practitioner should use these values to compare individual sessions/matches to each individual player to help longitudinally monitor their loading more effectively.

Informed Practice/Physical Performance Monitoring

For practitioners to effectively programme, they need to measure some physical performance parameters that are based on the key performance indicators of the sport that they perform in. While there is limited data surrounding the movement patterns of Para-football formats, there is even sparser data surrounding baseline data describing maximal physical performance parameters for para footballers. As with GPS based metrics, blind, amputee and CP football seem to have the most widely available data, although the study designs, methodologies, and sample size of the respective studies do not allow the reader to compare inter- or intra- impairment data (Table 16.5). This also impacts the practitioner, coach, and player who wants to compare physical performance variables to 'normative' values to determine what a high level of physical performance would be in Para footballers. In these cases, it is advised that any practitioner working with Para footballers use the

TABLE 16.5 Physical Performance Variables Found in the Literature within Para Football Players. Variables Stated as Mean (SD) or Median [25th–75th Percentile]

Reference	Impairment	No. of Players	Level of Play	Sprint Time (s)				Agility				Jumps			Power		Aerobic Capactiy
				5 meter	10 meter	20 meter	30 meter	20 m + 180 Turn Run (s)	Illinois	MAT (s)	RAST (s)	CMJ (cm)	SJ (cm)	SBJ (cm)	PPO (W)	PPO (W·kg⁻¹)	VO₂ max (ml·kg⁻¹·min⁻¹)
Henriquez et al. (2020)[c]	Cerebral Palsy	28	National		2.48 (0.31)		6.61 (0.87)	8.49 (0.46)	17.97 (1.22)								
Miyamoto et al. (2018)	Amputee	12	National														
Miyamoto et al. (2019)	Amputee	18	National		1.97 (0.99)		6.66 (0.38)					31.0 (4.4)					
Özkan et al. (2012)	Amputee	15	National		2.06 (0.2)	3.70 (0.40)	5.40 (0.70)					33.0 (9.7)					
Wieczorek et al. (2015)	Amputee	13	National	1.16 (0.09)	2.08 (0.11)	3.80 (0.19)	5.47 (0.29)										
Coswig et al. (2019)	Cerebral Palsy	40										27.8 (6.1)[a]	26.2 (6.2)[a]				
Yanci et al. (2016)[c]	Cerebral Palsy	12	National									23.9 (5.4)	20.0 (4.3)		490.6 (125.7)[c]	7.3 (1.5)[c]	
Reina et al. (2018)	Cerebral Palsy	13	National									38.4 (11.5)[b]					
Peña-Gónzalez et al. (2022)[d]	Cerebral Palsy	15	National	1.287 (0.141)	2.139 (0.213)					6.37 [6.17–7.09]							
Campos et al. (2014)[d]	Blind	7	National							22.50 (2.38)				218 (13)	518.9 (87.8)[f]		54.3 (5.5)
de Campos (2013)	Blind	4	National												491 (72.9)[f]		68.3 (11.3)
Papadopoulos et al. (2022)	Blind	6	National														41.15 [36.93–43.93]
Silva (2018)	Blind	8	National														46.3 (6.7)

MAT = Modified agility test; RAST = Running based anaerobic sprint test; CMJ = countermovement jump; SJ = squat jump; SBJ = standing broad jump; PPO = Peak Power Output; [a] Contact mat data; [b] jumps with arm swing; [c] data collected before classification rule change; [d] data post training intervention; [e] calculated from Wingate test; [f] calculated from 5 × repeated sprints

290 Strength and Conditioning for Football

data in Table 16.5 as a guide but make a conscious effort to collect and monitor their athlete with robust, reliable, and valid physical performance measures that they can longitudinally monitor to help inform programme and player development.

Programming

At present, there appears to be very little work in the literature where specific strength and conditioning programming is prescribed for different impairments. Of those discussed in the current chapter, the major consideration for the practitioner when programming should be with athletes with CP given the muscle architecture and contractile differences compared to able-bodied counterparts (Hussain, Onambélé, Williams, and Morse, 2014, 2017). This is potentially why, within the literature, only CP has any wealth of strength programming studies available (Fleeton, Sanders, and Fornusek, 2020). Of those available though, the vast majority are performed on children and sedentary populations with CP. A recent in-depth review by Fleeton et al. (2020) discussed >50 articles associated with CP strength training, without any commenting or reporting on athletic CP populations. Their main findings were that there is no consensus from CP-specific studies on how to develop athletic performance within CP populations and that traditional models adopted in able-bodied studies should be utilised to aid these athletes. Until there are more specific training studies in athletic CP populations, as well as other Para athlete-based populations, programming methods should be consistent with able-bodied studies. Therefore, the following section aims to introduce exercise modifications for Para footballers specifically, to help strength and conditioning practitioners overcome some potential obstacles when working with impairment groups and different classifications.

Exercise Modification

Given the lack of widely available literature and content available for elite athletic development with Para football, this portion of the chapter will break down some anecdotal problems when choosing exercises for micro- and mesocycles of a strength and conditioning programme. Given the physical impairment of CP, and that it seems to be the most investigated impairment within the literature, this section will predominantly focus on this impairment for the squat and hinge patterns of a strength programme while providing some derivatives of the movements to help the practitioner programme accordingly.

Squat

Squat-based movements are a staple in most strength and conditioning programmes for both strength and power development. Squat kinematics and kinetics have been studied extensively within able-bodied populations from sedentary to elite athletes with a consensus of stance width, squat depth, and torso lean (Schoenfeld,

2010). Both squat depth and torso lean are somewhat determined by ankle mobility and range of motion (Schoenfeld, 2010); the greater the ankle range of motion (dorsiflexion) the easier it is for individuals to attain appropriate squat depth and torso position. CP is a neurological condition and along with strength limitation compared to able-bodied individuals and unaffected limbs, they are also limited in coordination, through both an inactivity of agonists and overactivity of antagonists due to a high degree of muscle spasticity and tone in their affected limbs (Hussain, Onambélé, Williams, and Morse, 2014). These lead to an increased tone of muscle which limits joint range of motion and is particularly evident in the CP ankle, with FT1 and FT2 having limited passive and active dorsiflexion. Furthermore, individuals with CP are limited in strength capacity compared to able-bodied individuals as well as between affected and unaffected legs which can limit the force production of the unaffected leg due to the limitation in the affected leg (Hussain, Onambélé, Williams, and Morse, 2017).

There appears to be no empirical research outlining the squat kinematics and kinetics of CP athletes, but there is work done in children and results suggest that diplegic children are more flexed at the hip, while there was minimal anterior knee translation which resulted in significant trunk lean at the bottom position of the squat (Dan et al., 1999). Furthermore, squatting takes significantly longer to complete in the diplegic children, compared to able-bodied children (Dan et al., 1999). Importantly, as mentioned above, ankle mobility limits squat depth, and in spastic diplegic children, there is very limited ankle dorsiflexion at the bottom position of the squat (Dan et al., 1999).

The observations of Dan et al. (1999) are also observed anecdotally with CP footballers with diplegia and hemiplegia. Figure 16.1 shows this with a hemiplegic FT2, whilst Figure 16.2 shows this with a diplegic FT3 CP footballer. Both examples provide a simple kinematic schematic overlay of the squat without heel raises compared to when using 15° and 30° heel raises beneath both feet. In both classifications, there is a lower bottom position (here as hip joint centre), a more vertical trunk, and more inclined shin angle when using wedges, compared to without. This position would likely reduce the shear forces in the lumbar spine and transfer them to the gluteal and quadricep group, as the target muscles of the squat exercise.

The combination of low dorsiflexion and increased trunk lean during the squat movement, as well as a likely greater impulse observed during the squat in CP athletes (assuming CP and able-bodied were lifting the same mass as each other and CP athletes take longer to complete the squat, as observed in Dan et al. [1999]) would suggest a greater engagement of core musculature, particularly posteriorly, such as the erector spinae in CP athletes. This would likely put a greater shear force through their lumbar region and not load their gluteal and quadricep groups to the same extent as able-bodied players. Practitioners working with CP athletes should therefore encourage athletes to wear weightlifting shoes, that have been shown to improve trunk lean by adding dorsiflexion (Sato, Fortenbaugh, and Hydock, 2012; Legg, Glaister, Cleather, and Goodwin, 2017), which will then allow a greater length:tension within the gluteal and quadricep groups in the bottom position of

FIGURE 16.1 A 9 panel matrix of a hemiplegic FT2 footballer performing a goblet, front, and back squat on a flat ground, 15 and 30 wedges. White lines provide a simple kinematic observation of joint positions at the bottom position of the squat; joint centres are estimated as the lateral malleolus, lateral epicondyle, great trochanter, and acromion process.

the squat. While there is no empirical research into the squat kinematic and kinetic analysis of athletic CP populations though, practitioners should also adopt squat adaptations where the load is moved anteriorly, for example from a traditional high bar position to a front or goblet squat, which are shown to result in a move vertical trunk and lower bottom position (Yavuz, Erdağ, Amca, and Aritan, 2015); this is observed anecdotally for the readers in Figures 16.1 and 16.2.

Considerations for Disability Football **293**

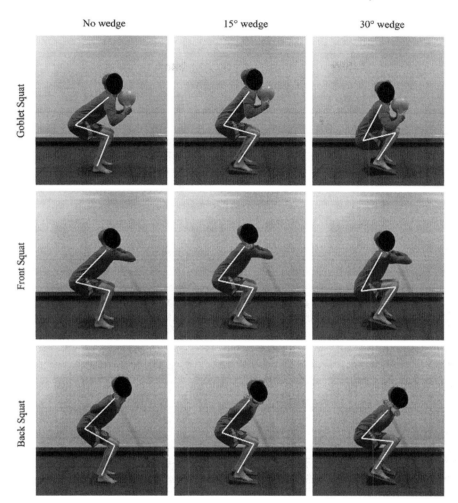

FIGURE 16.2 A 9 panel matrix of a diplegic FT1 footballer performing a goblet, front, and back squat on a flat ground, 15 and 30 wedges. White lines provide a simple kinematic observation of joint positions at the bottom position of the squat; joint centres are estimated as the lateral malleolus, lateral epicondyle, great trochanter, and acromion process.

Lastly, shoulder mobility of CP athletes should be a major consideration for practitioners when performing the squat exercise. Individuals with hemiplegia are affected throughout their left or right side. Therefore, the ability of individuals with hemiplegia to grip the barbell, when in a high or low-back barbell squat, could limit their ability to complete the squat effectively. For these athletes, it is advised that other squat variations where the athletes hand position is anterior to the shoulder, such as the front squat with a cross-over arm position or a safety bar squat, should be considered.

Hinge

The hinge exercise is another staple within a strength and conditioning coach's armoury. For CP footballers, unlike the squat exercise, the hinge is not limited by ankle dorsiflexion, but there are still some considerations as they will be unable to engage musculature through the full range of motion due to their respective spasticity and tone in their affected limbs.

As mentioned, individuals with CP are limited in strength capacity and coordination, due to spasticity and coactivation of antagonists. For hinge movements, such as Romanian Deadlifts (RDL), kinematic positions require flexion at the hip with minimal flexion at the knee and ankle (dorsiflexion). Due to muscle spasticity and increased tone in affected CP legs though, hamstrings appear to be overactive during the descending phase of the RDL meaning that individuals with CP will undergo a higher degree of flexion at the knee compared to able-bodied athletes. Anecdotally, when instructing CP footballers to 'try and maintain a more extended knee' during hinge-based exercises, there is an overcompensation of the lower back and the athlete reverts to a more kyphotic position along with a more posteriorly tilted pelvis. This in turn creates a 'Butt Wink' position at the bottom position of the RDL which increases compressive forces on the anterior aspects of the lumbar vertebrae, which is identified as an injury risk in the lower back (Schoenfeld, 2010). In turn, this overexcites the posterior core muscles, such as the iliocostalis, and longissimus, and takes emphasis away from the target muscle groups for the hinge, i.e., the hamstring group – see Figure 16.3 for an example of this in hemiplegic and diplegic CP football players. Where practitioners may be observing this in their athletes, an attempt should be made to ensure that the CP athletes' knees are at a constant angle throughout the descending and ascending phases of hinge exercises to maintain a stable lower back and pelvis position through the movement. This should then lengthen the proximal aspect of the hamstring group during the eccentric phase of the RDL. From there, other open chain exercises can be added to the athletes' programme to lengthen the proximal aspect of the hamstring, such as Swiss ball hamstring rollouts (Figures 16.4a and 16.4b).

Practical Applications: Putting It All Together

Due to the subtle, but important, differences in kinematics between CP and able-bodied footballers when performing strength exercises, the exercise selection within a programme can change vastly. The strength and conditioning coach therefore needs to acknowledge the capabilities and level of impairment their Para athlete has when they are working with them or designing a programme. Based on the exercise examples in the previous section of this chapter, there are example session plans below for an FT3 (less impaired) and FT1 (more impaired) Para footballer where the focus is strength development in the lower limbs; for this example, both athletes are assumed to have the same one repetition maximum, and the programme is designed at 80% of this one repetition maximum.

Considerations for Disability Football **295**

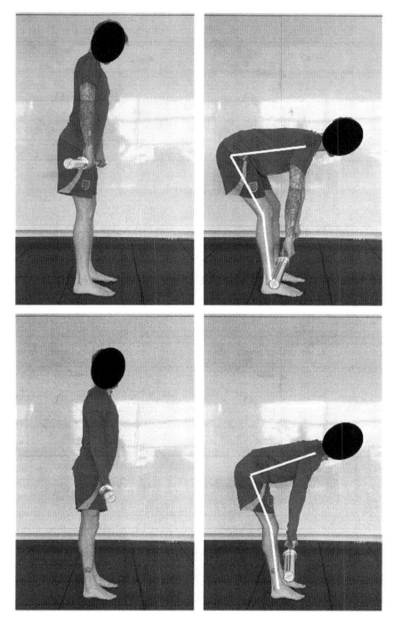

FIGURE 16.3 Demonstration of a Romanian Deadlift (RDL) in an FT2 (top two panels) and an FT1 CP footballer. Note in both the bottom positions, there is pronounced 'rounding' of the lumber to reach end range and excessive knee flexion in the FT2 athlete (top right panel). White lines provide a simple kinematic observation of joint positions at the bottom position; joint centres are estimated as the lateral malleolus, lateral epicondyle, great trochanter, and acromion process.

296 Strength and Conditioning for Football

FIGURE 16.4 Demonstration of a hamstring rollout in an FT2 (top two panels) and an FT1 CP footballer. Note in both athletes, there is good hip extension position at the end range (right panels) which help target the proximal aspect of the hamstring which may have a limited range due to spasticity, demonstrated here in the top right panel for the FT2 athlete who has increased knee flexion. White lines provide a simple kinematic observation of joint positions at the bottom position; joint centres are estimated as the lateral malleolus, lateral epicondyle, great trochanter, and acromion process.

For both athletes here (Tables 16.6 and 16.7), the movement patterns are the same for each exercise and where there can be a superset (same-coloured rows), the patterns are again the same. However, note that the main squat lift is different for each athlete where an FT3 will be able to perform a back rack position by not only having better shoulder and hand mobility but also a better bottom position due to less spasticity in the lower limbs compared to and FT1. Whereas the FT1 programme replaces the back rack position with a front rack position to mitigate issues with shoulder position but also to facilitate improved squat depth, as demonstrated in Figure 16.2. Note that the load for both exercises differs considerably, due to relative force development between squat variations, but also to mitigate the risk of injury/failure for the FT1 player. The main hinge lift also differs between classifications where the FT1 completes a machine-based lift to ensure the targeted musculature is activated with the weight moving along the correct plane and axis, whereas the FT3 is able to perform a more free-weight orientated exercise without the need for external guidance. Furthermore, the latter exercises

TABLE 16.6 Example Strength Session Plan for an FT3 Para Footballer with the Aim of the Session to Develop Lower Limb Strength

Theme	Exercise	Tempo	Reps/Sets	Rest (mins)	Weight (kg)	Equipment
Whole body	Static recumbent bike	HR zone 3	5 mins/1	0.0	N/A	Static recumbent bike
Mobility	Mobility – hip – lateral glide + abduction – long lunge	-	30 sec/2	0.5	Green power band	Power bands
Mobility	Mobility – hip – lateral glide – split squat	-	30 sec hold/2	0.5	Green power band	Power bands
Squat – Bi	Squats – barbell back rack	2-1-2-1	6/4	2.0	80	Rack, barbell + plates
Hinge	Hip thrust – barbell	2-1-2-1	6/4	2.0	48	Bench, barbell + plates
Hinge	Hamstring – nordic curls	2-1-2-1	6/4	2.0	Bodyweight	Heel anchor
Squat – Uni	Split squat – barbell Bulgarian	2-1-2-1	6/4	2.0	47	Barbell + plates + bench
Squat – Uni	Split squat – FFE BOSU bodyweight	2-1-2-1	12 each/4	1.5	Bodyweight	BOSU
Core	QL – lateral flexion/ extension – kettlebell	1-1-1-1	6/4	2.0	20	Kettlebell/dumbbell
Core	Plank – banded – pull through	1-1-1-1	12 each/4	1.5	Red power band	Power bands

Length: ~70 mins

TABLE 16.7 Example Strength Session Plan for an FT1 Para Footballer with the Aim of the Session to Develop Lower Limb Strength

Theme	Exercise	Tempo	Reps/Sets	Rest (mins)	Weight (kg)	Equipment
Whole body	Static recumbent bike	HR zone 3	5 mins/1	0.0	N/A	Static recumbent bike
Mobility	Mobility – hip – lateral glide + abduction – long lunge	-	30 sec/2	0.5	Green power band	Power bands
Mobility	Mobility – hip – lateral glide – split squat	-	30 sec hold/2	0.5	Green power band	Power bands
Squat – Bi	Squats – barbell front rack	2-1-2-1	6/4	2.0	63	Rack, barbell + plates
Hinge	Hip thrust – machine	2-1-2-1	6/4	2.0	64	Machine
Hinge	Hamstring – swiss ball roll outs double leg	2-1-2-1	10/4	2.0	Bodyweight	Swiss ball
Squat – Uni	Split squat – smith machine	2-1-2-1	6/4	2.0	48	Smith machine + Plates
Squat – Uni	Step ups – dumbbell alternate leg	2-1-2-1	6/4	2.0	24	Box + dumbbells
Core	QL – lateral flexion/extension – kettlebell	1-1-1-1	6/4	2.0	20	Kettlebell/dumbbell
Core	Plank – banded – pull through	1-1-1-1	12 each/4	1.5	Red power band	Power bands

Length: ~72 mins

within the session differ when unilateral and stability exercises are considered. For example, a Bulgarian split squat is used for an FT3 player, due to them likely having greater balance and control than an FT1. Whereas the FT1 completes a split squat exercise using a Smith Machine, where they can use the apparatus to again help themselves to perform the movement in the correct plane and axis. Note here too, that the FT1 has a greater load to lift that FT3 when machine exercises are used to help compensate for the removal of stability in the exercise. The FT1 athlete then completes loaded step-ups to challenge their stability while loading each leg independently, whereas the FT3 completes bodyweight front foot elevated split squats on a BOSU to further challenge their stability during a dynamic movement (there is scope to load this exercise with dumbbells if needed) which would be observed more in a match/training scenarios compared to an FT1.

References

Baird, M. F., Graham, S. M., Baker, J. S., and Bickerstaff, G. F. (2012). Creatine-kinase-and exercise-related muscle damage implications for muscle performance and recovery. *Journal of Nutrition and Metabolism, 2012*(1):960363.

Beato, M., Coratella, G., Schena, F., and Hulton, A. T. (2017). Evaluation of the external and internal workload in female futsal players. *Biology of Sport, 34*(3), 227–231.

Beattie, C. E., Fahey, J. T., Pullinger, S. A., Edwards, B. J., and Robertson, C. M. (2020). The sensitivity of countermovement jump, creatine kinase and urine osmolality to 90-min of competitive match-play in elite English Championship football players 48-h post-match. *Science and Medicine in Football, 5*(2), 1–9.

Boyd, C., Barnes, C., Eaves, S. J., Morse, C. I., Roach, N., and Williams, A. G. (2016). A time-motion analysis of Paralympic football for athletes with cerebral palsy. *International Journal of Sports Science and Coaching, 11*(4), 552–558.

Boyd RN, Davies PSW, Ziviani J, et al. PREDICT-CP: study protocol of implementation of comprehensive surveillance to predict outcomes for school-aged children with cerebral palsy. BMJ Open 2017;7:e014950. doi:10.1136/ bmjopen-2016-014950

Coswig, Victor, et al. "Assessing the validity of the MyJUMP2 app for measuring different jumps in professional cerebral palsy football players: An experimental study." *JMIR mHealth and uHealth* 7.1 (2019): e11099.s

de Borba Campos, Márcia, et al. "Usability evaluation of a mobile navigation application for blind users." *Universal Access in Human-Computer Interaction. Access to the Human Environment and Culture: 9th International Conference, UAHCI 2015, Held as Part of HCI International 2015, Los Angeles, CA, USA, August 2-7, 2015, Proceedings, Part IV 9.* Springer International Publishing, 2015.

Dan, B., Bouillot, E., Bengoetxea, A., Nöel, P., Kahn, A., and Cheron, G. (1999). Adaptive motor strategy for squatting in spastic diplegia. *European Journal of Paediatric Neurology, 3*(4), 159–165.

De Oliveira Bueno, Murilo José, et al. "Analysis of the distance covered by Brazilian professional futsal players during official matches." *Sports biomechanics* 13.3 (2014): 230–240.

Ekstand, J., Walden, M., and Haqqlund, M. (2004). A congested football calendar and the wellbeing of players: Correlation between match exposure of European footballers

300 Strength and Conditioning for Football

before the World Cup 2002 and their injuries and performances during that World Cup. *British Journal of Sports Medicine, 38*(4), 493–497.

Esatbeyoglu, F., Hazir, T., and İsler, A. K. (2022). Match characteristics of professional outfield amputee soccer players during official amputee soccer matches. *Turkish Journal of Sports Medicine, 57*(4), 189–195.

Fleeton, J. R., Sanders, R. H., and Fornusek, C. (2020). Strength training to improve performance in athletes with cerebral palsy: A systematic review of current evidence. *The Journal of Strength and Conditioning Research, 34*(6), 1774–1789.

Gamonales, J. M., León, K., Rojas-Valverde, D., Sánchez-Ureña, B., and Muñoz-Jiménez, J. (2021a). Data mining to select relevant variables influencing external and internal workload of elite blind 5-a-side soccer. *International Journal of Environmental Research and Public Health, 18*(6), 3155–3166.

Gamonales, J. M., Muñoz-Jiménez, J., Gómez-Carmona, C. D., and Ibáñez, S. J. (2022). Comparative external workload analysis based on the new functional classification in cerebral palsy football 7-a-side. A full-season study. *Research in Sports Medicine, 30*(3), 295–307.

Gamonales, J. M., Muñoz Jiménez, J., Mancha-Triguero, D., and Ibáñez, S. J. (2021b). The influence of the competition phase and the result of the match on the competitive demands in football 5-a-side for the visually impaired. *International Journal of Performance Analysis in Sport, 21*(1), 1–11.

González, I. P., Marin, J. M., Triguero, D. M., Ramon, M. M., and Puerto, J. G. (2021). Relationship between physical performance and match load and effects of two consecutive matches in cerebral palsy footballers. *Retos: Nuevas Tendencias en Educación Física, Deporte y Recreación, 41*, 728–734.

Gualtieri, A., Rampinini, E., Dello Iacono, A., and Beato, M. (2023). High-speed running and sprinting in professional adult soccer: Current thresholds definition, match demands and training strategies. A systematic review. *Frontiers in Sports and Active Living, 5*, 1116293.

Henríquez, M., Iturricastillo, A., González-Olguín, A., Herrera, F., Riquelme, S., and Reina, R. (2021). Time−motion characteristics and physiological responses of Para-footballers with cerebral palsy in two small-sided games and a simulated game. *Adapted Physical Activity Quarterly, 38*(2), 232–247.

Henriquez, M. J., Kokaly, M., Herrera, F., and Reina, R. (2020). The relationship among repeated sprint and change of direction abilities in football players with cerebral palsy. *Kinesiology, 52*(2), 208–216.

Howatson, G., and Milak, A. (2009). Exercise-induced muscle damage following a bout of sport specific repeated sprints. *The Journal of Strength and Conditioning Research, 23*(8), 2419–2424.

Hunkin, S. L., Fahrner, B., and Gastin, P. B. (2014). Creatine kinase and its relationship with match performance in elite Australian Rules football. *Journal of Science and Medicine in Sport, 17*(3), 332–336.

Hussain, A. W., Onambélé, G. L., Williams, A. G., and Morse, C. I. (2014). Muscle size, activation and coactivation in adults with cerebral palsy. *Muscle and Nerve, 49*(1), 76–85.

Hussain, A. W., Onambélé, G. L., Williams, A. G., and Morse, C. I. (2017). Medial gastrocnemius specific force of adult men with spastic cerebral palsy. *Muscle and Nerve, 56*(2), 298–306.

IBSA. (2017). *IBSA classification manual for IBSA members* (pp. 1–25). Internation Blind Sports Association.

IFCPF. (2018). *Classification rule and regulations.* Internation Federation of Cerebral Palsy Football.

Ingebrigtsen, J., Dalen, T., Hjelde, G. H., Drust, B., and& Wisløff, U. (2015). Acceleration and sprint profiles of a professional elite football team in match play. *European Journal of Sport Science, 15*(2), 101–110.

Legg, H. S., Glaister, M., Cleather, D. J., and Goodwin, J. E. (2017). The effect of weightlifting shoes on the kinetics and kinematics of the back squat. *Journal of Sports Sciences, 35*(5), 508–515.

Maehana, H. M., Suzuki, K., Koshiyama, K., and Yoshimura, M. (2018). Influence of amputation on match performance in amputee soccer. *Juntendo Medical Journal, 64*(1), 27–31.

Miyamoto, Aya, Hirofumi Maehana, and Toshio Yanagiya. "Characteristics of anaerobic performance in Japanese amputee soccer players." *Juntendo Medical Journal* 64.Suppl. 1 (2018): 22–26.

Mohr, M., Krustrup, P., and Bangsbo, J. (2003). Match performance of high-standard soccer players with special reference to development of fatigue. *Journal of Sports Sciences, 21*(7), 519–528.

Nédélec, M., McCall, A., Carling, C., Legall, F., Berthoin, S., and Dupont, G. (2012). Recovery in soccer: Part I – Post-match fatigue and time course of recovery. *Sports Medicine, 12*, 997–1015.

Özkan, Ali, et al. "The relationship between body composition, anaerobic performance and sprint ability of amputee soccer players." *Journal of human kinetics* 35 (2012): 141.

Panagiotopoulou, Maria, and Maria Tsirintani. "Accessibility and web quality information for people with disabilities in healthcare structures." *The Importance of Health Informatics in Public Health during a Pandemic*. IOS Press, 2020. 306-309.

Panagiotopoulo, F. V. (2020, April). Analysis of running performance and heart rate in soccer players with amputation. *MSc Thesis*. Thessaloniki: Aristotle University of Thessaloniki.

Papadopoulos, C., Metaxas, T. I., Fotiadou, E. G., Giagazoglou, P. F., Michailidis, Y., Christoulas, K., and Tsimaras, V. (2022). Correlations between VO_{2max} and match distance running performance of soccer players with visual impairment. *Research Square*, 1–12.

Papadopoulos, Konstantinos, et al. "3D haptic texture discrimination in individuals with and without visual impairments using a force feedback device." *Universal Access in the Information Society* (2025): 1–14

Peña-González I, Sarabia JM, Roldan A, Manresa-Rocamora A, Moya-Ramón M. Physical Performance Differences Between Spanish Selected and Nonselected Para-Footballers With Cerebral Palsy for the National Team. Int J Sports Physiol Perform. 2021 Nov 1;16(11):1676-1683. doi: 10.1123/ijspp.2020-0842. Epub 2021 May 5. PMID: 33952712.

Rago, V., Brito, J., Figueiredo, P., Costa, J., Barreira, D., Krustrup, P., and Rebelo, A. (2020). Methods to collect and interpret external training load using microtechnology incorporating GPS in professional football: A systematic review. *Research in Sports Medicine, 28*(3), 437–458.

Ravé, Guillaume, et al. "How to use global positioning systems (GPS) data to monitor training load in the "real world" of elite soccer." *Frontiers in physiology* 11 (2020): 944.

Ravé, G., Granacher, U., Boullosa, D., Hackney, A. C., and Zouhal, H. (2020). How to use global positioning systems (gps) data to monitor training load in the "real world" of elite soccer. *Frontiers in Physiology, 11*(944), 1–11.

Reina, R., Elvira, J. L., Valverde, M., Roldán, A., and& Yanci, J. (2018a). Kinematic and kinetic analyses of the vertical jump with and without header as performed by parafootballers with cerebral palsy. *Sports, 7*(9), 209–220.

Reina, R., Iturricastillo, A., Castillo, D., Roldan, A., Toledo, C., and Yanci, J. (2021). Is impaired coordination related to match physical load in footballers with cerebral palsy of different sport classes? *Journal of Sports Sciences, 39*(1), 140–149.

302 Strength and Conditioning for Football

Reina, R., Iturricastillo, A., Sabido, R., Campayo-Piernas, M., and& Yanci, J. (2018b). Vertical and horizontal jump capacity in international cerebral palsy football players. *International Journal of Sports Physiology and Performance, 13*(5), 597–603.

Reina, R., Sarabia, J. M., Yanic, J., García-Vaquero, M. P., and Campayo-Piernas, M. (2016). Change of direction ability performance in cerebral palsy football players according to functional profiles. *Frontiers in Physiology, 6*(409), 1–8.

Russell, M., Sparkes, W., Northeast, J., Cook, C. J., Bracken, R. M., and Kilduff, L. P. (2016). Relationships between match activities and peak power output and Creatine Kinase responses to professional reserve team soccer match-play. *Human Movement Science, 45*, 96–101.

Sánchez, Jaime, and Marcia de Borba Campos. "Development of Navigation Skills through Audio Haptic Videogaming in Learners who are Blind." *J. Univers. Comput.* Sci. 19.18 (2013): 2677-2697.

Sato, K., Fortenbaugh, D., and Hydock, D. S. (2012). Kinematic changes using weightlifting shoes on barbell back squat. *The Journal of Strength and Conditioning Research, 26*(1), 28–33.

Schoenfeld, B. J. (2010). Squatting kinematics and kinetics and their application to exercise performance. *The Journal of Strength and Conditioning Research, 24*(12), 3497–3506.

Schuth, G., Szigeti, G., Dobreff, G., Revisnyei, P., Pasic, A., Toka, L., . . . Pavlik, G. (2021). Factors influencing creatine kinase response in youth national team soccer players. *Sports Health, 13*(4), 332–340.

Serrano, Carlos, et al. "Physical demands in elite futsal referees during Spanish futsal cup." *Frontiers in Psychology* 12 (2021): 625154.

Simoes, Walter CSS, et al. "A guidance system for blind and visually impaired people via hybrid data fusion." 2018 *IEEE Symposium on Computers and Communications (ISCC)*. IEEE, 2018.

Thorpe, R., and Sunderland, C. (2012). Muscle damage, endocrine, and immune marker response to a soccer match. *The Journal of Strength and Conditioning Research, 10*, 2783–2790.

Wieczorek, Marta, et al. "Hand grip strength vs. sprint effectiveness in amputee soccer players." *Journal of Human kinetics* 48 (2015): 133.

Yanci, J., Castagna, C., Los Arcos, A., Santalla, A., Grande, I., Figueroa, J., and Camara, J. (2016). Muscle strength and anaerobic performance in football players with cerebral palsy. *Disability and Health Journal, 9*(2), 313–319.

Yanci, J., Castillo, D., Iturricastillo, A., and Reina, R. (2019). Evaluation of the official match external load in soccer players with cerebral palsy. *The Journal of Strength and Conditioning Research, 33*(3), 866–873.

Yanci, J., Castillo, D., Iturricastillo, A., Urbán, T., and Reina, R. (2018). External match loads of footballers with cerebral palsy: A comparison among sport classes. *International Journal of Sports Physiology and Performance, 15*(3), 590–596.

Yanci, J. C., Iturricastillo, A., Henríquez, M., Roldan, A., and Reina, R. (2022). Comparison of the physical response during official matches and small-sided games in international cerebral palsy footballers: Implications for evidence-based classification. *Adapted Physical Activity Quarterly, 40*(1), 4–18.

Yavuz, H. U., Erdağ, D., Amca, A. M., and Aritan, S. (2015). Kinematic and EMG activities during front and back squat variations in maximum loads. *Journal of Sports Sciences, 33*(10), 1058–1066.

POSTSCRIPT

Barry Drust

This postscript comes at the end of a book that is filled with detailed information related to strength and conditioning for football. The wide variety of content provided across each of the chapters covers a range of important considerations that support the physical performance of the modern footballer. The detailed content is a good reflection of the growth in academic research related to science and football. It also reflects developments in the applied expertise acquired by practitioners working in football across the last two to three decades. There is a general view amongst these groups that the sport of football is getting more demanding. Players need to work harder during individual games and repeat these efforts more frequently, with limited recovery times, across a high number of matches in multiple competitions. This has effectively changed the annual calendar previously experienced by teams by reducing the opportunities for rest and recovery between seasons. The globalisation of the game and the demand for matches to be accessible to audiences far beyond those within the stadium have also imposed additional demands around travel and performing at non-traditional times of the day on those involved. These changes within the sport have been driven by those who run the game to satisfy the public's interest as well as to maximise financial income to football organisations.

At the time of writing this postscript, there is substantial debate as to whether these requirements now surpass the abilities of players to perform. This has resulted in movements by players and their representatives to lobby against the match loads imposed on them. This challenge may signify a critical point in the sport, and the way in which teams and individuals support the development and performance of players. While the outcome of such debate is currently uncertain, it is clear that attempts to understand the impact of these demands on players, and the associated development of short, medium, and long-term strategies to support performance and reduce injury, is vital. Such knowledge will come from the collection,

DOI: 10.4324/9781003383475-18

304 Strength and Conditioning for Football

analysis, interpretation, and dissemination of relevant data in books like this. This emphasises the importance of these types of publications for the football industry.

It may be a testament to the effectiveness of our current knowledge and practical interventions that football has been able to progress so far and so quickly without too many negative considerations for performance and injury. Many of the potentially impactful approaches to intervene with players are described in the previous chapters of this book. We do, however, need to bear in mind that as good as the content of this book is, it is only largely reflective of one aspect of the performance model relevant to the sport. While there is an appreciation of the need to consider tactical, technical, and psychological factors within the chapters of the book, there remains a way to go before we have truly multi-disciplinary and inter-disciplinary understanding. All individuals involved in the sport are aware of the importance of the interconnectedness of the multiple factors that determine performance yet there is still little effort focussed on either this type of research or practice. There would, therefore, seem to be a clear need to better understand the performance of players from a more holistic perspective. Relevant projects in this area may well also include how all individuals working with players (e.g., coaches, science and medicine practitioners, and nutritionists) can work more collaboratively and effectively to support individual players and teams. As these insights may well be population-specific it may also lead to a need for us to complete different projects with the different groups of players (e.g., female, youth) currently involved in the sport.

Maybe the lack of research that directly mirrors the situations we see in football in the real world is one reason why we continue to see a gap between the scientific knowledge that is available and that which is directly translated to impact the day-to-day practice we see in the sport. While this gap has reduced in recent years, as a function of some great examples of collaborative partnerships between academics and football organisations, there are still improvements that should be targeted to limit the time between knowledge creation and application. The problems that the sport wants to answer are often very difficult to investigate scientifically. Appropriate research designs for such studies would test collaborative frameworks between organisations as well as theoretical approaches to experimental designs and the practicality/validity of methodological strategies for data collection to their limit. The science and football community should embrace this challenge and focus on developing knowledge that revolutionises our insights, not just "edge" us forward. While collaboration will lie at the heart of these endeavours, we should also encourage innovative thought and new research paradigms to create new understanding.

Those involved in developing both the chapters for this book and the research on which the content is based should be proud of the contribution they will make to developing the current and future generations of individuals involved in the sport. The constant evolution seen in football necessitates the need to challenge our understanding and to do work that attempts to generate greater awareness of the game. This drive for better knowledge will ensure that we can support those involved in the game as it develops. This will help the sport to continue to be one that we, and future generations, all love.

INDEX

Note: **Bold** page numbers refer to tables, *italic* page numbers refer to figures.

able bodied football 281–284, **282–283**
acceleration 4, 6, 8, 110, 116, 131, 187–188, 239, 256, 266–267; hard 42; mechanical demands of 41–42; metabolic demands of 41–42; training 69
accelerometers 94, 110
active pre-match warm-up 143–144
active recovery 163–164
adenosine-tri-phosphate (ATP) concentration 9–10
adolescent growth spurt 253
aerobic conditioning: football 21–34; HIIT for 22–23; number of players and pitch size 29–30, *30*
aerobic tests 92–93
aerobic training 75, 79
agility 144, 190–191, 258–261, **261–263**; and COD 191, 258; defined 190; and optimal fitness 224
agility performance: assessment of 57–59; determinants of 54–55; training methods for enhancing 65–67
agility training: in football 53–69; with a generic stimulus 66; with a specific stimulus 66–67
amputee football 273–274, 285
anaerobic conditioning: football 21–34; HIIT for 22–29; number of players and pitch size 29–30, *30*

anaerobic metabolism 9
anaerobic speed reserve (ASR) for HIIT 26–28, *27–28*
anaerobic training 1, 75, 79
anterior cruciate ligament (ACL) 242–244; injuries 100, 181–183, 185–186, 188–195
assessment: change-of-direction and agility performance 57–60; of physical capacities following injury 183; of reactive strength 185–186; sprint performance 55–57
athlete management system (AMS) 134–135
athletic development 254–255
athletic motor skill competencies (AMSC) 264

biochemical markers 126–127
biochemical measures 125–127
biomechanical framework: ball striking 44–45; braking 43; coupling and decoupling 43–44; for football 42–45; manipulating an opponent's body 44; sprinting 42–43
blind and partially sighted football 273
broad jump 130

carbohydrate (CHO) 202–205, *205, 207–210*; based breakfast 209; based meal 209; within blood 204;

306 Index

consumption during high-intensity intermittent protocol 204; containing beverages 210; drinks and juices 207; electrolyte drinks 206, 207; high glycaemic index (HGI) 207; ingestion of 211–212; low glycaemic index (LGI) 207, 209; nutritional plan to attain **208**; oxidation rates 209–211
cardiovascular measures 127–128
cerebral palsy (CP) football 273
change of direction (COD) ability 53, 189–190, 255, 258, 261; and agility 191, 258; assessment of 57–59; determinants of 54–55; in-effective 189; reactive agility test 60; re-developing 190; tests 59–60, 98–99; training methods for enhancing 65–67
change of direction deficit (CODD) 98
Charter of Player Data Rights 128
club culture 220–222, *221*
coach feedback *228,* 228–230
coaching staff's multidisciplinary mindset 223–225
cold water immersion (CWI) 156, 158, 161–163, 166–167
common injuries 99, 187
compression garments 164–165
cooling strategies 161–162
coping strategy selection *230,* 230–232
cortisol 126, 142
countermovement jump (CMJ) 95–96, 130–131, 185
COVID-19 pandemic 134
Creatine Kinase (CK) 125–126
criteria-based progression *182,* 182–183
cryotherapy 158, 161
cumulative fatigue 7–8, 12
curvilinear sprint test 57
Cutting Movement Assessment Score (CMAS) Qualitative Screening Tool 58–59
cycling assessments 129

Daily Analysis of Life Demands for Athletes 133
data analysis 102
deaf football 274
deceleration 188–189; re-developing 189
decision-making 191–192
delayed onset of muscle soreness (DOMS) 164, 166–167, 169
differentiated RPE (dRPE) 114–115
Disability Cup 272

disability football *see* Para football
dose-response investigations 109
drop jump (DJ) 95–96, 130

educational efforts 224
effort expenditure and fair-play 220–222, *221*
ego-oriented climate 221
elite football player: context 154; importance of recovery for 154
Elite Player Performance Plan 252
endurance training 244, 264–267
energy expenditure (EE) 203, 206–207
energy intake (EI) 207
English Football Association 272
English Premier League 89, 153, 165–166, 206, 211, 256
European Championships 2024 153
external load 4–7
external training load monitoring 115–120; reliability 117, *118*; speed zone calculation 118–119, *119*
extra time 148–149

fatigue 203–204, 224–227, 230, 265; cumulative 7–8, 12; described 203; neuromuscular 281, 284; post-match 242; residual 10–12; resistant 240, *240,* 242; temporary 7–9, 12, 14
Fédération Internationale de Football Association (FIFA) 128, 144, 238
feedback *228,* 228–230
female players 238–249, **247–249**; differences in recovery 242; evidence-based approach to practice *247*; growth and maturation 243–245; health considerations 245–246; injury epidemiology 242–243; match demands 238–239; overview 238; physiological differences in 239–241, *240*; training responses 241
fibres 203
'FIFA 11+' (Fédération Internationale de Football Association) program 144
FIFA Women's World Cups 239
FIFPRO 128
fitness testing: aerobic tests 92–93; changes of direction tests 98–99; football 89–102; injury screening assessments 99–102; linear speed testing 97; need for *91,* 91–92; physical demands 89–102; repeated sprint ability 99; strength testing 94–97

Index **307**

fitness training: categorization of **75.**
75–76; individual sessions 76–78, **77;**
international tournaments and cup
games 82–83; planning, in football
74–85; planning of injury prevention
83–84; planning preseason 78–79;
planning the season 79–82, **80–82;**
practical applications 84–85
flexibility and mobility 11, 76, 142, 166,
209, 254, 261, 273, 291, 293, 296
fluid considerations 206
flying-start tests 56
football: aerobic conditioning 21–34;
agility training in 53–69; anaerobic
conditioning 21–34; biomechanical
framework for 42–45; fitness testing
89–102; muscle and blood metabolites
during match **13**; physical demands
of 3–14; physical profiling 89–102;
physiological demands of 3–14;
planning fitness training in 74–85;
plyometric training 40–51; power
training 40–51; speed in 53–69; strength
training 40–51; training load monitoring
in 107–120; wellness monitoring and
readiness in 124–136
football performance: active pre-match
warm-up 143–144; extra time 147–149;
half-time 147–149; hormonal priming
142–143; match-day strategies to
enhance 140–150; morning priming
exercise 141–142; post-activation
performance enhancement (PAPE)
145–147; practical applications
149–150, *150*; protecting warm-up
benefits 144–145; strategies adopted less
than 3 h before player's entry 142–147;
strategies adopted more than 3 h before
player's entry 141–142; strategies
implemented after player's entry into
match 147–149
force development: and power 184–185;
rate of 184–185
free-unresisted sprinting methods 61–62
fundamental movement patterns (FMS) 258
fundamental movement skills (FMS) 254

General Data Protection Regulation 128
global positioning systems (GPS) 110, 112,
116, 284–286, **286,** 288
glutamate 126
glutamine 126
glycogen resynthesis 12

Ground Reaction Force (GRF) 187
guided prescription of recovery modalities
168–169, *169*
gyroscopes 110

half-time 147–148
half-time analysis *230,* 230–232
hamstring strain injury (HSI) risk 100
hand-held dynamometer (HHD) 100–101
heart rate (HR) 127; training load
monitoring 111–112, *113*
heating strategies 163
high glycaemic index (HGI) foods 207–209
high-intensity interval training (HIIT)
21–22, 241, 265; for aerobic
conditioning 22–23; for anaerobic
conditioning 22–23; anaerobic speed
reserve for 26–28; categorization of *23*;
maximal aerobic speed for 26–28; short
vs. long intervals 23–26, *24–26*
high-speed running (HSR) 256, 267; *see
also* sprinting ability/speed
hinge exercise 294
hormonal priming 142–143
HR recovery (HRR) 93, 127
HR variability (HRV) 127
hydration 111, 159, 161, 206, 210, 215
hypoglycaemia 203–204, 209–211

individualised GPS-derived external
training loads 118–119
injury/ies: acceleration 187; agility
190–191; change of direction
189–190; criteria-based progression
182, 182–183; deceleration 188–189;
decision-making 191–192; late phase
rehabilitation 187; maximal running
speed 187; optimizing return to
performance following 181–195; power/
rate of force development 184–185;
reactive strength 185–186; recovering
explosiveness 185; re-developing
COD ability 190; re-developing
deceleration 189; re-developing speed
187–188; re-developing strength 184;
re-development of physical capacities
183; restoring soccer-specific capacities
187; strength assessment 183–184;
targeting improvements in reactive
strength 186
injury screening assessments 99–102
intensity 49–50, **50**
internal load 8–10

308 Index

internal training load monitoring 111
International Olympic Committee 252
Internation Federation of Cerebral Palsy
  Football (IFCPF) 273
interrogative feedback 229
interval training 21–26, 241, 265
interventions driving recovery process
  following match-play 159–161, **160**
invisible monitoring 134
isokinetic dynamometry testing 100

jump assessments 130–131
jump testing 95, 129, 130

linear speed testing 97
linear sprint tests 56–57; flying-start tests
  56; practical case 68; static-start tests 56
load: external 4–7; internal 8–10;
  small-sided games (SSG) *see*
  small-sided games (SSG)
long-term athletic development (LTAD)
  models 254
low glycaemic index (LGI) 207, 209

massage 166–167
matches: progressing to extra time 148–149;
  recovery strategies after 153–171
maximal aerobic speed (MAS) 26–28,
  27–28, 187
medium-sided games (MSG) 266
menstrual cycle (MC) 245
modelling 223–224
monitoring: readiness with wearables
  128; training load 107–120; wellness
  124–136
morning priming exercise 141–142
motion strategies 165–166
motivation 29, 34, 92, 134, 141, 221,
  225–227, 230–232, 234
motivational climate 220–222, *221*
movement screening 100
multidisciplinary coaching to in-game
  performance *223,* 223–225
muscle fiber composition 7
muscle glycogen 9–12, 76, 82–83, 161,
  203–204, *204,* 207, 209, 210
muscle lactate concentration 9
muscle protein breakdown (MPB) 205, 210
muscle protein synthesis (MPS) 205, 213
muscle strength assessments 131–133
muscular strength, defined 261

neuromotor activation 224
neuromuscular fatigue (NMF) 128–129

non-specific training methods: plyometric
  jump training 63; power training 64;
  sprint performance 62–64; strength
  training 63–64
non-verbal feedback 228
Nordic Hamstring Exercise (NHE) 132
Nordic hamstring testing 100
nutrition 159, 161, 202–215, *215;*
  carbohydrates 203–204; energy
  expenditure 206–207; and fatigue
  203–204; fluid considerations 206; for
  match-day (during matches) 210–212;
  for match-day (post-match) 212–213;
  for match-day (pre-match) 208–210;
  overview 202–203; plan **208**; pre-match
  day (MD-1) 207–208; proteins 204–205;
  support **214**

objective methods 125–133
optimal fitness 224
optimal readiness 124
overload 49–50, **50**

Para football 272–299; *vs.* able bodied
  football 281–284, **282–283**; amputee
  football 273–274; blind and partially
  sighted football 273; cerebral palsy (CP)
  football 273; classification 274–281;
  deaf football 274; exercise modification
  290–294; formats 273–274, **275–280**;
  hinge exercise 294; impairment specific
  formats 285–288; informed practice/
  physical performance monitoring
  288–290, **289**; match and training
  load analysis 285–290; overview
  272; powerchair football (PF) 274;
  programming 290; speed zones to
  analyse movement patterns of **287**;
  squat-based movements 290–293;
  strength and conditioning 284
passive heat maintenance 145
peak height velocity (PHV) 244–245,
  253–257
performance-oriented climate 221
physical demands: external load 4–7;
  of football 3–14; internal load 8–10;
  residual fatigue 10–12
physical profiling 45–46; football 89–102;
  physical demands 89–102
physiological demands: external load 4–7;
  of football 3–14; internal load 8–10;
  residual fatigue 10–12
physiological mechanisms underpinning
  recovery 154

physiological resilience 11
planned change-of-direction movements 65–66
players' home environment *223,* 223–225
players' self-regulation *226*
plyometric: jump training 63, 64, 66; practical case 68–69; training 40–51, 186
positive reinforcement 224–225
post-activation performance enhancement (PAPE) 145–147
power: testing 95–97; training 40–51, 64
powerchair football (PF) 274
practical applications: football performance 149–150, *150*; of recovery strategies for footballers *170,* 170–171; training load monitoring 120; wellness monitoring and readiness 136
the Profile of Mood State (POMS) 133
protecting warm-up benefits 144–145
proteins 204–205
#PsychMapping model 220
psychological loads in training designs 225–227, *226*
psychological mechanisms underpinning recovery 154
psychology for coaches in talent development 219–234; action accuracy 223–225; club culture 220–222, *221*; coach feedback *228,* 228–230; coaching staff's multidisciplinary mindset *223,* 223–225; coping strategy selection 230–232; effort expenditure and fair-play 220–222, *221*; emotion expression and performance 225–227; half-time analysis 230–232; home environment *223,* 223–225; motivational climate 220–222, *221*; overview 219–220; psychological loads in training designs 225–227, *226*; self-talk/ self-control/performance 228–230

range of motion (ROM) 182–183
rate of force development (RFD) 185
Ratings of Perceived Exertion (RPE) 110–111, 113–115, *115*
reactive agility test 60
reactive agility training (RAT) 258
reactive strength: assessment of 185–186; targeting improvements in 186
reactive strength index modified (RSImod) 130
readiness, defined 124, 128
recovering explosiveness 185

recovery 14; defined 154; physiological mechanisms 154; psychological mechanisms 154
recovery strategies after matches 153–171; active recovery 163–164; athletes' perception 158; compression garments 164–165; context 154; cooling strategies 161–162; elite football player 154; environmental stress 158; guided prescription 168–169, *169*; heating strategies 163; individual considerations 156–159; influence of recovery and adaptation 154–156; interventions used 159–161, **160**; massage 166–167; nutrition 161; physiological/ psychological mechanisms 154; practical application *170,* 170–171; range of motion strategies 165–166; sequencing of multiple strategies 167–168, *168*; sleep 159–161; timing/proximity of next session 158–159; training cycle and aim of session 157–158; training load and frequency of sessions 158
Recovery-Stress Questionnaire for athletes 133
re-developing: COD ability 190; deceleration 189; physical capacities following injury 183; speed 187–188; strength 184
rehabilitation 2, 76, 78, 181–192, 195, 243
reliability: defined 117; external training load monitoring 117, *118*
repeated sprint ability (RSA) 22, 99
residual fatigue 10–12; *see also* fatigue
resistance exercise 141
resistance training 62, 84, 94, 131, 141, 162, 184, 190, 241, 243, 244, 255, 257, 261, 264, **265**
resisted and assisted sprinting methods 62
rest 159–161
"return to participation" 181
return to performance following injury 181–195
return to play (RTP) 181, 187–188
"return to sport" 181
Romanian Deadlifts (RDL) 294, *295*

self-confidence 221–222
self-efficacy 221–222
self-talk/self-control/performance 228–230
session RPE (sRPE) 113–115, *115*
single-leg CMJ (SLCMJ) 95–96
single leg drop jump (SLDJ) performance 186

310 Index

single-leg repeated hops 95–96
sleep 159–161
small-sided games (SSG) 21, *23,* 265,
  267;-based HIIT types 28–29; impact of
  encouragement during *32*; physiological
  responses of **33**; task constraints of
  31–34
soccer-specific capacities: late phase
  rehabilitation 187; restoring 187
specificity: defined 46; and exercise
  selection 46–47, **47–49**
specific training methods: defined 61;
  free-unresisted sprinting methods
  61–62; resisted and assisted sprinting
  methods 62; sprint performance 61–62
speed 256–258, **259–260**; and agility
  53–69; in football 53–69; re-developing
  187–188; zone calculation 118–119, *119*
sport, exercise, and performance
  psychologist (SEPPist) 219, 232
Sport, Exercise, and Performance
  Psychology (SEPP) 219; practical
  application 220; principles 219;
  #PsychMapping model of 220; for
  psychological needs of athletes 220;
  theoretical knowledge 220
sport-specific movements 143, 255
sprint acceleration 63, 187
sprint assessments 129–130
sprinting ability 256–258, **259–260**; *see
  also* high-speed running (HSR)
sprint interval training (SIT) 23, 26
sprint performance 7; assessment of 55–57;
  combined training methods 64–65;
  curvilinear sprint test 57; determinants
  of 53–54; instruments for measuring 55;
  linear sprint tests 56–57; non-specific
  training methods 62–64; setup of tests
  55–56; specific training methods 61–62;
  stride length 53–54; stride rate 54;
  training methods for enhancing 60–65
squat-based movements 290–293
squat jump (SJ) 95–96, 130
standing broad jump (SBJ) 95–96
static-start tests 56
strategies: adopted less than 3 h before
  player's entry 142–147; adopted more
  than 3 h before player's entry 141–142;
  to enhance football performance
  140–150; implemented after player's
  entry 147–149; match-day 140–150
strength: assessment 183–184; contralateral
  limb 184; defined 46; re-developing 184

strength testing: fitness testing 94–97;
  power testing 95–97; repetition
  maximum (RM) testing 94
strength training 40–51, 63–64; practical
  case 68–69
stretch-shortening cycle (SSC) activities
  185–186
stride length 53–54
stride rate 54
subjective methods 133–134
submaximal fitness test (SMFT) 127

task-oriented climate 221, 222
temporary fatigue 7–9, 12, 14
testosterone 126, 141
Total Recovery Scale 133
Total Score of Athleticism (TSA) 191
training impulse score (TRIMP) 112, 114
training load monitoring: external training
  load monitoring 115–120; in football
  107–120; heart rates 111–112, *113*;
  internal training load monitoring 111;
  practical applications 120; ratings of
  perceived exertion 113–115
Training Load Tactics Whiteboard *120*
training principles: intensity 49–50, **50**;
  overload 49–50, **50**; specificity and
  exercise selection 46–47, **47–49**; volume
  49–50, **50**

Union of European Football Associations
  (UEFA) Europa League 159

Velocity-Based Training (VBT) 131, 135
verbal feedback 228
vertical stiffness 187
VO2max measurement 92
volume 49–50, **50**

warm-up: active pre-match 143–144;
  benefits 144–145
well-being 124
wellness monitoring and readiness:
  biochemical measures 125–127;
  cardiovascular measures 127–128;
  cycling assessments 129; in football
  124–136; implementation 135–136;
  invisible monitoring 134; jump
  assessments 130–131; methods for
  assessing readiness 125; monitoring
  readiness with wearables 128; muscle
  strength assessments 131–133;
  neuromuscular fatigue (NMF) 128–129;

Index **311**

objective methods 125–133; practical applications 136; sprint assessments 129–130; subjective methods 133–134; Velocity-Based Training (VBT) 131

Y-Balance test 100
youth football/training: agility 258–261, **261–263**; athletic development 254–255; endurance 264–267; growth and maturation 253; injury prevalence 253–254; overview 252–253; resistance training guidance **265**; speed 256–258, **259–260**; speed development **257**; strength and conditioning (S and C) for 252–267; strength and power 261–264, **266**
Yo-Yo intermittent endurance test 244
Yo-Yo intermittent recovery tests 93, 212

Printed in the United States
by Baker & Taylor Publisher Services